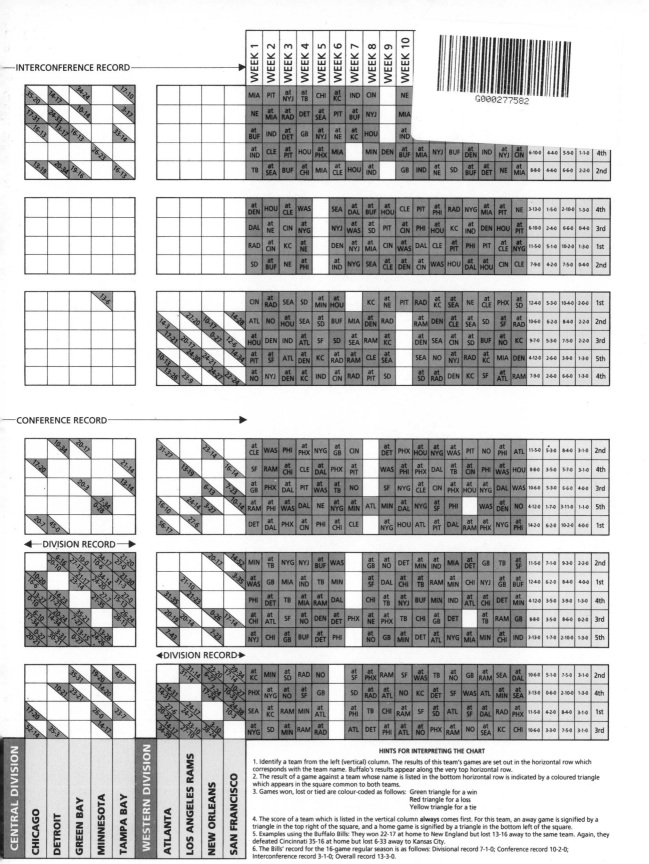

INTERCONFERENCE RECORD

CONFERENCE RECORD

DIVISION RECORD

DIVISION RECORD

| | WEEK 1 | WEEK 2 | WEEK 3 | WEEK 4 | WEEK 5 | WEEK 6 | WEEK 7 | WEEK 8 | WEEK 9 | WEEK 10 |

**CENTRAL DIVISION:** CHICAGO, DETROIT, GREEN BAY, MINNESOTA, TAMPA BAY

**WESTERN DIVISION:** ATLANTA, LOS ANGELES RAMS, NEW ORLEANS, SAN FRANCISCO

G000277582

### HINTS FOR INTERPRETING THE CHART

1. Identify a team from the left (vertical) column. The results of this team's games are set out in the horizontal row which corresponds with the team name. Buffalo's results appear along the very top horizontal row.

2. The result of a game against a team whose name is listed in the bottom horizontal row is indicated by a coloured triangle which appears in the square common to both teams.

3. Games won, lost or tied are colour-coded as follows: Green triangle for a win
Red triangle for a loss
Yellow triangle for a tie

4. The score of a team which is listed in the vertical column **always** comes first. For this team, an away game is signified by a triangle in the top right of the square, and a home game is signified by a triangle in the bottom left of the square.

5. Examples using the Buffalo Bills: They won 22-17 at home to New England but lost 13-16 away to the same team. Again, they defeated Cincinnati 35-16 at home but lost 6-33 away to Kansas City.

6. The Bills' record for the 16-game regular season is as follows: Divisional record 7-1-0; Conference record 10-2-0; Interconference record 3-1-0; Overall record 13-3-0.

# THE OFFICIAL CHANNEL FOUR
# AMERICAN FOOTBALL
## ANNUAL 1992-93

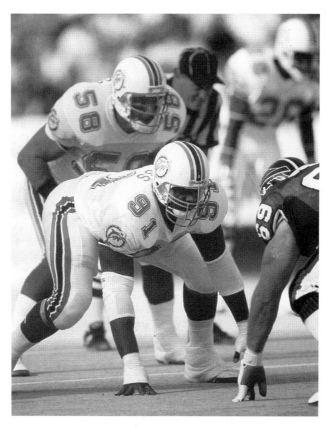

# THE OFFICIAL CHANNEL FOUR

# AMERICAN FOOTBALL

## ANNUAL 1992-93

### KEN THOMAS

**STANLEY PAUL**
LONDON

# ACKNOWLEDGEMENTS

For the tenth year I have the opportunity of thanking the many people who are of invaluable assistance in putting together this annual.

Readers of previous editions will be aware of the debt which I owe to Nick Wridgway, whose influence has grown steadily to the extent that he is now my most trusted adviser. For this, and the sheer donkey work, Nick has my grateful thanks.

When it comes to reflecting on the NFL's history, I can either spend a day poring over my research material or I can simply phone Beau Riffenburgh, in which case the answer comes immediately. Similarly, if ever I did write a 'good line', the chances are that Larry Eldridge, Jr., wrote it first. To both Beau and Larry I extend my usual appreciation. I am also most grateful to John Herrera, a Senior Executive with the Los Angeles Raiders, who introduced me to the combined delights of the Raiders' preseason camp and Mexican food.

Several NFL officials, among them Pete Abitante and Leslie Hammond, continue to tolerate my many requests for information. Despite the intense demands on their time, the answers always come whistling through the wires. Both Pete and Leslie have my sincere thanks. Thanks also go to Paul Spinelli and Kevan Burks who select photographic material for me and deliver it, in perfect condition, ahead of time.

On the home front, Susanna Yager and Sandy Holton of Channel Four Television offer a constant source of reassurance which has come in handy over recent years. Thankyou, ladies. Roddy Bloomfield, Marion Paull and Louise Speller of Stanley Paul have managed to survive their first encounter with me, as has the designer Roger Walker, and that has to merit some form of thanks.

Finally, my wife Janie continues to put up with me. I don't know why, but thanks anyway, love.

K.T., June 1992

# PHOTOGRAPHIC ACKNOWLEDGEMENTS

The author and the publishers would like to thank the following photographers and agencies for allowing them to use their copyright photographs: Paul Spinelli/NFLP/NFL Photos pp. 1, 5, 6, 17, 23, 30, 40, 46/47 (top), 51 (bottom), 56 (left), 58 (top), 77, 83, 89, 93, 95, 96, 98, 101, 102, 104, 107, 109, 111, 112, 119, 126, 128, 131, 132, 135, 136, 138, 141, 142, 145, 147, 149, 153; Paul Spinelli/Allsport USA p. 58 (bottom); David Boss/NFL Photos pp. 2/3, 64, 114, 150; Jonathan Daniel/Allsport USA pp. 9 (left), 41, 70, 71, 73 (both), 74 (right); Andy Hayt/NFL Photos pp. 51 (top), 52, 53; Michael Zagaris/NFL Photos p. 9; Bruce Dierdorff/NFL Photos p. 10; Mitchell B Riebel/NFL Photos pp. 11, 14; Mickey Pfleger/NFL Photos p. 12; James D Smith/NFL Photos pp. 13, 35; Jim Turner/NFL Photos pp. 15, 34, 38 (bottom); Al Messerschmidt/NFL Photos pp. 16, 44, 45, 81; Tim De Frisco/Allsport p. 18; Robert B Shaver/NFL Photos p. 19; Tony Tomsic/NFL Photos p. 22; Bob Rosato/NFL Photos pp. 24, 90, 123, 125; William R Sallaz/NFL Photos p. 25; Markus Boesch/Allsport USA p. 26 (top); Perry McIntyre JR/NFL Photos pp. 28, 29, 36; Pete J Groh/NFL Photos p. 31; Long Photography/NFL Photos p. 32; Tom Croke/NFL Photos p. 33; George Rose/NFL Photos p. 37; Allsport p. 38 (top); Kevin Terrell/NFL Photos p. 42; Rick Stewart/NFL Photos p. 43; Paul Jasienski/NFL Photos p. 47 (bottom); John Elway/NFL Photos p. 48; Scott Cunningham/NFL Photos pp. 49, 50 (top), 55, 79; Rob Brown/NFL Photos pp. 50 (bottom), 56 (right), 124; Corky Trewin/NFL Photos p. 60; David Drapkin/NFL Photos pp. 26 (bottom), 65; Tony Duffy/Allsport p. 67; Stephen Dunn/Allsport p. 68; Joe Patromite/Allsport USA p. 69; Otto Greule JR/Allsport p. 72 (both); Mike Kullen/Allsport USA p. 74 (left); NFL Photos p. 78; Ron Vesely/NFL Photos p. 80; Ed Webber/NFL p. 82; Al Kooistra/NFL Photos p. 84; Thearou Henderson/NFL Photos p. 87; Brian Drake/NFL Photos p. 88; Mike Moore/NFL Photos p. 91; Mark Sherengo/NFL Photos p. 116; Doug Pensinger/Allsport p. 122.

Stanley Paul & Co. Ltd

An imprint of Random House UK Ltd
20 Vauxhall Bridge Road, London SW1V 2SA

Random House Australia (Pty) Ltd
20 Alfred Street, Milsons Point, Sydney, NSW 2061

Random House, New Zealand (Pty) Ltd
18 Poland Road, PO Box 40-86, Glenfield, Auckland

Random House South Africa (Pty) Ltd
PO Box 337, Bergvlei 2012, South Africa

First published 1992
Copyright © Ken Thomas 1992

The right of Ken Thomas to be identified as the author of this work has been asserted by him in accordance with the Copyright, Design and Patents Act, 1988

*All rights reserved*

*The Official Channel Four American Football Annual 1992-93* is associated with Channel Four Television coverage of the sport

Set in Futura by SX Composing Ltd, Rayleigh, Essex
Printed in England by Clays Ltd, St Ives plc

A catalogue record for this book is available upon request from the British Library

ISBN 0 09 177531 0

# CONTENTS

# INTRODUCTION

Eleven years ago, it was an excited fan, your writer, who savoured the prospect of watching his favourite sport in the comfort of his own living room. That he might be given the opportunity of sharing his enjoyment, to the extent that this has occurred, was nothing more than a dream. It is, then, a particular pleasure for me to welcome readers, many of whom have become friends, to the tenth in the series of the American Football Annual.

Its publication has coincided with a period of growth which has seen NFL teams contest 18 preseason games outside the United States, the first four being played at Wembley Stadium. In 1983, the NFL tested the water, and London quickly became the key city in the league's plans for international expansion. Even the gods gave their approval, as the Monarchs were victorious in the in-augural 1991 World Bowl. One wonders if those same gods are now putting us to the test, for the Monarchs struggled through a difficult 1992 campaign which culminated in a World Bowl victory for the Sacramento Surge. More than a few eyes will be monitoring attendance figures in the 1993 season. For what it is worth, my view is that the future of the World League lies in the affiliation of each team with a parent NFL franchise, along the lines successfully developed by Major League Baseball.

As for expansion of the NFL's membership to 30 teams, scheduled for the 1994 season, it is certain that the two new franchises will be located in the United States. The best guess is that there will be at least five years before any further expansion, but wouldn't it be a truly stylish move if the NFL opened the 21st century by awarding its first overseas franchise to the city of London?

Returning to the 1992 edition, we felt that it was about time that NFL head coaches were given a little more exposure. Accordingly, eight of the most promi-nent members of this respected fraternity are offered for your consideration. Also, it made sense to take a much closer look at the outstanding 1992 draftees.

Otherwise, the formula is unchanged. Please be assured that I take very careful note of every suggestion on how the book might be improved. After all, it is written for you.

# CHAPTER ONE
# A REVIEW OF THE 1991 SEASON

## PROLOGUE

Every time an AFC team wins the Super Bowl Championship the Dow Jones Index rises. Or does it fall? Not many people can remember. For not since the 1983 Los Angeles Raiders humbled the Washington Redskins in Super Bowl XVIII has the NFC representative tasted defeat. In the second half of the 1980s the maxim became a reminiscence, while these days it has taken the form of legend.

In the 1990 renewal of the rivalry, Super Bowl XXV, the AFC's Buffalo Bills actually were fancied to win. But they were first checked by the disciplined New York Giants defense and then pounded into submission by a remorseless ball-control offense spearheaded by running back Ottis Anderson. Certainly, the Bills did have a late chance for glory, but there was an inevitability about the manner in which Scott Norwood's last-gasp 47-yard field goal attempt drifted wide to the right.

By way of consolation for AFC fans, the suggestion was that the Bills simply had lacked big-game temperament and, for sure, no club in the entire league except, perhaps, San Francisco had better talent. And few disagreed that the AFC contingent did offer a more serious threat as the 28 clubs entered the NFL's 72nd season.

As part of the annual strengthening process which, for more than half a century, had been restricted to the Collegiate Draft, the clubs now had access to a pool of veteran free agents under the system known as Plan B. In what was its third year of operation, the early months of 1991 saw 139 players sign for new teams. For most of the travellers the best hope was to secure a roster spot as a benchwarmer, but, for a few, there was a point to be made. Left unprotected by San Francisco, a club he had helped to win four Super Bowl titles on the way to becoming the NFL's premier safety, Ronnie Lott was quickly picked up by the Raiders, whose signing also of Lott's teammate, four-time Pro Bowl running back Roger Craig, was considered only marginally less of a coup. Another highly respected safety, Felix Wright, moved from Cleveland to Minnesota, while

Houston's Tony Zendejas was seen by the Rams as the immediate solution to their placekicking problems.

For all its promise of longer-term benefits, the Collegiate Draft, the process by which college students graduate to the professional ranks, is a much more risky business. It is not unknown for the 'sensational prospect – a superb physical specimen with a rare combination of speed, agility, hand-eye coordination and presence' to burst into tears at the first sight of an unshaven, wizened pro, growling and fulminating as he settles into his action stance. Yet Draft Day, or rather the two-day period in the Marriott Marquis Hotel in New York City where each selection is greeted with near insanity by 500 devotees draped about the gallery, is one of the most exciting in the calendar. In the 1991 draft, Dallas dealt with New England for the prime spot and used it to pick Russell Maryland, whom they saw as forming the core of their defensive line for the next decade.

A novel feature of the 1990 draft had been the opening of the door to 'juniors', namely, those students with a year of collegiate eligibility remaining. It had not led to an avalanche of aspirants and, following the selection of eight juniors in the 1990 first round, of the 31 juniors who were available in 1991, only two, wide receiver Herman Moore and running back Leonard Russell, were top selections. More interesting, intriguing even, was the first-round selection by the Raiders of quarterback Todd Marinovich, who had entered the draft still with two years of collegiate eligibility remaining, while the Cardinals used their prime option to pick defensive lineman Eric Swann, who had never played college football.

On the coaching front, Miami's Don Shula entered the campaign needing just two victories to reach 300, a total exceeded by only the late George Halas (325). On the other hand, for each of Bill Belichick, Ray Handley, Rich Kotite and Dick MacPherson, it was a first turn at the wheel.

Belichick joined the Cleveland Browns in early February and, at 38, would be the NFL's youngest active head coach.

He was in charge of the Giants' defense in two victorious Super Bowls and, had he stayed in New York, he might have assumed seniority following the surprise departure of Bill Parcells in mid-May. As it was, Handley, who had been the Giants' running backs coach, was expected to step up without too many problems. Kotite advanced with the firing of the expressive Buddy Ryan in Philadelphia. While Ryan had seldom minced his words, Kotite was looking to mince the opposition. The choice of MacPherson, 60 years old, by the Patriots ownership raised a few eyebrows. His curriculum vitae showed experience with Cleveland and Denver, but for the last ten years he had been head coach at Syracuse University.

It was for the final three games of the 1990 season that Richard Williamson had been temporary head coach of the Tampa Bay Buccaneers. His reward for holding the team together was the permanent spot, confirmed by owner Hugh Culverhouse on 4 February.

When it came to predicting the Super Bowl Champion, most eyes turned to San Francisco and Washington from the NFC, with Buffalo and an emerging Houston club expected to carry the AFC's banner. Your writer, whose track record in these matters is deplorable, was hoping to register a first by opting for Buffalo.

*'Only in America can a fat kid from Chicago become the first pick in the NFL draft,'*
*said Russell Maryland upon his selection by the Cowboys.*

*The Raiders snapped up All-Pro safety Ronnie Lott as a Plan-B free agent.*

# WEEK ONE

## American Football Conference
Cincinnati 14 at Denver 45
Los Angeles Raiders 17 at Houston 47
Miami 31 at Buffalo 35
New England 16 at Indianapolis 7
San Diego 20 at Pittsburgh 26

## National Football Conference
Detroit 0 at Washington 45
Minnesota 6 at Chicago 10
Philadelphia 20 at Green Bay 3
Phoenix 24 at Los Angeles Rams 14
San Francisco 14 at New York Giants 16

## Interconference Games
Atlanta 3 at Kansas City 14
Dallas 26 at Cleveland 14
Seattle 24 at New Orleans 27
Tampa Bay 13 at New York Jets 16

## Interconference Play
AFC 2 – NFC 2

*The Eagles lost Randall Cunningham for the season after just one quarter.*

## Game of The Week
## San Francisco 14 – New York Giants 16

In San Francisco they frighten children with the prospect of meeting Matt Bahr, the former Cleveland placekicker who was signed as a free agent by the Giants three weeks into the 1990 season, after Raul Allegre had gone out with an injury. In the NFC Championship Game of that year, against San Francisco, Bahr kicked all the Giants' points in a 15–13 win, settling the issue with a 42-yard field goal as time ran out.

When the re-match took place in the showpiece Monday Night Game to complete Week One, the script had a familiar ring. Of course, Bahr opened the scoring with a 35-yard field goal but the response, a 73-yard touchdown play involving reserve quarterback Steve Young, who was standing in for the injured Joe Montana, and pro football's best wide receiver, Jerry Rice, was equally predictable.

Playing to their strengths or perhaps within their limits, the Giants pounded away, controlling possession with running back Ottis Anderson playing the part of steamhammer and quarterback Jeff Hostetler tidying up the loose ends. Entering the final quarter, Anderson's one-yard touchdown run and Bahr's second field goal had built a six-point cushion but, as often they do in the final quarter, back came the 49ers, Young rounding off a 42-yard drive with his five-yard touchdown run.

The clock was winding down but the Giants didn't panic. Hostetler used all of 13 plays to nudge inexorably 60 yards down to the San Francisco 18-yard line, before handing over to Bahr. And wouldn't you just know that Bahr would step up calmly and plant the ball between the uprights, leaving the 49ers just five seconds of game time to curse their luck and to contemplate the ending of their NFL-record string of away victories at 18?

### The Road To Super Bowl XXVI

Thurman Thomas became the first player in Buffalo history to both rush and catch passes for 100 or more yards in a game, as the Bills overcame a 14-point deficit to beat Miami.

The Redskins unleashed the full fury of their awesome strength as they routed the Detroit Lions. 'Everything we did worked. It was a perfect night,' reflected Redskins head coach Joe Gibbs.

*Albert Lewis foiled the Falcons with three interceptions.*

## OUTSTANDING INDIVIDUAL PERFORMANCES

**100 Yards Rushing**
Thurman Thomas (Buffalo) 25-165-20-1
Mark Higgs (Miami) 30-146-20-1
Allen Pinkett (Houston) 26-144-27-1
Christian Okoye (Kansas City) 22-143-48-1
Gaston Green (Denver) 24-116-43-0
Emmitt Smith (Dallas) 32-112-12-0

**100 Yards Pass Receiving**
Brian Blades (Seattle) 12-160-31-2
Andre Reed (Buffalo) 11-154-54t-1
Mark Clayton (Miami) 6-138-43t-2
Dwight Stone (Pittsburgh) 4-124-89t-1
Michael Irvin (Dallas) 9-123-23-1
Henry Ellard (L.A. Rams) 7-116-24-0
Robert Delpino (L.A. Rams) 10-113-41-0
Keith Byars (Philadelphia) 8-111-32t-1
Gary Clark (Washington) 6-107-38t-1
Thurman Thomas (Buffalo) 8-103-50t-1
Sam Graddy (L.A. Raiders) 3-103-80t-1

**Passing**
Dan Marino (Miami) 28-17-267-0-43t-3
Mark Rypien (Washington) 19-15-183-1-38t-2
John Elway (Denver) 28-18-262-0-52t-2
Tommy Hodson (New England) 18-13-136-0-23t-1
Jim Kelly (Buffalo) 39-29-381-1-54t-2
Jim Harbaugh (Chicago) 24-17-186-0-37t-1
Bernie Kosar (Cleveland) 31-22-249-0-62t-1
Troy Aikman (Dallas) 37-24-274-0-23-2

## STANDINGS

| AFC East | W | L | T | PF | PA | Pct. | NFC East | W | L | T | PF | PA | Pct. |
|---|---|---|---|---|---|---|---|---|---|---|---|---|---|
| Buffalo | 1 | 0 | 0 | 35 | 31 | 1.000 | Dallas | 1 | 0 | 0 | 26 | 14 | 1.000 |
| New England | 1 | 0 | 0 | 16 | 7 | 1.000 | N.Y. Giants | 1 | 0 | 0 | 16 | 14 | 1.000 |
| N.Y. Jets | 1 | 0 | 0 | 16 | 13 | 1.000 | Philadelphia | 1 | 0 | 0 | 20 | 3 | 1.000 |
| Indianapolis | 0 | 1 | 0 | 7 | 16 | 0.000 | Phoenix | 1 | 0 | 0 | 24 | 14 | 1.000 |
| Miami | 0 | 1 | 0 | 31 | 35 | 0.000 | Washington | 1 | 0 | 0 | 45 | 0 | 1.000 |
| **AFC Central** | **W** | **L** | **T** | **PF** | **PA** | **Pct.** | **NFC Central** | **W** | **L** | **T** | **PF** | **PA** | **Pct.** |
| Houston | 1 | 0 | 0 | 47 | 17 | 1.000 | Chicago | 1 | 0 | 0 | 10 | 6 | 1.000 |
| Pittsburgh | 1 | 0 | 0 | 26 | 20 | 1.000 | Detroit | 0 | 1 | 0 | 0 | 45 | 0.000 |
| Cincinnati | 0 | 1 | 0 | 14 | 45 | 0.000 | Green Bay | 0 | 1 | 0 | 3 | 20 | 0.000 |
| Cleveland | 0 | 1 | 0 | 14 | 26 | 0.000 | Minnesota | 0 | 1 | 0 | 6 | 10 | 0.000 |
| **AFC West** | **W** | **L** | **T** | **PF** | **PA** | **Pct.** | Tampa Bay | 0 | 1 | 0 | 13 | 16 | 0.000 |
| Denver | 1 | 0 | 0 | 45 | 14 | 1.000 | **NFC West** | **W** | **L** | **T** | **PF** | **PA** | **Pct.** |
| Kansas City | 1 | 0 | 0 | 14 | 3 | 1.000 | New Orleans | 1 | 0 | 0 | 27 | 24 | 1.000 |
| L.A. Raiders | 0 | 1 | 0 | 17 | 47 | 0.000 | Atlanta | 0 | 1 | 0 | 3 | 14 | 0.000 |
| San Diego | 0 | 1 | 0 | 20 | 26 | 0.000 | L.A. Rams | 0 | 1 | 0 | 14 | 24 | 0.000 |
| Seattle | 0 | 1 | 0 | 24 | 27 | 0.000 | San Francisco | 0 | 1 | 0 | 14 | 16 | 0.000 |

# WEEK TWO

## Game of The Week
## Washington 33 – Dallas 31

There is always something special about a meeting between these two rivals who have been banging helmets since 1960, over which time Dallas had established a 34–26–2 lead in the series. And it was hardly surprising that ABC paraded the contest as its Monday Night Game.

The Redskins had opened their 1991 campaign with a 45–0 rout of Detroit but, against a resurgent Dallas club filled to the brim with young talent and widely predicted to reach the playoffs, they faced a severe test. Also, there was the added spice that Washington was carrying the burden of six consecutive losses in front of the Monday evening television audience.

Even in an era when America's late-nineteenth-century history west of the Mississippi is in the process of re-evaluation, it was difficult not to think of those days when most things, it seems, were decided by a shoot-out, as a furious series of exchanges saw the teams amass a total of 64 points. Among the Dallas sharpshooters was running back Emmitt Smith, who scored on a 75-yard run and would catch a five-yard touchdown pass before leaving for good with a stomach upset. Washington quarterback Mark Rypien responded with a second scoring pass, but it was the boot of Chip Lohmiller that first kept the Redskins in touch and then eased them into a 23–21 lead with field goals covering 53, 52 and 45 yards.

Yet Dallas, too, had its siege-gun in the form of Ken Willis, whose 51-yard field goal restored the Cowboys' one-point advantage. And they appeared to have established a grip, late in the third quarter, when they had the Redskins in trouble on fourth-and-one at midfield.

However, Washington head coach Joe Gibbs called a fake punt and blocking back Brian Mitchell responded, scurrying three yards to keep alive a drive which culminated in Gerald Riggs' one-yard touchdown plunge. Lohmiller's fourth field goal, a 46-yarder, gave Washington a position of comfort from which to play prevent defense, safe in the knowledge that a late Dallas touchdown could be to no avail.

## The Road To Super Bowl XXVI

Buffalo quarterback Jim Kelly set a club record with six touchdown passes as the Bills outlasted the Pittsburgh Steelers by the score of 52–34. While establishing personal-best marks with ten catches and 112 yards receiving, wide receiver Don Beebe also tied the club record with four touchdown receptions.

*Steve Young led the 49ers to their first victory of the season by passing for 348 yards and three touchdowns.*

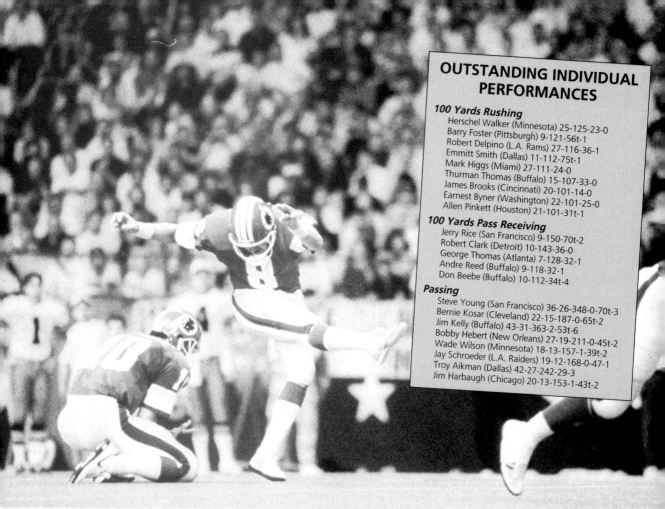

## OUTSTANDING INDIVIDUAL PERFORMANCES

**100 Yards Rushing**
Herschel Walker (Minnesota) 25-125-23-0
Barry Foster (Pittsburgh) 9-121-56t-1
Robert Delpino (L.A. Rams) 27-116-36-1
Emmitt Smith (Dallas) 11-112-75t-1
Mark Higgs (Miami) 27-111-24-0
Thurman Thomas (Buffalo) 15-107-33-0
James Brooks (Cincinnati) 20-101-14-0
Earnest Byner (Washington) 22-101-25-0
Allen Pinkett (Houston) 21-101-31t-1

**100 Yards Pass Receiving**
Jerry Rice (San Francisco) 9-150-70t-2
Robert Clark (Detroit) 10-143-36-0
George Thomas (Atlanta) 7-128-32-1
Andre Reed (Buffalo) 9-118-32-1
Don Beebe (Buffalo) 10-112-34t-4

**Passing**
Steve Young (San Francisco) 36-26-348-0-70t-3
Bernie Kosar (Cleveland) 22-15-187-0-65t-2
Jim Kelly (Buffalo) 43-31-363-2-53t-6
Bobby Hebert (New Orleans) 27-19-211-0-45t-2
Wade Wilson (Minnesota) 18-13-157-1-39t-2
Jay Schroeder (L.A. Raiders) 19-12-168-0-47-1
Troy Aikman (Dallas) 42-27-242-29-3
Jim Harbaugh (Chicago) 20-13-153-1-43t-2

*Chip Lohmiller kept the Redskins ahead of the Cowboys with field goals of 53, 52, 45 and 46 yards.*

## STANDINGS

| AFC East | W | L | T | PF | PA | Pct. | NFC East | W | L | T | PF | PA | Pct. |
|---|---|---|---|---|---|---|---|---|---|---|---|---|---|
| Buffalo | 2 | 0 | 0 | 87 | 65 | 1.000 | Phoenix | 2 | 0 | 0 | 50 | 24 | 1.000 |
| Miami | 1 | 1 | 0 | 48 | 41 | .500 | Washington | 2 | 0 | 0 | 78 | 31 | 1.000 |
| New England | 1 | 1 | 0 | 16 | 27 | .500 | Dallas | 1 | 1 | 0 | 57 | 47 | .500 |
| N.Y. Jets | 1 | 1 | 0 | 29 | 33 | .500 | N.Y. Giants | 1 | 1 | 0 | 29 | 33 | .500 |
| Indianapolis | 0 | 2 | 0 | 13 | 33 | 0.000 | Philadelphia | 1 | 1 | 0 | 30 | 29 | .500 |
| **AFC Central** | **W** | **L** | **T** | **PF** | **PA** | **Pct.** | **NFC Central** | **W** | **L** | **T** | **PF** | **PA** | **Pct.** |
| Houston | 2 | 0 | 0 | 77 | 24 | 1.000 | Chicago | 2 | 0 | 0 | 31 | 26 | 1.000 |
| Cleveland | 1 | 1 | 0 | 34 | 26 | .500 | Detroit | 1 | 1 | 0 | 23 | 59 | .500 |
| Pittsburgh | 1 | 1 | 0 | 60 | 72 | .500 | Minnesota | 1 | 1 | 0 | 26 | 29 | .500 |
| Cincinnati | 0 | 2 | 0 | 21 | 75 | 0.000 | Green Bay | 0 | 2 | 0 | 17 | 43 | 0.000 |
| **AFC West** | **W** | **L** | **T** | **PF** | **PA** | **Pct.** | Tampa Bay | 0 | 2 | 0 | 33 | 37 | 0.000 |
| Denver | 1 | 1 | 0 | 58 | 30 | .500 | **NFC West** | **W** | **L** | **T** | **PF** | **PA** | **Pct.** |
| Kansas City | 1 | 1 | 0 | 24 | 20 | .500 | New Orleans | 2 | 0 | 0 | 44 | 34 | 1.000 |
| L.A. Raiders | 1 | 1 | 0 | 33 | 60 | .500 | L.A. Rams | 1 | 1 | 0 | 33 | 37 | .500 |
| Seattle | 1 | 1 | 0 | 44 | 40 | .500 | San Francisco | 1 | 1 | 0 | 48 | 30 | .500 |
| San Diego | 0 | 2 | 0 | 34 | 60 | 0.000 | Atlanta | 0 | 2 | 0 | 22 | 34 | 0.000 |

# WEEK THREE

## Game of The Week
## New York Giants 17 – Chicago 20

After making a fine start with an opening victory against San Francisco, on Week Two the Giants had been upset by a Rams team which, even though going through a lean patch, usually finds an extra gear against a rival which it now leads 20–9–0 in a series stretching back to 1938.

Chicago is usually quick off the mark and that pattern had been maintained, comfortably against Minnesota and less so in a 21–20 squeaker with Tampa Bay. If the Giants would offer the first acid test, there was an added incentive for the Bears who were still feeling the effects of being slammed 31–3 by New York in the 1990 playoffs.

As most would expect, the Giants dominated the time of possession by almost two to one, but in the first half it was Chicago which took its chances, quarterback Jim Harbaugh combining with wide receiver Wendell Davis for a 75-yard touchdown play sandwiched between Kevin Butler field goals. However, what might be a 13-point deficit for some is more a target for New York. Capitalizing on a fumble by Bears running back Neal Anderson, Matt Bahr kicked a 35-yard field goal and two poor Chicago punts were punished when, twice, New York's Rodney Hampton ran into the end zone from close range.

It was against the flow when Anderson atoned for his fumble, scampering 42 yards on a counter-trap for the touchdown which gave the Bears a three-point margin with just over six minutes remaining in regulation time. Yet they could hardly feel comfortable, knowing full well that the Giants are virtually unstoppable when it comes to driving into range for a field goal which, in this case, would take the game into overtime. And when the Giants did slug their

way down to the Chicago 18-yard line the tying kick appeared to be a formality.

Remember William (The Refrigerator) Perry? He was the 1985 rookie defensive lineman, grossly overweight but with great talent, who found a way of attracting the headlines. And now, with just 15 seconds remaining, he hurled his mass through the Giants' line to block Bahr's 35-yard field goal attempt and preserve the win. 'Maybe he did it with his stomach,' offered Bears head coach Mike Ditka.

## The Road To Super Bowl XXVI

The Redskins were not troubled in handing out their thirteenth consecutive home win in the series against the Phoenix Cardinals. For the first time since the 1977 season, Washington registered its second shutout.

While the Redskins coasted to victory, Buffalo had no end of bother against the Jets and came through only when Thurman Thomas scored to complete a hair-raising fourth-quarter drive in which Jim Kelly converted on fourth-and-six with his ten-yard pass to James Lofton. For the Jets, Pat Leahy failed on a late 51-yard field goal attempt.

14

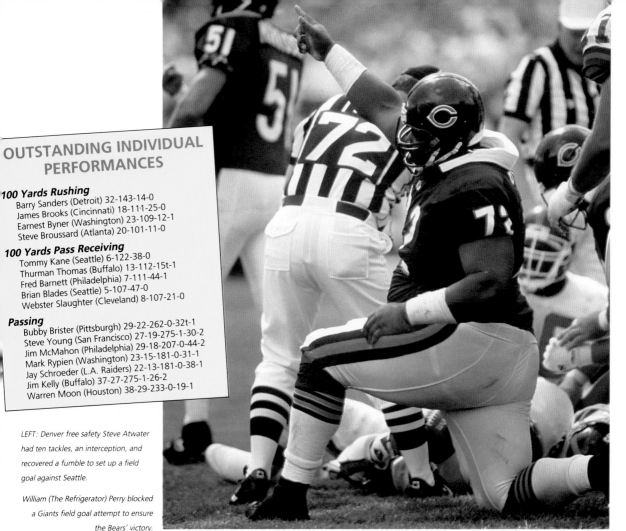

## OUTSTANDING INDIVIDUAL PERFORMANCES

### 100 Yards Rushing
Barry Sanders (Detroit) 32-143-14-0
James Brooks (Cincinnati) 18-111-25-0
Earnest Byner (Washington) 23-109-12-1
Steve Broussard (Atlanta) 20-101-11-0

### 100 Yards Pass Receiving
Tommy Kane (Seattle) 6-122-38-0
Thurman Thomas (Buffalo) 13-112-15t-1
Fred Barnett (Philadelphia) 7-111-44-1
Brian Blades (Seattle) 5-107-47-0
Webster Slaughter (Cleveland) 8-107-21-0

### Passing
Bubby Brister (Pittsburgh) 29-22-262-0-32t-1
Steve Young (San Francisco) 27-19-275-1-30-2
Jim McMahon (Philadelphia) 29-18-207-0-44-2
Mark Rypien (Washington) 23-15-181-0-31-1
Jay Schroeder (L.A. Raiders) 22-13-181-0-38-1
Jim Kelly (Buffalo) 37-27-275-1-26-2
Warren Moon (Houston) 38-29-233-0-19-1

LEFT: Denver free safety Steve Atwater had ten tackles, an interception, and recovered a fumble to set up a field goal against Seattle.

William (The Refrigerator) Perry blocked a Giants field goal attempt to ensure the Bears' victory.

## STANDINGS

| AFC East | W | L | T | PF | PA | Pct. | NFC East | W | L | T | PF | PA | Pct. |
|---|---|---|---|---|---|---|---|---|---|---|---|---|---|
| Buffalo | 3 | 0 | 0 | 110 | 85 | 1.000 | Washington | 3 | 0 | 0 | 112 | 31 | 1.000 |
| Miami | 1 | 2 | 0 | 61 | 58 | .333 | Philadelphia | 2 | 1 | 0 | 54 | 29 | .667 |
| New England | 1 | 2 | 0 | 22 | 47 | .333 | Phoenix | 2 | 1 | 0 | 50 | 58 | .667 |
| N.Y. Jets | 1 | 2 | 0 | 49 | 56 | .333 | Dallas | 1 | 2 | 0 | 57 | 71 | .333 |
| Indianapolis | 0 | 3 | 0 | 13 | 49 | 0.000 | N.Y. Giants | 1 | 2 | 0 | 46 | 53 | .333 |
| **AFC Central** | **W** | **L** | **T** | **PF** | **PA** | **Pct.** | **NFC Central** | **W** | **L** | **T** | **PF** | **PA** | **Pct.** |
| Houston | 3 | 0 | 0 | 94 | 31 | 1.000 | Chicago | 3 | 0 | 0 | 51 | 43 | 1.000 |
| Cleveland | 2 | 1 | 0 | 48 | 39 | .667 | Detroit | 2 | 1 | 0 | 40 | 72 | .667 |
| Pittsburgh | 2 | 1 | 0 | 80 | 78 | .667 | Minnesota | 2 | 1 | 0 | 43 | 43 | .667 |
| Cincinnati | 0 | 3 | 0 | 34 | 89 | 0.000 | Green Bay | 1 | 2 | 0 | 32 | 56 | .333 |
| **AFC West** | **W** | **L** | **T** | **PF** | **PA** | **Pct.** | Tampa Bay | 0 | 3 | 0 | 46 | 52 | 0.000 |
| Denver | 2 | 1 | 0 | 74 | 40 | .667 | **NFC West** | **W** | **L** | **T** | **PF** | **PA** | **Pct.** |
| L.A. Raiders | 2 | 1 | 0 | 49 | 60 | .667 | New Orleans | 3 | 0 | 0 | 68 | 41 | 1.000 |
| Kansas City | 1 | 2 | 0 | 31 | 37 | .333 | Atlanta | 1 | 2 | 0 | 35 | 44 | .333 |
| Seattle | 1 | 2 | 0 | 54 | 56 | .333 | L.A. Rams | 1 | 2 | 0 | 40 | 61 | .333 |
| San Diego | 0 | 3 | 0 | 44 | 73 | 0.000 | San Francisco | 1 | 2 | 0 | 62 | 47 | .333 |

# WEEK FOUR

## American Football Conference
Houston 20 at New England 24
San Diego 19 at Denver 27
Seattle 13 at Kansas City 20

## National Football Conference
Dallas 17 at Phoenix 9
Los Angeles Rams 10 at San Francisco 27
Minnesota 0 at New Orleans 26

## Interconference Games
Buffalo 17 at Tampa Bay 10
Cleveland 10 at New York Giants 13
Detroit 33 at Indianapolis 24
Green Bay 13 at Miami 16
Los Angeles Raiders 17 at Atlanta 21
New York Jets 13 at Chicago 19 (OT)
Pittsburgh 14 at Philadelphia 23
Washington 34 at Cincinnati 27

## Interconference Play
AFC 4 – NFC 12

*'It was cold, but I enjoyed it,' said Don Shula, whose players doused him in celebration of the Miami head coach's 300th career win.*

## Game of The Week
## Houston 20 – New England 24

The portents could hardly have been better for the unbeaten Houston Oilers, who travelled to Massachusetts with the best start in their 32-year history. A decade of careful reconstruction, given the finishing touch by imaginative head coach Jack Pardee, had produced a squad which comfortably had rolled over the Raiders, Cincinnati and Kansas City, and now stood alongside Buffalo as the class of the AFC.

The Patriots, on the other hand, were in a prolonged slump. In their previous 24 games they had scored only three victories, all at the expense of the modest Indianapolis Colts. In front of their home crowd, they were riding a ten-game losing streak. The Week-One euphoria which came with their victory over the Colts had quickly evaporated with losses to Cleveland and Pittsburgh.

Jason Staurovsky's field goal, just over six minutes into the first quarter, was, then, a welcome boost. And even after Oilers placekicker Ian Howfield had responded, there was a gathering feeling that 'something might be on' when touchdowns by tight end Marv Cook and rookie running back Leonard Russell, against a second Howfield intervention, took New England into the fourth quarter with a 17–6 lead.

For much of the way, Houston quarterback Warren Moon had faltered, searching for, but never quite finding, the right gear. But it couldn't last for ever and, on consecutive possessions, Moon drove the offense 69 yards, rounding off with touchdown passes of 35 and five yards to wide receiver Curtis Duncan.

With 1:52 remaining in the game and 83 yards to go against not the worst defense in the NFL, New England fans were looking at a probable 11th straight disappointment.

## OUTSTANDING INDIVIDUAL PERFORMANCES

### 100 Yards Rushing
Emmitt Smith (Dallas) 23-182-60t-2
Barry Sanders (Detroit) 30-179-42-2
Gaston Green (Denver) 24-127-63t-3
Blair Thomas (N.Y. Jets) 27-125-17-0
Gill Fenerty (New Orleans) 20-106-54-0
Rodney Hampton (N.Y. Giants) 17-104-44-1
Rod Bernstine (San Diego) 18-103-18-0

### 100 Yards Pass Receiving
Eric Green (Pittsburgh) 8-158-49-1
Roy Green (Philadelphia) 6-114-42-0
Anthony Johnson (Indianapolis) 9-105-15-0
Tom Waddle (Chicago) 8-102-31-0

### Passing
Steve Young (San Francisco) 31-21-288-0-62t-2
Steve DeBerg (Kansas City) 32-21-214-0-26-2
Jeff George (Indianapolis) 40-29-348-1-38-2

Yet it didn't bother quarterback Hugh Millen, a free-agent signing who boasted only three previous starts in his NFL career (they were for the Atlanta Falcons) and was making his first for New England. Passes of 23 yards to Cook and 16 to wide receiver Michael Timpson prised open the door before, with just six seconds left, he combined with wide receiver Greg McMurtry for a stunning 34-yard touchdown.

'People were wondering who we were,' said Patriots head coach Dick MacPherson.

## The Road To Super Bowl XXVI

Although outgaining Tampa Bay by 421 yards to 303, the Bills needed a late scoring drive to break a 10–10 tie. The winning touchdown came with 5:21 remaining when Jim Kelly fired a 29-yard pass to tight end Keith McKeller.

After establishing a 27–10 lead, 2:59 into the second half, the Redskins were reined in by a spirited Cincinnati rally. Gerald Riggs' seven-yard touchdown run, with 2:02 left, broke a 27–27 deadlock.

*Pro Bowl linebacker Sam Mills led the Saints to a shutout of the Vikings with 11 tackles, an interception and a forced fumble.*

# STANDINGS

| AFC East | W | L | T | PF | PA | Pct. | NFC East | W | L | T | PF | PA | Pct. |
|---|---|---|---|---|---|---|---|---|---|---|---|---|---|
| Buffalo | 4 | 0 | 0 | 127 | 95 | 1.000 | Washington | 4 | 0 | 0 | 146 | 58 | 1.000 |
| Miami | 2 | 2 | 0 | 77 | 71 | .500 | Philadelphia | 3 | 1 | 0 | 77 | 43 | .750 |
| New England | 2 | 2 | 0 | 46 | 67 | .500 | Dallas | 2 | 2 | 0 | 74 | 80 | .500 |
| N.Y. Jets | 1 | 3 | 0 | 62 | 75 | .250 | N.Y. Giants | 2 | 2 | 0 | 59 | 63 | .500 |
| Indianapolis | 0 | 4 | 0 | 37 | 82 | 0.000 | Phoenix | 2 | 2 | 0 | 59 | 75 | .500 |
| **AFC Central** | W | L | T | PF | PA | Pct. | **NFC Central** | W | L | T | PF | PA | Pct. |
| Houston | 3 | 1 | 0 | 114 | 55 | .750 | Chicago | 4 | 0 | 0 | 70 | 56 | 1.000 |
| Cleveland | 2 | 2 | 0 | 58 | 52 | .500 | Detroit | 3 | 1 | 0 | 73 | 96 | .750 |
| Pittsburgh | 2 | 2 | 0 | 94 | 101 | .500 | Minnesota | 2 | 2 | 0 | 43 | 69 | .500 |
| Cincinnati | 0 | 4 | 0 | 61 | 123 | 0.000 | Green Bay | 1 | 3 | 0 | 45 | 72 | .250 |
| **AFC West** | W | L | T | PF | PA | Pct. | Tampa Bay | 0 | 4 | 0 | 56 | 69 | 0.000 |
| Denver | 3 | 1 | 0 | 101 | 59 | .750 | **NFC West** | W | L | T | PF | PA | Pct. |
| Kansas City | 2 | 2 | 0 | 51 | 50 | .500 | New Orleans | 4 | 0 | 0 | 94 | 41 | 1.000 |
| L.A. Raiders | 2 | 2 | 0 | 66 | 81 | .500 | Atlanta | 2 | 2 | 0 | 56 | 61 | .500 |
| Seattle | 1 | 3 | 0 | 67 | 76 | .250 | San Francisco | 2 | 2 | 0 | 89 | 57 | .500 |
| San Diego | 0 | 4 | 0 | 63 | 100 | 0.000 | L.A. Rams | 1 | 3 | 0 | 50 | 88 | .250 |

# WEEK FIVE

### American Football Conference
Indianapolis 3 at Seattle 31
Kansas City 14 at San Diego 13
Miami 23 at New York Jets 41

### National Football Conference
Green Bay 21 at Los Angeles Rams 23
New Orleans 27 at Atlanta 6
New York Giants 16 at Dallas 21
Philadelphia 0 at Washington 23
Tampa Bay 3 at Detroit 31

### Interconference Games
Chicago 20 at Buffalo 35
Denver 13 at Minnesota 6
New England 10 at Phoenix 24
San Francisco 6 at Los Angeles Raiders 12

### Interconference Play
AFC 7 – NFC 13

## Game of The Week
## New York Giants 16 – Dallas 21

After four weeks, it was clear that the Giants would have to keep an eye on the undefeated Washington Redskins while the Cowboys, their Week Five opponents, had shown every evidence of being a contender. At the heart of the Cowboys' offense, quarterback Troy Aikman had shown signs of developing maturity, and in running back Emmitt Smith and wide receiver Michael Irvin he had the NFL's best pair of strikers at his disposal. Both teams were 2–2 and now was the time either for New York to halt a threat or for the Cowboys to announce their arrival.

It was expected to be close and was indeed decided by turnovers, but both teams had their periods of momentum. With Aikman in sharp form, Dallas moved steadily to a 14–3 third-quarter lead, helped by an important turnover which saw safety Ray Horton force and return a fumble 20 yards for a touchdown. A response was expected and it came when Matt Bahr, whose 43-yard field goal had opened the scoring, rewarded a 78-yard drive with his 29-yard chip-shot. At 3:48 into the final quarter, Bahr reduced the deficit to five points from 25 yards out. On the Giants' next possession, quarterback Jeff Hostetler, whose seniority over backup Phil Simms was coming under consideration, took charge. Completing a 41-yard pass to wide receiver Mark Ingram, Hostetler then ran for a 20-yard gain to place himself in position for the final act, a 19-yard scoring pass to wide receiver Stephen Baker.

One good defensive series might have saved the day for New York, but Aikman would not be denied. At 84 yards from his goal he trusted his arm, completing five of six passes, including a 30-yarder to Irvin, and salvaging a tricky third-and-three play with a 13-yard nerve-tester to tight

*Gaston Green gained his third rushing 'century' for the Broncos.*

end Jay Novacek. Riding the wave, Irvin was Aikman's choice for the 23-yard pass which gave Dallas the lead.

Only 2:13 remained, but it was long enough for the Giants to move ominously into scoring range. Trailing by five points, Hostetler's only option was to generate a touchdown. And when he made his move, Dallas cornerback Issiac Holt, hovering inside the end zone, pounced to intercept the pass.

Astonishingly, Aikman had completed at least one pass to ten different receivers as Dallas became the first team to score three touchdowns against the 1991 Giants. It had to mean something.

## The Road To Super Bowl XXVI

After the Bills had struggled through a first half from which they emerged with a one-point lead, Jim Kelly turned up the heat, passing for his second and third touchdowns of the game as Buffalo overcame the tough Chicago Bears.

On Monday evening the Redskins overcame a brave Philadelphia club which lost starting quarterback Jim McMahon in the early going. Ominously, this was the Redskins' third shutout of the campaign.

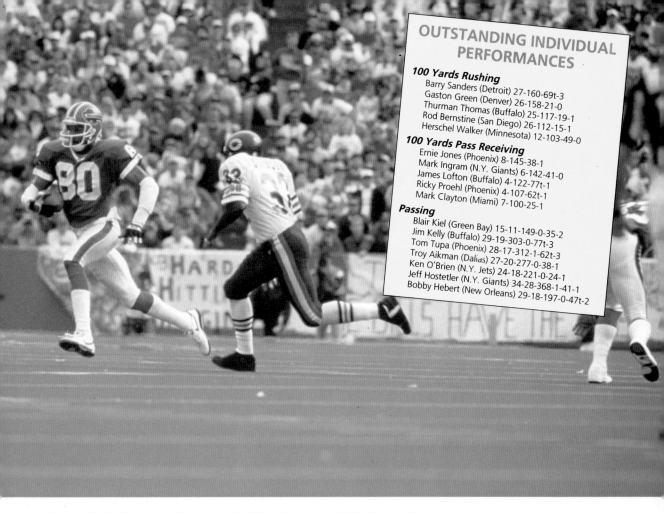

## OUTSTANDING INDIVIDUAL PERFORMANCES

### 100 Yards Rushing
Barry Sanders (Detroit) 27-160-69t-3
Gaston Green (Denver) 26-158-21-0
Thurman Thomas (Buffalo) 25-117-19-1
Rod Bernstine (San Diego) 26-112-15-1
Herschel Walker (Minnesota) 12-103-49-0

### 100 Yards Pass Receiving
Ernie Jones (Phoenix) 8-145-38-1
Mark Ingram (N.Y. Giants) 6-142-41-0
James Lofton (Buffalo) 4-122-77t-1
Ricky Proehl (Phoenix) 4-107-62t-1
Mark Clayton (Miami) 7-100-25-1

### Passing
Blair Kiel (Green Bay) 15-11-149-0-35-2
Jim Kelly (Buffalo) 29-19-303-0-77t-3
Tom Tupa (Phoenix) 28-17-312-1-62t-3
Troy Aikman (Dallas) 27-20-277-0-38-1
Ken O'Brien (N.Y. Jets) 24-18-221-0-24-1
Jeff Hostetler (N.Y. Giants) 34-28-368-1-41-1
Bobby Hebert (New Orleans) 29-18-197-0-47t-2

*James Lofton moved into fourth spot on the all-time receiving list with four catches, including this 77-yarder, against the Bears.*

# STANDINGS

| AFC East | W | L | T | PF | PA | Pct. | NFC East | W | L | T | PF | PA | Pct. |
|---|---|---|---|---|---|---|---|---|---|---|---|---|---|
| Buffalo | 5 | 0 | 0 | 162 | 115 | 1.000 | Washington | 5 | 0 | 0 | 169 | 58 | 1.000 |
| Miami | 2 | 3 | 0 | 100 | 112 | .400 | Dallas | 3 | 2 | 0 | 95 | 96 | .600 |
| New England | 2 | 3 | 0 | 56 | 91 | .400 | Philadelphia | 3 | 2 | 0 | 77 | 66 | .600 |
| N.Y. Jets | 2 | 3 | 0 | 103 | 98 | .400 | Phoenix | 3 | 2 | 0 | 83 | 85 | .600 |
| Indianapolis | 0 | 5 | 0 | 40 | 113 | 0.000 | N.Y. Giants | 2 | 3 | 0 | 75 | 84 | .400 |
| **AFC Central** | W | L | T | PF | PA | Pct. | **NFC Central** | W | L | T | PF | PA | Pct. |
| Houston** | 3 | 1 | 0 | 114 | 55 | .750 | Chicago | 4 | 1 | 0 | 90 | 91 | .800 |
| Cleveland** | 2 | 2 | 0 | 58 | 52 | .500 | Detroit | 4 | 1 | 0 | 104 | 99 | .800 |
| Pittsburgh** | 2 | 2 | 0 | 94 | 101 | .500 | Minnesota | 2 | 3 | 0 | 49 | 82 | .400 |
| Cincinnati** | 0 | 4 | 0 | 61 | 123 | 0.000 | Green Bay | 1 | 4 | 0 | 66 | 95 | .200 |
| **AFC West** | W | L | T | PF | PA | Pct. | Tampa Bay | 0 | 5 | 0 | 59 | 100 | 0.000 |
| Denver | 4 | 1 | 0 | 114 | 65 | .800 | **NFC West** | W | L | T | PF | PA | Pct. |
| Kansas City | 3 | 2 | 0 | 65 | 63 | .600 | New Orleans | 5 | 0 | 0 | 121 | 47 | 1.000 |
| L.A. Raiders | 3 | 2 | 0 | 78 | 87 | .600 | Atlanta | 2 | 3 | 0 | 62 | 88 | .400 |
| Seattle | 2 | 3 | 0 | 98 | 79 | .400 | L.A. Rams | 2 | 3 | 0 | 73 | 109 | .400 |
| San Diego | 0 | 5 | 0 | 76 | 114 | 0.000 | San Francisco | 2 | 3 | 0 | 95 | 69 | .400 |

**Did not play on Week Five

# Week Six

*Rodney Peete led the Lions to 21 fourth-quarter points as Detroit came back to beat the Vikings.*

## Game of The Week
## Minnesota 20 – Detroit 24

Each year the Minnesota Vikings, a team of ample talent and well coached by Jerry Burns, promise a return to the authority they showed in the late 1960s and throughout the 1970s when, essentially, they owned the NFC Central division. But a series of questionable decisions and some disappointments, the most recent of which was a costly trade with Dallas for running back Herschel Walker, have always deflected them off course.

For Detroit's purple patch we have to search back to the 1950s. Since then the Lions have surfaced occasionally but mostly have flattered only to deceive. However, head coach Wayne Fontes has had a rejuvenating effect and his 1991 squad had brushed off a dreadful opening-day loss to score four straight wins.

In the Lions' den Minnesota began well, drawing first blood on Darrin Nelson's 11-yard touchdown run and establishing a hold when tight end Steve Jordan capitalized on Joey Browner's interception by catching a two-yard touchdown pass. The hold became a grip as placekicker Fuad Reveiz responded to a lone Detroit field goal and then took the Vikings further ahead with his 25-yarder. With less than nine minutes remaining and having shown little more than honest toil, the Lions were all but defeated.

But nobody told Detroit's Rodney Peete, more a battler than the classic quarterback. After three probing plays, he combined with wide receiver Robert Clark for a 68-yard touchdown play – 6:50 to go. Following a fumble recovery by Derek Tennell on the ensuing kickoff, Peete took his time to move 41 yards in seven plays before connecting with Willie Green for a 16-yard touchdown – 4:22 left. And on the drive for the coup de grâce he was even more circumspect, using all of nine plays as he nudged the offense 57 yards before handing off to running back Barry Sanders on a draw play, 15 yards from the Minnesota end zone. The great running back already had caught nine passes for 76 yards and had just taken his personal rushing total over 100 yards for the fourth successive game. With Sanders in that kind of mood, not even Pro Bowl safety Joey Browner presented a problem and the 21-point rally was duly completed with 36 seconds to spare.

## The Road To Super Bowl XXVI

Kansas City running backs Christian Okoye and Harvey Williams rushed for 130 and 103 yards respectively, Jim Kelly was sacked six times and the Bills lost possession on five fumbles. It wasn't a nightmare, it was real, as the Bills were demolished for their first loss of the campaign.

Playing some way below their best and being held to less than 300 yards offense for the first time in the season, the Redskins nonetheless overcame an error-prone Chicago Bears team to remain as one of only two undefeated teams in the entire league.

*Ernest Givins gained 151 yards receiving as the Oilers crushed the Broncos.*

## OUTSTANDING INDIVIDUAL PERFORMANCES

**100 Yards Rushing**
Rodney Hampton (N.Y. Giants) 22-137-37-1
Christian Okoye (Kansas City) 29-122-14-2
Emmitt Smith (Dallas) 32-122-26-0
Barry Sanders (Detroit) 25-116-15t-1
Harvey Williams (Kansas City) 20-103-21-0

**100 Yards Pass Receiving**
Ernest Givins (Houston) 5-151-49-0
Jay Novacek (Dallas) 11-121-26-1
Eddie Brown (Cincinnati) 7-117-43-0
Mark Jackson (Denver) 7-111-43-0
Ron Morris (Chicago) 5-106-33-0

**Passing**
Jeff Hostetler (N.Y. Giants) 18-14-200-0-30-1
Dan Marino (Miami) 38-25-321-0-34-2
Bubby Brister (Pittsburgh) 16-13-181-2-28-2
Ken O'Brien (N.Y. Jets) 23-19-195-0-32-0
Warren Moon (Houston) 31-19-334-1-49-2
Troy Aikman (Dallas) 41-31-287-0-26-1
Steve DeBerg (Kansas City) 23-16-150-0-21-1

# STANDINGS

| AFC East | W | L | T | PF | PA | Pct. | NFC East | W | L | T | PF | PA | Pct. |
|---|---|---|---|---|---|---|---|---|---|---|---|---|---|
| Buffalo | 5 | 1 | 0 | 168 | 148 | .833 | Washington | 6 | 0 | 0 | 189 | 65 | 1.000 |
| Miami | 3 | 3 | 0 | 120 | 122 | .500 | Dallas | 4 | 2 | 0 | 115 | 113 | .667 |
| N.Y. Jets | 3 | 3 | 0 | 120 | 112 | .500 | N.Y. Giants | 3 | 3 | 0 | 95 | 93 | .500 |
| New England | 2 | 4 | 0 | 66 | 111 | .333 | Philadelphia | 3 | 3 | 0 | 90 | 80 | .500 |
| Indianapolis | 0 | 6 | 0 | 43 | 134 | 0.000 | Phoenix | 3 | 3 | 0 | 92 | 105 | .500 |
| **AFC Central** | **W** | **L** | **T** | **PF** | **PA** | **Pct.** | **NFC Central** | **W** | **L** | **T** | **PF** | **PA** | **Pct.** |
| Houston | 4 | 1 | 0 | 156 | 69 | .800 | Detroit | 5 | 1 | 0 | 128 | 119 | .833 |
| Pittsburgh | 3 | 2 | 0 | 115 | 104 | .600 | Chicago | 4 | 2 | 0 | 97 | 111 | .667 |
| Cleveland | 2 | 3 | 0 | 72 | 69 | .400 | Minnesota | 2 | 4 | 0 | 69 | 106 | .333 |
| Cincinnati | 0 | 5 | 0 | 68 | 136 | 0.000 | Green Bay | 1 | 5 | 0 | 83 | 115 | .167 |
| **AFC West** | **W** | **L** | **T** | **PF** | **PA** | **Pct.** | Tampa Bay | 1 | 5 | 0 | 73 | 113 | .167 |
| Denver | 4 | 2 | 0 | 128 | 107 | .667 | **NFC West** | **W** | **L** | **T** | **PF** | **PA** | **Pct.** |
| Kansas City | 4 | 2 | 0 | 98 | 69 | .667 | New Orleans** | 5 | 0 | 0 | 121 | 47 | 1.000 |
| L.A. Raiders | 3 | 3 | 0 | 91 | 108 | .500 | Atlanta** | 2 | 3 | 0 | 62 | 88 | .400 |
| Seattle | 3 | 3 | 0 | 111 | 86 | .500 | L.A. Rams** | 2 | 3 | 0 | 73 | 109 | .400 |
| San Diego | 1 | 5 | 0 | 97 | 127 | .167 | San Francisco** | 2 | 3 | 0 | 95 | 69 | .400 |

*\*\*Did not play on Week Six*

# WEEK SEVEN

**American Football Conference**
>Houston 23 at New York Jets 20
>Indianapolis 6 at Buffalo 42
>Los Angeles Raiders 23 at Seattle 20 (OT)
>Miami 7 at Kansas City 42

**National Football Conference**
>New Orleans 13 at Philadelphia 6
>Phoenix 7 at Minnesota 34
>Atlanta 39 at San Francisco 34 (venue switched)

**Interconference Games**
>Cincinnati 23 at Dallas 35
>Cleveland 17 at Washington 42
>New York Giants 23 at Pittsburgh 20
>San Diego 24 at Los Angeles Rams 30

**Interconference Play**
>AFC 7 – NFC 17

## Game of The Week
## Los Angeles Raiders 23 – Seattle 20 (Overtime)

It is a measure of the Raiders' historic greatness that, in their series against the other 27 clubs, they lead in all but four. In games with New England and Philadelphia they were tied while they trailed Buffalo by one game out of 27 and Seattle by two out of 28. Six weeks into the 1991 season, both the Raiders and Seattle were at 3–3. Ask anyone in El Segundo, the Raiders' power base, and even he will admit that he always expects trouble when they face the Seahawks. As for the fans in the Seattle Kingdome, the venue for this game, they always have a special strain of vituperation 'on ice' for the visits of the hated 'Silver and Black'.

And they had quite a time dishing out the taunts as the Raiders made a series of errors, resulting in five early turn-overs, the last of which, an interception, was returned 32 yards by cornerback Patrick Hunter for the touchdown which gave Seattle a 17–0 halftime lead.

'I used some choice words,' understated Raiders head coach Art Shell when describing his halftime comments to his charges. Whatever they were, they had the desired effect. Putting together his drive carefully, Los Angeles quarterback Jay Schroeder used 12 plays in the 76-yard march climaxed by tight end Ethan Horton's eight-yard touchdown catch. At 1:12 inside the final quarter, after Schroeder and Horton had combined for plays of eight and nine yards on key third-downs, placekicker Jeff Jaeger re-duced the deficit to seven points with a 47-yard field goal. Little more than eight minutes later, after Schroeder had switched his attention to wide receiver Mervyn Fernandez, the scores were level, when wide receiver Tim Brown hauled in a 12-yard touchdown pass.

Placekicker John Kasay's 45-yard field goal took Seattle back into the lead, but by now Schroeder was directing his offense with real authority. In a whirlwind series of ten plays, he moved the ball 53 yards, and only one second of regulation time remained when Jaeger's 49-yard field goal took the teams into overtime.

Six minutes into the extra period, pressure from the Raiders' defense harried Seahawks quarterback Jeff Kemp into an errant pass, which was intercepted by the diving Ronnie Lott on the Seattle 19-yard line. After nudging into position on one play, Shell opted for a 37-yard field goal attempt and Jaeger duly obliged.

## The Road To Super Bowl XXVI

Despite the loss of Jim Kelly, who left the field with mild concussion in the second quarter, the Bills bounced back from their loss to Kansas City, scoring six touchdowns against the winless Indianapolis Colts.

Against Cleveland, Washington unveiled yet another weapon in the form of rookie running back Ricky Ervins, who carried 13 times for 133 yards, including touchdown runs of 12 and 65 yards. At the other end of the spectrum, veteran wide receiver Art Monk raised his total of catches to 751, moving him into second place in the all-time list.

FAR LEFT: Christian Okoye, 'The Nigerian Nightmare', battered the Dolphins with 153 yards rushing and two touchdowns.

LEFT: Washington's Art Monk moved past Charlie Joiner into second place in the NFL's all-time receiving list.

## OUTSTANDING INDIVIDUAL PERFORMANCES

### 100 Yards Rushing
Christian Okoye (Kansas City) 23-153-38t-2
Ricky Ervins (Washington) 13-133-65t-2
Harold Green (Cincinnati) 12-124-75t-1
Thurman Thomas (Buffalo) 20-117-19-2
Kenneth Davis (Buffalo) 9-108-78t-1
Steve Broussard (Atlanta) 10-104-36-0

### 100 Yards Pass Receiving
Haywood Jeffires (Houston) 13-186-35-0
Anthony Miller (San Diego) 7-149-43-1
Michael Irvin (Dallas) 6-148-61-0
Jerry Rice (San Francisco) 7-138-57t-1
Cris Carter (Minnesota) 6-118-42t-1
Art Monk (Washington) 7-106-46-1
Tony Martin (Miami) 4-104-54-0

### Passing
Steve DeBerg (Kansas City) 12-9-177-0-41t-3
Jim Everett (L.A. Rams) 25-19-219-0-31-2
Rich Gannon (Minnesota) 31-23-254-0-42t-2
Chris Miller (Atlanta) 28-16-208-0-41-3
Mark Rypien (Washington) 22-16-190-0-46-1
Neil O'Donnell (Pittsburgh) 21-11-152-0-25-2
John Friesz (San Diego) 33-21-306-1-49t-2
Bernie Kosar (Cleveland) 29-21-266-0-45-0

## STANDINGS

| AFC East | W | L | T | PF | PA | Pct. | NFC East | W | L | T | PF | PA | Pct. |
|---|---|---|---|---|---|---|---|---|---|---|---|---|---|
| Buffalo | 6 | 1 | 0 | 210 | 154 | .857 | Washington | 7 | 0 | 0 | 231 | 82 | 1.000 |
| Miami | 3 | 4 | 0 | 127 | 164 | .429 | Dallas | 5 | 2 | 0 | 150 | 136 | .714 |
| N.Y. Jets | 3 | 4 | 0 | 140 | 135 | .429 | N.Y. Giants | 4 | 3 | 0 | 118 | 113 | .571 |
| New England** | 2 | 4 | 0 | 66 | 111 | .333 | Philadelphia | 3 | 4 | .0 | 96 | 93 | .429 |
| Indianapolis | 0 | 7 | 0 | 49 | 176 | 0.000 | Phoenix | 3 | 4 | 0 | 99 | 139 | .429 |
| **AFC Central** | W | L | T | PF | PA | Pct. | **NFC Central** | W | L | T | PF | PA | Pct. |
| Houston | 5 | 1 | 0 | 179 | 89 | .833 | Detroit** | 5 | 1 | 0 | 128 | 119 | .833 |
| Pittsburgh | 3 | 3 | 0 | 135 | 127 | .500 | Chicago** | 4 | 2 | 0 | 97 | 111 | .667 |
| Cleveland | 2 | 4 | 0 | 89 | 111 | .333 | Minnesota | 3 | 4 | 0 | 103 | 113 | .429 |
| Cincinnati | 0 | 6 | 0 | 91 | 171 | 0.000 | Green Bay** | 1 | 5 | 0 | 83 | 115 | .167 |
| **AFC West** | W | L | T | PF | PA | Pct. | Tampa Bay** | 1 | 5 | 0 | 73 | 113 | .167 |
| Kansas City | 5 | 2 | 0 | 140 | 76 | .714 | **NFC West** | W | L | T | PF | PA | Pct. |
| Denver** | 4 | 2 | 0 | 128 | 107 | .667 | New Orleans | 6 | 0 | 0 | 134 | 53 | 1.000 |
| L.A. Raiders | 4 | 3 | 0 | 114 | 128 | .571 | Atlanta | 3 | 3 | 0 | 101 | 122 | .500 |
| Seattle | 3 | 4 | 0 | 131 | 109 | .429 | L.A. Rams | 3 | 3 | 0 | 103 | 133 | .500 |
| San Diego | 1 | 6 | 0 | 121 | 157 | .143 | San Francisco | 2 | 4 | 0 | 129 | 108 | .333 |

**Did not play on Week Seven

# WEEK EIGHT

### American Football Conference
Cincinnati 16 at Buffalo 35
Cleveland 30 at San Diego 24 (OT)
Houston 17 at Miami 13
Kansas City 16 at Denver 19
New York Jets 17 at Indianapolis 6
Seattle 27 at Pittsburgh 7

### National Football Conference
Atlanta 10 at Phoenix 16
Chicago 10 at Green Bay 0
Detroit 3 at San Francisco 35
Tampa Bay 7 at New Orleans 23

### Interconference Games
Los Angeles Rams 17 at Los Angeles Raiders 20
Minnesota 23 at New England 26 (OT)

### Interconference Play
AFC 9 – NFC 17

## Game of The Week
## Minnesota 23 – New England 26 (Overtime)

Following their Week-Four upset of Houston, the Patriots reverted to mediocrity, losing to Phoenix and Miami. Against the Dolphins, quarterback Hugh Millen had been sacked six times and he, together with one or two more, welcomed the break in their schedule on Week Seven.

The Vikings, on the other hand, were coming off a handsome 34–7 victory at the expense of Phoenix. Encouragingly, newly promoted quarterback Rich Gannon was settling in and the once-feared defense was warming to the task, having registered five sacks. With Herschel Walker back to full fitness, the signs were good but they could hardly afford a loss in what clearly had become a competitive NFC Central division.

Right from the start, the Vikings were rocked back on their heels as Patriots wide receiver Greg McMurtry capped an 11-play drive with his 18-yard touchdown reception. Five minutes into the second period, Minnesota was on level terms when Walker scored from the one, but New England responded immediately with Leonard Russell making the final step of a 70-yard march. Yet the Vikings hung on tenaciously and, though they could not punch into the end zone following drives of 70 and 57 yards, field goals of 23 and 32 yards by Fuad Reveiz left them only one point adrift.

New England had a stroke of luck when guard Freddie Childress recovered a fumble by a teammate in the Vikings' end zone. The extra point attempt failed but, after New England's Marvin Allen recovered possession following a fumble by Minnesota punt returner Leo Lewis, Jason Staurovsky was on target with a 38-yard field goal to give New England a ten-point lead.

*Miami's Sammie Smith coughs up the ball as he dives for the end zone. Cris Dishman recovered for Houston.*

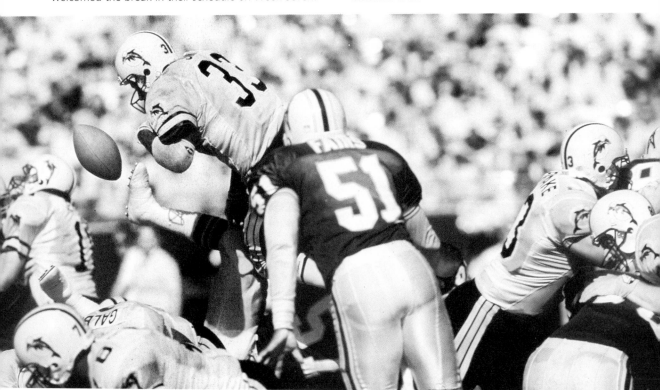

*John Elway's 71-yard completion on 3rd-and-17 set up Denver's winning field goal.*

But the Vikings were not yet ready to concede. Gannon rounded off a 58-yard drive with a four-yard touchdown pass to wide receiver Anthony Carter and, following the inevitable onside kick, Minnesota's Solomon Wilcots recovered possession. In barely more than a minute, Gannon took the offense 38 yards in nine plays, including a 14-yard completion to Hassan Jones on fourth-and-ten. Just 20 seconds of regulation time remained when Reveiz's 23-yard chip took the game into overtime.

In the extra period, after failing on a relatively simple 36-yard field goal attempt, with his second chance Staurovsky was on the mark, splitting the uprights as time ran out.

## The Road To Super Bowl XXVI

With Washington inactive on Week Eight, the Bills overcame the winless Cincinnati Bengals, who gave up a series of penalties and intercepted Jim Kelly three times. Kelly did throw five touchdown passes, including those for 74 and 48 yards to wide receiver James Lofton, whose game total of 220 yards receiving was a career best.

# STANDINGS

| AFC East | W | L | T | PF | PA | Pct. | NFC East | W | L | T | PF | PA | Pct. |
|---|---|---|---|---|---|---|---|---|---|---|---|---|---|
| Buffalo | 7 | 1 | 0 | 245 | 170 | .875 | Washington** | 7 | 0 | 0 | 231 | 82 | 1.000 |
| N.Y. Jets | 4 | 4 | 0 | 157 | 141 | .500 | Dallas** | 5 | 2 | 0 | 150 | 136 | .714 |
| New England | 3 | 4 | 0 | 92 | 134 | .429 | N.Y. Giants** | 4 | 3 | 0 | 118 | 113 | .571 |
| Miami | 3 | 5 | 0 | 140 | 181 | .375 | Phoenix | 4 | 4 | 0 | 115 | 149 | .500 |
| Indianapolis | 0 | 8 | 0 | 55 | 193 | 0.000 | Philadelphia** | 3 | 4 | 0 | 96 | 93 | .429 |
| **AFC Central** | **W** | **L** | **T** | **PF** | **PA** | **Pct.** | **NFC Central** | **W** | **L** | **T** | **PF** | **PA** | **Pct.** |
| Houston | 6 | 1 | 0 | 196 | 102 | .857 | Chicago | 5 | 2 | 0 | 107 | 111 | .714 |
| Cleveland | 3 | 4 | 0 | 119 | 135 | .429 | Detroit | 5 | 2 | 0 | 131 | 154 | .714 |
| Pittsburgh | 3 | 4 | 0 | 142 | 154 | .429 | Minnesota | 3 | 5 | 0 | 126 | 139 | .375 |
| Cincinnati | 0 | 7 | 0 | 107 | 206 | 0.000 | Green Bay | 1 | 6 | 0 | 83 | 125 | .143 |
| **AFC West** | **W** | **L** | **T** | **PF** | **PA** | **Pct.** | Tampa Bay | 1 | 6 | 0 | 80 | 136 | .143 |
| Denver | 5 | 2 | 0 | 147 | 123 | .714 | **NFC West** | **W** | **L** | **T** | **PF** | **PA** | **Pct.** |
| Kansas City | 5 | 3 | 0 | 156 | 95 | .625 | New Orleans | 7 | 0 | 0 | 157 | 60 | 1.000 |
| L.A. Raiders | 5 | 3 | 0 | 134 | 145 | .625 | Atlanta | 3 | 4 | 0 | 111 | 138 | .429 |
| Seattle | 4 | 4 | 0 | 158 | 116 | .500 | L.A. Rams | 3 | 4 | 0 | 120 | 153 | .429 |
| San Diego | 1 | 7 | 0 | 145 | 187 | .125 | San Francisco | 3 | 4 | 0 | 164 | 111 | .429 |

***Did not play on Week Eight*

# WEEK NINE

## American Football Conference
Cincinnati 3 at Houston 35
Denver 9 at New England 6
Los Angeles Raiders 21 at Kansas City 24
Pittsburgh 14 at Cleveland 17
San Diego 9 at Seattle 20

## National Football Conference
Chicago 20 at New Orleans 17
Dallas 10 at Detroit 34
Green Bay 27 at Tampa Bay 0
Los Angeles Rams 14 at Atlanta 31
Minnesota 28 at Phoenix 0
San Francisco 23 at Philadelphia 7
Washington 17 at New York Giants 13

## Interconference Play
AFC 9 – NFC 17

RIGHT: Seattle's John Kasay kicked field goals of 51 and 54 yards.
BELOW: Charles Haley (94) had three sacks against Philadelphia.

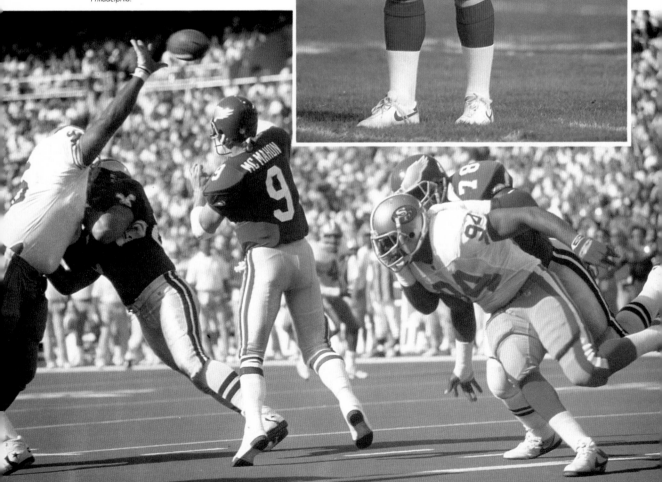

## Game of The Week
## Chicago 20 – New Orleans 17

Chicago opened the season with four victories before losing consecutive games against Buffalo and Washington. Despite the reverses they stood equal first with the surprising Detroit Lions in the NFC Central division. Even so, they had to avoid too many setbacks if they were to retain the title they'd held for a seven-year period, punctuated only by Minnesota in 1989.

On Week Nine they faced a formidable opponent in New Orleans, a club which was one of only two remaining unbeaten teams after seven games. For the Saints, Bobby Hebert was re-established at quarterback after a year's absence because of a contractual dispute, but the true strength of the team lay in defense in perhaps the finest quartet of linebackers in football.

And, for much of the game, Bears quarterback Jim Harbaugh was a believer as he was hounded with unrelenting fury by the foursome. Three times he was sacked and only twice did his first 19 passing attempts find their mark. The Saints, meanwhile, totted up the points on what was Floyd Turner's best day as a pro. On the way to a total of nine receptions in the game, the third-year wide receiver opened the scoring with a 65-yard catch. The Bears responded, but only by picking up the bits in establishing position for a pair of Kevin Butler field goals. Butler's second effort was a highly respectable 48-yarder but his New Orleans counterpart, Morten Andersen, responded on the stroke of half-time by kicking the equal third-longest field goal in NFL history, a 60-yarder, extending the lead to four points.

Shortly after the resumption, Chicago took the lead for the first time on Brad Muster's six-yard touchdown run, but it had been with the assistance of a 37-yard pass interference penalty on Saints cornerback Vince Buck. Less than eight minutes later, Hebert and Turner combined for the eight-yard touchdown play which re-established a lead. Only with less than two minutes remaining did the 'real Chicago Bears' stand up. After a poor punt had given Chicago possession on their own 48-yard line, Harbaugh completed all three of his passes in a four-play drive culminating in wide receiver Tom Waddle's 12-yard scoring catch.

'I got mad at him out there but he's trying to make the plays. That's a war zone,' reflected Bears head coach Mike Ditka.

## The Road To Super Bowl XXVI

On Week Nine it was Buffalo's turn for rest and recuperation.

For the first time in the season, the Redskins were taken to the limit by a Giants team which led 13–0 until just 42 seconds before the end of the third quarter. However, with outstanding ball-control offense which saw Washington convert nine consecutive third-down plays in the second half, twice for touchdown passes from Mark Rypien to wide receiver Gary Clark, the reigning Super Bowl Champions were gradually overpowered.

### OUTSTANDING INDIVIDUAL PERFORMANCES

**100 Yards Pass Receiving**
Jay Novacek (Dallas) 10-191-49-0
Floyd Turner (New Orleans) 9-179-65t-2
Michael Irvin (Dallas) 8-143-22-0
Drew Hill (Houston) 6-129-61t-1
Michael Haynes (Atlanta) 4-110-55t-1
Mervyn Fernandez (L.A. Raiders) 3-107-59-0

**Passing**
Chris Miller (Atlanta) 19-14-237-0-55t-3
Erik Kramer (Detroit) 16-9-108-0-26t-2
Steve Young (San Francisco) 15-10-96-0-22-1

### STANDINGS

| AFC East | W | L | T | PF | PA | Pct. |
|---|---|---|---|---|---|---|
| Buffalo** | 7 | 1 | 0 | 245 | 170 | .875 |
| N.Y. Jets** | 4 | 4 | 0 | 157 | 141 | .500 |
| Miami** | 3 | 5 | 0 | 140 | 181 | .375 |
| New England | 3 | 5 | 0 | 98 | 143 | .375 |
| Indianapolis** | 0 | 8 | 0 | 55 | 193 | 0.000 |

| AFC Central | W | L | T | PF | PA | Pct. |
|---|---|---|---|---|---|---|
| Houston | 7 | 1 | 0 | 231 | 105 | .875 |
| Cleveland | 4 | 4 | 0 | 136 | 149 | .500 |
| Pittsburgh | 3 | 5 | 0 | 156 | 171 | .375 |
| Cincinnati | 0 | 8 | 0 | 110 | 241 | 0.000 |

| AFC West | W | L | T | PF | PA | Pct. |
|---|---|---|---|---|---|---|
| Denver | 6 | 2 | 0 | 156 | 129 | .750 |
| Kansas City | 6 | 3 | 0 | 180 | 116 | .667 |
| L.A. Raiders | 5 | 4 | 0 | 155 | 169 | .556 |
| Seattle | 5 | 4 | 0 | 178 | 125 | .556 |
| San Diego | 1 | 8 | 0 | 154 | 207 | .111 |

| NFC East | W | L | T | PF | PA | Pct. |
|---|---|---|---|---|---|---|
| Washington | 8 | 0 | 0 | 248 | 95 | 1.000 |
| Dallas | 5 | 3 | 0 | 160 | 170 | .625 |
| N.Y. Giants | 4 | 4 | 0 | 131 | 130 | .500 |
| Phoenix | 4 | 5 | 0 | 115 | 177 | .444 |
| Philadelphia | 3 | 5 | 0 | 103 | 116 | .375 |

| NFC Central | W | L | T | PF | PA | Pct. |
|---|---|---|---|---|---|---|
| Chicago | 6 | 2 | 0 | 127 | 128 | .750 |
| Detroit | 6 | 2 | 0 | 165 | 164 | .750 |
| Minnesota | 4 | 5 | 0 | 154 | 139 | .444 |
| Green Bay | 2 | 6 | 0 | 110 | 125 | .250 |
| Tampa Bay | 1 | 7 | 0 | 80 | 163 | .125 |

| NFC West | W | L | T | PF | PA | Pct. |
|---|---|---|---|---|---|---|
| New Orleans | 7 | 1 | 0 | 174 | 80 | .875 |
| Atlanta | 4 | 4 | 0 | 142 | 152 | .500 |
| San Francisco | 4 | 4 | 0 | 187 | 118 | .500 |
| L.A. Rams | 3 | 5 | 0 | 134 | 184 | .375 |

**Did not play on Week Nine

# WEEK TEN

**American Football Conference**
Cleveland 21 at Cincinnati 23
Miami 10 at Indianapolis 6
New England 17 at Buffalo 22
Pittsburgh 13 at Denver 20

**National Football Conference**
San Francisco 14 at Atlanta 17 (venue switched)
Detroit 10 at Chicago 20
New Orleans 24 at Los Angeles Rams 17
New York Giants 7 at Philadelphia 30
Phoenix 7 at Dallas 27
Tampa Bay 13 at Minnesota 28

**Interconference Games**
Green Bay 16 at New York Jets 19 (OT)
Houston 13 at Washington 16 (OT)

**Interconference Play**
AFC 10 – NFC 18

## Game of The Week
## San Francisco 14 – Atlanta 17

Entering Week Ten, San Francisco was 4–4, three games
behind the leader in the NFC West and level with Atlanta, to
whom they'd lost 34–39 in a wild one on Week Seven. But
despite their lowly spot in the order of things, the 49ers still
represented the benchmark against which true progress

was measured. Was their previous loss to Atlanta genuine?
After all, Falcons cornerback Tim McKyer intercepted two
passes in the final three minutes. That was unusual, and
so was Deion Sanders' 100-yard kickoff return for a
touchdown.

There was no question that, under head coach Jerry
Glanville, Atlanta no longer was a team which expected to
lose. They'd become a tough, even mean, outfit and, in
addition to beating the 49ers, they had knocked off San
Diego, the Raiders and the Rams. No one felt that they were
yet title contenders but maybe soon . . .

Perhaps later . . . the casual observer might have reflected, when the other half of the NFL's best pairing at
wide receiver, John Taylor, caught a 97-yard touchdown
pass. And bad became worse for Atlanta when quarterback
Chris Miller, who'd unravelled the 49ers with three touchdown passes three weeks earlier, left the game with a

*Michael Haynes
secured an unlikely win
for the Falcons.*

## OUTSTANDING INDIVIDUAL PERFORMANCES

### 100 Yards Rushing
Harold Green (Cincinnati) 24-135-29-0
Terry Allen (Minnesota) 14-127-55t-2
Thurman Thomas (Buffalo) 32-126-22-1
Earnest Byner (Washington) 21-112-23t-1
Greg Lewis (Denver) 19-111-27-1
Leonard Russell (New England) 27-106-19-2

### 100 Yards Pass Receiving
John Taylor (San Francisco) 2-127-97t-2
Andre Reed (Buffalo) 5-121-55-0
Al Toon (N.Y. Jets) 8-109-21-0
Webster Slaughter (Cleveland) 5-107-43-0

### Passing
Jim McMahon (Philadelphia) 26-16-229-0-73t-1
Jim Harbaugh (Chicago) 31-17-205-0-29-2
Billy Joe Tolliver (Atlanta) 22-11-120-0-44t-2
Rich Gannon (Minnesota) 28-19-160-0-22-1

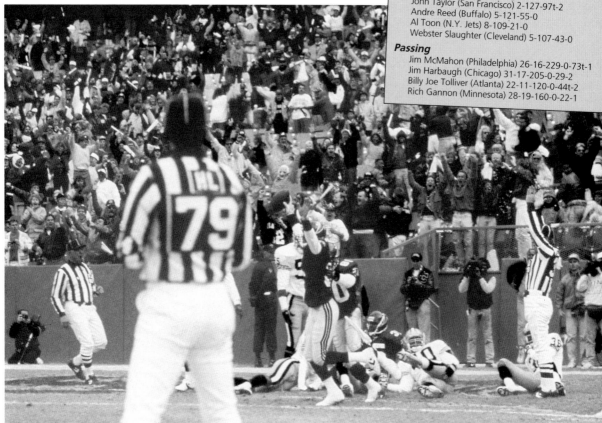

bruised shoulder. His departure meant that Billy Joe Tolliver, who had been traded by San Diego following a miserable preseason showing, faced the test of his life.

Tolliver took time to settle but, astonishingly, towards the end of the third quarter, he started out on what would be an 18-play drive which bore fruit 6:37 into the fourth, when wide receiver Andre Rison caught a three-yard touchdown pass. With 2:39 remaining in the game, following a botched 49ers punt recovered by the Falcons, Norm Johnson's 29-yard field goal gave Atlanta an unlikely three-point lead.

But the 49ers were not out of ideas and Steve Bono, who had come in for injured starter Steve Young, applied the 49ers' formula, and with just 53 seconds left his 30-yard touchdown pass to Taylor rounded off an eight-play drive.

Given the circumstances it was some way beyond reason to expect the Falcons to mount a rally, but they did. After six plays, including a fourth-and-six completion to Rison, Tolliver found himself 44 yards out and with time for one more shot. With what is known as a 'Hail Mary' pass, somewhere among a clutch of bodies, he found wide receiver Michael Haynes, who made the game-winning catch in the end zone.

## The Road To Super Bowl XXVI

Houston missed an outstanding opportunity to hand Washington its first loss of the campaign when placekicker Ian Howfield failed on a 33-yard field goal attempt with one second left in regulation time.

*Both of John Taylor's receptions against Atlanta went for touchdowns.*

In overtime, Chip Lohmiller's 41-yard field goal settled the issue after Darrell Green had intercepted a Warren Moon pass.

Buffalo's Scott Norwood was on target with three field goals, while Jason Staurovsky failed with attempts from 46 and 35 yards, as the Bills held off a spirited New England team.

| STANDINGS | | | | | | | | | | | | | |
|---|---|---|---|---|---|---|---|---|---|---|---|---|---|
| **AFC East** | **W** | **L** | **T** | **PF** | **PA** | **Pct.** | **NFC East** | **W** | **L** | **T** | **PF** | **PA** | **Pct.** |
| Buffalo | 8 | 1 | 0 | 267 | 187 | .889 | Washington | 9 | 0 | 0 | 264 | 108 | 1.000 |
| N.Y. Jets | 5 | 4 | 0 | 176 | 157 | .556 | Dallas | 6 | 3 | 0 | 187 | 177 | .667 |
| Miami | 4 | 5 | 0 | 150 | 187 | .444 | N.Y. Giants | 4 | 5 | 0 | 138 | 160 | .444 |
| New England | 3 | 6 | 0 | 115 | 165 | .333 | Philadelphia | 4 | 5 | 0 | 133 | 123 | .444 |
| Indianapolis | 0 | 9 | 0 | 61 | 203 | 0.000 | Phoenix | 4 | 6 | 0 | 122 | 204 | .400 |
| **AFC Central** | **W** | **L** | **T** | **PF** | **PA** | **Pct.** | **NFC Central** | **W** | **L** | **T** | **PF** | **PA** | **Pct.** |
| Houston | 7 | 2 | 0 | 244 | 121 | .778 | Chicago | 7 | 2 | 0 | 147 | 138 | .778 |
| Cleveland | 4 | 5 | 0 | 157 | 172 | .444 | Detroit | 6 | 3 | 0 | 175 | 184 | .667 |
| Pittsburgh | 3 | 6 | 0 | 169 | 191 | .333 | Minnesota | 5 | 5 | 0 | 182 | 152 | .500 |
| Cincinnati | 1 | 8 | 0 | 133 | 262 | .111 | Green Bay | 2 | 7 | 0 | 126 | 144 | .222 |
| **AFC West** | **W** | **L** | **T** | **PF** | **PA** | **Pct.** | Tampa Bay | 1 | 8 | 0 | 93 | 191 | .111 |
| Denver | 7 | 2 | 0 | 176 | 142 | .778 | **NFC West** | **W** | **L** | **T** | **PF** | **PA** | **Pct.** |
| Kansas City** | 6 | 3 | 0 | 180 | 116 | .667 | New Orleans | 8 | 1 | 0 | 198 | 97 | .889 |
| L.A. Raiders** | 5 | 4 | 0 | 155 | 169 | .556 | Atlanta | 5 | 4 | 0 | 159 | 166 | .556 |
| Seattle** | 5 | 4 | 0 | 178 | 125 | .556 | San Francisco | 4 | 5 | 0 | 201 | 135 | .444 |
| San Diego** | 1 | 8 | 0 | 154 | 207 | .111 | L.A. Rams | 3 | 6 | 0 | 151 | 208 | .333 |
| **Did not play on Week Ten | | | | | | | | | | | | | |

# WEEK ELEVEN

### American Football Conference
Indianapolis 28 at New York Jets 27
Los Angeles Raiders 17 at Denver 16
New England 20 at Miami 30
Pittsburgh 33 at Cincinnati 27 (OT)
Seattle 14 at San Diego 17

### National Football Conference
Atlanta 17 at Washington 56
Chicago 34 at Minnesota 17
Detroit 21 at Tampa Bay 30
New York Giants 21 at Phoenix 14
San Francisco 3 at New Orleans 10

### Interconference Games
Buffalo 34 vs Green Bay 24 (at Milwaukee)
Dallas 23 at Houston 26 (OT)
Kansas City 27 at Los Angeles Rams 20
Philadelphia 32 at Cleveland 30

### Interconference Play
AFC 13 – NFC 19

## Game of The Week
## Philadelphia 32 – Cleveland 30

The season had started badly for Philadelphia. Catastrophically might be a better way of describing the effect of an opening-day injury which sidelined starting quarterback Randall Cunningham for the entire year. For Cunningham was not only one of the NFL's best passers, he was also the Eagles' most prolific rusher. His loss meant that the club had turned to Jim McMahon, who'd led the Bears to victory in Super Bowl XX but now was bothered by so many injuries that his status was reviewed by the week. An hour before this game, he still wasn't sure if he could play.

By contrast, Cleveland quarterback Bernie Kosar had rebounded from a slump in 1990 and was only one short of equalling the NFL record for consecutive passes without an interception (294), held by the fabled Bart Starr. His problem was that he would be facing the league's best defense.

But it didn't seem to bother Kosar as he quickly relegated Starr into second place and added to an early ten-point lead with touchdown passes of 65 and 18 yards to Leroy Hoard and Webster Slaughter respectively. Fifteen seconds into the second quarter, then, the Browns led 23–0. McMahon's initial response, a 16-yard touchdown pass to tight end Keith Jackson, was hardly a sign of impending disaster for Cleveland, but then things started to unravel, just a little.

McMahon combined with wide receiver Fred Barnett for a 70-yard touchdown and, following Ben Smith's interception of Kosar's pass, ending the sequence at a new record 308, placekicker Roger Ruzek reduced the deficit to just six points. But the Browns did surface briefly to regain the initiative with Kosar's touchdown pass to Reggie Langhorne.

Cleveland's points total of 30 was more than the Eagles had conceded in any *full* game over the season thus far. And perhaps it was this which sparked a fury which would restrict the Browns to just 24 offensive yards the rest of the way. McMahon, meanwhile, struggled on, fighting through the pain as he grubbed out drives of 60, 89 and 78 yards for three further Ruzek field goals. Then, with the Eagles trailing by four points and time ebbing away, he was left with only five yards to go following the recovery of a fumble at the Browns' two-yard line. Three plays later, his touchdown pass to wide receiver Calvin Williams won the game, recording the 13th-best comeback in league history. For the Browns, the loss of a 23–0 lead was the worst collapse ever.

*Jeff George led the Colts to an upset over the Jets.*

## The Road To Super Bowl XXVI

After sitting out a few plays during the third quarter with an injured back, Jim Kelly returned to re-establish the momentum as Buffalo stayed comfortably clear of the Green Bay Packers.

Atlanta's tactic was to mount an all-out blitz, daring the Redskins to pass. Mark Rypien accepted the challenge, delivered a personal, single-game-best six touchdown passes and even ran for a touchdown as the Falcons were handed a lesson.

RIGHT: Bernie Kosar set a new NFL record before he was halted by the Eagles.

## OUTSTANDING INDIVIDUAL PERFORMANCES

### 100 Yards Rushing
Reggie Cobb (Tampa Bay) 21-139-59t-3
Barry Sanders (Detroit) 23-118-40-2
Thurman Thomas (Buffalo) 24-106-21-1
Gaston Green (Denver) 18-103-21-0

### 100 Yards Pass Receiving
Gary Clark (Washington) 4-203-82t-3
Art Monk (Washington) 7-164-64t-2
Henry Ellard (L.A. Rams) 8-160-27-1
Fred Barnett (Philadelphia) 8-146-70t-1
Sterling Sharpe (Green Bay) 8-133-58t-1
Brian Blades (Seattle) 8-131-39-0
Brett Perriman (Detroit) 6-127-42-0
Anthony Miller (San Diego) 5-124-58-0
James Lofton (Buffalo) 6-114-29-0
Michael Haynes (Atlanta) 2-105-75t-1
Tim McGee (Cincinnati) 3-101-52-0
Jessie Hester (Indianapolis) 5-100-49t-2

### Passing
Mark Rypien (Washington) 31-16-442-0-82t-6
Hugh Millen (New England) 26-20-257-1-40t-2
Dan Marino (Miami) 29-19-263-1-32t-3
Jim Everett (L.A. Rams) 37-26-329-1-27-3
Neil O'Donnell (Pittsburgh) 39-24-309-0-35t-3
Dave Krieg (Seattle) 38-28-376-1-49-2
Jay Schroeder (L.A. Raiders) 19-12-140-0-27-1
Ken O'Brien (N.Y. Jets) 36-23-329-0-31-1
Steve DeBerg (Kansas City) 26-17-199-0-31-1

## STANDINGS

| AFC East | W | L | T | PF | PA | Pct. | NFC East | W | L | T | PF | PA | Pct. |
|---|---|---|---|---|---|---|---|---|---|---|---|---|---|
| Buffalo | 9 | 1 | 0 | 301 | 211 | .900 | Washington | 10 | 0 | 0 | 320 | 125 | 1.000 |
| Miami | 5 | 5 | 0 | 180 | 207 | .500 | Dallas | 6 | 4 | 0 | 210 | 203 | .600 |
| N.Y. Jets | 5 | 5 | 0 | 203 | 185 | .500 | N.Y. Giants | 5 | 5 | 0 | 159 | 174 | .500 |
| New England | 3 | 7 | 0 | 135 | 195 | .300 | Philadelphia | 5 | 5 | 0 | 165 | 153 | .500 |
| Indianapolis | 1 | 9 | 0 | 89 | 230 | .100 | Phoenix | 4 | 7 | 0 | 136 | 225 | .364 |
| **AFC Central** | **W** | **L** | **T** | **PF** | **PA** | **Pct.** | **NFC Central** | **W** | **L** | **T** | **PF** | **PA** | **Pct.** |
| Houston | 8 | 2 | 0 | 270 | 144 | .800 | Chicago | 8 | 2 | 0 | 181 | 155 | .800 |
| Cleveland | 4 | 6 | 0 | 187 | 204 | .400 | Detroit | 6 | 4 | 0 | 196 | 214 | .600 |
| Pittsburgh | 4 | 6 | 0 | 202 | 218 | .400 | Minnesota | 5 | 6 | 0 | 199 | 186 | .455 |
| Cincinnati | 1 | 9 | 0 | 160 | 295 | .100 | Green Bay | 2 | 8 | 0 | 150 | 178 | .200 |
| **AFC West** | **W** | **L** | **T** | **PF** | **PA** | **Pct.** | Tampa Bay | 2 | 8 | 0 | 123 | 212 | .200 |
| Denver | 7 | 3 | 0 | 192 | 159 | .700 | **NFC West** | **W** | **L** | **T** | **PF** | **PA** | **Pct.** |
| Kansas City | 7 | 3 | 0 | 207 | 136 | .700 | New Orleans | 9 | 1 | 0 | 208 | 100 | .900 |
| L.A. Raiders | 6 | 4 | 0 | 172 | 185 | .600 | Atlanta | 5 | 5 | 0 | 176 | 222 | .500 |
| Seattle | 5 | 5 | 0 | 192 | 142 | .500 | San Francisco | 4 | 6 | 0 | 204 | 145 | .400 |
| San Diego | 2 | 8 | 0 | 171 | 221 | .200 | L.A. Rams | 3 | 7 | 0 | 171 | 235 | .300 |

# WEEK TWELVE

### American Football Conference
Buffalo 41 at Miami 27
Cleveland 24 at Houston 28
Denver 24 at Kansas City 20
New York Jets 28 at New England 21
Seattle 7 at Los Angeles Raiders 31

### National Football Conference
Dallas 9 at New York Giants 22
Los Angeles Rams 10 at Detroit 21
Minnesota 35 at Green Bay 21
Phoenix 10 at San Francisco 14
Tampa Bay 7 at Atlanta 43

### Interconference Games
Chicago 31 at Indianapolis 17
Cincinnati 10 at Philadelphia 17
New Orleans 21 at San Diego 24
Washington 41 at Pittsburgh 14

### Interconference Play
AFC 14 – NFC 22

## Game of The Week
## New York Jets 28 – New England 21

After a respectable 3–4 start, New England was halfway along 'murder row', a six-game sequence against potential playoff teams. They had fared badly, losing to all three of

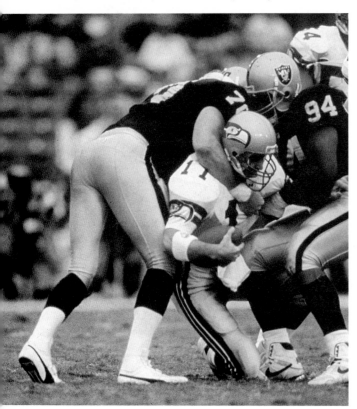

Denver, Buffalo and Miami, and had little hope of earning a playoff berth. The Jets had hardly set the world on fire but, under second-year head coach Bruce Coslet, they had discovered a sense of purpose. Having taken advantage of the weak spots in their schedule, the Jets were at 5–5 and in contention for an AFC wild-card spot. But they were coming off an upset loss to the lowly Indianapolis Colts and a setback against the Patriots could have dealt a severe blow to their ambitions.

The opening exchanges were even but New England did make two critical errors, a pass interference by cornerback Maurice Hurst which gave New York possession on the Patriots' one-yard line, and an interception picked off by Scott Mersereau on the Patriots' 33-yard line. Both times the Jets moved in for touchdowns. Halfway through the third quarter, the lead was extended to 21 points when quarterback Ken O'Brien, now in full flow, hit wide receiver Terance Mathis with a 35-yard touchdown pass.

Almost three minutes into the final quarter, with the home fans beginning to file out of Foxboro Stadium, the Patriots struck back when wide receiver Irving Fryar caught a 56-yard touchdown pass. With 4:28 left, running back Jon Vaughn ploughed into the end zone, capitalizing on a fumble by Jets running back Brad Baxter. And little more than two minutes later, the scores were level on Vaughn's second short-yardage touchdown run following a second fumble by poor Baxter.

Casting caution aside, O'Brien went after the Patriots, taking the offense 71 yards in six quick-fire plays culminating in a three-yard touchdown pass, unusually, by tackle-eligible Trevor Matich. Surely that had slammed the door.

Yet the drama was only just beginning. In the 57 seconds that remained, incredibly, quarterback Hugh Millen drove the Patriots down to the New York one-yard line, from where he opted for the play that had worked twice before in the game. But this time Vaughn was stopped cold by the combined efforts of defensive end Jeff Lageman and middle linebacker Kyle Clifton.

## The Road To Super Bowl XXVI

Applying the 'no-huddle' offense to perfection, Buffalo had an astonishing 80 plays from scrimmage as they both confused and wore down the Miami defense. For Jim Kelly, who delivered three touchdown passes in a performance of serene maturity, Thurman Thomas was the perfect foil, rushing for 135 yards and a touchdown, in addition to catching a touchdown pass.

Washington became the first team to earn a playoff berth as the Pittsburgh Steelers were put to the sword. Leading by the score of 27–0 at the end of the third quarter, the Redskins eased up before rekindling the fire with late touchdown passes by Mark Rypien and backup Jeff Rutledge.

*The Raiders' Scott Davis (left) and Anthony Smith each had 2.5 sacks.*

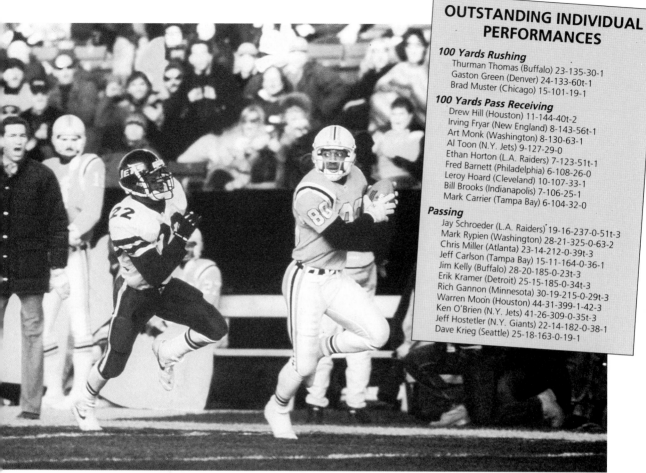

*Patriots receiver Irving Fryar was a thorn in the Jets' side.*

## STANDINGS

| AFC East | W | L | T | PF | PA | Pct. | NFC East | W | L | T | PF | PA | Pct. |
|---|---|---|---|---|---|---|---|---|---|---|---|---|---|
| Buffalo | 10 | 1 | 0 | 342 | 238 | .909 | Washington*** | 11 | 0 | 0 | 361 | 139 | 1.000 |
| N.Y. Jets | 6 | 5 | 0 | 231 | 206 | .545 | Dallas | 6 | 5 | 0 | 219 | 225 | .545 |
| Miami | 5 | 6 | 0 | 207 | 248 | .455 | N.Y. Giants | 6 | 5 | 0 | 181 | 183 | .545 |
| New England | 3 | 8 | 0 | 156 | 223 | .273 | Philadelphia | 6 | 5 | 0 | 182 | 163 | .545 |
| Indianapolis | 1 | 10 | 0 | 106 | 261 | .091 | Phoenix | 4 | 8 | 0 | 146 | 239 | .333 |
| **AFC Central** | **W** | **L** | **T** | **PF** | **PA** | **Pct.** | **NFC Central** | **W** | **L** | **T** | **PF** | **PA** | **Pct.** |
| Houston | 9 | 2 | 0 | 298 | 168 | .818 | Chicago | 9 | 2 | 0 | 212 | 172 | .818 |
| Cleveland | 4 | 7 | 0 | 211 | 232 | .364 | Detroit | 7 | 4 | 0 | 217 | 224 | .636 |
| Pittsburgh | 4 | 7 | 0 | 216 | 259 | .364 | Minnesota | 6 | 6 | 0 | 234 | 207 | .500 |
| Cincinnati | 1 | 10 | 0 | 170 | 312 | .091 | Green Bay | 2 | 9 | 0 | 171 | 213 | .182 |
| **AFC West** | **W** | **L** | **T** | **PF** | **PA** | **Pct.** | Tampa Bay | 2 | 9 | 0 | 130 | 255 | .182 |
| Denver | 8 | 3 | 0 | 216 | 179 | .727 | **NFC West** | **W** | **L** | **T** | **PF** | **PA** | **Pct.** |
| Kansas City | 7 | 4 | 0 | 227 | 160 | .636 | New Orleans | 9 | 2 | 0 | 229 | 124 | .818 |
| L.A. Raiders | 7 | 4 | 0 | 203 | 192 | .636 | Atlanta | 6 | 5 | 0 | 219 | 229 | .545 |
| Seattle | 5 | 6 | 0 | 199 | 173 | .455 | San Francisco | 5 | 6 | 0 | 218 | 155 | .455 |
| San Diego | 3 | 8 | 0 | 195 | 242 | .273 | L.A. Rams | 3 | 8 | 0 | 181 | 256 | .273 |

***Clinched Playoff Spot*

# WEEK THIRTEEN

**American Football Conference**

> Buffalo 13 at New England 16
> Denver 10 at Seattle 13
> Houston 14 at Pittsburgh 26
> Kansas City 15 at Cleveland 20
> Los Angeles Raiders 38 at Cincinnati 14
> San Diego 3 at New York Jets 24

**National Football Conference**

> Atlanta 23 at New Orleans 20 (OT)
> Dallas 24 at Washington 21
> Detroit 34 at Minnesota 14
> New York Giants 21 at Tampa Bay 14
> San Francisco 33 at Los Angeles Rams 10
> Philadelphia 34 at Phoenix 14

**Interconference Games**

> Indianapolis 10 vs Green Bay 14 (at Milwaukee)
> Miami 16 at Chicago 13 (OT)

**Interconference Play**

> AFC 15 – NFC 23

## Game of The Week
## Miami 16 – Chicago 13 (Overtime)

Entering Week Thirteen, five consecutive wins for Chicago, coupled with only two by Detroit over the same period, had seen the Bears move into a two-game lead on top of the NFC Central. With games against Green Bay and Tampa Bay among the five remaining, a victory for the Bears might give them one hand on the division crown. Miami was in a much less secure position. With little hope of challenging the pack-leading Buffalo Bills, the Dolphins' best prospects lay in a six-team scramble for three wild-card places.

Perhaps still a little shell-shocked from their Week Twelve loss against Buffalo, the Dolphins were listless. Running back Sammie Smith could generate no real momentum and not even the great Dan Marino could produce a spark. They offered little in response to a Bears team which, as usual, went about its task in a workmanlike fashion. A steady 59-yard drive ended with running back Brad Muster's three-yard scoring carry, and it was a booster when Kevin Butler responded to an opening shot by Miami placekicker Pete Stoyanovich with a 32-yard field goal as time ran out in the first half.

Chicago wasn't heading for a comprehensive win but the signs were that they could handle anything offered by the Dolphins. And the task eased even further with Butler's second field goal. It wasn't a problem when, just inside the fourth quarter, Stoyanovich brought Miami to within seven points with his 22-yard field goal. With the clock ticking away, Chicago retained control. It came to the point when one decent punt would put the Dolphins way out of range and everyone could go home to enjoy dinner. But the snap

went over the head of punter Maury Buford. He raced back, gathered the ball and punted under pressure, only to see the ball blocked by Miami special-teamer Marc Logan. Miami regained possession just four yards from the Chicago goal line.

From that position even an out-of-sorts Marino can find a way, and tight end Ferrell Edmunds proved to be an easy target for the equalizing score. Butler had one last chance to clinch the result but his 50-yarder fell short with four seconds left in regulation time. The momentum had shifted and it was not unpredictable when Stoyanovich rewarded an excellent catch by Mark Clayton with the game-winning 27-yard field goal.

## The Road To Super Bowl XXVI

It wasn't for the first time in the history of this great rivalry that Dallas upset the Redskins, putting an end to their dreams of a perfect season. With Emmitt Smith rushing for 132 yards and both Michael Irvin and Alvin Harper catching passes for more than 100 yards, Washington could have no complaints.

On the day that all six division leaders lost, Buffalo's defeat at the hands of New England was the major shock. After holding the Bills to just 13 points, the Patriots won on quarterback Hugh Millen's fourth-quarter two-yard touchdown run.

*Pepper Johnson had a Giants' club-record 4.5 sacks and an interception against Tampa Bay.*

## OUTSTANDING INDIVIDUAL PERFORMANCES

**100 Yards Rushing**
Barry Sanders (Detroit) 23-220-45t-4
Fred McAfee (New Orleans) 28-138-34-1
Emmitt Smith (Dallas) 34-132-32t-1
Reggie Cobb (Tampa Bay) 22-110-27t-1
John L. Williams (Seattle) 17-109-42-0

**100 Yards Pass Receiving**
Michael Haynes (Atlanta) 6-187-80t-2
Emile Harry (Kansas City) 11-159-36-1
Irving Fryar (New England) 6-134-50t-1
Michael Irvin (Dallas) 9-130-23t-1
Haywood Jeffires (Houston) 8-122-26-1
John Taylor (San Francisco) 6-121-78-0
Cris Carter (Minnesota) 7-116-34-0
Floyd Turner (New Orleans) 5-115-61-0
Alvin Harper (Dallas) 4-101-39-1

**Passing**
Steve Beuerlein (Dallas) 12-7-109-0-23t-1
Phil Simms (N.Y. Giants) 14-10-100-0-30t-1

*Alvin Harper caught this 34-yard touchdown pass as Dallas ended the Redskins' winning streak.*

## STANDINGS

| AFC East | W | L | T | PF | PA | Pct. | NFC East | W | L | T | PF | PA | Pct. |
|---|---|---|---|---|---|---|---|---|---|---|---|---|---|
| Buffalo | 10 | 2 | 0 | 355 | 254 | .833 | Washington*** | 11 | 1 | 0 | 382 | 163 | .917 |
| N.Y. Jets | 7 | 5 | 0 | 255 | 209 | .583 | Dallas | 7 | 5 | 0 | 243 | 246 | .583 |
| Miami | 6 | 6 | 0 | 223 | 261 | .500 | N.Y. Giants | 7 | 5 | 0 | 202 | 197 | .583 |
| New England | 4 | 8 | 0 | 172 | 236 | .333 | Philadelphia | 7 | 5 | 0 | 216 | 177 | .583 |
| Indianapolis | 1 | 11 | 0 | 116 | 275 | .083 | Phoenix | 4 | 9 | 0 | 160 | 273 | .308 |
| **AFC Central** | **W** | **L** | **T** | **PF** | **PA** | **Pct.** | **NFC Central** | **W** | **L** | **T** | **PF** | **PA** | **Pct.** |
| Houston | 9 | 3 | 0 | 312 | 194 | .750 | Chicago | 9 | 3 | 0 | 225 | 188 | .750 |
| Cleveland | 5 | 7 | 0 | 231 | 247 | .417 | Detroit | 8 | 4 | 0 | 251 | 238 | .667 |
| Pittsburgh | 5 | 7 | 0 | 242 | 273 | .417 | Minnesota | 6 | 7 | 0 | 248 | 241 | .462 |
| Cincinnati | 1 | 11 | 0 | 184 | 350 | .083 | Green Bay | 3 | 9 | 0 | 185 | 223 | .250 |
| **AFC West** | **W** | **L** | **T** | **PF** | **PA** | **Pct.** | Tampa Bay | 2 | 10 | 0 | 144 | 276 | .167 |
| Denver | 8 | 4 | 0 | 226 | 192 | .667 | **NFC West** | **W** | **L** | **T** | **PF** | **PA** | **Pct.** |
| L.A. Raiders | 8 | 4 | 0 | 241 | 206 | .667 | New Orleans | 9 | 3 | 0 | 249 | 147 | .750 |
| Kansas City | 7 | 5 | 0 | 242 | 180 | .583 | Atlanta | 7 | 5 | 0 | 242 | 249 | .583 |
| Seattle | 6 | 6 | 0 | 212 | 183 | .500 | San Francisco | 6 | 6 | 0 | 251 | 165 | .500 |
| San Diego | 3 | 9 | 0 | 198 | 266 | .250 | L.A. Rams | 3 | 9 | 0 | 191 | 289 | .250 |

*** *Clinched Playoff Spot*

# WEEK FOURTEEN

### American Football Conference
Cleveland 31 at Indianapolis 0
Kansas City 19 at Seattle 6
Los Angeles Raiders 9 at San Diego 7
New England 3 at Denver 20
New York Jets 13 at Buffalo 24

### National Football Conference
Chicago 6 at Detroit 16
Green Bay 31 at Atlanta 35
New Orleans 24 at San Francisco 38
Washington 27 at Los Angeles Rams 6

### Interconference Games
Pittsburgh 10 at Dallas 20
New York Giants 24 at Cincinnati 27
Philadelphia 13 at Houston 6
Tampa Bay 14 at Miami 33

### Interconference Play
AFC 17 – NFC 25

## Game of The Week
## Green Bay 31 – Atlanta 35

With four weeks of the regular season remaining, the Green Bay Packers were out of serious contention, but with games against Chicago, Detroit and Minnesota to come, they could still play the rôle of spoiler, not only in the NFC Central division but also in the NFC wild-card race. It was in this that Atlanta had a clear stake. One of a seven-team cluster, the Falcons even held out hopes of a division title, as they'd beaten the front-running New Orleans Saints on Week Thirteen and trailed by only two games.

The Falcons took the field without normal starting quarterback Chris Miller, who was suffering with a 102-degree fever and was kept back in the locker room on an intravenous fluid drip. He would have heard on the radio that the gift of an early Packers fumble at their own 22-yard line was quickly converted into an Atlanta touchdown by running back Erric Pegram. However, by half time the Packers were in control, leading by the score of 21–7 on a pair of touchdown passes by Mike Tomczak either side of a 40-yard scoring run by Darrell Thompson.

In his team's moment of need, on came Miller and he had an immediate effect, taking the offense 85 yards in seven plays, climaxed by Steve Broussard's three-yard touchdown run. Seconds into the fourth quarter, however, Green Bay's margin was restored when wide receiver Sterling Sharpe caught his second touchdown pass of the day.

But Miller wasn't yet ready to give up. Nine plays later, including an 18-yard completion on fourth-and-ten to wide receiver Andre Rison, he'd reduced the deficit to seven with his 20-yard touchdown pass to the same player.

Astonishingly, on the ensuing kickoff, Green Bay returner Charles Wilson fumbled the ball, allowing Falcons special-teamer Joe Fishback to recover possession and race 16 yards into the end zone for the tying score.

Atlanta's joy was short-lived when Chris Jacke's 27-yard field goal left Green Bay needing to protect a three-point lead for not much more than three minutes. Yet there was time for one more Green Bay error, a mishandle by punter Paul McJulien, who subsequently ran out of bounds well short of the first-down marker. Presented with the chance of one more trip to the well, Miller again looked to Rison, first with a 21-yard pass and then for the game-clinching 16-yarder with just 41 seconds remaining.

## The Road To Super Bowl XXVI

Both Washington and Buffalo rebounded on Week Fourteen, though the Bills were pressured by the New York Jets and needed a fourth-quarter touchdown pass from Jim Kelly to James Lofton for comfort.

Washington, too, needed time to shake off a tenacious opponent, the Rams, who led 3–0 and trailed by only one point entering the second half. A pair of Mark Rypien touchdown passes and two field goals gave Washington the title in the NFC East.

*LEFT: Chris Miller shrugged off a bout of influenza to rally the Falcons for victory.*

*ABOVE: Steve Bono inspired the 49ers to 21 points in the final four minutes.*

## OUTSTANDING INDIVIDUAL PERFORMANCES

**100 Yards Rushing**
Mark Higgs (Miami) 25-131-19t-1
Thurman Thomas (Buffalo) 23-124-21-0
Eric Dickerson (Indianapolis) 16-117-28-0
Emmitt Smith (Dallas) 32-109-14-1

**100 Yards Pass Receiving**
Michael Irvin (Dallas) 8-157-66t-1
Jerry Rice (San Francisco) 9-154-52-1
Floyd Turner (New Orleans) 10-132-41-2
Andre Rison (Atlanta) 8-124-21-2
Mark Ingram (N.Y. Giants) 7-116-28-1
James Lofton (Buffalo) 5-109-54-1
Tony Martin (Miami) 5-106-51-1
Lawrence Dawsey (Tampa Bay) 8-100-17t-1

**Passing**
Chris Miller (Atlanta) 18-12-186-0-28-2
Mark Rypien (Washington) 24-15-269-1-47t-3
Steve Bono (San Francisco) 41-27-347-0-52-3
Bernie Kosar (Cleveland) 23-18-189-0-25-1
Mike Tomczak (Green Bay) 35-22-276-0-23-3
Dan Marino (Miami) 32-20-307-0-51-2
John Elway (Denver) 25-18-215-0-21t-1
Phil Simms (N.Y. Giants) 44-26-296-0-28-3

## STANDINGS

| AFC East | W | L | T | PF | PA | Pct. | NFC East | W | L | T | PF | PA | Pct. |
|---|---|---|---|---|---|---|---|---|---|---|---|---|---|
| Buffalo* | 11 | 2 | 0 | 379 | 267 | .846 | Washington* | 12 | 1 | 0 | 409 | 169 | .923 |
| Miami | 7 | 6 | 0 | 256 | 275 | .538 | Dallas | 8 | 5 | 0 | 263 | 256 | .615 |
| N.Y. Jets | 7 | 6 | 0 | 268 | 233 | .538 | Philadelphia | 8 | 5 | 0 | 229 | 183 | .615 |
| New England | 4 | 9 | 0 | 175 | 256 | .308 | N.Y. Giants | 7 | 6 | 0 | 226 | 224 | .538 |
| Indianapolis | 1 | 12 | 0 | 116 | 306 | .077 | Phoenix** | 4 | 9 | 0 | 160 | 273 | .308 |
| **AFC Central** | **W** | **L** | **T** | **PF** | **PA** | **Pct.** | **NFC Central** | **W** | **L** | **T** | **PF** | **PA** | **Pct.** |
| Houston | 9 | 4 | 0 | 318 | 207 | .692 | Chicago | 9 | 4 | 0 | 231 | 204 | .692 |
| Cleveland | 6 | 7 | 0 | 262 | 247 | .462 | Detroit | 9 | 4 | 0 | 267 | 244 | .692 |
| Pittsburgh | 5 | 8 | 0 | 252 | 293 | .385 | Minnesota** | 6 | 7 | 0 | 248 | 241 | .462 |
| Cincinnati | 2 | 11 | 0 | 211 | 374 | .154 | Green Bay | 3 | 10 | 0 | 216 | 258 | .231 |
| **AFC West** | **W** | **L** | **T** | **PF** | **PA** | **Pct.** | Tampa Bay | 2 | 11 | 0 | 158 | 309 | .154 |
| Denver | 9 | 4 | 0 | 246 | 195 | .692 | **NFC West** | **W** | **L** | **T** | **PF** | **PA** | **Pct.** |
| L.A. Raiders | 9 | 4 | 0 | 250 | 213 | .692 | New Orleans | 9 | 4 | 0 | 273 | 185 | .692 |
| Kansas City | 8 | 5 | 0 | 261 | 186 | .615 | Atlanta | 8 | 5 | 0 | 277 | 280 | .615 |
| Seattle | 6 | 7 | 0 | 218 | 202 | .462 | San Francisco | 7 | 6 | 0 | 289 | 189 | .538 |
| San Diego | 3 | 10 | 0 | 205 | 275 | .231 | L.A. Rams | 3 | 10 | 0 | 197 | 316 | .231 |

*Division Champion                    **Did not play on Week Fourteen

# Week Fifteen

### American Football Conference
Buffalo 30 at Los Angeles Raiders 27 (OT)
Cincinnati 13 at Miami 37
Denver 17 at Cleveland 7
Indianapolis 17 at New England 23 (OT)
Pittsburgh 6 at Houston 31
San Diego 17 at Kansas City 20 (OT)

### National Football Conference
Atlanta 31 at Los Angeles Rams 14
Green Bay 13 at Chicago 27
Minnesota 26 at Tampa Bay 24
New Orleans 14 at Dallas 23
Philadelphia 19 at New York Giants 14
Washington 20 at Phoenix 14

### Interconference Games
New York Jets 20 at Detroit 34
San Francisco 24 at Seattle 22

### Interconference Play
AFC 17 − NFC 27

*RIGHT: Mark Duper tormented the Bengals. BELOW: Jeff Kemp catalysed the Eagles to a crucial victory.*

## Game of The Week
## Buffalo 30 – Los Angeles Raiders 27 (Overtime)

On Week Fourteen Buffalo had clinched the title in the AFC East and now they sought the victories which would bring home-field advantage in the playoffs. There was, then, every reason for not letting up; not that they would against a Raiders club which manages to bring out the competitiveness in every opponent it faces. Art Shell's team had flirted with the lead in the AFC West for most of the campaign. Their list of victims, including as it did San Francisco and both Denver and Seattle twice, was impressive. Yet, despite this and the abundance of big-name players, they didn't inspire total confidence.

But there wasn't much wrong with the way they set about the Bills, wide receiver Tim Brown hauling in a 78-yard touchdown pass as they moved out to a 10–0 first-quarter lead. Buffalo's response was of the shocking type, Al Edwards returning the ensuing kickoff 91 yards for a score. That sort of thing can happen to any team and was answered quickly by rookie Nick Bell's 12-yard scoring run. And even after Bills tight end Keith McKeller had scored following a 59-yard punt return by Clifford Hicks, Jeff Jaeger's second field goal and Marcus Allen's one-yard touchdown run left the Raiders in apparent control with a 27–14 lead. Not until 10:54 into the fourth quarter did the Bills reply as Kenneth Davis rounded off a 67-yard drive.

However, alarmingly, the Raiders had run out of offensive ideas. Possession became almost an embarrassment. With one minute left in regulation time, wide receiver James Lofton's nine-yard touchdown reception brought the Bills on level terms. After being outplayed for much of the game, astonishingly, the Bills could even have been home and dry. But their placekicker, Scott Norwood, was having a poor day. Already he had missed an extra point and field goal attempts from 49 and 32 yards, and he would miss a 36-yarder with just 11 seconds to go.

In overtime the Raiders still could not re-establish their momentum, and finally Norwood corrected his sights. An interception by Bills safety Mark Kelso gave Buffalo possession on its 36-yard line and a quick 31-yard completion by Jim Kelly to wide receiver Andre Reed helped to place Norwood in position for the clinching 42-yard field goal.

## The Road To Super Bowl XXVI

While the Bills were mounting a rally to overcome the Raiders, Washington was having trouble with the Phoenix Cardinals, who jumped out to a 14–0 halftime lead on a pair of touchdown runs by Johnny Johnson. However, Mark Rypien threw two touchdown passes and Chip Lohmiller responded with a brace of field goals as the Redskins confirmed their strength of character.

### OUTSTANDING INDIVIDUAL PERFORMANCES

**100 Yards Rushing**
Herschel Walker (Minnesota) 16-126-71t-1
Earnest Byner (Washington) 25-116-32-0
Barry Sanders (Detroit) 20-114-51t-2
Emmitt Smith (Dallas) 27-112-10-0

**100 Yards Pass Receiving**
Mark Duper (Miami) 7-134-43t-1
Greg McMurtry (New England) 8-119-25-0
John Taylor (San Francisco) 7-113-41-1
Michael Haynes (Atlanta) 6-112-52-1
Mark Carrier (Tampa Bay) 6-110-32-1
Andre Reed (Buffalo) 8-107-31-0
Tim Brown (L.A. Raiders) 2-106-78t-1
Michael Irvin (Dallas) 5-101-29-0

**Passing**
Dan Marino (Miami) 33-24-281-0-43t-3
Mark Vlasic (Kansas City) 18-12-150-0-30-1
Mark Rypien (Washington) 33-22-256-0-30-2
Chris Miller (Atlanta) 28-19-271-1-52-2
Jim Harbaugh (Chicago) 25-16-209-1-35t-2
Steve Walsh (New Orleans) 39-26-238-0-19-2

## STANDINGS

| AFC East | W | L | T | PF | PA | Pct. | NFC East | W | L | T | PF | PA | Pct. |
|---|---|---|---|---|---|---|---|---|---|---|---|---|---|
| Buffalo* | 12 | 2 | 0 | 409 | 294 | .857 | Washington* | 13 | 1 | 0 | 429 | 183 | .929 |
| Miami | 8 | 6 | 0 | 293 | 288 | .571 | Dallas | 9 | 5 | 0 | 286 | 270 | .643 |
| N.Y. Jets | 7 | 7 | 0 | 288 | 267 | .500 | Philadelphia | 9 | 5 | 0 | 248 | 197 | .643 |
| New England | 5 | 9 | 0 | 198 | 273 | .357 | N.Y. Giants | 7 | 7 | 0 | 240 | 243 | .500 |
| Indianapolis | 1 | 13 | 0 | 133 | 329 | .071 | Phoenix | 4 | 10 | 0 | 174 | 293 | .286 |
| **AFC Central** | **W** | **L** | **T** | **PF** | **PA** | **Pct.** | **NFC Central** | **W** | **L** | **T** | **PF** | **PA** | **Pct.** |
| Houston* | 10 | 4 | 0 | 349 | 213 | .714 | Chicago | 10 | 4 | 0 | 258 | 217 | .714 |
| Cleveland | 6 | 8 | 0 | 269 | 264 | .429 | Detroit | 10 | 4 | 0 | 301 | 264 | .714 |
| Pittsburgh | 5 | 9 | 0 | 258 | 324 | .357 | Minnesota | 7 | 7 | 0 | 274 | 265 | .500 |
| Cincinnati | 2 | 12 | 0 | 224 | 411 | .143 | Green Bay | 3 | 11 | 0 | 229 | 285 | .214 |
| **AFC West** | **W** | **L** | **T** | **PF** | **PA** | **Pct.** | Tampa Bay | 2 | 12 | 0 | 182 | 335 | .143 |
| Denver** | 10 | 4 | 0 | 263 | 202 | .714 | **NFC West** | **W** | **L** | **T** | **PF** | **PA** | **Pct.** |
| Kansas City** | 9 | 5 | 0 | 281 | 203 | .643 | Atlanta | 9 | 5 | 0 | 308 | 294 | .643 |
| L.A. Raiders** | 9 | 5 | 0 | 277 | 243 | .643 | New Orleans | 9 | 5 | 0 | 287 | 208 | .643 |
| Seattle | 6 | 8 | 0 | 240 | 226 | .429 | San Francisco | 8 | 6 | 0 | 313 | 211 | .571 |
| San Diego | 3 | 11 | 0 | 222 | 295 | .214 | L.A. Rams | 3 | 11 | 0 | 211 | 347 | .214 |

*Division Champion
**Clinched Playoff Spot

# WEEK SIXTEEN

### American Football Conference
Buffalo 35 at Indianapolis 7
Cincinnati 10 at Pittsburgh 17
Houston 17 at Cleveland 14
Miami 30 at San Diego 38
New England 6 at New York Jets 3

### National Football Conference
Dallas 25 at Philadelphia 13
Detroit 21 at Green Bay 17
Los Angeles Rams 14 at Minnesota 20
New York Giants 17 at Washington 34
Tampa Bay 0 at Chicago 27

### Interconference Games
Kansas City 14 at San Francisco 28
Los Angeles Raiders 0 at New Orleans 27
Phoenix 19 at Denver 24
Seattle 13 at Atlanta 26

### Interconference Play
AFC 18 – NFC 30

## Game of The Week
## Houston 17 – Cleveland 14

The Browns were not yet out of contention, though their prospects were not better than those usually described as 'mathematical' by 'experts' who do not have a proper understanding of that term.

The Houston Oilers, on the other hand, had clinched the first division title in their history the previous weekend but still there was the quest for some kind of home-field advantage, at least for one playoff game. That was an obvious goal but there was another, namely, to test themselves in unfriendly weather conditions. Playing their home games in the Astrodome, they were seen by many as a cosseted outfit and their ability to operate the complexities of the run-and-shoot offense, their staple fare, on the frozen tundra they were likely to meet in the playoffs was questioned. They'd have their chance in the icy wastes of Cleveland Stadium.

Interestingly, quarterbacks Warren Moon (40a, 26c, 250 yds, 1i, 2td) and Bernie Kosar (40a, 28c, 258 yds, 1i, 2td) had almost identical passing figures, reflecting the closeness of the game as a whole. Indeed, it was decided in the final seconds by a slip of the foot.

With characteristic care, Kosar took the Browns 43 yards in seven plays for the opening touchdown but Moon, with the pressure off, was a little more carefree. He completed a 44-yard pass to Haywood Jeffires, scrambled 11 yards on a third-and-12 play and, with the help of Allen Pinkett's seven-yard run, converted a fourth-and-one in the drive for Ernest Givins' seven-yard touchdown catch. It encouraged Kosar, whose eight-yard touchdown pass to Brian Brennan came less than six minutes later. Brennan was a factor on

*Rod Bernstine's third touchdown run, a 63-yarder, clinched the Chargers' comeback victory over Miami.*

the ensuing kickoff, being charged with an unsportsmanlike penalty which granted Houston 15 yards in the drive which ended when Al Del Greco connected on a 27-yard field goal with 2:26 remaining in the half.

The barometer was falling and, by the final quarter, it had plummeted. The blinding snow offered Moon the challenge and he accepted, driving 80 yards in 12 plays before zipping a two-yard touchdown pass to Jeffires with 2:19 left. But Kosar was at home in the conditions. A Browns fan all his life, antifreeze keeping his vital organs active, Kosar

40

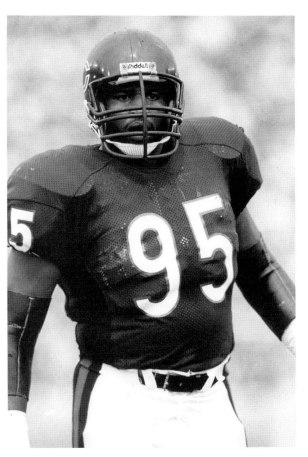

charged the offense down to within two yards of the Houston end zone before handing over to placekicker Matt Stover with four seconds remaining. Stover must have chipped a hundred field goals from the 19 in practice but this time he was betrayed by the icy conditions – not by much but enough to send the ball wide.

## The Road To Super Bowl XXVI

With home-field advantage throughout the AFC playoffs the reward for victory, the Bills made certain, coming away with the bonus of a new club single-season record for points, passing yardage and total offense. Leading the way, Jim Kelly passed for three touchdowns.

The Redskins, meanwhile, confirmed their authority in the NFC by dealing a mortal blow to the Giants. With typical grit, the Giants led 3–0 and 10–7, but their lack of finishing strength was exposed as Washington pressed the button and moved into the clear.

*Richard Dent had three sacks as the Bears shut out Tampa Bay.*

### OUTSTANDING INDIVIDUAL PERFORMANCES

**100 Yards Rushing**
Barry Word (Kansas City) 17-115-37-1
Leonard Russell (New England) 26-112-15-0
Rod Bernstine (San Diego) 13-104-63t-3

**100 Yards Pass Receiving**
Gary Clark (Washington) 3-129-65t-2
Quinn Early (New Orleans) 4-127-52-0
Mark Duper (Miami) 9-123-39-0
Flipper Anderson (L.A. Rams) 7-103-23-0

**Passing**
Jim Kelly (Buffalo) 11-9-119-0-26-3
Mark Rypien (Washington) 19-9-230-0-65t-3
Steve Bono (San Francisco) 33-24-220-0-24-3
John Friesz (San Diego) 25-17-185-0-29-2
Dan Marino (Miami) 42-27-313-1-39-3

# STANDINGS

| AFC East | W | L | T | PF | PA | Pct. |
|---|---|---|---|---|---|---|
| Buffalo* | 13 | 2 | 0 | 444 | 301 | .867 |
| Miami | 8 | 7 | 0 | 323 | 326 | .533 |
| N.Y. Jets | 7 | 8 | 0 | 291 | 273 | .467 |
| New England | 6 | 9 | 0 | 204 | 276 | .400 |
| Indianapolis | 1 | 14 | 0 | 140 | 364 | .067 |

| AFC Central | W | L | T | PF | PA | Pct. |
|---|---|---|---|---|---|---|
| Houston* | 11 | 4 | 0 | 366 | 227 | .733 |
| Cleveland | 6 | 9 | 0 | 283 | 281 | .400 |
| Pittsburgh | 6 | 9 | 0 | 275 | 334 | .400 |
| Cincinnati | 2 | 13 | 0 | 234 | 428 | .133 |

| AFC West | W | L | T | PF | PA | Pct. |
|---|---|---|---|---|---|---|
| Denver* | 11 | 4 | 0 | 287 | 221 | .733 |
| Kansas City** | 9 | 6 | 0 | 295 | 231 | .600 |
| L.A. Raiders** | 9 | 6 | 0 | 277 | 270 | .600 |
| Seattle | 6 | 9 | 0 | 253 | 252 | .400 |
| San Diego | 4 | 11 | 0 | 260 | 325 | .267 |

*Division Champion
**Wild Card

| NFC East | W | L | T | PF | PA | Pct. |
|---|---|---|---|---|---|---|
| Washington* | 14 | 1 | 0 | 463 | 200 | .933 |
| Dallas** | 10 | 5 | 0 | 311 | 283 | .667 |
| Philadelphia | 9 | 6 | 0 | 261 | 222 | .600 |
| N.Y. Giants | 7 | 8 | 0 | 257 | 277 | .467 |
| Phoenix | 4 | 11 | 0 | 193 | 317 | .267 |

*Division Champion  **Wild Card

| NFC Central | W | L | T | PF | PA | Pct. |
|---|---|---|---|---|---|---|
| Chicago** | 11 | 4 | 0 | 285 | 217 | .733 |
| Detroit** | 11 | 4 | 0 | 322 | 281 | .733 |
| Minnesota | 8 | 7 | 0 | 294 | 279 | .533 |
| Green Bay | 3 | 12 | 0 | 246 | 306 | .200 |
| Tampa Bay | 2 | 13 | 0 | 182 | 362 | .133 |

**Clinched Playoff Spot

| NFC West | W | L | T | PF | PA | Pct. |
|---|---|---|---|---|---|---|
| Atlanta** | 10 | 5 | 0 | 334 | 307 | .667 |
| New Orleans** | 10 | 5 | 0 | 314 | 208 | .667 |
| San Francisco | 9 | 6 | 0 | 341 | 225 | .600 |
| L.A. Rams | 3 | 12 | 0 | 225 | 367 | .200 |

**Clinched Playoff Spot

# Week Seventeen

### American Football Conference
Cleveland 10 at Pittsburgh 17
Denver 17 at San Diego 14
Kansas City 27 at Los Angeles Raiders 21
New England 7 at Cincinnati 29
New York Jets 23 at Miami 20 (OT)

### National Football Conference
Atlanta 27 at Dallas 31
Chicago 14 at San Francisco 52
Green Bay 27 at Minnesota 7
New Orleans 27 at Phoenix 3
Washington 22 at Philadelphia 24

### Interconference Games
Detroit 17 at Buffalo 14 (OT)
Houston 20 at New York Giants 24
Indianapolis 3 at Tampa Bay 17
Los Angeles Rams 9 at Seattle 23

### Interconference Play
AFC 19 – NFC 33

## Game of The Week
## Atlanta 27 – Dallas 31

The Atlanta Falcons had won five straight games and victory on Week Seventeen would have guaranteed them the title in the NFC West for, even should New Orleans win, the Falcons held the superior intradivisional record. At the very least, they were assured of a wild-card spot. Dallas was in a similar position. Though unable to win the division title, the Cowboys, too, had secured a playoff berth and were seeking a possible home fixture in the first round. Interestingly, there was the possibility that the two teams could meet in the playoffs.

With so many spectacular individuals on parade, the chances of pyrotechnics were good and, barely two minutes into the contest, Dallas quarterback Steve Beuerlein ignited the fuse with a 58-yard touchdown pass to wide receiver Michael Irvin. Less than two minutes later, Atlanta's Chris Miller responded in even more spectacular fashion, connecting with wide receiver Michael Haynes for a 67-yard touchdown.

Still in the first quarter, the exchanges continued as, first, Dallas running back Emmitt Smith scored from the four-yard line, followed shortly afterwards by Andre Rison, who hauled in a 28-yard scoring pass. Just 19 seconds later, the Cowboys' Alexander Wright strode into the Atlanta end zone on a Dallas club-record 102-yard kickoff return.

In a comparatively calm second quarter, each team took advantage of turnovers for field goals which saw Dallas head for the locker room leading by the score of 24–17.

The pendulum of fortune had shown no particular preference but it was given a nudge when Falcons placekicker Norm Johnson reduced the deficit with a 29-yard field goal. And it continued in the same direction when Haynes caught a 43-yard pass to give Atlanta its first lead at 27–24, just over halfway through the third quarter.

*Three touchdown passes from rookie Todd Marinovich were not enough for the Raiders, who lost 27-21 to the Chiefs and had to travel to Kansas City for the playoffs.*

## OUTSTANDING INDIVIDUAL PERFORMANCES

### 100 Yards Rushing
Emmitt Smith (Dallas) 32-160-24-2
Barry Word (Dallas) 35-152-15-1
Rodney Hampton (N.Y. Giants) 28-140-24-1
Johnny Hector (N.Y. Jets) 13-132-47-0
Kenneth Davis (Buffalo) 25-118-35-0
Barry Sanders (Detroit) 26-108-20-1

### 100 Yards Pass Receiving
J.J. Birden (Kansas City) 8-188-57t-2
Michael Irvin (Dallas) 10-169-58t-1
Michael Timpson (New England) 7-150-60t-1
Michael Haynes (Atlanta) 5-148-67t-2
Webster Slaughter (Cleveland) 11-138-27-0
Cris Carter (Minnesota) 7-112-50-0

### Passing
Steve DeBerg (Kansas City) 20-14-277-0-57t-2
Phil Simms (N.Y. Giants) 17-15-200-0-38-1
Boomer Esiason (Cincinnati) 40-20-333-0-53-3
Chris Miller (Atlanta) 39-19-325-0-67t-3
Todd Marinovich (L.A. Raiders) 40-23-243-0-26t-3

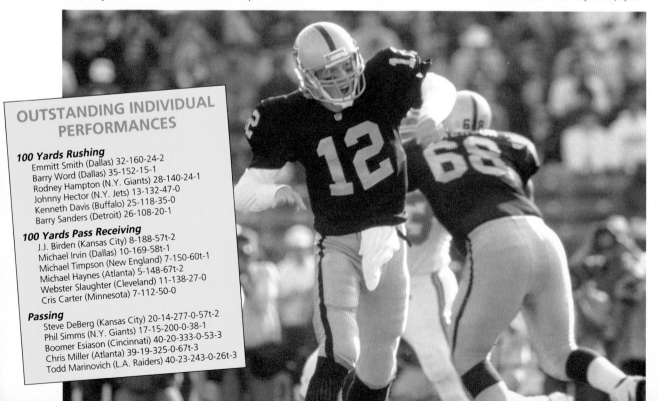

The sub-plot involved the destination of the NFL individual pass receiving and rushing titles. Earlier in the game Irvin had done enough to confirm himself as the leading receiver, but Smith was in a close race with Detroit's Barry Sanders for the rushing crown. In the event, Smith's six-yard touchdown run, early in the final quarter, was vital in helping him to the much-coveted title of leading rusher. It also gave Dallas a four-point advantage, though this looked increasingly precarious as the clock wound down. Yet the defense was up to the task, batting away Miller's three passing attempts from the 16-yard line, the final one as time ran out.

## The Road To Super Bowl XXVI

Eddie Murray missed two field goals in the final 35 seconds of regulation time but chipped the 21-yard winner in overtime as Detroit set a franchise record with its 12th win of the regular season. It came on a day that Buffalo rested Jim Kelly, Thurman Thomas and James Lofton.

Although the Redskins outplayed Philadelphia, the Midas touch was missing as, for once, the other team timed its finish to perfection. Roger Ruzek kicked the game-winning field goal with 13 seconds left.

*Barry Sanders helped to sustain Detroit's momentum with 108 yards rushing against Buffalo.*

## STANDINGS

| AFC East | W | L | T | PF | PA | Pct. |
|---|---|---|---|---|---|---|
| Buffalo* | 13 | 3 | 0 | 458 | 318 | .813 |
| N.Y. Jets** | 8 | 8 | 0 | 314 | 293 | .500 |
| Miami | 8 | 8 | 0 | 343 | 349 | .500 |
| New England | 6 | 10 | 0 | 211 | 305 | .375 |
| Indianapolis | 1 | 15 | 0 | 143 | 381 | .063 |

*Division Champion
**Wild Card

| AFC Central | W | L | T | PF | PA | Pct. |
|---|---|---|---|---|---|---|
| Houston* | 11 | 5 | 0 | 386 | 251 | .688 |
| Pittsburgh | 7 | 9 | 0 | 292 | 344 | .438 |
| Cleveland | 6 | 10 | 0 | 293 | 298 | .375 |
| Cincinnati | 3 | 13 | 0 | 263 | 435 | .188 |

*Division Champion

| AFC West | W | L | T | PF | PA | Pct. |
|---|---|---|---|---|---|---|
| Denver* | 12 | 4 | 0 | 304 | 235 | .750 |
| Kansas City** | 10 | 6 | 0 | 322 | 252 | .625 |
| L.A. Raiders** | 9 | 7 | 0 | 298 | 297 | .563 |
| Seattle | 7 | 9 | 0 | 276 | 261 | .438 |
| San Diego | 4 | 12 | 0 | 274 | 342 | .250 |

*Division Champion
**Wild Card

| NFC East | W | L | T | PF | PA | Pct. |
|---|---|---|---|---|---|---|
| Washington* | 14 | 2 | 0 | 485 | 224 | .875 |
| Dallas** | 11 | 5 | 0 | 342 | 310 | .688 |
| Philadelphia | 10 | 6 | 0 | 285 | 244 | .625 |
| N.Y. Giants | 8 | 8 | 0 | 281 | 297 | .500 |
| Phoenix | 4 | 12 | 0 | 196 | 344 | .250 |

*Division Champion
**Wild Card

| NFC Central | W | L | T | PF | PA | Pct. |
|---|---|---|---|---|---|---|
| Detroit* | 12 | 4 | 0 | 339 | 295 | .750 |
| Chicago** | 11 | 5 | 0 | 299 | 269 | .688 |
| Minnesota | 8 | 8 | 0 | 301 | 306 | .500 |
| Green Bay | 4 | 12 | 0 | 273 | 313 | .250 |
| Tampa Bay | 3 | 13 | 0 | 199 | 365 | .188 |

*Division Champion
**Wild Card

| NFC West | W | L | T | PF | PA | Pct. |
|---|---|---|---|---|---|---|
| New Orleans* | 11 | 5 | 0 | 341 | 211 | .688 |
| Atlanta** | 10 | 6 | 0 | 361 | 338 | .625 |
| San Francisco | 10 | 6 | 0 | 393 | 239 | .625 |
| L.A. Rams | 3 | 13 | 0 | 234 | 390 | .188 |

*Division Champion
**Wild Card

# WEEK EIGHTEEN

## FIRST-ROUND PLAYOFFS

### AFC Los Angeles Raiders 6 – Kansas City 10

Power rushing by Barry Word, who gained 130 yards on 33 carries, and a defensive effort which recovered two fumbles and intercepted four passes, took Kansas City to Buffalo for the Divisional Playoffs.

Twice during the regular season the Raiders had lost games which they felt they could have won, and this contest had a similar pattern. Now in the playoffs, they actually outgained the Chiefs and had every chance to win as the game drew to a close.

Earlier, Kansas City had capitalized on an interception and 29-yard return by safety Deron Cherry. From the 11-yard line, one pass from Steve DeBerg to Fred Jones did the trick. Los Angeles drew to within a point on field goals of 32 and 26 yards by Jeff Jaeger. And even after Kansas City's Nick Lowery had extended the margin to four points with his final-quarter field goal, a win was in prospect as the Raiders set up a second-and-one at the Kansas City 24-yard line. But a succession of errors, four penalties on consecutive plays, took the Raiders out of threatening distance. An interception by Lonnie Marts ended the threat with 2:14 left.

### AFC New York Jets 10 – Houston 17

Against New York, an outstanding performance by a less than healthy defense preserved the lead and took Houston to Denver for the AFC Divisional Playoffs.

Houston quarterback Warren Moon was in confident mood, smoothly directing an 80-yard drive for his touchdown pass to wide receiver Ernest Givins. For the Jets, Ken O'Brien, too, replied with style, levelling the scores with his ten-yard scoring pass to wide receiver Al Toon following an interception of Moon's pass by safety Erik McMillan. Undeterred, Moon bounced back, again combining with Givins for a touchdown after O'Brien's pass had been intercepted by Oilers safety Bo Orlando.

An exchange of field goals, Houston's Al Del Greco booming a 53-yarder after Raul Allegre had cut the deficit to four points, left the Oilers needing to protect a seven-point lead with 13:29 remaining. Enter the defense.

First, with the Jets at fourth-and-one on the Oilers' three-yard line, Orlando hit Jets running back Freeman McNeil in the air for no gain. On the next Jets series, Toon, under pressure, couldn't hold on to a fourth-and-six pass from the Houston 22-yard line. And on the game's final play, safety Bubba McDowell intercepted a pass at the Houston one.

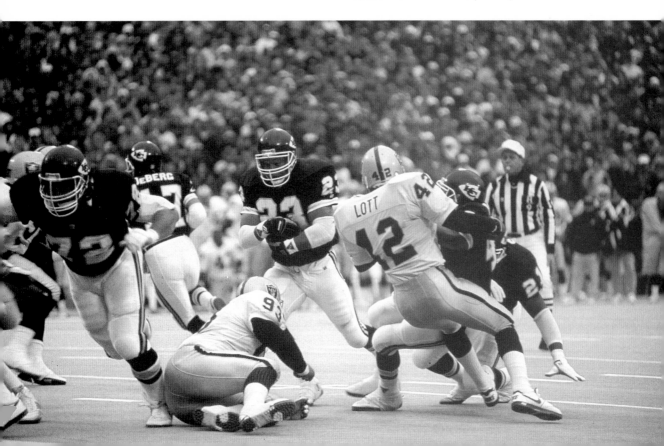

## NFC Atlanta 27 – New Orleans 20

Atlanta wide receiver Michael Haynes caught six passes for 144 yards and two touchdowns as the Falcons rallied for victory against New Orleans.

Playing with authority, New Orleans jumped out to a ten-point lead on a 26-yard scoring catch by wide receiver Floyd Turner and Morten Andersen's 45-yard field goal. And after Atlanta had replied in like kind, on Andre Rison's 24-yard touchdown reception and Norm Johnson's 45-yard field goal, the Saints went into half time with a three-point cushion thanks to Andersen's 35-yard kick three seconds before the break.

The Falcons' first lead came after 5:01 of the third quarter, when Michael Haynes's 20-yard reception capped a nine-play, 84-yard drive. However, a minute into the final quarter, New Orleans nosed back into the lead when Dalton Hilliard took the final step of an 80-yard march.

In all five of their regular-season losses, the Saints had led in the final quarter and perhaps it was this which bolstered the Falcons. Johnson's 36-yard chip, with 7:43 remaining, tied the scores, before Haynes broke the deadlock in majestic style, searing into the end zone with a 61-yard scoring pass from quarterback Chris Miller.

## NFC Dallas 17 – Chicago 13

Dallas took advantage of turnovers for ten first-quarter points, and solid defense hurled back the Bears more than a few times as the Cowboys marched on.

The opening field goal came after Dallas defensive end Tony Hill had recovered a Jim Harbaugh fumble at midfield and, five plays after linebacker Ken Norton had recovered possession at the Chicago ten-yard line following a blocked punt, Emmitt Smith powered in from the one.

In its entire history, no Chicago team has ever come back from a deficit of seven-or-more points to win a playoff game, and perhaps it was this legacy that persuaded head coach Mike Ditka to chance his luck. It didn't pay off when Neal Anderson was stopped on fourth-and-one at the Dallas two-yard line in the second quarter. Kevin Butler field goals cut the deficit to four points but Cowboys tight end Jay Novacek countered with interest, catching a three-yard touchdown pass with 23 seconds left in the third quarter.

Even more desperate as the clock wound down, the Bears tried, and failed, on fourth-and-four from the Dallas seven-yard line. A late Tom Waddle touchdown reception brought Chicago to within four points but they could summon up no further threat.

*FAR LEFT: Barry Word (23) follows the blocking of Dave Lutz (72) as he surges through the Raiders' line on yet another punishing run.*

*LEFT: The best efforts of Raiders wide receiver Mervyn Fernandez were all in vain.*

# WEEK NINETEEN

## DIVISIONAL PLAYOFFS

### NFC Dallas 6 – Detroit 38

With each team riding a six-game winning streak, a close contest was anticipated. But it was with extraordinary ease that Detroit coasted smoothly to its first championship game since winning the NFL title in 1957.

Mindful of the threat posed by Detroit running back Barry Sanders, the Cowboys attacked the line of scrimmage. And the ploy worked in one sense, with Sanders restricted to a below-par 69 yards rushing, 47 of those coming on a scoring run when the result was beyond doubt. But it meant that the back door was always open, a weakness exploited to the full by Lions quarterback Erik Kramer.

In the eighth game of the regular season, Kramer had replaced an injured Rodney Peete, coincidentally against Dallas, and threw a pair of touchdowns in the Lions' 34–10 win. Now, with just a little more on offer from the Cowboys' pass defense, he was virtually flawless, completing 29 of 38 passes for 341 yards and three touchdowns. The out-of-touch Cowboys lost two fumbles, saw two passes intercepted and troubled the scorer with just two field goals.

### NFC Atlanta 7 – Washington 24

The combination of hostile weather conditions, and just the suggestion that the Redskins might have peaked too early, led some observers to predict a close game – even an upset. But the NFL front runners banished such notions with a ground-game dominance in the best traditions of teams coached by Joe Gibbs.

In their regular-season match with Washington, in early November, the Falcons risked all on a blitzing defense and were buried 56–17. Having learnt their lesson, they packed the defensive backfield, often using seven- or eight-man zones. But the Redskins adjusted quickly. Ploughing through the mud behind one of the NFL's great offensive lines, running backs Ricky Ervins and Earnest Byner repeatedly punched into the Atlanta backfield. And when it came to short-yardage time, on came specialist Gerald Riggs. The formula brought second-quarter touchdowns by Ervins and Riggs.

Atlanta did put together a solid drive, helped by a nullified interception by Washington cornerback Darrell Green, to halve the deficit 57 seconds before half time.

However, the unrelenting Washington pressure, not only from the offense, brought further scores, a 24-yard Chip Lohmiller field goal and Riggs' second short-yardage thrust. Long before the end, Atlanta was well beaten.

### AFC Houston 24 – Denver 26

Against the favoured Houston Oilers, Denver quarterback John Elway evoked memories of the 1986 AFC title game and 'The Drive', as he rallied the Broncos for a heroic last-minute win.

For Houston, the opening series, indeed most of the game, went according to plan as Warren Moon passed effortlessly for touchdowns to wide receivers Haywood Jeffires, Drew Hill and Curtis Duncan. They led 14–0, 21–6 and, after 1:35 of the final quarter, 24–16. The Broncos, who always trailed, were made to work hard for everything, driving 65, 88 and 80 yards for touchdowns as they stuck to the task. However, with 2:07 left and starting at their own two-yard line with no timeouts remaining, all appeared lost.

Early in the march Elway scrambled seven yards to convert a fourth-and-six. On fourth-and-ten at his own 35-yard line with 59 seconds remaining, he found Vance Johnson open at midfield from where the wide receiver ran down to the Houston 21. The twelfth play of the drive took Denver down to the Houston 11-yard line and, with the help of holder Gary Kubiak, who calmly rescued a bad snap, David Treadwell slotted the game-winning field goal.

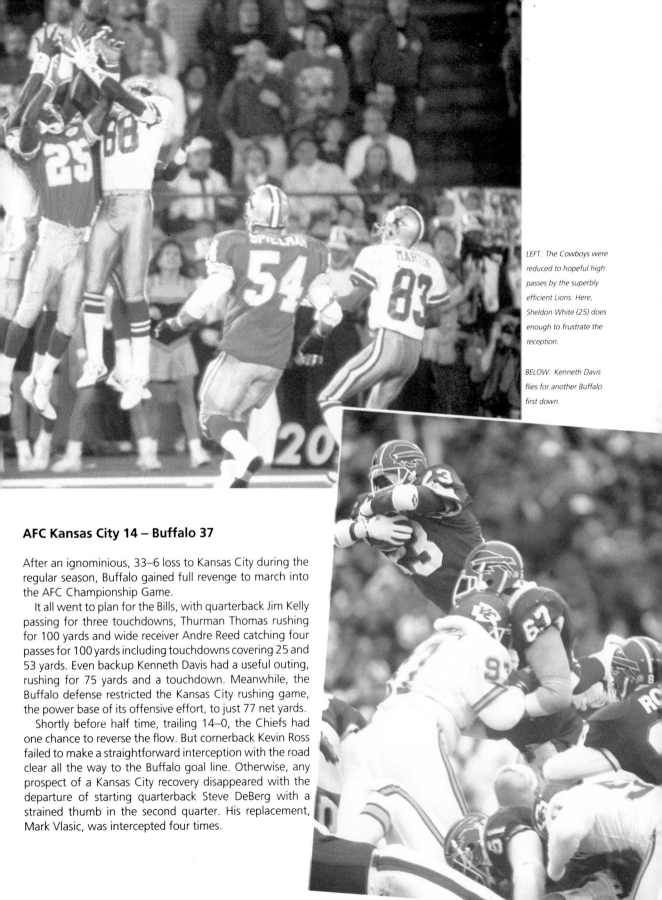

## AFC Kansas City 14 – Buffalo 37

After an ignominious, 33–6 loss to Kansas City during the regular season, Buffalo gained full revenge to march into the AFC Championship Game.

It all went to plan for the Bills, with quarterback Jim Kelly passing for three touchdowns, Thurman Thomas rushing for 100 yards and wide receiver Andre Reed catching four passes for 100 yards including touchdowns covering 25 and 53 yards. Even backup Kenneth Davis had a useful outing, rushing for 75 yards and a touchdown. Meanwhile, the Buffalo defense restricted the Kansas City rushing game, the power base of its offensive effort, to just 77 net yards.

Shortly before half time, trailing 14–0, the Chiefs had one chance to reverse the flow. But cornerback Kevin Ross failed to make a straightforward interception with the road clear all the way to the Buffalo goal line. Otherwise, any prospect of a Kansas City recovery disappeared with the departure of starting quarterback Steve DeBerg with a strained thumb in the second quarter. His replacement, Mark Vlasic, was intercepted four times.

# Week Twenty

## CONFERENCE CHAMPIONSHIPS

### AFC Denver 7 – Buffalo 10

Denver is not a flashy club. Its players often are best described as workmanlike. After an uncharacteristically poor 1990 campaign, when the Broncos finished dead last in the AFC West, they had come back to win the division title with honest determination. In the playoffs they'd refused to be blinded by the glitter of the Houston Oilers' offense, and by the end of that contest they were showing

*John Elway ponders one that got away.*

quite a sparkle of their own. Leading his club in playoff experience, head coach Dan Reeves had been to a record eight Super Bowls, as either a player or a coach, including three losses in a recent four-year period while in charge of the Broncos. He knew how to give good advice.

The Bills had underlined their position as favourites to retain the title in the AFC East, taking the crown by a huge five-game margin. Their only losses, three, came in a mistake-ridden nightmare against Kansas City, a shocker to New England and an end-of-term lapse to Detroit. Had there been any doubts over their sharpness, these were dispelled in a clinical dismantling of Kansas City in the Divisional Playoffs. Entertaining a Denver team which relied heavily on the audacious talents of quarterback John Elway, they were favoured to represent the AFC in the Super Bowl for the second year in a row.

In a game dominated by defense, in the first half alone Denver failed to capitalize on six forays into Buffalo territory as placekicker David Treadwell missed on field goal attempts from 47, 42 and 37 yards. Twice, his kicks were deflected by the uprights. On Denver's first possession of the second half, Elway suffered a bruised thigh. He remained in the trenches but his lack of mobility was a factor, nine minutes inside the third quarter, when his attempted screen pass was tipped into the arms of Bills linebacker Carlton Bailey. The least known of that quartet returned the ball 11 yards for a touchdown.

In the final quarter, trailing by ten points following Scott Norwood's 44-yard field goal, Broncos reserve quarterback Gary Kubiak came on to complete five of six passes and rush for 14 yards, the last three of which were for a touchdown with 1:43 left in regulation time. A field goal would tie the game and the tension reached fever pitch when Denver's Steve Atwater recovered possession on the ensuing onside kick. Kubiak even hit the target with his next pass but the receiver, Steve Sewell, had the ball stripped by Buffalo cornerback Kirby Jackson, who also had the presence of mind to recover possession and preserve the win.

### NFC Detroit 10 – Washington 41

It was against the odds that Detroit even reached the playoffs. They were smashed 45–0 by Washington on opening day and suffered through a mid-season stretch when they lost to all three of San Francisco, Chicago and Tampa Bay in a four-week spell. However, under third-string quarterback Erik Kramer, who had moved ahead of Andre Ware as senior backup to the injured Rodney Peete, they regrouped to win the final six games before routing Dallas in the Divisional Playoffs. Barry Sanders had been absent for the loss to Washington but subsequently he had confirmed his class as one of the top three running backs in the NFL. Detroit was the underdog, but a win was not out of the question.

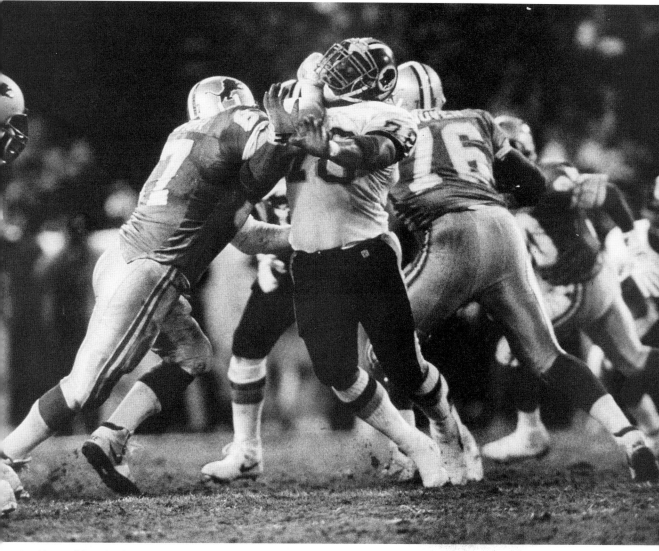

*Detroit's Ken Dallafior and Washington's Tim Johnson engage in battle.*

The Redskins hadn't needed a boost but, against Atlanta in the Divisional Playoffs, even with their long-range guns having been spiked by the difficult playing conditions, their authority had not been under much threat. Barry Sanders was almost certain to present a problem but it was clear that Detroit had weaknesses which would be difficult to hide. On offense, Lions backup tackle Scott Conover was expected to have problems handling the pass rush, led by Charles Mann and Wilber Marshall, while the absence of Detroit's Pro Bowl nose tackle Jerry Ball could only be an advantage when the Redskins rushers chose to attack up the middle.

From the start, Conover's inexperience was cruelly exploited by Mann, who, on the second play from scrimmage, sacked Kramer to force a fumble. Two plays later, Gerald Riggs smashed into the end zone. Another forced error saw

Washington linebacker Kurt Gouveia intercept Kramer's pass and return 38 yards to the Detroit ten-yard line. Yet the Lions achieved a moral victory of sorts when Washington was forced to settle for Chip Lohmiller's 20-yard field goal.

A touchdown pass from Kramer to wide receiver Willie Green was quickly followed by Riggs' second score but Eddie Murray's 30-yard field goal, 37 seconds before half time, reduced the deficit to just seven points.

Sadly, however, the Lions left their momentum in the locker room. Redskins quarterback Mark Rypien opened up, passing 45 yards to tight end Terry Orr, setting up Lohmiller's 28-yard field goal, before he unfurled touchdown passes of 45 and 21 yards to Gary Clark and Art Monk respectively. Cornerback Darrell Green's 32-yard interception return for a touchdown completed the scoring with ten minutes remaining.

# SUPER BOWL

**XXVI**

*Washington 37
Buffalo 24*

**Hubert H. Humphrey Metrodome,
Minneapolis, Minnesota,
January 26th, 1992**

The Super Bowl usually brings together the NFL's best two teams and this year was no exception.

Predominantly on the strength of its offense, which ranked first in the entire NFL, Buffalo logged the AFC's best regular-season record. Quarterback Jim Kelly won the AFC passing title by a huge ten rating points ahead of Cleveland's Bernie Kosar. If that was impressive, so were the credentials of Thurman Thomas, who was the AFC leading rusher by an equally staggering margin of 370 yards over Denver's Gaston Green. The primary targets for Kelly's rockets, wide receivers Andre Reed and James Lofton, each had caught passes for over 1,000 yards and scored ten and eight touchdowns respectively. Kelly, Reed and Thomas had been picked to start in the 1992 Pro Bowl, with Lofton and guard Jim Ritcher selected as backups. If Buffalo had a worry it was in the defense, which had slipped precipitously from eighth in the NFL in 1990 to 27th in 1991. A major factor was a persistent injury to starting defensive right end Bruce Smith, a regular All-Pro who might have been expected to register anywhere upwards of a dozen quarterback sacks. He had 1.5. Certainly, Pro Bowl linebackers

Cornelius Bennett and Darryl Talley had helped to fill the void, but only in part. Against the run the Bills were very vulnerable, despite the commitment of nose tackle Jeff Wright and inside linebackers Shane Conlan and Carlton Bailey. Wright had registered a creditable six sacks, while Conlan led the team with 122 tackles. The Bills, then, would have to be at their best on defense but, to the advantage of the whole squad, there was a factor of unknown value, namely, the bitter memory of defeat in Super Bowl XXV. Head coach Marv Levy would have them ready to put that matter straight.

*Action from Super Bowl XXVI.*

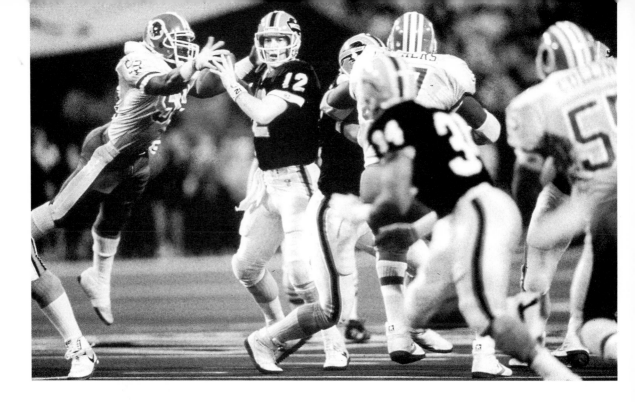

In the regular season the Washington Redskins had been the unchallenged class team of the NFC with losses only to Dallas, in a close three-pointer, and by two points at Philadelphia on the final weekend.

The platform for their success began with a powerful offensive line, anchored by All-Pro left tackle Jim Lachey, and it had been a feature of the season that quarterback Mark Rypien had blossomed. Rypien entered the year with his rough edges still showing but, doubtless benefiting from a choice of terrific receivers, he came second in the NFC passing list with a rating slightly better than that of Jim Kelly. When Rypien surveyed the field, usually he'd see all of wide receivers Art Monk, Ricky Sanders and Gary Clark available. Both Monk, who is coming to the end of a Hall-of-Fame career, and Clark caught passes for over 1,000 yards. In running backs Earnest Byner, Ricky Ervins and Gerald Riggs, the Redskins had a response to most eventualities. The stock rusher, Byner, nonetheless was one of only seven players in the league to rush for over 1,000 yards, Ervins had a burst of speed, while Riggs was the master on short-yardage plays near the end zone. Defensively Washington had settled into a pattern which gave away little and ranked third in the NFL behind Philadelphia and New Orleans. Assuming the leadership rôle, defensive end Charles Mann was the club's premier pass rusher with 11 quarterback sacks. A step behind at linebacker, Wilber Marshall finally had started to play like the Pro Bowler for whom the Redskins sent two first-round draft options to Chicago in a 1988 trade. The defensive secondary focused around All-Pro cornerback Darrell Green, who was far more than just the speedster who regularly wins the title of NFL's Fastest

Man. Essentially, Green closed off a huge parcel of real estate. Joe Gibbs was seeking his third win in four trips to the Super Bowl as head coach.

Early in the game, the signs were that Buffalo was 'in for a long day', as they say. Thurman Thomas was absent from the Bills' first scrimmage downs, trying to find his helmet! Washington saw an apparent Art Monk touchdown reception overruled by the instant-replay official, and the normally efficient Redskins special team managed to botch a straightforward field goal attempt at the end of an 87-yard drive. But this couldn't last for long, and on the final play of the opening quarter Rypien initiated the first of three consecutive scoring drives. Coming out for the second half, on the wrong end of a 17–0 scoreline, the Bills continued in self-destruct mode when Kelly's first pass was intercepted and returned down to the Buffalo two-yard line. On the very next play, Riggs completed the formalities.

Briefly, Kelly slipped into gear, and a few hopes were raised as the Bills drew to within 14 points on Scott Norwood's 21-yard field goal and Thomas's one-yard touchdown run. But any optimism was dashed when the Redskins responded in like kind. Lohmiller subsequently extended the lead to 37–10 before the Redskins settled back to see out the clock in yet another one-sided triumph for the NFC.

On the day, the Redskins were the better team; they were better organized; they came to play. Anyone looking for the real Buffalo Bills should perhaps focus on the Divisional Playoffs. It would be of little consolation that they will start out the 1992 season strongly favoured once more to carry the AFC banner.

# THE GAME

**Scoring By Quarters**

**2nd Quarter**
Washington: Lohmiller, 34-yard field goal (1:58)
**Washington 3 – Buffalo 0**
Washington: Byner, 10-yard pass from Rypien;
Lohmiller kick (5:06)
**Washington 10 – Buffalo 0**
Washington: Riggs, 1-yard run;
Lohmiller kick (7:43)
**Washington 17 – Buffalo 0**

**3rd Quarter**
Washington: Riggs, 2-yard run;
Lohmiller kick (0:16)
**Washington 24 – Buffalo 0**
Buffalo: Norwood, 21-yard field goal (3:01)
**Washington 24 – Buffalo 3**
Buffalo: Thomas, 1-yard run; Norwood kick (9:02)
**Washington 24 – Buffalo 10**
Washington: Clark, 30-yard pass from Rypien;
Lohmiller kick (13:36)
**Washington 31 – Buffalo 10**

**4th Quarter**
Washington: Lohmiller, 25-yard field goal (0:06)
**Washington 34 – Buffalo 10**
Washington: Lohmiller, 39-yard field goal (3:24)
**Washington 37 – Buffalo 10**
Buffalo: Metzelaars, 2-yard pass from Kelly;
Norwood kick (9:01)
**Washington 37 – Buffalo 17**
Buffalo: Beebe, 4-yard pass from Kelly;
Norwood kick (11:05)
**Washington 37 – Buffalo 24**

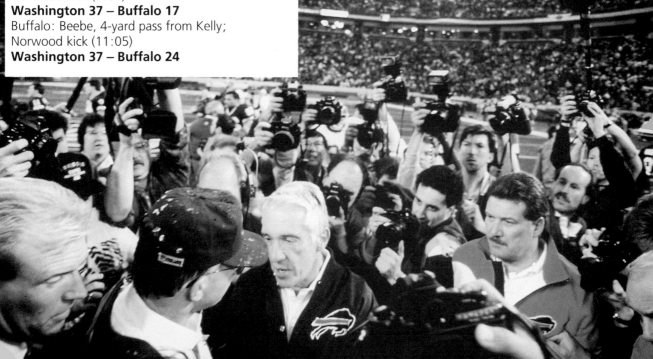

# ANATOMY OF
# SUPER BOWL XXVI

## 1st QUARTER

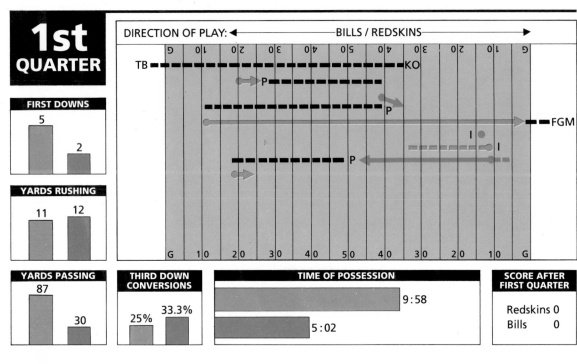

**DIRECTION OF PLAY:** ◄——— BILLS / REDSKINS ———►

**FIRST DOWNS**
5
2

**YARDS RUSHING**
11
12

**YARDS PASSING**
87
30

**THIRD DOWN CONVERSIONS**
25%
33.3%

**TIME OF POSSESSION**
9:58
5:02

**SCORE AFTER FIRST QUARTER**
Redskins 0
Bills    0

## 2nd QUARTER

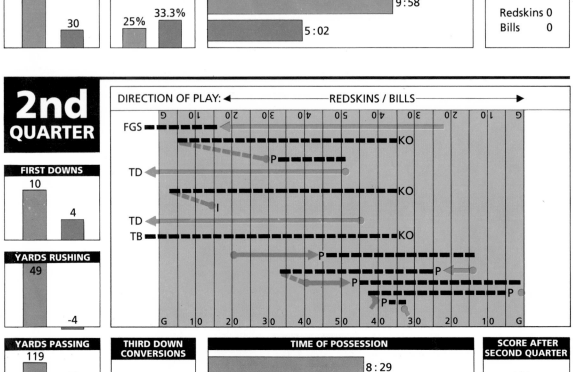

**DIRECTION OF PLAY:** ◄——— REDSKINS / BILLS ———►

**FIRST DOWNS**
10
4

**YARDS RUSHING**
49
-4

**YARDS PASSING**
119
69

**THIRD DOWN CONVERSIONS**
25%
33.3%

**TIME OF POSSESSION**
8:29
6:31

**SCORE AFTER SECOND QUARTER**
Redskins 17
Bills    0

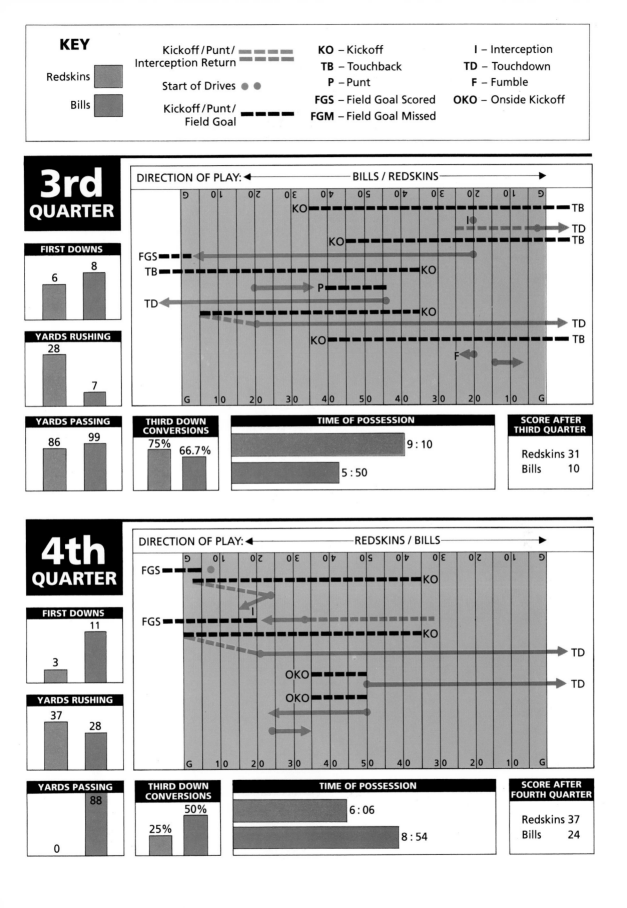

**KEY**

Redskins
Bills

Kickoff / Punt / Interception Return
Start of Drives ● ●
Kickoff / Punt / Field Goal

**KO** – Kickoff
**TB** – Touchback
**P** – Punt
**FGS** – Field Goal Scored
**FGM** – Field Goal Missed

**I** – Interception
**TD** – Touchdown
**F** – Fumble
**OKO** – Onside Kickoff

## 3rd QUARTER

DIRECTION OF PLAY: ← BILLS / REDSKINS →

G 10 20 30 40 50 40 30 20 10 G

KO — TB
I — TD
KO — TB
FGS — 
TB — KO
P — 
TD — 
— KO
— TD
KO — TB
F — 

**FIRST DOWNS**
6 | 8

**YARDS RUSHING**
28 | 7

**YARDS PASSING**
86 | 99

**THIRD DOWN CONVERSIONS**
75% | 66.7%

**TIME OF POSSESSION**
9 : 10
5 : 50

**SCORE AFTER THIRD QUARTER**
Redskins 31
Bills 10

## 4th QUARTER

DIRECTION OF PLAY: ← REDSKINS / BILLS →

G 10 20 30 40 50 40 30 20 10 G

FGS — 
— KO
I — 
FGS — 
— KO
— TD
OKO — 
OKO — 
— TD

**FIRST DOWNS**
3 | 11

**YARDS RUSHING**
37 | 28

**YARDS PASSING**
0 | 88

**THIRD DOWN CONVERSIONS**
25% | 50%

**TIME OF POSSESSION**
6 : 06
8 : 54

**SCORE AFTER FOURTH QUARTER**
Redskins 37
Bills 24

# THE PRO BOWL

At the end of each season, the best players from each conference assemble in Hawaii to give the fans out there a treat. The teams are selected by a ballot of head coaches and players in each conference. Each team has two equal votes, those being the head coach's and a consensus of players' selections. Coaches and players may vote only for players from their own conference and may not vote for players from their own team. In the most recent AFC-NFC Pro Bowl, Dallas wide receiver Michael Irvin equalled a record with eight pass receptions, one of which was for a touchdown, to earn the Most Valuable Player award as the NFC extended its lead to 13–9 in the series.

### AFC-NFC Pro Bowl Results – NFC leads series 13–9

| Year | Date | Winner | Loser | Site | Attendance |
|------|------|--------|-------|------|------------|
| 1992 | Feb. 2 | NFC 21 | AFC 15 | Honolulu | 50,209 |
| 1991 | Feb. 3 | AFC 23 | NFC 21 | Honolulu | 50,345 |
| 1990 | Feb. 4 | NFC 27 | AFC 21 | Honolulu | 50,445 |
| 1989 | Jan. 29 | NFC 34 | AFC 3 | Honolulu | 50,113 |
| 1988 | Feb. 7 | AFC 15 | NFC 6 | Honolulu | 50,113 |
| 1987 | Feb. 1 | AFC 10 | NFC 6 | Honolulu | 50,101 |
| 1986 | Feb. 2 | NFC 28 | AFC 24 | Honolulu | 50,101 |
| 1985 | Jan. 27 | AFC 22 | NFC 14 | Honolulu | 50,385 |
| 1984 | Jan. 29 | NFC 45 | AFC 3 | Honolulu | 50,445 |
| 1983 | Feb. 6 | NFC 20 | AFC 19 | Honolulu | 49,883 |
| 1982 | Jan. 31 | AFC 16 | NFC 13 | Honolulu | 50,402 |
| 1981 | Feb. 1 | NFC 13 | AFC 7 | Honolulu | 50,360 |
| 1980 | Jan. 27 | NFC 37 | AFC 27 | Honolulu | 49,800 |
| 1979 | Jan. 29 | NFC 13 | AFC 7 | Los Angeles | 46,281 |
| 1978 | Jan. 23 | NFC 14 | AFC 13 | Tampa | 51,337 |
| 1977 | Jan. 17 | AFC 24 | NFC 14 | Seattle | 64,752 |
| 1976 | Jan. 26 | NFC 23 | AFC 20 | New Orleans | 30,546 |
| 1975 | Jan. 20 | NFC 17 | AFC 10 | Miami | 26,484 |
| 1974 | Jan. 20 | AFC 15 | NFC 13 | Kansas City | 66,918 |
| 1973 | Jan. 21 | AFC 33 | NFC 28 | Dallas | 37,091 |
| 1972 | Jan. 23 | AFC 26 | NFC 13 | Los Angeles | 53,647 |
| 1971 | Jan. 24 | NFC 24 | AFC 6 | Los Angeles | 48,222 |

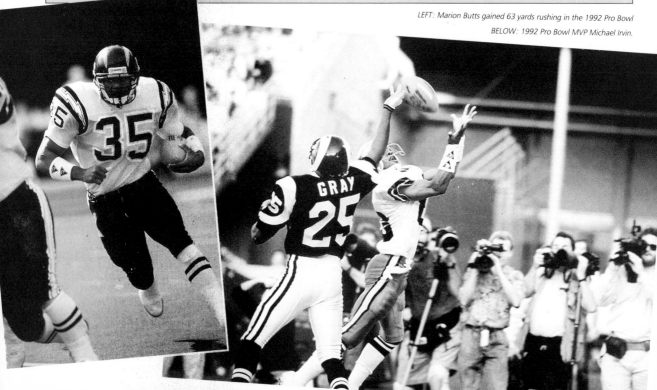

*LEFT: Marion Butts gained 63 yards rushing in the 1992 Pro Bowl*

*BELOW: 1992 Pro Bowl MVP Michael Irvin.*

# PRO BOWL ROSTERS

**(Original selections – starters in capitals)**

| OFFENSE | AMERICAN FOOTBALL CONFERENCE | | NATIONAL FOOTBALL CONFERENCE | |
|---|---|---|---|---|
| Wide Receivers | HAYWOOD JEFFIRES | Houston | MICHAEL IRVIN | Dallas |
| | ANDRE REED | Buffalo | JERRY RICE | San Francisco |
| | James Lofton | Buffalo | Andre Rison | Atlanta |
| | Mark Clayton | Miami | Gary Clark | Washington |
| Tackles | ANTHONY MUÑOZ | Cincinnati | JIM LACHEY | Washington |
| | BRUCE ARMSTRONG | New England | LOMAS BROWN | Detroit |
| | Richmond Webb | Miami | Chris Hinton | Atlanta |
| Guards | MIKE MUNCHAK | Houston | RANDALL McDANIEL | Minnesota |
| | STEVE WISNIEWSKI | L.A. Raiders | GUY McINTYRE | San Francisco |
| | Jim Ritcher | Buffalo | Mark Schlereth | Washington |
| Centers | BRUCE MATTHEWS | Houston | JAY HILGENBERG | Chicago |
| | Don Mosebar | L.A. Raiders | Bart Oates | N.Y. Giants |
| Tight Ends | MARV COOK | New England | JAY NOVACEK | Dallas |
| | Ethan Horton | L.A. Raiders | Steve Jordan | Minnesota |
| Quarterbacks | JIM KELLY | Buffalo | MARK RYPIEN | Washington |
| | Warren Moon | Houston | Troy Aikman | Dallas |
| | Dan Marino | Miami | Chris Miller | Atlanta |
| Running Backs | THURMAN THOMAS | Buffalo | BARRY SANDERS | Detroit |
| | CHRISTIAN OKOYE | Kansas City | EMMITT SMITH | Dallas |
| | Gaston Green | Denver | Earnest Byner | Washington |
| | Marion Butts | San Diego | Neal Anderson | Chicago |

| DEFENSE | | | | |
|---|---|---|---|---|
| Defensive Ends | WILLIAM FULLER | Houston | REGGIE WHITE | Philadelphia |
| | GREG TOWNSEND | L.A. Raiders | CLYDE SIMMONS | Philadelphia |
| | Neil Smith | Kansas City | Charles Mann | Washington |
| Interior Linemen | MICHAEL DEAN PERRY | Cleveland | JEROME BROWN | Philadelphia |
| | Ray Childress | Houston | Jerry Ball | Detroit |
| Outside Linebackers | CORNELIUS BENNETT | Buffalo | PAT SWILLING | New Orleans |
| | DERRICK THOMAS | Kansas City | SETH JOYNER | Philadelphia |
| | Darryl Talley | Buffalo | Charles Haley | San Francisco |
| | Greg Lloyd* | Pittsburgh | | |
| Inside Linebackers | AL SMITH | Houston | VAUGHAN JOHNSON | New Orleans |
| | JUNIOR SEAU | San Diego | SAM MILLS | New Orleans |
| | Karl Mecklenburg | Denver | Mike Singletary | Chicago |
| | | | Chris Spielman* | Detroit |
| Cornerbacks | CRIS DISHMAN | Houston | DARRELL GREEN | Washington |
| | GILL BYRD | San Diego | DEION SANDERS | Atlanta |
| | Rod Woodson | Pittsburgh | Eric Allen | Philadelphia |
| Safeties | RONNIE LOTT | L.A. Raiders | TIM McDONALD | Phoenix |
| | STEVE ATWATER | Denver | MARK CARRIER | Chicago |
| | Dennis Smith | Denver | Bennie Blades | Detroit |

| SPECIALISTS | | | | |
|---|---|---|---|---|
| Punter | JEFF GOSSETT | L.A. Raiders | RICH CAMARILLO | Phoenix |
| Kicker | JEFF JAEGER | L.A. Raiders | CHIP LOHMILLER | Washington |
| Kick Return Specialist | TIM BROWN | L.A. Raiders | MEL GRAY | Detroit |
| Special Teamer | STEVE TASKER | Buffalo | BENNIE THOMPSON | New Orleans |
| Head Coach | DAN REEVES | Denver | WAYNE FONTES | Detroit |

*Special selection made by head coach

# AN ALL-PRO TEAM

Just about every publication produces its All-Pro team. Here's my contribution to the controversy.

| | | |
|---|---|---|
| Wide Receivers | Jerry Rice | San Francisco |
| | Michael Irvin | Dallas |
| Tight End | Eric Green | Pittsburgh |
| Tackles | Bruce Armstrong | New England |
| | Jim Lachey | Washington |
| Guards | Mike Munchak | Houston |
| | Steve Wisniewski | L.A. Raiders |
| Center | Jay Hilgenberg | Chicago |
| Quarterback | Steve Young | San Francisco |
| Running Backs | Thurman Thomas | Buffalo |
| | Barry Sanders | Detroit |
| Defensive Ends | William Fuller | Houston |
| | Reggie White | Philadelphia |
| Defensive Tackles | Jerome Brown | Philadelphia |
| | Michael Dean Perry | Cleveland |
| Outside Linebackers | Cornelius Bennett | Buffalo |
| | Pat Swilling | New Orleans |
| Inside Linebackers | Vincent Brown | New England |
| | Vaughan Johnson | New Orleans |
| Safeties | Tim McDonald | Phoenix |
| | Steve Atwater | Denver |
| Cornerbacks | Darrell Green | Washington |
| | Deion Sanders | Atlanta |
| Placekicker | Jeff Jaeger | L.A. Raiders |
| Punter | Jeff Gossett | L.A. Raiders |
| Punt Returner | Mel Gray | Detroit |
| Kickoff Returner | Mel Gray | Detroit |
| Special-team Specialist | Steve Tasker | Buffalo |
| Head Coach | Joe Gibbs | Washington |

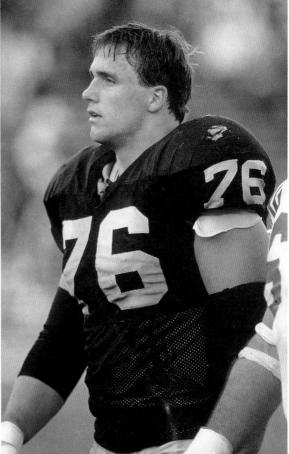

*ABOVE: Wide receiver Jerry Rice, a unanimous All-Pro, is on course to re-write the record books.*

*BELOW RIGHT: Raiders guard Steve Wisniewski is one of the game's rising stars.*

# CHAPTER TWO
# ALL-TIME RECORDS

## CHAMPIONS 1920-1991

### National Football League 1920-1969

(Until 1933 based solely on regular-season play)

1920    Akron Pros
1921    Chicago Staleys
1922    Canton Bulldogs
1923    Canton Bulldogs
1924    Cleveland Bulldogs
1925    Chicago Cardinals
1926    Frankford Yellow Jackets
1927    New York Giants
1928    Providence Steam Roller
1929    Green Bay Packers
1930    Green Bay Packers
1931    Green Bay Packers
1932    Chicago Bears 9 – Portsmouth Spartans 0
        (Championship Playoff)

### NFL Championship Games 1933-69

1933    Chicago Bears 23 – New York Giants 21
1934    New York Giants 30 – Chicago Bears 13
1935    Detroit Lions 26 – New York Giants 7
1936    Green Bay Packers 21 – Boston Redskins 6
1937    Washington Redskins 28 – Chicago Bears 21
1938    New York Giants 23 – Green Bay Packers 17
1939    Green Bay Packers 27 – New York Giants 0
1940    Chicago Bears 73 – Washington Redskins 0
1941    Chicago Bears 37 – New York Giants 9
1942    Washington Redskins 14 – Chicago Bears 6
1943    Chicago Bears 41 – Washington Redskins 21
1944    Green Bay Packers 14 – New York Giants 7
1945    Cleveland Rams 15 – Washington Redskins 14
1946    Chicago Bears 24 – New York Giants 14
1947    Chicago Cardinals 28 – Philadelphia Eagles 21
1948    Philadelphia Eagles 7 – Chicago Cardinals 0
1949    Philadelphia Eagles 14 – Los Angeles Rams 0
1950    Cleveland Browns 30 – Los Angeles Rams 28
1951    Los Angeles Rams 24 – Cleveland Browns 17
1952    Detroit Lions 17 – Cleveland Browns 7
1953    Detroit Lions 17 – Cleveland Browns 16
1954    Cleveland Browns 56 – Detroit Lions 10
1955    Cleveland Browns 38 – Los Angeles Rams 14
1956    New York Giants 47 – Chicago Bears 7
1957    Detroit Lions 59 – Cleveland Browns 14

1958    Baltimore Colts 23 – New York Giants 17 (OT)
1959    Baltimore Colts 31 – New York Giants 16
1960    Philadelphia Eagles 17 – Green Bay Packers 13
1961    Green Bay Packers 37 – New York Giants 0
1962    Green Bay Packers 16 – New York Giants 7
1963    Chicago Bears 14 – New York Giants 10
1964    Cleveland Browns 27 – Baltimore Colts 0
1965    Green Bay Packers 23 – Cleveland Browns 12
1966    Green Bay Packers 34 – Dallas Cowboys 27
1967    Green Bay Packers 21 – Dallas Cowboys 17
1968    Baltimore Colts 34 – Cleveland Browns 0
1969    Minnesota Vikings 27 – Cleveland Browns 7

### AFL Championship Games 1960-1969

1960    Houston Oilers 24 – Los Angeles Chargers 16
1961    Houston Oilers 10 – San Diego Chargers 3
1962    Dallas Texans 20 – Houston Oilers 17 (OT)
1963    San Diego Chargers 51 – Boston Patriots 10
1964    Buffalo Bills 20 – San Diego Chargers 7
1965    Buffalo Bills 23 – San Diego Chargers 0
1966    Kansas City Chiefs 31 – Buffalo Bills 7
1967    Oakland Raiders 40 – Houston Oilers 7
1968    New York Jets 27 – Oakland Raiders 23
1969    Kansas City Chiefs 17 – Oakland Raiders 7

## CONFERENCE CHAMPIONSHIP GAMES 1970-1991

### NFC

1970    Dallas Cowboys 17 – San Francisco 49ers 10
1971    Dallas Cowboys 14 – San Francisco 49ers 3
1972    Washington Redskins 26 – Dallas Cowboys 3
1973    Minnesota Vikings 27 – Dallas Cowboys 10
1974    Minnesota Vikings 14 – Los Angeles Rams 10
1975    Dallas Cowboys 37 – Los Angeles Rams 7
1976    Minnesota Vikings 24 – Los Angeles Rams 13
1977    Dallas Cowboys 23 – Minnesota Vikings 6
1978    Dallas Cowboys 28 – Los Angeles Rams 0
1979    Los Angeles Rams 9 – Tampa Bay Buccaneers 0
1980    Philadelphia Eagles 20 – Dallas Cowboys 7
1981    San Francisco 49ers 28 – Dallas Cowboys 27
1982    Washington Redskins 31 – Dallas Cowboys 17
1983    Washington Redskins 24 – San Francisco 49ers 21
1984    San Francisco 49ers 23 – Chicago Bears 0

| 1985 | Chicago Bears 24 – Los Angeles Rams 0 |
|---|---|
| 1986 | New York Giants 17 – Washington Redskins 0 |
| 1987 | Washington Redskins 17 – Minnesota Vikings 10 |
| 1988 | San Francisco 49ers 28 – Chicago Bears 3 |
| 1989 | San Francisco 49ers 30 – Los Angeles Rams 3 |
| 1990 | New York Giants 15 – San Francisco 49ers 13 |
| 1991 | Washington Redskins 41 – Detroit Lions 10 |

**AFC**

| 1970 | Baltimore Colts 27 – Oakland Raiders 17 |
|---|---|
| 1971 | Miami Dolphins 21 – Baltimore Colts 0 |
| 1972 | Miami Dolphins 21 – Pittsburgh Steelers 17 |
| 1973 | Miami Dolphins 27 – Oakland Raiders 10 |
| 1974 | Pittsburgh Steelers 24 – Oakland Raiders 13 |
| 1975 | Pittsburgh Steelers 16 – Oakland Raiders 10 |
| 1976 | Oakland Raiders 24 – Pittsburgh Steelers 7 |
| 1977 | Denver Broncos 20 – Oakland Raiders 17 |
| 1978 | Pittsburgh Steelers 34 – Houston Oilers 5 |
| 1979 | Pittsburgh Steelers 27 – Houston Oilers 13 |
| 1980 | Oakland Raiders 34 – San Diego Chargers 27 |
| 1981 | Cincinnati Bengals 27 – San Diego Chargers 7 |
| 1982 | Miami Dolphins 14 – New York Jets 0 |
| 1983 | Los Angeles Raiders 30 – Seattle Seahawks 14 |
| 1984 | Miami Dolphins 45 – Pittsburgh Steelers 28 |
| 1985 | New England Patriots 31 – Miami Dolphins 14 |
| 1986 | Denver Broncos 23 – Cleveland Browns 20 (OT) |
| 1987 | Denver Broncos 38 – Cleveland Browns 33 |

*A number of Steve Largent's receiving records are in jeopardy.*

| 1988 | Cincinnati Bengals 21 – Buffalo Bills 10 |
|---|---|
| 1989 | Denver Broncos 37 – Cleveland Browns 21 |
| 1990 | Buffalo Bills 51 – Los Angeles Raiders 3 |
| 1991 | Buffalo Bills 10 – Denver Broncos 7 |

# SUPER BOWL 1966-1991

| Season | SB | Winner | | Loser | | Stadium | Attendance |
|---|---|---|---|---|---|---|---|
| 1966 | I | Green Bay | 35 | Kansas City | 10 | Los Angeles Coliseum | 61,946 |
| 1967 | II | Green Bay | 33 | Oakland | 14 | Miami Orange Bowl | 75,546 |
| 1968 | III | N.Y. Jets | 16 | Baltimore | 7 | Miami Orange Bowl | 75,389 |
| 1969 | IV | Kansas City | 23 | Minnesota | 7 | New Orleans Tulane Stadium | 80,562 |
| 1970 | V | Baltimore | 16 | Dallas | 13 | Miami Orange Bowl | 79,204 |
| 1971 | VI | Dallas | 24 | Miami | 3 | New Orleans Tulane Stadium | 81,023 |
| 1972 | VII | Miami | 14 | Washington | 7 | Los Angeles Coliseum | 90,182 |
| 1973 | VIII | Miami | 24 | Minnesota | 7 | Houston Rice Stadium | 71,882 |
| 1974 | IX | Pittsburgh | 16 | Minnesota | 6 | New Orleans Tulane Stadium | 80,997 |
| 1975 | X | Pittsburgh | 21 | Dallas | 17 | Miami Orange Bowl | 80,187 |
| 1976 | XI | Oakland | 32 | Minnesota | 14 | Pasadena Rose Bowl | 103,438 |
| 1977 | XII | Dallas | 27 | Denver | 10 | New Orleans Superdome | 75,583 |
| 1978 | XIII | Pittsburgh | 35 | Dallas | 31 | Miami Orange Bowl | 79,484 |
| 1979 | XIV | Pittsburgh | 31 | L.A. Rams | 19 | Pasadena Rose Bowl | 103,985 |
| 1980 | XV | Oakland | 27 | Philadelphia | 10 | New Orleans Superdome | 76,135 |
| 1981 | XVI | San Francisco | 26 | Cincinnati | 21 | Pontiac Silverdome | 81,270 |
| 1982 | XVII | Washington | 27 | Miami | 17 | Pasadena Rose Bowl | 103,667 |
| 1983 | XVIII | L.A. Raiders | 38 | Washington | 9 | Tampa Stadium | 72,920 |
| 1984 | XIX | San Francisco | 38 | Miami | 16 | Stanford Stadium | 84,059 |
| 1985 | XX | Chicago | 46 | New England | 10 | New Orleans Superdome | 73,818 |
| 1986 | XXI | N.Y. Giants | 39 | Denver | 20 | Pasadena Rose Bowl | 101,063 |
| 1987 | XXII | Washington | 42 | Denver | 10 | San Diego Jack Murphy Stadium | 73,302 |
| 1988 | XXIII | San Francisco | 20 | Cincinnati | 16 | Miami Joe Robbie Stadium | 75,179 |
| 1989 | XXIV | San Francisco | 55 | Denver | 10 | New Orleans Superdome | 72,919 |
| 1990 | XXV | N.Y. Giants | 20 | Buffalo | 19 | Tampa Stadium | 73,813 |
| 1991 | XXVI | Washington | 37 | Buffalo | 24 | Hubert H. Humphrey Metrodome | 63,130 |

# ALL-TIME INDIVIDUAL RECORDS

(Regular Season only — New Records and Records tied are in bold type)

## CAREER BEST

| | | |
|---|---|---|
| **SEASONS PLAYED** | 26 | George Blanda |
| **GAMES PLAYED** | 340 | George Blanda |
| **POINTS** | 2,002 | George Blanda (9-TD, 943-EP, 335-FG) |
| **EXTRA POINTS** | 943 | George Blanda |
| **FIELD GOALS** | 373 | Jan Stenerud |
| **TOUCHDOWNS** | | |
| **Rushing and Pass Receiving** | 126 | Jim Brown (106-R, 20-P) |
| **Rushing** | 110 | Walter Payton |
| **Pass Receiving** | 100 | Steve Largent |
| **Passes Thrown** | 342 | Fran Tarkenton |
| **By Interception Return** | 9 | Ken Houston |
| **By Punt Return** | 8 | Jack Christiansen |
| | | Rick Upchurch |
| **By Kickoff Return** | 6 | Ollie Matson |
| | | Gale Sayers |
| | | Travis Williams |
| **By Fumble Recovery Return** | 4 | Billy Thompson |
| **YARDAGE** | | |
| **Rushing** | 16,726 | Walter Payton |
| **Pass Receiving** | 13,089 | Steve Largent |
| **Passing** | 47,003 | Fran Tarkenton |
| **HOW MANY TIMES** | | |
| **Pass Receptions** | 819 | Steve Largent |
| **Passes Completed** | 3,686 | Fran Tarkenton |
| **Interceptions** | 81 | Paul Krause |
| **100-Yard Rushing Games** | 77 | Walter Payton |
| **100-Yard Pass Receiving Games** | 50 | Don Maynard |
| **1,000-Yard Rushing Seasons** | 10 | Walter Payton |
| **1,000-Yard Pass Receiving Seasons** | 8 | Steve Largent |
| **MOST SEASONS LEADING LEAGUE** | | |
| **Points** | 5 | Don Hutson, Green Bay 1940-44 |
| | | Gino Cappelletti, Boston 1961, 1963-66 |
| **Extra Points** | 8 | George Blanda, Chicago Bears 1956, Houston 1961-62, |
| | | Oakland 1967-69, 1972, 1974 |
| **Field Goals** | 5 | Lou Groza, Cleveland Browns 1950, 1952-54, 1957 |
| **Touchdowns** | 8 | Don Hutson, Green Bay 1935-38, 1941-44 |
| **Touchdowns, Rushing** | 5 | Jim Brown, Cleveland Browns 1957-59, 1963, 1965 |
| **Touchdowns, Pass Receiving** | 9 | Don Hutson, Green Bay 1935-38, 1940-44 |
| **Touchdowns, Passes Thrown** | 4 | Johnny Unitas, Baltimore 1957-60 |
| | | Len Dawson, Dallas Texans 1962, Kansas City 1963, 1965-66 |
| **Yards, Rushing** | 8 | Jim Brown, Cleveland Browns 1957-61, 1963-65 |
| **Yards, Pass Receiving** | 7 | Don Hutson, Green Bay 1936, 1938-39, 1941-44 |
| **Yards, Passing** | 5 | Sonny Jurgensen, Philadelphia 1961-62, Washington 1966-67, 1969 |
| **Pass Receptions** | 8 | Don Hutson, Green Bay 1936-37, 1939, 1941-45 |
| **Passes Completed** | 5 | Sammy Baugh, Washington 1937, 1943, 1945, 1947-48 |
| **Pass Interceptions** | 3 | Everson Walls, Dallas 1981-82, 1985 |

## SEASON BEST

| | | |
|---|---|---|
| **POINTS** | 176 | Paul Hornung, Green Bay 1960 (15-TD, 41-EP, 15-FG) |
| **EXTRA POINTS** | 66 | Uwe von Schamann, Miami 1984 |
| **FIELD GOALS** | 35 | Ali Haji-Sheikh, N.Y. Giants 1983 |

**TOUCHDOWNS**

| | | |
|---|---|---|
| Rushing and Pass Receiving | 24 | John Riggins, Washington 1983 (24-R) |
| Rushing | 24 | John Riggins, Washington 1983 |
| Pass Receiving | 22 | Jerry Rice, San Francisco 1987 |
| Passes Thrown | 48 | Dan Marino, Miami 1984 |
| By Interception Return | 4 | Ken Houston, Houston 1971 |
| | | Jim Kearney, Kansas City 1972 |
| By Punt Return | 4 | Jack Christiansen, Detroit 1951 |
| | | Rick Upchurch, Denver 1976 |
| By Kickoff Return | 4 | Travis Williams, Green Bay 1967 |
| | | Cecil Turner, Chicago 1970 |
| By Fumble Recovery Return | 2 | By many players |

**YARDAGE**

| | | |
|---|---|---|
| Rushing | 2,105 | Eric Dickerson, L.A. Rams 1984 |
| Pass Receiving | 1,746 | Charley Hennigan, Houston 1961 |
| Passing | 5,084 | Dan Marino, Miami 1984 |

**HOW MANY TIMES**

| | | |
|---|---|---|
| Pass Receptions | 106 | Art Monk, Washington 1984 |
| Passes Completed | **404** | **Warren Moon, Houston 1991** |
| Interceptions | 14 | Dick (Night Train) Lane, L.A. Rams 1952 |

# GAME BEST

| | | |
|---|---|---|
| POINTS | 40 | Ernie Nevers (6-TD, 4-EP), Chicago Cardinals v Chicago Bears 1929 |
| EXTRA POINTS | 9 | Pat Harder, Chicago Cardinals v N.Y. Giants 1948 |
| | | Bob Waterfield, L.A. Rams v Baltimore 1950 |
| | | Charlie Gogolak, Washington v N.Y. Giants 1966 |
| FIELD GOALS | 7 | Jim Bakken, St Louis v Pittsburgh 1967 |
| | | Rich Karlis, Minnesota v L.A. Rams 1989 |

**TOUCHDOWNS**

| | | |
|---|---|---|
| All methods of scoring | 6 | Ernie Nevers (6-R), Chicago Cardinals v Chicago Bears 1929 |
| | | Dub Jones (4-R, 2-P), Cleveland v Chicago Bears 1951 |
| | | Gale Sayers (4-R, 1-P, 1-Ret), Chicago Bears v San Francisco 1965 |
| Rushing | 6 | Ernie Nevers, Chicago Cardinals v Chicago Bears 1929 |
| Pass Receiving | 5 | Bob Shaw, Chicago Cardinals v Baltimore 1950 |
| | | Kellen Winslow, San Diego v Oakland 1981 |
| | | Jerry Rice, San Francisco v Atlanta 1990 |
| Passes Thrown | 7 | Sid Luckman, Chicago Bears v N.Y. Giants 1943 |
| | | Adrian Burk, Philadelphia v Washington 1954 |
| | | George Blanda, Houston v N.Y. Titans 1961 |
| | | Y.A. Tittle, N.Y. Giants v Washington 1962 |
| | | Joe Kapp, Minnesota v Baltimore 1969 |

**YARDAGE**

| | | |
|---|---|---|
| Rushing | 275 | Walter Payton, Chicago v Minnesota 1977 |
| Pass Receiving | 336 | Willie (Flipper) Anderson, L.A. Rams v New Orleans 1989 |
| Passing | 554 | Norm Van Brocklin, L.A. Rams v N.Y. Yanks 1951 |

**HOW MANY TIMES**

| | | |
|---|---|---|
| Rushing Attempts | 45 | Jamie Morris, Washington v Cincinnati 1988 |
| Pass Receptions | 18 | Tom Fears, L.A. Rams v Green Bay 1950 |
| Passes Completed | 42 | Richard Todd, N.Y. Jets v San Francisco 1980 |
| Interceptions | 4 | By many players |

**LONGEST**

| | | |
|---|---|---|
| Touchdown Rushing | 99 yds | Tony Dorsett, Dallas v Minnesota 1983 |
| Touchdown Pass Receiving | 99 yds | Andy Farkas (from Filchock), Washington v Pittsburgh 1939 |
| | | Bobby Mitchell (from Izo), Washington v Cleveland 1963 |
| | | Pat Studstill (from Sweetan), Detroit v Baltimore 1966 |
| | | Gerry Allen (from Jurgensen), Washington v Chicago 1968 |
| | | Cliff Branch (from Plunkett), L.A. Raiders v Washington 1983 |
| | | Mike Quick (from Jaworski), Philadelphia v Atlanta 1985 |
| Field Goal | 63 yds | Tom Dempsey, New Orleans v Detroit 1970 |
| Punt Return (All TDs) | 98 yds | Gil LeFebvre, Cincinnati v Brooklyn 1933 |

|  |  | Charlie West, Minnesota v Washington 1968 |
| | | Dennis Morgan, Dallas v St Louis 1974 |
| | | Terance Mathis, N.Y. Jets v Dallas 1990 |
| **Kickoff Return** (All TDs) | 106 yds | Al Carmichael, Green Bay v Chicago Bears 1956 |
| | | Noland Smith, Kansas City v Denver 1967 |
| | | Roy Green, St Louis v Dallas 1979 |
| **Interception Return** (TD) | 103 yds | Vencie Glenn, San Diego v Denver 1987 |
| **Fumble Recovery Return** (TD) | 104 yds | Jack Tatum, Oakland v Green Bay 1972 |

# TEAM RECORDS

| | | |
|---|---|---|
| **Most Championships** | 11 | Green Bay, 1929-31, 1936, 1939, 1944, 1961-62, 1965-67 |
| | 9 | Chicago Staleys/Bears, 1921, 1932-33, 1940-41, 1943, 1946, 1963, 1985 |
| | 6 | N.Y. Giants, 1927, 1934, 1938, 1956, 1986, 1990 |
| | 5 | **Washington, 1937, 1942, 1982, 1987, 1991** |
| | 4 | Baltimore, 1958-59, 1968, 1970 |
| | | Cleveland Browns, 1950, 1954-55, 1964 |
| | | Detroit, 1935, 1952-53, 1957 |
| | | Oakland/L.A. Raiders, 1967, 1976, 1980, 1983 |
| | | Pittsburgh, 1974-75, 1978-79 |
| | | San Francisco, 1981, 1984, 1988-89 |
| **Most Consecutive Games Won** (inc. playoffs) | 18 | Chicago Bears, 1933-34 and 1941-42 |
| | | Miami, 1972-73 |
| | | San Francisco, 1989-90 |
| **Most Consecutive Games Won** | 17 | Chicago Bears, 1933-34 (exc. playoffs) |
| **Most Consecutive Games Lost** | 26 | Tampa Bay, 1976-77 |
| **Most Points in a Season** | 541 | Washington, 1983 |
| **Fewest Points in a Season** (Since 1932) | 37 | Cincinnati-St Louis, 1934 |
| **Most Points in a Game** | 72 | Washington v N.Y. Giants, 1966 |
| **Most Points (Both Teams) in a Game** | 113 | Washington v N.Y. Giants, 1966 |
| **Fewest Points (Both Teams) in a Game** | 0 | Many teams; last time N.Y. Giants v Detroit, 1943 |

# ALL-TIME TOP TWENTY

(1991 Active players in capitals)

| All-Time Leading Rushers | Yrs. | Att. | Yards | Ave. | TDs |
|---|---|---|---|---|---|
| 1. Walter Payton | 13 | 3,838 | 16,726 | 4.4 | 110 |
| 2. Tony Dorsett | 12 | 2,936 | 12,739 | 4.3 | 77 |
| 3. ERIC DICKERSON | 9 | 2,783 | 12,439 | 4.5 | 88 |
| 4. Jim Brown | 9 | 2,359 | 12,312 | 5.2 | 106 |
| 5. Franco Harris | 13 | 2,949 | 12,120 | 4.1 | 91 |
| 6. John Riggins | 14 | 2,916 | 11,352 | 3.9 | 104 |
| 7. O.J. Simpson | 11 | 2,404 | 11,236 | 4.7 | 61 |
| 8. OTTIS ANDERSON | 13 | 2,552 | 10,242 | 4.0 | 81 |
| 9. Earl Campbell | 8 | 2,187 | 9,407 | 4.3 | 74 |
| 10. Jim Taylor | 10 | 1,941 | 8,597 | 4.4 | 83 |
| 11. Joe Perry | 14 | 1,737 | 8,378 | 4.8 | 53 |
| 12. MARCUS ALLEN | 10 | 2,023 | 8,244 | 4.1 | 77 |
| 13. GERALD RIGGS | 10 | 1,989 | 8,188 | 4.1 | 69 |
| 14. Larry Csonka | 11 | 1,891 | 8,081 | 4.3 | 64 |
| 15. JAMES BROOKS | 11 | 1,667 | 7,918 | 4.7 | 49 |
| 16. FREEMAN McNEIL | 11 | 1,755 | 7,904 | 4.5 | 38 |
| 17. ROGER CRAIG | 9 | 1,848 | 7,654 | 4.1 | 51 |
| 18. Mike Pruitt | 11 | 1,844 | 7,378 | 4.0 | 51 |
| 19. Leroy Kelly | 10 | 1,727 | 7,274 | 4.2 | 74 |
| 20. George Rogers | 7 | 1,692 | 7,176 | 4.2 | 54 |

## All-Time Leading Receivers

| | | Yrs. | No. | Yards | Ave. | TDs |
|---|---|---|---|---|---|---|
| 1. | Steve Largent | 14 | 819 | 13,089 | 16.0 | 100 |
| 2. | ART MONK | 12 | 801 | 10,984 | 13.7 | 60 |
| 3. | Charlie Joiner | 18 | 750 | 12,146 | 16.2 | 65 |
| 4. | JAMES LOFTON | 14 | 699 | 13,035 | 18.6 | 69 |
| 5. | Ozzie Newsome | 13 | 662 | 7,980 | 12.1 | 47 |
| 6. | Charley Taylor | 13 | 649 | 9,110 | 14.0 | 79 |
| 7. | Don Maynard | 15 | 633 | 11,834 | 18.7 | 88 |
| 8. | Raymond Berry | 13 | 631 | 9,275 | 14.7 | 68 |
| 9. | Harold Carmichael | 14 | 590 | 8,985 | 15.2 | 79 |
| 10. | Fred Biletnikoff | 14 | 589 | 8,974 | 15.2 | 76 |
| 11. | Harold Jackson | 16 | 579 | 10,372 | 17.9 | 76 |
| 12. | Lionel Taylor | 10 | 567 | 7,195 | 12.7 | 45 |
| 13. | Wes Chandler | 11 | 559 | 8,966 | 16.0 | 56 |
| 14. | Stanley Morgan | 14 | 557 | 10,716 | 19.2 | 72 |
| 15. | ROY GREEN | 13 | 551 | 8,860 | 16.1 | 66 |
| 16. | J.T. Smith | 13 | 544 | 6,974 | 12.8 | 35 |
| 17. | Lance Alworth | 11 | 542 | 10,266 | 18.9 | 85 |
| 18. | Kellen Winslow | 9 | 541 | 6,741 | 12.5 | 45 |
| 19. | DREW HILL | 12 | 540 | 8,824 | 16.3 | 57 |
| 20. | John Stallworth | 14 | 537 | 8,723 | 16.2 | 63 |

*Dan Marino continues to amass passing yardage.*

## All-Time Passer Ratings

| | | Yrs. | Att. | Comp. | Yards | TDs | Int. | Rating |
|---|---|---|---|---|---|---|---|---|
| 1. | JOE MONTANA | 12 | 4,579 | 2,914 | 34,998 | 242 | 123 | 93.4 |
| 2. | DAN MARINO | 9 | 4,730 | 2,798 | 35,386 | 266 | 149 | 88.2 |
| 3. | JIM KELLY | 6 | 2,562 | 1,555 | 19,574 | 138 | 89 | 88.0 |
| 4. | BOOMER ESIASON | 8 | 3,100 | 1,753 | 24,264 | 163 | 114 | 84.0 |
| 5. | Roger Staubach | 11 | 2,958 | 1,685 | 22,700 | 153 | 109 | 83.4 |
| 6. | Neil Lomax | 8 | 3,153 | 1,817 | 22,771 | 136 | 90 | 82.7 |
| 7. | Len Dawson | 19 | 3,741 | 2,136 | 28,711 | 239 | 183 | 82.6 |
| | Sonny Jurgensen | 18 | 4,262 | 2,433 | 32,224 | 255 | 189 | 82.6 |
| 9. | DAVE KRIEG | 12 | 3,576 | 2,096 | 26,132 | 195 | 148 | 82.3 |
| 10. | Ken Anderson | 16 | 4,475 | 2,654 | 32,838 | 197 | 160 | 81.9 |
| 11. | Danny White | 13 | 2,950 | 1,761 | 21,959 | 155 | 132 | 81.7 |
| 12. | BERNIE KOSAR | 7 | 2,857 | 1,671 | 19,937 | 103 | 71 | 81.6 |
| 13. | KEN O'BRIEN | 10 | 3,367 | 1,984 | 23,744 | 119 | 89 | 81.3 |
| 14. | Bart Starr | 16 | 3,149 | 1,808 | 24,718 | 152 | 138 | 80.5 |
| 15. | Fran Tarkenton | 18 | 6,467 | 3,686 | 47,003 | 342 | 266 | 80.4 |
| 16. | WARREN MOON | 8 | 3,680 | 2,105 | 27,679 | 157 | 133 | 80.3 |
| 17. | Dan Fouts | 15 | 5,604 | 3,297 | 43,040 | 254 | 242 | 80.2 |
| 18. | JIM EVERETT | 6 | 2,528 | 1,431 | 18,783 | 112 | 93 | 79.7 |
| | Tony Eason | 8 | 1,564 | 911 | 11,142 | 61 | 51 | 79.7 |
| 20. | JIM McMAHON | 10 | 2,151 | 1,243 | 15,637 | 89 | 77 | 79.4 |

(Minimum 1,500 attempts)

## Passes Completed

| | | No. |
|---|---|---|
| 1. | Fran Tarkenton | 3,686 |
| 2. | Dan Fouts | 3,297 |
| 3. | JOE MONTANA | 2,914 |
| 4. | Johnny Unitas | 2,830 |
| 5. | DAN MARINO | 2,798 |
| 6. | Ken Anderson | 2,654 |
| 7. | STEVE DeBERG | 2,632 |
| 8. | Jim Hart | 2,593 |
| 9. | John Brodie | 2,469 |
| 10. | Sonny Jurgensen | 2,433 |
| 11. | Joe Ferguson | 2,369 |
| 12. | Roman Gabriel | 2,366 |
| 13. | John Hadl | 2,363 |
| 14. | Norm Snead | 2,276 |
| 15. | Ken Stabler | 2,270 |
| 16. | PHIL SIMMS | 2,246 |
| 17. | JOHN ELWAY | 2,201 |
| 18. | Ron Jaworski | 2,187 |
| 19. | Len Dawson | 2,136 |
| 20. | Y.A. Tittle | 2,118 |

## Yards Passing

| | | Yards |
|---|---|---|
| 1. | Fran Tarkenton | 47,003 |
| 2. | Dan Fouts | 43,040 |
| 3. | Johnny Unitas | 40,239 |
| 4. | DAN MARINO | 35,386 |
| 5. | JOE MONTANA | 34,998 |
| 6. | Jim Hart | 34,665 |
| 7. | John Hadl | 33,503 |
| 8. | Ken Anderson | 32,838 |
| 9. | Sonny Jurgensen | 32,224 |
| 10. | John Brodie | 31,548 |
| 11. | STEVE DeBERG | 31,455 |
| 12. | Norm Snead | 30,797 |
| 13. | Joe Ferguson | 29,817 |
| 14. | PHIL SIMMS | 29,512 |
| 15. | Roman Gabriel | 29,444 |
| 16. | Len Dawson | 28,711 |
| 17. | Y.A. Tittle | 28,339 |
| 18. | Ron Jaworski | 28,190 |
| 19. | Terry Bradshaw | 27,989 |
| 20. | JOHN ELWAY | 27,974 |

## Touchdown Passes

| | | No. |
|---|---|---|
| 1. | Fran Tarkenton | 342 |
| 2. | Johnny Unitas | 290 |
| 3. | DAN MARINO | 266 |
| 4. | Sonny Jurgensen | 255 |
| 5. | Dan Fouts | 254 |
| 6. | John Hadl | 244 |
| 7. | JOE MONTANA | 242 |
| 8. | Len Dawson | 239 |
| 9. | George Blanda | 236 |
| 10. | John Brodie | 214 |
| 11. | Terry Bradshaw | 212 |
| | Y.A. Tittle | 212 |
| 13. | Jim Hart | 209 |
| 14. | Roman Gabriel | 201 |
| 15. | Ken Anderson | 197 |
| 16. | Joe Ferguson | 196 |
| | Bobby Layne | 196 |
| | Norm Snead | 196 |
| 19. | DAVE KRIEG | 195 |
| 20. | Ken Stabler | 194 |

## All-Time Leading Scorers

| | | Yrs. | TDs | EPs | FGs | Total |
|---|---|---|---|---|---|---|
| 1. | George Blanda | 26 | 9 | 943 | 335 | 2,002 |
| 2. | Jan Stenerud | 19 | 0 | 580 | 373 | 1,699 |
| 3. | PAT LEAHY | 18 | 0 | 558 | 304 | 1,470 |
| 4. | Jim Turner | 16 | 1 | 521 | 304 | 1,439 |
| 5. | Mark Moseley | 16 | 0 | 482 | 300 | 1,382 |
| 6. | Jim Bakken | 17 | 0 | 534 | 282 | 1,380 |
| 7. | Fred Cox | 15 | 0 | 519 | 282 | 1,365 |
| 8. | Lou Groza | 17 | 1 | 641 | 234 | 1,349 |
| 9. | NICK LOWERY | 13 | 0 | 410 | 284 | 1,262 |
| 10. | Chris Bahr | 14 | 0 | 490 | 241 | 1,213 |
| 11. | JIM BREECH | 13 | 0 | 486 | 224 | 1,158 |
| 12. | Gino Cappelletti* | 11 | 42 | 350 | 176 | 1,130 |
| 13. | Ray Wersching | 15 | 0 | 456 | 222 | 1,122 |
| 14. | EDDIE MURRAY | 12 | 0 | 381 | 244 | 1,113 |
| 15. | Don Cockroft | 13 | 0 | 432 | 216 | 1,080 |
| 16. | Garo Yepremian | 14 | 0 | 444 | 210 | 1,074 |
| 17. | MATT BAHR | 13 | 0 | 402 | 221 | 1,065 |
| 18. | Bruce Gossett | 11 | 0 | 374 | 219 | 1,031 |
| 19. | GARY ANDERSON | 10 | 0 | 323 | 229 | 1,010 |
| 20. | Sam Baker | 15 | 2 | 428 | 179 | 977 |

* Includes four two-point conversions

*Bills wide receiver James Lofton may surpass 700 career receptions and Steve Largent's receiving yardage record in his first game of 1992.*

# INDEX OF RETIRED PLAYERS
## LISTED IN THE ALL-TIME STATISTICS

(1962-68)
MORGAN Dennis, Dallas (1974), Philadelphia (1975)
MORGAN Stanley, New England (1977-89), Indianapolis (1990)
MORRIS Jamie, Washington (1988-89), New England (1990)
MOSELEY Mark, Philadelphia (1970), Houston (1971-72), Washington (1974-86), Cleveland (1986)
NEVERS Ernie, Duluth Eskimos (1926-27), Chicago Cardinals (1929-31)
NEWSOME Ozzie, Cleveland (1978-90)
PAYTON Walter, Chicago (1975-87)
PERRY Joe, San Francisco (1948-60 and 1963), Baltimore (1961-62)
PLUNKETT Jim, New England (1971-75), San Francisco (1976-77), Oakland/L.A. Raiders (1978-85)
PRUITT Mike, Cleveland (1976-84), Buffalo (1985), Kansas City (1985-86)
QUICK Mike, Philadelphia (1982-90)
RIGGINS John, N.Y. Jets (1971-75), Washington (1976-79 and 1981-85)
ROGERS George, New Orleans (1981-84), Washington (1985-87)
SAYERS Gale, Chicago (1965-71)
SHAW Bob, Cleveland/L.A. Rams (1945-49), Chicago Cardinals (1950)
SIMPSON O.J., Buffalo (1969-77), San Francisco (1978-79)
SMITH J.T., Washington (1978), Kansas City (1978-84), St Louis/Phoenix (1985-90)
SMITH Noland, Kansas City (1967-69), San Francisco (1969)
SNEAD Norm, Washington (1961-63), Philadelphia (1964-70), Minnesota (1971), N.Y. Giants (1972-74 and 1976), San Francisco (1974-75)
STABLER Ken, Oakland (1970-79), Houston (1980-81), New Orleans (1982-84)
STALLWORTH John, Pittsburgh (1974-87)
STARR Bart, Green Bay (1956-71)
STAUBACH Roger, Dallas (1969-79)
STENERUD Jan, Kansas City (1967-79), Green Bay (1980-83), Minnesota (1984-85)
STUDSTILL Pat, Detroit (1961-62 and 1964-67), L.A. Rams (1968-71), New England (1972)
SWEETAN Karl, Detroit (1966-67), New Orleans (1968), L.A. Rams (1969-70)
TARKENTON Fran, Minnesota (1961-66 and 1972-78), N.Y. Giants (1967-71)
TATUM Jack, Oakland (1971-79), Houston (1980)
TAYLOR Charley, Washington (1964-75 and 1977)
TAYLOR Jim, Green Bay (1958-66), New Orleans (1967)
TAYLOR Lionel, Chicago Bears (1959), Denver (1960-66), Houston (1967-68)
THOMPSON Billy, Denver (1969-81)
TITTLE Y.A., Baltimore (1948-50), San Francisco (1951-60), N.Y. Giants (1961-64)
TODD Richard, N.Y. Jets (1976-83), New Orleans (1984-85)

TURNER Cecil, Chicago (1968-73)
TURNER Jim, N.Y. Jets (1964-70), Denver (1971-79)
UNITAS Johnny, Baltimore (1956-72), San Diego (1973)
UPCHURCH Rick, Denver (1975-83)
VAN BROCKLIN Norm, L.A. Rams (1949-57), Philadelphia (1958-60)
von SCHAMANN Uwe, Miami (1979-84)
WATERFIELD Bob, Cleveland/L.A. Rams (1945-52)
WERSCHING Ray, San Diego (1973-76), San Francisco (1977-87)
WEST Charlie, Minnesota (1968-73), Detroit (1974-77), Denver (1978-79)
WHITE Danny, Dallas (1976-88)
WILLIAMS Travis, Green Bay (1967-70), L.A. Rams (1971)
WINSLOW Kellen, San Diego (1979-87)
YEPREMIAN Garo, Detroit (1966-67), Miami (1970-78), New Orleans (1979), Tampa Bay (1980-81)

*John Riggins.*

# CHAPTER THREE

# THE CLASS OF '92

With the unenviable status of being the weakest team in the NFL in 1991, the Colts gained the premier pick in the draft. And they came up with an unexpected bonus, the second option overall, as their part of the trade which sent backup quarterback Chris Chandler to Tampa Bay prior to the 1990 regular season. In **Steve Emtman** they have a dominant defensive tackle whose impact may be compared to those of All-Pro defensive linemen Bruce Smith and Reggie White. Noted for the power of his initial surge and relentless pursuit, even from his position of defensive tackle Emtman is likely to log a clutch of sacks. However, significantly for the Colts, who are adjusting to the 4–3 formation to accommodate his talents, he is expected to help secure the defense against the run immediately. Astonishingly for a 21-stoner, Emtman can turn reverse somersaults as just one component of a package which earned him both the Outland and Lombardi awards as college football's best down lineman.

For sheer aggression and intimidation the Colts could have done no better than select **Quentin Coryatt**, who is the latest in a line of Texas A&M hitting machines, following the likes of John Roper and Aaron Wallace. Primarily an inside linebacker in college, Coryatt has great lateral speed and pursuit, qualities which may see him play the outside position in the NFL. He had a late start to his collegiate career, missing his first two years because of academic ineligibility. It has led some scouts to regard him as 'raw', but this didn't deter the selectors who made him Southwestern Conference Defensive Player of the Year. Coryatt signed a four-year contract for a reported $8.8 million, valuing him just a couple of digits behind Emtman.

Joining Coryatt in the first round was former teammate **Kevin Smith**, who was the first of two selections by the Dallas Cowboys. Entering the 1991 season, the NCAA record for career interceptions (29) was a possible target for the ball-hawking Smith, who, with 18, had surpassed Lester Hayes's A&M record of 14 and was tied for the SWC

*Top pick Steve Emtman should become a firm favourite with the Colts' faithful.*

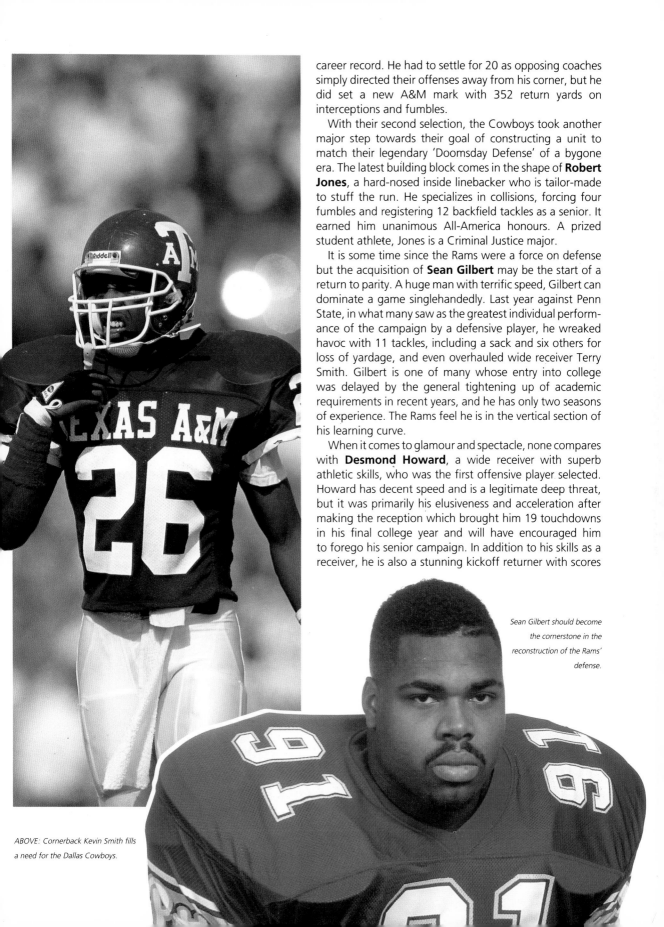

career record. He had to settle for 20 as opposing coaches simply directed their offenses away from his corner, but he did set a new A&M mark with 352 return yards on interceptions and fumbles.

With their second selection, the Cowboys took another major step towards their goal of constructing a unit to match their legendary 'Doomsday Defense' of a bygone era. The latest building block comes in the shape of **Robert Jones**, a hard-nosed inside linebacker who is tailor-made to stuff the run. He specializes in collisions, forcing four fumbles and registering 12 backfield tackles as a senior. It earned him unanimous All-America honours. A prized student athlete, Jones is a Criminal Justice major.

It is some time since the Rams were a force on defense but the acquisition of **Sean Gilbert** may be the start of a return to parity. A huge man with terrific speed, Gilbert can dominate a game singlehandedly. Last year against Penn State, in what many saw as the greatest individual performance of the campaign by a defensive player, he wreaked havoc with 11 tackles, including a sack and six others for loss of yardage, and even overhauled wide receiver Terry Smith. Gilbert is one of many whose entry into college was delayed by the general tightening up of academic requirements in recent years, and he has only two seasons of experience. The Rams feel he is in the vertical section of his learning curve.

When it comes to glamour and spectacle, none compares with **Desmond Howard**, a wide receiver with superb athletic skills, who was the first offensive player selected. Howard has decent speed and is a legitimate deep threat, but it was primarily his elusiveness and acceleration after making the reception which brought him 19 touchdowns in his final college year and will have encouraged him to forego his senior campaign. In addition to his skills as a receiver, he is also a stunning kickoff returner with scores

*Sean Gilbert should become the cornerstone in the reconstruction of the Rams' defense.*

*ABOVE: Cornerback Kevin Smith fills a need for the Dallas Cowboys.*

*The Redskins coveted the home-run threat of Desmond Howard.*

nonetheless is the devil-may-care type, who strikes with cat-quick certainty and is coming off an astounding final year in which he surpassed both Sanders and another former Florida State All-America, LeRoy Butler, with 12 interceptions for 238 return yards. He won the Jim Thorpe Award as college football's best defensive back. With four career touchdowns on interception returns, he is tied with Sanders for the Florida State record and is only one short of the NCAA record held by Jackie Walker and Ken Thomas (really!). At Green Bay, Buckley will be reunited with Butler.

Cincinnati selection **David Klingler** chose to remain in college for his senior year and may have missed out on being the premier selection of 1990. As a precaution, he insured himself against injury for $1.5 million and for most of the season he had a chance of collecting as, playing behind a weak offensive line, he was often reduced to running for his life as he tried desperately to operate the run-and-shoot offense. In the eyes of many his stock fell, but he is still regarded as having the strongest arm of all the draftees and he does hold or share an astronomic 51 NCAA Division I records. Much is expected of an athlete who can high jump 6 ft 9 in and can long jump 24 feet, but for the moment he'll have to bide his time behind Boomer Esiason.

Cincinnati's second first-round pick, **Darryl Williams**, who came with the option which was acquired as part of the trade which enabled Washington to move up to fourth place, could give the Bengals excellent depth for the safety positions. A consensus All-America, Williams is seen by some scouts as lacking strength, while others place him in the class of Bennie Blades, who is another former first-round pick from the same stable and is now making an impact with the Detroit Lions. For certain, there are no doubts over Williams' ability to match a wide receiver stride for stride. An instinctive tackler, he comes with the bonus of having been schooled in the techniques of zone defense much used by NFL teams.

Over the last decade, defense has been a problem for the Miami Dolphins and more than a few high-round draftees, particularly at linebacker, proved disappointing. Slowly, however, the defense is firming up and this trend is expected to continue with the arrival of **Troy Vincent** and **Marco Coleman**. Vincent was the second defensive back selected and brings with him the extra skill of punt returning. For his primary rôle of cornerback he has smooth, graceful speed, long arms and sure hands. Important to the pros, he has a natural instinct for man-to-man coverage. His combination of speed and spatial awareness earmark him for the kick coverage teams, and here he is likely to specialize on punt returns following his career average of 11.4 yards on 68 returns including touchdowns covering 71, 71 and 90 yards.

Coleman may be the most prolific backfield tackler of the entire rookie crop. Over his career at Georgia Tech he had 28 sacks, breaking the team record of 23 set by subsequent New Orleans All-Pro Pat Swilling and tying the Atlantic

on runs of 93 and 95 yards. In 1991 he won college football's most coveted award, the Heisman Trophy, with more than four times the number of votes gained by the runner-up, quarterback Casey Weldon.

Unanimous All-America selection **Terrell Buckley** is in the mould of Deion Sanders, the Atlanta Falcons cornerback and kick returner who would win the title of NFL's Flashiest Man, were there to be such an award. Not quite as expressive as Sanders, who is also his mentor, Buckley

Coast Conference mark established by Michael Dean Perry (Cleveland), who has also been picked All-Pro. Coleman's figure of 50 tackles-for-loss erased Swilling's total (37) by some way. At 6 ft 2 in and 259 pounds he is too small for the position of down lineman in the NFL, and the signs are that he will operate as a blitzing outside linebacker for Miami.

Offensive linemen are often more intelligent than the average and that is true of **Bob Whitfield**, the unanimous All-America and Economics major from Stanford who is rated as the best offensive lineman to emerge since Jim Lachey and, before him, the peerless Anthony Munoz. Whitfield has never been placed under pressure to dominate opponents, taking care of his quarterback from the crucial left tackle position. Teak-tough, he played every offensive down through his three-year college career and regularly graded out with the highest performance marks despite being totally blind in his left eye. His strength lies in pass protection with a slight comparative weakness on run blocking. But this is not unusual in collegians. He'll still be only 20 years old on opening day.

*The Bengals' personnel department was not put off by David Klingler's gruelling senior season.*

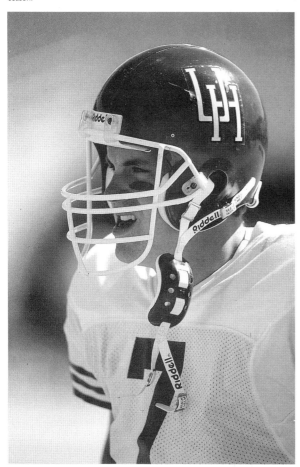

Whitfield was followed in the draft by the player for whom he blocked at Stanford, **Tommy Vardell**, who leapt to prominence as a senior when he set Cardinal records by rushing for 1,084 yards, scoring 20 touchdowns and accumulating 120 points. He was only the fourth rusher in Stanford history to gain over 1,000 yards. Even so, not many scouts felt that he was a top-ten prospect and perhaps his elevation is more a recognition of need by the Cleveland Browns, who see a rôle for a punishing, slashing back who also brings secure blocking. On the down side, he is recuperating from a broken collarbone suffered in the Aloha Bowl.

Seattle's choice of an offensive lineman was unexpected but it could be that **Ray Roberts** was just too good to overlook. Roberts gained some All-America attention but, perhaps with not the versatility of some in an excellent year for offensive linemen, others were preferred for that accolade. In common with Whitfield, Roberts has never been seriously extended in college football and has led some scouts to question just how far he can progress. But the prospect of owning a player who rarely loses his balance, and who delivers such great power as a drive blocker from the left tackle position, encouraged the Seahawks to make him the second of his breed to be selected.

In contrast to Seattle, Pittsburgh was widely expected to look for an offensive lineman and the search brought **Leon Searcy**, whose ability to play tackle or guard on either side of center may have attracted a club which, under new head coach Bill Cowher, will ring the changes. Under former head coach Chuck Noll the Steelers looked for speed, quickness and finesse in linemen who, usually, were not as big as some around the NFL. While it is not suggested that Searcy lacks these, he does bring great strength and the instincts to demolish his opponent. It is praise indeed that he is considered to be the Miami Hurricanes' best player in his position since Dennis Harrah.

With **Eugene Chung** still undrafted and the 13th option imminent, New England traded with Dallas to move up the order and they got their man. A leading member of the Virginia Tech 'Iron Hokies' strength and conditioning club, Chung has developed immense power though not at the expense of quickness and balance which were developed as part of his judo training programme. Some scouts feel that his agility may suit him for the guard position in the NFL as his experience develops. In college he specialized on the left side of the line from where he gave up less than a handful of sacks over two years. Whether on pass protection or blocking for the runner in open field and near the goal line, he seems to be equally effective.

Unusually, each New York club selected a tight end. In the quest to replace retired All-Pro Mark Bavaro, the Giants went to Notre Dame, the nursery which produced Bavaro, and found **Derek Brown**. At 6 ft 5 in and 243 pounds when he arrived in South Bend in 1988, Brown was the most heralded high school player of his year, but the Fight-

*Tommy Vardell.*

*Leon Searcy joins Pittsburgh.*

ing Irish were committed to a 'Wishbone Offense' driven by quarterback Tony Rice. Even with Rick Mirer calling signals, only rarely was Brown featured as a receiver. 'I get a lot of mail because we don't use Derek Brown the way everybody thinks we ought to,' said head coach Lou Holtz. Brown has, then, spent his time largely improving his blocking skills, but his ability to catch the ball is unquestioned. Few doubt his rapid emergence in the NFL.

The Jets' selection, **Johnny Mitchell**, is another who should develop well in the pros after being used sparingly at Nebraska and emerging as the team's leading receiver with 31 catches only in 1991. Because of academic ineligibility in 1989, Mitchell has played just two full seasons and is one of many underclassmen considered by some scouts to be too inexperienced. But he responds well to the big occasion, as he showed with five receptions for 138 yards and a touchdown against Georgia Tech in the Citrus Bowl at the end of the 1990 season.

The Raiders are hoping that **Chester McGlockton** will turn out to be the next in a long sequence of great defensive linemen and will be quite satisfied if he can reproduce the

form of another former Clemson defensive lineman, William (The Refrigerator) Perry, who made headlines as a rookie when he switched to offense on short-yardage plays near the goal line and now starts for the Bears. In common with Perry, the enormous McGlockton may have difficulty controlling his diet and is seen by some as an underachiever. But he does appear to have limitless potential and the Raiders can point to a history of enthusing young men.

It seems impossible that San Francisco needs to rebuild any section of its defense or even carry out running repairs, but there is a weakness at safety which, they feel, will be solved by **Dana Hall**. An interesting character, Hall played mostly at cornerback for the National Champion Washington Huskies, first on the right and then on the left. With good size, aggression and terrific range, he could play either the weak or strong spots but his speed may be put to best use at free safety. As a track athlete Hall is a high-class hurdler with a best time of 13.75 over 110 metres.

Atlanta's second selection in the first round brought **Tony Smith**, who represents a continuation of Falcons head coach Jerry Glanville's liking for big halfbacks. But

*LEFT: Vaughn Dunbar heads off for New Orleans.*

*BELOW: Dale Carter takes his big-play potential to Kansas City.*

that's not all, for Smith has the kind of speed which could be used on kickoff returns, a rôle in which he led the nation with an average of 32.5 yards in 1989. As a senior Smith rushed for 998 yards at an impressive 5.1-yard average and was robbed of cracking the four-figure barrier by a hand injury which forced him to miss two games. A decent receiver, he is a multi-purpose prospect and should fill the void created by the release of veteran Mike Rozier.

Strength in the defensive secondary is a Kansas City tradition stretching back to the 1960s, and the selection of **Dale Carter** represents a commitment to the continuation of this. The emotional leader of the Volunteer defense, Carter's 1991 campaign was littered with big moments generated by his tremendous speed and sensational open-field tackling. A consensus All-America for his play at free safety as a senior, Carter combined with teammate Carl Pickens to form arguably the best pair of kick returners in college football. In 1990 Carter led the nation, returning 17 kickoffs for a huge 507 yards. In the short term his goal is to challenge incumbent Chiefs free safety Deron Cherry.

To a New Orleans club which was short of consistent productivity at running back in 1991, **Vaughn Dunbar** brings excellent credentials. After spending a year as backup to Anthony Thompson, in 1990 Dunbar used his promotion to feature back to rush for 1,143 yards at an average of 5.0 and went even better as a senior with 1,699 yards at 5.1 per carry. A brave, consistent runner, Dunbar is hungry, always striving for a few more inches at the end of a surge. It is the sort of style which brought him 24 touchdowns over his last two years and could propel him directly into a starting spot for the Saints.

For the second consecutive year, the Bears sought to improve their defensive line with a high pick, this time elevating the importance to round one with the selection of the predatory **Alonzo Spellman**. A High-School All-America, Spellman began as an outside linebacker but moved forward a step for his last two years. At 6 ft 4 in and 20 stone with no evidence of fat, Spellman delivers his tackles with startling ferocity, particularly in the trenches. There is, however, some question over his development, with some scouts feeling that he may need two or three years to be a factor in the NFL.

San Diego did not have a first-round pick, having traded it to Washington during the 1991 draft. But with the option they acquired by trading defensive end Lee Williams to Houston, they selected **Chris Mims**, who came through as one of the premier pass rushers with six sacks and 14 tackles-for-loss as a senior. It was in 1991 that Mims beefed up by 20 pounds to confirm his position as a defensive end when some felt that he was best suited at outside linebacker. A spirited young man, Mims was suspended for the opening game of last season after putting on his own (real) fireworks display in the hall of residence. Boys will be boys.

It is one of the certainties for 1992 that, barring injury, **Tommy Maddox** is not going to displace John Elway. But to be his heir is the greatest compliment to the former UCLA star who was thrust into the starting lineup as a second-year freshman in the third game of the 1990 season and was an immediate success. Although an outstanding ball-handler with a field generalship often compared to that of the great Hall-of-Famer Roger Staubach, Maddox is a drop-back passer, not yet with Elway's ability as a runner. Maddox follows the lead given by Todd Marinovich in 1991 by coming out with two years of eligibility remaining.

The Detroit Lions felt the loss of several defensive starters in their 1991 charge and they may have found at least a

*BELOW LEFT: Alonzo Spellman joins the Bears. BELOW RIGHT: Chris Mims adds yet more talent to San Diego's fearsome-looking defensive front seven.*

# The First-Round Selections in the 1992 Collegiate Draft

| No. | Player | Club | Pos. | College |
|---|---|---|---|---|
| 1 | Steve Emtman | Indianapolis | DT | Washington |
| 2 | Quentin Coryatt | Indianapolis | LB | Texas A&M |
| 3 | Sean Gilbert | L.A. Rams | DE | Pittsburgh |
| 4 | Desmond Howard | Washington | WR-KR | Michigan |
| 5 | Terrell Buckley | Green Bay | CB | Florida State |
| 6 | David Klingler | Cincinnati | QB | Houston |
| 7 | Troy Vincent | Miami | CB-PR | Wisconsin |
| 8 | Bob Whitfield | Atlanta | T | Stanford |
| 9 | Tommy Vardell | Cleveland | RB | Stanford |
| 10 | Ray Roberts | Seattle | T | Virginia |
| 11 | Leon Searcy | Pittsburgh | T-G | Miami |
| 12 | Marco Coleman | Miami | LB | Georgia Tech |
| 13 | Eugene Chung | New England | T | Virginia Tech |
| 14 | Derek Brown | N.Y. Giants | TE | Notre Dame |
| 15 | Johnny Mitchell | N.Y. Jets | TE | Nebraska |
| 16 | Chester McGlockton | L.A. Raiders | DT | Clemson |
| 17 | Kevin Smith | Dallas | CB | Texas A&M |
| 18 | Dana Hall | San Francisco | CB-S | Washington |
| 19 | Tony Smith | Atlanta | RB | Southern Mississippi |
| 20 | Dale Carter | Kansas City | S | Tennessee |
| 21 | Vaughn Dunbar | New Orleans | RB | Indiana |
| 22 | Alonzo Spellman | Chicago | DE | Ohio State |
| 23 | Chris Mims | San Diego | DE | Tennessee |
| 24 | Robert Jones | Dallas | LB | East Carolina |
| 25 | Tommy Maddox | Denver | QB | UCLA |
| 26 | Robert Porcher | Detroit | DE | South Carolina State |
| 27 | John Fina | Buffalo | T | Arizona |
| 28 | Darryl Williams | Cincinnati | S | Miami |

specialist pass rusher in **Robert Porcher**. In his one full year of college football, 1991, Porcher's figures were hardly believable, showing 15 quarterback sacks, nine fumbles caused, eight fumble recoveries and even a touchdown following an interception. It brought him the award of Mid-Eastern Athletic Conference Defensive Player of the Year. The reservation is that he was playing in the modest company offered by Division I-AA opponents.

It may have been the memory of hordes of Washington players assaulting the ramparts in Super Bowl XXVI that led Buffalo to select help for the offensive line. For his final three years in college, **John Fina**, a fifth-year senior, was the mainstay of the Arizona line after starting out as a defensive lineman in 1988. He helped out when the opposition needed stopping at the goal line and, with this additional contribution, earned the Arizona Bronko Nagurski Award. Fina brings the high intelligence of an honour student to a rôle which asks as much of timing and composure as it does the sheer delivery of mass. His speciality lies in open-field blocking, particularly on screen plays.

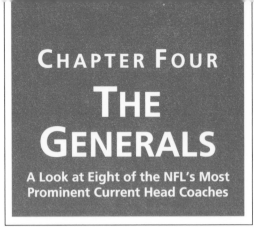

## All-Time Head Coaches – Career Records (including postseason) (Minimum 100 victories – order based on percentage)

| Coach | Teams | Yrs. | Won | Lost | Tied | Pct. |
|---|---|---|---|---|---|---|
| Vince Lombardi | G.B., Wash. | 10 | 105 | 35 | 6 | .740 |
| John Madden | Raiders | 10 | 112 | 39 | 7 | .731 |
| Joe Gibbs | Wash. | 11 | 130 | 57 | 0 | .695 |
| George Allen | Rams, Wash. | 12 | 118 | 54 | 5 | .681 |
| Don Shula | Balt., Mia. | 29 | 306 | 145 | 6 | .676 |
| George Halas | Chi. | 40 | 325 | 151 | 31 | .672 |
| Mike Ditka | Chi. | 10 | 107 | 57 | 0 | .652 |
| Curly Lambeau | G.B., Cards., Wash. | 33 | 229 | 134 | 22 | .623 |
| Bill Walsh | S.F. | 10 | 102 | 63 | 1 | .617 |
| Paul Brown | Clev., Cin. | 21 | 170 | 108 | 6 | .609 |
| Bud Grant | Minn. | 18 | 168 | 108 | 5 | .607 |
| Dan Reeves | Den. | 11 | 109 | 71 | 1 | .605 |
| Tom Landry | Dall. | 29 | 270 | 178 | 6 | .601 |
| Chuck Knox | Rams, Buff., Sea. | 19 | 178 | 125 | 1 | .587 |
| Steve Owen | Giants | 23 | 153 | 108 | 17 | .581 |
| Buddy Parker | Cards., Det., Pitt. | 15 | 107 | 76 | 9 | .581 |
| Hank Stram | K.C., N.O. | 17 | 136 | 100 | 10 | .573 |
| Chuck Noll | Pitt. | 23 | 209 | 156 | 1 | .572 |
| Don Coryell | Cards., S.D. | 14 | 114 | 89 | 1 | .561 |
| Sid Gillman | Rams, S.D., Hou. | 18 | 123 | 104 | 7 | .541 |
| Weeb Ewbank | Balt., Jets | 20 | 134 | 130 | 7 | .507 |

## Active Head Coaches – Career Records (including postseason) (Order based on number of victories)

| Coach | Teams | Yrs. | Won | Lost | Tied | Pct. |
|---|---|---|---|---|---|---|
| Don Shula | Balt., Mia. | 29 | 306 | 145 | 6 | .676 |
| Chuck Knox | Rams, Buff., Sea. | 19 | 178 | 125 | 1 | .587 |
| Joe Gibbs | Wash. | 11 | 130 | 57 | 0 | .695 |
| Dan Reeves | Den. | 11 | 109 | 71 | 1 | .605 |
| Mike Ditka | Chi. | 10 | 107 | 57 | 0 | .652 |
| Marv Levy | K.C., Buff. | 11 | 92 | 76 | 0 | .548 |
| Tom Flores | Raiders, Sea. | 9 | 91 | 56 | 0 | .619 |
| Marty Schottenheimer | Clev., K.C. | 8 | 76 | 51 | 1 | .598 |
| Jack Pardee | Chi., Wash., Hou. | 8 | 65 | 61 | 0 | .516 |
| Sam Wyche | Cin., T.B. | 8 | 64 | 68 | 0 | .485 |
| Jim Mora | N.O. | 6 | 57 | 41 | 0 | .582 |
| Jerry Glanville | Hou., Atl. | 7 | 51 | 53 | 0 | .490 |
| George Seifert | S.F. | 3 | 42 | 11 | 0 | .792 |
| Ted Marchibroda | Balt., Ind. | 5 | 41 | 36 | 0 | .532 |
| Art Shell | Raiders | 3 | 29 | 18 | 0 | .617 |
| Wayne Fontes | Det. | 3 | 28 | 27 | 0 | .509 |
| Jimmy Johnson | Dall. | 3 | 20 | 30 | 0 | .400 |
| Bruce Coslet | Jets | 2 | 14 | 19 | 0 | .424 |
| Rich Kotite | Phil. | 1 | 10 | 6 | 0 | .625 |
| Joe Bugel | Phoe. | 2 | 9 | 23 | 0 | .281 |
| Ray Handley | Giants | 1 | 8 | 8 | 0 | .500 |
| Bill Belichick | Clev. | 1 | 6 | 10 | 0 | .375 |
| Dick MacPherson | N.E. | 1 | 6 | 10 | 0 | .375 |

## Don Shula (Miami Dolphins)

'He can take his'n and beat your'n, and he could take your'n and beat his'n,' reflected former Oilers and Saints head coach O.A. (Bum) Phillips. It was his rustic style of saying that Don Shula could coach either team and win the game. And, for more than a quarter of a century, that's what Shula has been doing in a steady march that could see him achieve what, not long ago, was inconceivable, namely, to surpass the league-record career total of 325 wins amassed by the legendary George Halas.

After a solid playing career as a defensive back with Cleveland, Baltimore and Washington (he had 21 interceptions over seven years), Shula spent two years as an assistant in collegiate football and just three in that capacity with the Detroit Lions before, at the age of 33, he became the youngest head coach in NFL history when he took charge of the Baltimore Colts. Within two years he took the Colts to the 1964 NFL Championship Game, which they lost to Cleveland, and in 1968 it was as the (pre-merger) NFL Champion that his team was upset by the underdog AFL Champion New York Jets in Super Bowl III.

| | Don Shula – Career Record (Regular Season) | | | | |
|---|---|---|---|---|---|
| **Year** | **Team** | **W** | **L** | **T** | **Div. Stand.** |
| 1963 | Baltimore | 8 | 6 | 0 | 3rd |
| 1964 | Baltimore | 12 | 2 | 0 | 1st |
| 1965 | Baltimore | 10 | 3 | 1 | 1st equal |
| 1966 | Baltimore | 9 | 5 | 0 | 2nd |
| 1967 | Baltimore | 11 | 1 | 2 | 2nd |
| 1968 | Baltimore | 13 | 1 | 0 | 1st |
| 1969 | Baltimore | 8 | 5 | 1 | 2nd |
| 1970 | Miami | 10 | 4 | 0 | 2nd |
| 1971 | Miami | 10 | 3 | 1 | 1st |
| 1972 | Miami | 14 | 0 | 0 | 1st |
| 1973 | Miami | 12 | 2 | 0 | 1st |
| 1974 | Miami | 11 | 3 | 0 | 1st |
| 1975 | Miami | 10 | 4 | 0 | 2nd |
| 1976 | Miami | 6 | 8 | 0 | 3rd |
| 1977 | Miami | 10 | 4 | 0 | 2nd |
| 1978 | Miami | 11 | 5 | 0 | 2nd |
| 1979 | Miami | 10 | 6 | 0 | 1st |
| 1980 | Miami | 8 | 8 | 0 | 3rd |
| 1981 | Miami | 11 | 4 | 1 | 1st |
| 1982 | Miami* | 7 | 2 | 0 | 1st* |
| 1983 | Miami | 12 | 4 | 0 | 1st |
| 1984 | Miami | 14 | 2 | 0 | 1st |
| 1985 | Miami | 12 | 4 | 0 | 1st |
| 1986 | Miami | 8 | 8 | 0 | 3rd |
| 1987 | Miami* | 8 | 7 | 0 | 3rd |
| 1988 | Miami | 6 | 10 | 0 | 5th |
| 1989 | Miami | 8 | 8 | 0 | 3rd |
| 1990 | Miami | 12 | 4 | 0 | 2nd |
| 1991 | Miami | 8 | 8 | 0 | 3rd |
| **Totals** | | **289** | **131** | **6** | |

*Strike-shortened seasons

By now seen as one of the league's premier coaches, in 1970 he was signed by Miami, a team which had been in existence just four years and had a mere 15 wins to its credit. But there were questions surrounding the ethics of his acquisition and, after having found the Dolphins guilty of 'tampering' in their attempts to lure Shula, NFL Commissioner Pete Rozelle awarded Miami's 1971 first-round draft option to Baltimore.

However, Rozelle did allow the move and it would transpire that the loss of the draft pick, costly though it was seen at the time, was worth the price. In Shula's second season, Miami contested the Super Bowl, a 24–3 loss to Dallas, but they won the following two Super Bowl Championships, the first of which, a 14–7 victory over Washington, crowned a perfect 17–0 season, which remains as the only undefeated, untied campaign in NFL history.

In the face of an NFL policy which, primarily through the collegiate draft, offers every advantage to the weaker teams, Shula mostly has kept the Dolphins in the forefront of competition. Even when the squad is out of balance, never can Miami be taken lightly. The last decade has seen two further trips to the Super Bowl and, though they have resulted in losses, it means that Shula has become the only head coach in league history to contest the NFL's showpiece six times.

Throughout, he has remained the perfect gentleman. 'If I'm remembered for anything as a coach,' says Shula, 'I hope it's for playing within the rules. I also hope it will be said that my teams showed class and dignity in victory or defeat.' It is with this philosophy and the accomplishments of his teams that Don Shula has set the standards of excellence against which the rest will be measured.

Yet his sternest test may be yet to come, for his elder son, David, is entering his first year as an NFL head coach with Cincinnati while the other, Mike, is being tutored as a Dolphins assistant by dad. In a brilliantly witty article on a futuristic NFL (Super Bowl XXVI Programme), Phil Barber projected the first female head coach in NFL history to be one Dawn Shula-Rodriguez. Naturally, she coached her team to victory in Super Bowl LXII.

## Chuck Knox (Los Angeles Rams)

In 1992, his 20th NFL year, Chuck Knox will rejoin the Los Angeles Rams to complete a job which he began in 1973.

An offensive line coach, Knox started out as an assistant with the New York Jets in 1963, moving to Detroit in that capacity in 1967 and spending six years with the NFC Central club before taking on one of the most glamorous, and yet demanding, posts in the entire league, when he became head coach of the Los Angeles Rams. Under George Allen the Rams had emerged from a ten-year slump but his replacement, Tommy Prothro, couldn't maintain the momentum, and it was following 8–5–1 and 6–7–1 campaigns that Knox received the call.

Basing his philosophy on the rushing game, Knox bolstered a backfield, which already featured Lawrence McCutcheon and Jim Bertelsen, with draftees Cullen Bryant and Heisman Trophy winner John Cappelletti. Later, the draft would yield two future All-Pro linemen, Jackie Slater and Dennis Harrah, another regular for the offensive line, Doug France, and yet another classy halfback, Wendell Tyler. The early trade of quarterback Roman Gabriel to Philadelphia didn't go down well at the time but the partnership of his replacement, John Hadl, and wide receiver Harold Jackson softened the blow. At the end of his debut campaign, Knox was voted NFL Coach of the Year, Hadl was selected NFC Most Valuable Player and the Rams had the best record in franchise history as they won the first of five consecutive titles.

But success is relative. Before long, the Rams simply accepted winning as the norm. Knox's ground game wasn't the most exciting spectacle in pro football – he was nicknamed 'Ground Chuck' – and the club still craved the biggest title of all. Shocking as it may seem 20 years on,

| Year | Team | W | L | T | Div. Stand. |
|---|---|---|---|---|---|
| 1973 | L.A. Rams | 12 | 2 | 0 | 1st |
| 1974 | L.A. Rams | 10 | 4 | 0 | 1st |
| 1975 | L.A. Rams | 12 | 2 | 0 | 1st |
| 1976 | L.A. Rams | 10 | 3 | 1 | 1st |
| 1977 | L.A. Rams | 10 | 4 | 0 | 1st |
| 1978 | Buffalo | 5 | 11 | 0 | 4th |
| 1979 | Buffalo | 7 | 9 | 0 | 4th |
| 1980 | Buffalo | 11 | 5 | 0 | 1st |
| 1981 | Buffalo | 10 | 6 | 0 | 3rd |
| 1982 | Buffalo* | 4 | 5 | 0 | 4th |
| 1983 | Seattle | 9 | 7 | 0 | 2nd |
| 1984 | Seattle | 12 | 4 | 0 | 2nd |
| 1985 | Seattle | 8 | 8 | 0 | 3rd |
| 1986 | Seattle | 10 | 6 | 0 | 3rd |
| 1987 | Seattle* | 9 | 6 | 0 | 2nd |
| 1988 | Seattle | 9 | 7 | 0 | 1st |
| 1989 | Seattle | 7 | 9 | 0 | 4th |
| 1990 | Seattle | 9 | 7 | 0 | 3rd |
| 1991 | Seattle | 7 | 9 | 0 | 4th |
| **Totals** | | **171** | **114** | **1** | |

Chuck Knox – Career Record (Regular Season)

*Strike-shortened seasons

Knox, who shared with Paul Brown the distinction of being the only two men to take their teams to division titles in each of their first five years, departed.

Inheriting a Buffalo team that had won only five games over its previous two seasons, Knox used two campaigns to build before, in 1980, the Bills won their first division title since 1966. The 1982 players' strike disrupted more than one programme around the league and Buffalo did not escape, sinking to 4–5.

It was time to move on and there was a job to be done in the Pacific Northwest, where the seven-year-old Seattle Seahawks had flickered without ever bursting into flame. In the 1983 draft the Rams selected Eric Dickerson with the second pick, but Knox was more than satisfied to take Curt Warner, a running back of great speed with dazzling open-field moves, in third place overall. With the Penn State All-America in place, Knox needed only to light the fuse. In that season, Knox's first, the Seahawks earned their first playoff berth, falling to the eventual Super Bowl Champion Raiders in the AFC title game. And there would be two more wild-card playoff berths before, in 1988, Seattle won its first division title, making Knox the only head coach in league history to win division titles with three different clubs.

You wonder if destiny has simply been put on hold for Knox to return to Los Angeles and it might just be that someone in Anaheim Stadium will unfurl a banner reading 'Welcome Home'.

## Joe Gibbs (Washington Redskins)

It is not by chance that the eleven-year tenure of Joe Gibbs as head coach has seen the most successful era in the history of this great club. Under Gibbs, the Redskins have contested four Super Bowl Championship Games, winning three, the most recent of which was a dismantling of the AFC's Buffalo Bills. Also, over this period, only San Francisco has a better record (136–50–1) than Washington's 130–57–0.

The assiduous care with which he approaches every game – he is said to schedule meetings with his assistants for midnight when necessary – is mirrored in the programme of his personal development, which has seen him pick his way meticulously through the ranks. For much of the route, as his mentor, he has had the innovative, expressive Don Coryell, the former head coach of St Louis and San Diego. It was as a graduate assistant under Coryell at San Diego State that he took his first steps as offensive line coach in 1964. Valuable experience as an assistant came from two-year stints with each of Florida State, a USC powerhouse coached by John McKay and the Arkansas Razorbacks, before Coryell beckoned once again.

This time, it was to take the major step of bringing his expertise as an offensive backfield coach to the NFL's St Louis Cardinals. It was during the tenure of the Coryell-Gibbs partnership, in 1974 and 1975, that the Cardinals won the two division titles which represent their only successes from 1948 to the present day.

After one year with Tampa Bay, Gibbs was reunited with Coryell, taking the post of offensive coordinator – air-traffic controller – of a San Diego offense known as the 'Air Force' for its prolific passing attack.

It was inevitable that Gibbs would be summoned to a top job but still it was a surprise when, as the Redskins describe

| Joe Gibbs – Career Record (Regular Season) | | | | | |
|---|---|---|---|---|---|
| Year | Team | W | L | T | Div. Stand. |
| 1981 | Washington | 8 | 8 | 0 | 4th |
| 1982 | Washington* | 8 | 1 | 0 | 1st |
| 1983 | Washington | 14 | 2 | 0 | 1st |
| 1984 | Washington | 11 | 5 | 0 | 1st |
| 1985 | Washington | 10 | 6 | 0 | 3rd |
| 1986 | Washington | 12 | 4 | 0 | 2nd |
| 1987 | Washington* | 11 | 4 | 0 | 1st |
| 1988 | Washington | 7 | 9 | 0 | 3rd |
| 1989 | Washington | 10 | 6 | 0 | 3rd |
| 1990 | Washington | 10 | 6 | 0 | 3rd |
| 1991 | Washington | 14 | 2 | 0 | 1st |
| **Totals** | | **115** | **53** | **0** | |

*Strike-shortened seasons

it, 'this obscure coach' was signed by Redskins owner Jack Kent Cooke.

His start was hardly auspicious as he lost his first five games, but he set a pattern for strong finishing by ending the season at 8–8. The following year he started out fast and ended in triumph with a dramatic victory over Miami in Super Bowl XVII, which was the very first title game viewed on Channel Four TV.

With typical modesty, Gibbs sums up his time with the Redskins with the words, 'I have been fortunate to work in a great situation over the years.'

## Dan Reeves (Denver Broncos)

Judged on his single-season records or his overall impact since joining the Broncos in 1981, Dan Reeves is firmly established in the exclusive company of the NFL's premier head coaches. Under Reeves, the Broncos have registered six of the seven best single-season records in franchise history and have won five divisional titles, a dominance all the more remarkable for having been in the tough AFC West. Three times in a four-year span, Denver went to the Super Bowl.

Although having the imperious John Elway at quarterback, the Broncos have never been blessed with talent in abundance and mostly have had to defy the odds, whether it be a problem at running back, a modest offensive line or defensive weaknesses. However, disadvantage seems not to discourage a man who has come up the hard way.

Entering the NFL as a rookie with the unenviable status of undrafted free agent, Reeves, who had played quarterback in college at South Carolina, won a place on the roster of the mighty Dallas Cowboys as an all-purpose offensive back. Here, 'all-purpose' meant being the odd-job man who'd block for the star, be it Don Perkins, Duane Thomas or Calvin Hill, catch passes, return kickoffs and punts and even throw a few passes. He held on to his spot for eight seasons (1965-72), even becoming the fifth-ranked rusher in Dallas history. Unusually, over his final three years, he eased smoothly into the demanding rôle of player-coach, developing his skills as a running backs tutor. After spending a year out of football to pursue private business, he returned to Dallas as a full-time assistant. All told during his association with the Cowboys, he went to five Super Bowls, winning one and losing one as a player, and winning one and losing two as an assistant. As the latter, he could have had no finer apprenticeship than under the watchful eye of Tom Landry, the 'Dean' of head coaches, and in 1981 he beat the competition to take over from Red Miller in Denver.

Eleven seasons on, he stands alone as the only man to participate in eight Super Bowls as either player or coach, but sadly the persisting memory of Reeves is of a man patrolling the sideline, bearing the anguish of watching his Broncos overwhelmed in three title game defeats. A more perceptive observer might detect the defiance of the intense competitor who refuses to accept the status of loser. It is with the absolute confidence that, one day, he will hold aloft the Vince Lombardi Trophy that Reeves enters the 1992 season.

| Dan Reeves – Career Record (Regular Season) | | | | | |
|---|---|---|---|---|---|
| Year | Team | W | L | T | Div. Stand. |
| 1981 | Denver | 10 | 6 | 0 | 2nd |
| 1982 | Denver* | 2 | 7 | 0 | 5th |
| 1983 | Denver | 9 | 7 | 0 | 3rd |
| 1984 | Denver | 13 | 3 | 0 | 1st |
| 1985 | Denver | 11 | 5 | 0 | 2nd |
| 1986 | Denver | 11 | 5 | 0 | 1st |
| 1987 | Denver* | 10 | 4 | 1 | 1st |
| 1988 | Denver | 8 | 8 | 0 | 2nd |
| 1989 | Denver | 11 | 5 | 0 | 1st |
| 1990 | Denver | 5 | 11 | 0 | 5th |
| 1991 | Denver | 12 | 4 | 0 | 1st |
| **Totals** | | **102** | **65** | **1** | |

*Strike-shortened seasons

## Mike Ditka (Chicago Bears)

If it is rare in professional sports that great players become equally great head coaches, Mike Ditka may be more than just the exception; he probably is unique. Over 32 seasons in the league, Ditka has exemplified true excellence in every facet of the game.

Entering the NFL as the Bears' first-round draft choice in 1961, playing at tight end, Ditka had an immediate impact, not only blocking with awesome ferocity and timing but also as a receiver, to earn the award of NFL Rookie of the Year. With great foresight, head coach George Halas had adjusted the position of tight end from that of the nominal 'third tackle', who primarily was a blocker, to one of a dual-purpose tackle-receiver. Ditka was the prototype, catching 56 passes, an astronomic figure for a tight end in those days and good enough for equal fifth place in the NFL receiving list. He reached a peak in 1964 with 75 receptions to rank second in the league behind teammate Johnny Morris.

His prodigious talents brought five Pro Bowl selections as part of a package which, in 1988, encouraged the NFL Hall of Fame selection committee to make him the 21st Chicago Bear and the very first tight end to be inducted into that select group of the league's all-time heroes. Before his retirement as a player, he would earn a Super Bowl winners' ring with Dallas, catching a touchdown pass in the Cowboys' 24–3 victory over Miami.

As an assistant coach with Dallas he was an integral part of the Cowboys' victory in Super Bowl XII. And in 1982, when Halas sought the man to lead the Bears out of a slump that had lasted almost 20 years, he looked no further than Ditka.

Quickly he fashioned a team in his own image and by the end of his third season, the Bears won the NFC Central division title. It was to be the first of five in a row, the second of which saw the Bears go on to maul New England by the score of 46–10 in Super Bowl XX. Four times in a seven-year span from 1984 to 1990, the Bears have lost in the playoffs to the team which eventually went on to win the Super Bowl.

Now entering his 11th season in charge, Ditka is one of only two men to win a Super Bowl ring in all three rôles of player, assistant and head coach. The other, Seattle's Tom Flores, was on the Chiefs' roster in Game IV but did not play a down. Again, amongst his peers, together with Art Shell and Dan Reeves, he is one of only three to have been selected to the Pro Bowl and, with Shell, is one of just two in the Hall of Fame.

Outside of football he is an avid golfer, playing to a handicap of eight despite the difficulties of arthritic hips which have required replacement surgery. He collects antique cars and has even dabbled in television, playing himself in the TV series, LA Law. But more than anything else, Ditka is a football man. Uncompromising in his quest for continued success and more than a little mean, he's a true Chicago Bear.

| Mike Ditka – Career Record (Regular Season) | | | | |
|---|---|---|---|---|
| Year | Team | W | L | T | Div. Stand. |
| 1982 | Chicago* | 3 | 6 | 0 | 5th |
| 1983 | Chicago | 8 | 8 | 0 | 3rd |
| 1984 | Chicago | 10 | 6 | 0 | 1st |
| 1985 | Chicago | 15 | 1 | 0 | 1st |
| 1986 | Chicago | 14 | 2 | 0 | 1st |
| 1987 | Chicago* | 11 | 4 | 0 | 1st |
| 1988 | Chicago | 12 | 4 | 0 | 1st |
| 1989 | Chicago | 6 | 10 | 0 | 4th |
| 1990 | Chicago | 11 | 5 | 0 | 1st |
| 1991 | Chicago | 11 | 5 | 0 | 2nd |
| **Totals** | | **101** | **51** | **0** | |

*Strike-shortened seasons

## Marv Levy (Buffalo Bills)

In the past two seasons, Marv Levy has taken Buffalo close to the summit of NFL superiority by contesting Super Bowls XXV and XXVI. And it has been an achievement only marginally less impressive that he has kept Don Shula's Miami at bay as the Bills have established a dominance of the AFC Eastern division.

Just a breath of wind could have made the difference when Scott Norwood's 47-yard field goal attempt drifted wide, with four seconds remaining, allowing the New York Giants to retain their one-point margin in Super Bowl XXV. One week earlier, in a performance of breathtaking efficiency, ingenuity and verve, the Bills had dismantled the Los Angeles Raiders by the record score of 51–3 in the AFC Championship Game.

Levy's rise to the top has followed the standard procedure step by step, beginning as a high school coach in 1951 before moving quickly through the college system with the University of New Mexico and on through California. He entered the professional ranks as an assistant with the Philadelphia Eagles. Subsequently, with the Rams, he came under the influence of the late, much respected George Allen, with whom he moved when Allen went to Washington. As the Redskins' special teams coach, Levy was a vital cog in the machine which lost in Super Bowl VII to Miami.

The period 1973-77 saw Levy blossom in the exciting, wide-open play of the Canadian Football League, where he guided the Montreal Alouettes to two Grey Cup titles. His growing reputation impressed the ownership of the Kansas City Chiefs, who hired him in 1977 to rehabilitate a team which had slipped into mediocrity following its victory in Super Bowl IV. Gradually, Levy brought the team back into contention, coming within a game of winning the division title in 1981.

Following his release by Kansas City in 1982, Levy's engaging wit took him into television commentary for three years, between times filling in as a coach in the ill-fated USFL.

It was once more as a rebuilder that he accepted the post of head coach with Buffalo for the final seven games of the 1986 season. The Bills were coming off back-to-back 2–14 campaigns and hadn't had a winning record since 1981. But there was a sprinkling of talent milling around the likes of quarterback Jim Kelly and defensive end Bruce Smith. Levy kick-started the engine with the acquisition of outside linebacker Cornelius Bennett, who came via a merry-go-round trade with Indianapolis and the Rams involving draft choices and major players, not the least of whom was Rams running back Eric Dickerson, whose part in the arrangement was to join the Colts. The following year the Bills took charge of the AFC East and, for the last two seasons, haven't been seriously challenged.

A gentleman in every respect, Levy holds a master's degree in English History from Harvard and soothes away the mental bruises with his passion for English literature.

| Marv Levy – Career Record (Regular Season) | | | | | |
|---|---|---|---|---|---|
| Year | Team | W | L | T | Div. Stand. |
| 1978 | Kansas City | 4 | 12 | 0 | 5th |
| 1979 | Kansas City | 7 | 9 | 0 | 5th |
| 1980 | Kansas City | 8 | 8 | 0 | 3rd |
| 1981 | Kansas City | 9 | 7 | 0 | 3rd |
| 1982 | Kansas City* | 3 | 6 | 0 | 4th |
| 1986 | Buffalo** | 2 | 5 | 0 | 4th |
| 1987 | Buffalo* | 7 | 8 | 0 | 4th |
| 1988 | Buffalo | 12 | 4 | 0 | 1st |
| 1989 | Buffalo | 9 | 7 | 0 | 1st |
| 1990 | Buffalo | 13 | 3 | 0 | 1st |
| 1991 | Buffalo | 13 | 3 | 0 | 1st |
| **Totals** | | **87** | **72** | **0** | |

*Strike-shortened seasons
**Appointed head coach after nine games

## Marty Schottenheimer (Kansas City Chiefs)

In seven full seasons as an NFL head coach, Marty Schottenheimer has never had a losing campaign. Over that span, Schottenheimer and Chicago's Mike Ditka are the only two head coaches to reach the playoffs six times. Schottenheimer has not yet won a major title – twice in succession he was foiled by John Elway and the Denver Broncos in the AFC Championship Game – but he may be the best in the league when it comes to extracting the most from his players.

Taking charge of the slumping Cleveland Browns halfway through the 1984 season, he rallied the team to 4–4

| Marty Schottenheimer – Career Record (Regular Season) | | | | | |
|---|---|---|---|---|---|
| Year | Team | W | L | T | Div. Stand. |
| 1984 | Cleveland** | 4 | 4 | 0 | 3rd |
| 1985 | Cleveland | 8 | 8 | 0 | 1st |
| 1986 | Cleveland | 12 | 4 | 0 | 1st |
| 1987 | Cleveland* | 10 | 5 | 0 | 1st |
| 1988 | Cleveland | 10 | 6 | 0 | 2nd |
| 1989 | Kansas City | 8 | 7 | 1 | 2nd |
| 1990 | Kansas City | 11 | 5 | 0 | 2nd |
| 1991 | Kansas City | 10 | 6 | 0 | 2nd |
| **Totals** | | **73** | **45** | **1** | |

*Strike-shortened season
**Appointed head coach after eight games

over the remainder of the campaign. And though he followed up with a modest 8–8 record, it was good enough for the title in the AFC Central division. It was to be the first of three in a row for a team which had topped the division only twice since the two leagues merged in 1970. The Browns were back where they belonged.

It was one of the surprises of early 1989 when he resigned his position and, subsequently, joined Kansas City. Not unlike Cleveland, it was some time since the Chiefs had been a true contender. John Mackovic had taken an opportunistic squad to the playoffs in 1986 but his replacement, Frank Gansz, had laboured through seasons of 4–11 and 4–11–1. With barely a pause, Schottenheimer generated a disciplined sense of purpose, strengthening a few weak spots, and immediately brought the team into genuine contention. In each of the last two seasons the Chiefs have gone to the playoffs as a wild card.

His story is that of a multi-sports honour student in high school who went on to become an All-America linebacker at the University of Pittsburgh, where he was selected to the Panthers' all-time team. After a solid playing career with Buffalo and the Patriots, he began the climb through the NFL's coaching ranks as linebackers coach under Bill Arnsparger of the Giants. Promotion to defensive coordinator under John McVay came in 1977. A two-year stint with Detroit led to his 1980 appointment as defensive coordinator with Cleveland, where he built a defense which, in 1984, led the AFC and ranked second only to Chicago in the entire NFL.

Hardly the sort to seek the headlines, Schottenheimer is a teacher with a special gift for communication. He inspires great loyalty in his players. 'It is evident up front that he has complete faith in what he's doing,' said all-time great veteran center Mike Webster, who continued, 'There is no doubt that he knows where he's going and he makes you want to come along for the ride.'

## Jerry Glanville (Atlanta Falcons)

Jerry Glanville is one of pro football's great motivators but he is equally well known for being quite the most colourful and easily the most controversial of his profession.

There can be no doubting Glanville's ability to 'straighten things out'. Having assumed control of a Houston club which, following the departure of head coach 'Bum' Phillips after the 1980 season, had gone into precipitous decline, Glanville was well on the way to regenerating a serious title contender. But after five full seasons, in three of which he took the Oilers to the playoffs as a wild card, he was released. Even so, the team which, in 1991, won Houston's first AFC Central division title, still bore the stamp of its architect.

For Glanville, who joined the Atlanta Falcons, the trip to Georgia was a homecoming, since it was with the Falcons as defensive backs coach and, subsequently, defensive coordinator, that over the period 1977 to 1982 he confirmed the promise he had shown as an assistant with his home-town club, Detroit. Known for his liking of inspirational nicknames, in 1977 Glanville had installed his so-called 'Gritz Blitz', an audacious style of defensive pass rush. Now he would introduce the 'Red Gun' offense, while the defense has become known as the 'Black Wave'.

Off the field he is no less expressive, alternating between a Corvette convertible, a Dodge van and a black Stealth for the journey to work. His garage protects a black 1950 Mercury and, for those times when it is a little bronchitic, there's an identical model at its side. He drag-races a Harley Davidson Low Rider. Glanville loves country music and is often seen at concerts with Kris Kristofferson, Travis Tritt, Jerry Jeff Walker and John Cougar Mellencamp. An avid fan of both Elvis Presley and James Dean, Glanville boasts '1-Elvis' licence plates from the states of Tennessee and Hawaii, and a pair of Texas plates bearing the names '4-Elvis' and 'James Dean'.

Two seasons ago, he left a pair of tickets at the Atlanta box office for Elvis (deceased). The next week he left a pair for James Dean (deceased). Shortly afterwards, his team suffered a heavy defeat, leading the joker in Glanville to have addressed the gathered newshounds thus: 'Gentlemen, I went out to buy you all free 'plane tickets for our trip to the West Coast but there were none available. You see, they had first-class tickets and second-class tickets, but they didn't have any no-class tickets.'

Almost hidden away behind all the quips and memorabilia is the serious side of Glanville. He approaches his job with deadly earnest and it works. No longer the soft touch, the Falcons are coming off a season in which they beat San Francisco twice and almost took the title in the NFC West. Glanville enters the 1992 campaign poised for the final thrust.

| Jerry Glanville – Career Record (Regular Season) | | | | | |
|---|---|---|---|---|---|
| Year | Team | W | L | T | Div. Stand. |
| 1985 | Houston** | 0 | 2 | 0 | 4th |
| 1986 | Houston | 5 | 11 | 0 | 4th |
| 1987 | Houston* | 9 | 6 | 0 | 2nd |
| 1988 | Houston | 10 | 6 | 0 | 3rd |
| 1989 | Houston | 9 | 7 | 0 | 2nd |
| 1990 | Atlanta | 5 | 11 | 0 | 4th |
| 1991 | Atlanta | 10 | 6 | 0 | 2nd |
| **Totals** | | **48** | **49** | **0** | |

*Strike-shortened season
**Interim head coach

# CHAPTER FIVE
# AMERICAN FOOTBALL CONFERENCE

## TEAM RANKINGS

| | OFFENSE | | | | | | DEFENSE | | | | | |
| | Total Yds. | Rushing | Passing | Points For | No. Intercepted | No. Sacked | Total Yds. | Rushing | Passing | Points Against | Interceptions | Sacks |
|---|---|---|---|---|---|---|---|---|---|---|---|---|
| Buffalo | 1 | 1 | 3 | 1 | 10 | =7 | 13 | 12 | 9 | 9 | =1 | 10 |
| Cincinnati | 8 | 6 | 5 | 12 | =12 | =4 | 14 | 5 | 14 | 14 | 9 | 14 |
| Cleveland | 9 | 12 | 4 | 8 | 1 | =9 | 6 | 10 | 6 | 7 | =10 | =7 |
| Denver | 6 | 5 | 10 | 6 | =2 | 12 | 1 | 9 | 1 | 1 | =1 | 1 |
| Houston | 2 | 11 | 1 | 2 | 11 | 2 | 3 | 2 | 5 | 2 | 3 | 2 |
| Indianapolis | 14 | 14 | 14 | 14 | =6 | 13 | 8 | 14 | 2 | 13 | =10 | =11 |
| Kansas City | 3 | 3 | 8 | 4 | =4 | 1 | 5 | 8 | 7 | 3 | =10 | 4 |
| L.A. Raiders | 13 | 7 | 13 | 7 | 9 | =4 | 9 | 11 | 8 | 6 | =6 | 3 |
| Miami | 5 | 13 | 2 | 3 | =4 | 3 | 11 | 13 | 4 | 12 | =13 | =7 |
| New England | 12 | 9 | 9 | 13 | =12 | 14 | 12 | 3 | 13 | 8 | =13 | 13 |
| N.Y. Jets | 4 | 4 | 6 | 5 | =2 | =4 | 4 | 1 | 11 | 5 | =6 | =7 |
| Pittsburgh | 10 | 8 | 11 | 9 | =6 | 11 | 10 | 4 | 12 | 11 | =4 | 5 |
| San Diego | 7 | 2 | 12 | 11 | =6 | =7 | 7 | 6 | 10 | 10 | =4 | =11 |
| Seattle | 11 | 10 | 7 | 10 | 14 | =9 | 2 | 7 | 3 | 4 | =6 | 6 |

## AFC PASSERS

| | Att | Comp | % Comp | Yards | Ave Gain | TD | % TD | Long | Int | % Int | Rating Points |
|---|---|---|---|---|---|---|---|---|---|---|---|
| Kelly, Jim, *Buff.* | 474 | 304 | 64.1 | 3844 | 8.11 | 33 | 7.0 | t77 | 17 | 3.3 | 97.6 |
| Kosar, Bernie, *Clev.* | 494 | 307 | 62.1 | 3487 | 7.06 | 18 | 3.6 | t71 | 9 | 1.8 | 87.8 |
| Marino, Dan, *Mia.* | 549 | 318 | 57.9 | 3970 | 7.23 | 25 | 4.6 | 54 | 13 | 2.4 | 85.8 |
| Krieg, Dave, *Sea.* | 285 | 187 | 65.6 | 2080 | 7.30 | 11 | 3.9 | 60 | 12 | 4.2 | 82.5 |
| Moon, Warren, *Hou.* | 655 | 404 | 61.7 | 4690 | 7.16 | 23 | 3.5 | t61 | 21 | 3.2 | 81.7 |
| DeBerg, Steve, *K.C.* | 434 | 256 | 59.0 | 2965 | 6.83 | 17 | 3.9 | 63 | 14 | 3.2 | 79.3 |
| O'Donnell, Neil, *Pitt.* | 286 | 156 | 54.5 | 1963 | 6.86 | 11 | 3.8 | t89 | 7 | 2.4 | 78.8 |
| O'Brien, Ken, *Jets* | 489 | 287 | 58.7 | 3300 | 6.75 | 10 | 2.0 | 53 | 11 | 2.2 | 76.6 |
| Elway, John, *Den.* | 451 | 242 | 53.7 | 3253 | 7.21 | 13 | 2.9 | 71 | 12 | 2.7 | 75.4 |
| George, Jeff, *Ind.* | 485 | 292 | 60.2 | 2910 | 6.00 | 10 | 2.1 | t49 | 12 | 2.5 | 73.8 |
| Esiason, Boomer, *Cin.* | 413 | 233 | 56.4 | 2883 | 6.98 | 13 | 3.1 | 53 | 16 | 3.9 | 72.5 |
| Millen, Hugh, *N.E.* | 409 | 246 | 60.1 | 3073 | 7.51 | 9 | 2.2 | t60 | 18 | 4.4 | 72.5 |
| Schroeder, Jay, *Raiders* | 357 | 189 | 52.9 | 2562 | 7.18 | 15 | 4.2 | t78 | 16 | 4.5 | 71.4 |
| Friesz, John, *S.D.* | 487 | 262 | 53.8 | 2896 | 5.95 | 12 | 2.5 | 58 | 15 | 3.1 | 67.1 |
| **Non-qualifiers** | | | | | | | | | | | |
| Reich, Frank, *Buff.* | 41 | 27 | 65.9 | 305 | 7.44 | 6 | 14.6 | 29 | 2 | 4.9 | 107.2 |
| Marinovich, Todd, *Raiders* | 40 | 23 | 57.5 | 243 | 6.08 | 3 | 7.5 | t26 | 0 | 0.0 | 100.3 |
| Vlasic, Mark, *K.C.* | 44 | 28 | 63.6 | 316 | 7.18 | 2 | 4.5 | 30 | 0 | 0.0 | 100.2 |
| Brister, Bubby, *Pitt.* | 190 | 103 | 54.2 | 1350 | 7.11 | 9 | 4.7 | t65 | 9 | 4.7 | 72.9 |
| Wilhelm, Erik, *Cin.* | 42 | 24 | 57.1 | 217 | 5.17 | 0 | 0.0 | 29 | 2 | 4.8 | 51.4 |
| Hollas, Donald, *Cin.* | 55 | 32 | 58.2 | 310 | 5.64 | 1 | 1.8 | t23 | 4 | 7.3 | 49.8 |
| Hodson, Tom, *N.E.* | 68 | 36 | 52.9 | 345 | 5.07 | 1 | 1.5 | 32 | 4 | 5.9 | 47.7 |
| Gagliano, Bob, *S.D.* | 23 | 9 | 39.1 | 76 | 3.30 | 0 | 0.0 | 17 | 1 | 4.3 | 30.3 |

t = touchdown
Leader based on rating points, minimum 224 attempts

## AFC RECEIVERS – Most Receptions

| | No | Yards | Ave | Long | TD |
|---|---|---|---|---|---|
| Jeffires, Haywood, *Hou.* | 100 | 1181 | 11.8 | 44 | 7 |
| Hill, Drew, *Hou.* | 90 | 1109 | 12.3 | t61 | 4 |
| Cook, Marv, *N.E.* | 82 | 808 | 9.9 | 49 | 3 |
| Reed, Andre, *Buff.* | 81 | 1113 | 13.7 | 55 | 10 |
| Toon, Al, *Jets* | 74 | 963 | 13.0 | 32 | 0 |
| Brooks, Bill, *Ind.* | 72 | 888 | 12.3 | 46 | 4 |
| Duper, Mark, *Mia.* | 70 | 1085 | 15.5 | t43 | 5 |
| Clayton, Mark, *Mia.* | 70 | 1053 | 15.0 | t43 | 12 |
| Blades, Brian, *Sea.* | 70 | 1003 | 14.3 | 52 | 2 |
| Givins, Ernest, *Hou.* | 70 | 996 | 14.2 | 49 | 5 |
| Moore, Rob, *Jets* | 70 | 987 | 14.1 | 53 | 5 |
| Fryar, Irving, *N.E.* | 68 | 1014 | 14.9 | t56 | 3 |
| Slaughter, Webster, *Clev.* | 64 | 906 | 14.2 | t62 | 3 |
| Thomas, Thurman, *Buff.* | 62 | 631 | 10.2 | t50 | 5 |
| Williams, John L., *Sea.* | 61 | 499 | 8.2 | 35 | 1 |
| Hester, Jessie, *Ind.* | 60 | 753 | 12.6 | t49 | 5 |
| Brown, Eddie, *Cin.* | 59 | 827 | 14.0 | 53 | 2 |
| Harmon, Ronnie, *S.D.* | 59 | 555 | 9.4 | 36 | 1 |
| Lofton, James, *Buff.* | 57 | 1072 | 18.8 | t77 | 8 |
| Paige, Tony, *Mia.* | 57 | 469 | 8.2 | 26 | 1 |
| Lipps, Louis, *Pitt.* | 55 | 671 | 12.2 | 35 | 2 |
| Duncan, Curtis, *Hou.* | 55 | 588 | 10.7 | 42 | 4 |
| Horton, Ethan, *Raiders* | 53 | 650 | 12.3 | 52 | 5 |
| McGee, Tim, *Cin.* | 51 | 802 | 15.7 | t52 | 4 |
| Kane, Tommy, *Sea.* | 50 | 763 | 15.3 | 60 | 2 |
| Hoge, Merril, *Pitt.* | 49 | 379 | 7.7 | 25 | 1 |
| Hoard, Leroy, *Clev.* | 48 | 567 | 11.8 | t71 | 9 |
| Fernandez, Mervyn, *Raiders* | 46 | 694 | 15.1 | 59 | 1 |
| Miller, Anthony, *S.D.* | 44 | 649 | 14.8 | 58 | 3 |

t = touchdown

## AFC RECEIVERS – Most Yards

| | Yards | No | Ave | Long | TD |
|---|---|---|---|---|---|
| Jeffires, Haywood, *Hou.* | 1181 | 100 | 11.8 | 44 | 7 |
| Reed, Andre, *Buff.* | 1113 | 81 | 13.7 | 55 | 10 |
| Hill, Drew, *Hou.* | 1109 | 90 | 12.3 | t61 | 4 |
| Duper, Mark, *Mia.* | 1085 | 70 | 15.5 | t43 | 5 |
| Lofton, James, *Buff.* | 1072 | 57 | 18.8 | t77 | 8 |
| Clayton, Mark, *Mia.* | 1053 | 70 | 15.0 | t43 | 12 |
| Fryar, Irving, *N.E.* | 1014 | 68 | 14.9 | t56 | 3 |
| Blades, Brian, *Sea.* | 1003 | 70 | 14.3 | 52 | 2 |
| Givins, Ernest, *Hou.* | 996 | 70 | 14.2 | 49 | 5 |
| Moore, Rob, *Jets* | 987 | 70 | 14.1 | 53 | 5 |
| Toon, Al, *Jets* | 963 | 74 | 13.0 | 32 | 0 |
| Slaughter, Webster, *Clev.* | 906 | 64 | 14.2 | t62 | 3 |
| Brooks, Bill, *Ind.* | 888 | 72 | 12.3 | 46 | 4 |
| Brown, Eddie, *Cin.* | 827 | 59 | 14.0 | 53 | 2 |
| Cook, Marv, *N.E.* | 808 | 82 | 9.9 | 49 | 3 |
| McGee, Tim, *Cin.* | 802 | 51 | 15.7 | t52 | 4 |
| Kane, Tommy, *Sea.* | 763 | 50 | 15.3 | 60 | 2 |
| Hester, Jessie, *Ind.* | 753 | 60 | 12.6 | t49 | 5 |
| Fernandez, Mervyn, *Raiders* | 694 | 46 | 15.1 | 59 | 1 |
| Lipps, Louis, *Pitt.* | 671 | 55 | 12.2 | 35 | 2 |
| Horton, Ethan, *Raiders* | 650 | 53 | 12.3 | 52 | 5 |
| Miller, Anthony, *S.D.* | 649 | 44 | 14.8 | 58 | 3 |
| Stone, Dwight, *Pitt.* | 649 | 32 | 20.3 | t89 | 5 |
| Thomas, Thurman, *Buff.* | 631 | 62 | 10.2 | t50 | 5 |
| Young, Mike, *Den.* | 629 | 44 | 14.3 | t52 | 2 |
| McMurtry, Greg, *N.E.* | 614 | 41 | 15.0 | 40 | 2 |
| Jackson, Mark, *Den.* | 603 | 33 | 18.3 | 71 | 1 |
| Duncan, Curtis, *Hou.* | 588 | 55 | 10.7 | 42 | 4 |

t = touchdown

*Haywood Jeffires led the AFC in receptions for the second consecutive year.*

## AFC RUSHERS

| | Att | Yards | Ave | Long | TD |
|---|---|---|---|---|---|
| Thomas, Thurman, *Buff.* | 288 | 1407 | 4.9 | 33 | 7 |
| Green, Gaston, *Den.* | 261 | 1037 | 4.0 | t63 | 4 |
| Okoye, Christian, *K.C.* | 225 | 1031 | 4.6 | 48 | 9 |
| Russell, Leonard, *N.E.* | 266 | 959 | 3.6 | 24 | 4 |
| Higgs, Mark, *Mia.* | 231 | 905 | 3.9 | 24 | 4 |
| Butts, Marion, *S.D.* | 193 | 834 | 4.3 | 44 | 6 |
| Bernstine, Rod, *S.D.* | 159 | 766 | 4.8 | t63 | 8 |
| Williams, John L., *Sea.* | 188 | 741 | 3.9 | 42 | 4 |
| Green, Harold, *Cin.* | 158 | 731 | 4.6 | t75 | 2 |
| Thomas, Blair, *Jets* | 189 | 728 | 3.9 | 25 | 3 |
| Mack, Kevin, *Clev.* | 197 | 726 | 3.7 | t51 | 8 |
| Pinkett, Allen, *Hou.* | 171 | 720 | 4.2 | 32 | 9 |
| Word, Barry, *K.C.* | 160 | 684 | 4.3 | 37 | 4 |
| Baxter, Brad, *Jets* | 184 | 666 | 3.6 | 31 | 11 |
| Davis, Kenneth, *Buff.* | 129 | 624 | 4.8 | t78 | 4 |
| Hoge, Merril, *Pitt.* | 165 | 610 | 3.7 | 24 | 2 |
| Craig, Roger, *Raiders* | 162 | 590 | 3.6 | 15 | 1 |
| Brooks, James, *Cin.* | 152 | 571 | 3.8 | 25 | 2 |
| Harmon, Ronnie, *S.D.* | 89 | 544 | 6.1 | 33 | 1 |
| Dickerson, Eric, *Ind.* | 167 | 536 | 3.2 | 28 | 2 |
| Foster, Barry, *Pitt.* | 96 | 488 | 5.1 | t56 | 1 |
| White, Lorenzo, *Hou.* | 110 | 465 | 4.2 | 20 | 4 |
| Williams, Harvey, *K.C.* | 97 | 447 | 4.6 | 21 | 1 |
| Lewis, Greg, *Den.* | 99 | 376 | 3.8 | 27 | 4 |
| Clark, Ken, *Ind.* | 114 | 366 | 3.2 | 25 | 0 |
| Hector, Johnny, *Jets* | 62 | 345 | 5.6 | 47 | 0 |
| Bell, Nick, *Raiders* | 78 | 307 | 3.9 | 15 | 3 |
| McNeil, Freeman, *Jets* | 51 | 300 | 5.9 | 58 | 2 |
| Smith, Sammie, *Mia.* | 83 | 297 | 3.6 | 18 | 1 |
| Morris, Joe, *Clev.* | 93 | 289 | 3.1 | 15 | 2 |
| Allen, Marcus, *Raiders* | 63 | 287 | 4.6 | 26 | 2 |
| Fenner, Derrick, *Sea.* | 91 | 267 | 2.9 | 15 | 4 |
| Smith, Steve, *Raiders* | 62 | 265 | 4.3 | 19 | 1 |
| Williams, Warren, *Pitt.* | 57 | 262 | 4.6 | 21 | 4 |
| Elway, John, *Den.* | 55 | 255 | 4.6 | t17 | 6 |
| Sewell, Steve, *Den.* | 50 | 211 | 4.2 | 26 | 2 |
| Stephens, John, *N.E.* | 63 | 163 | 2.6 | 13 | 2 |
| Hoard, Leroy, *Clev.* | 37 | 154 | 4.2 | 52 | 2 |
| Jones, James, *Sea.* | 45 | 154 | 3.4 | 22 | 3 |
| Taylor, Craig, *Cin.* | 33 | 153 | 4.6 | t34 | 2 |
| Gardner, Carwell, *Buff.* | 42 | 146 | 3.5 | 18 | 4 |
| Vaughn, Jon, *N.E.* | 31 | 146 | 4.7 | 23 | 2 |
| Manoa, Tim, *Ind.* | 27 | 144 | 5.3 | 44 | 1 |
| Reed, Andre, *Buff.* | 12 | 136 | 11.3 | 46 | 0 |
| Worley, Tim, *Pitt.* | 22 | 117 | 5.3 | 16 | 0 |
| McCallum, Napoleon, *Raiders* | 31 | 110 | 3.5 | 9 | 1 |
| Metcalf, Eric, *Clev.* | 30 | 107 | 3.6 | 15 | 0 |

t = touchdown

## AFC SCORING – Kickers

| | XP | XPA | FG | FGA | PTS |
|---|---|---|---|---|---|
| Stoyanovich, Pete, *Mia.* | 28 | 29 | 31 | 37 | 121 |
| Jaeger, Jeff, *Raiders* | 29 | 30 | 29 | 34 | 116 |
| Treadwell, David, *Den.* | 31 | 32 | 27 | 36 | 112 |
| Lowery, Nick, *K.C.* | 35 | 35 | 25 | 30 | 110 |
| Norwood, Scott, *Buff.* | 56 | 58 | 18 | 29 | 110 |
| Leahy, Pat, *Jets* | 30 | 30 | 26 | 37 | 108 |
| Kasay, John, *Sea.* | 27 | 28 | 25 | 31 | 102 |
| Anderson, Gary, *Pitt.* | 31 | 31 | 23 | 33 | 100 |
| Breech, Jim, *Cin.* | 27 | 27 | 23 | 29 | 96 |
| Carney, John, *S.D.* | 31 | 31 | 19 | 29 | 88 |
| Stover, Matt, *Clev.* | 33 | 34 | 16 | 22 | 81 |
| Howfield, Ian, *Hou.* | 25 | 29 | 13 | 18 | 64 |
| Biasucci, Dean, *Ind.* | 14 | 14 | 15 | 26 | 59 |
| Staurovsky, Jason, *N.E.* | 10 | 11 | 13 | 19 | 49 |
| Del Greco, Al, *Hou.* | 16 | 16 | 10 | 13 | 46 |
| Baumann, Charlie, *Mia.-N.E.* | 15 | 16 | 9 | 12 | 42 |
| Allegre, Raul, *Giants-Jets* | 7 | 7 | 5 | 6 | 22 |
| Aguiar, Louie, *Jets* | 0 | 0 | 1 | 2 | 3 |
| Johnson, Lee, *Cin.* | 0 | 0 | 1 | 3 | 3 |

*Thurman Thomas dominated the AFC rushing list.*

# AFC SCORING – Touchdowns

| | TD | TDR | TDP | TDM | PTS |
|---|---|---|---|---|---|
| Clayton, Mark, *Mia.* | 12 | 0 | 12 | 0 | 72 |
| Thomas, Thurman, *Buff.* | 12 | 7 | 5 | 0 | 72 |
| Baxter, Brad, *Jets* | 11 | 11 | 0 | 0 | 66 |
| Hoard, Leroy, *Clev.* | 11 | 2 | 9 | 0 | 66 |
| Mack, Kevin, *Clev.* | 10 | 8 | 2 | 0 | 60 |
| Pinkett, Allen, *Hou.* | 10 | 9 | 1 | 0 | 60 |
| Reed, Andre, *Buff.* | 10 | 0 | 10 | 0 | 60 |
| Okoye, Christian, *K.C.* | 9 | 9 | 0 | 0 | 54 |
| Bernstine, Rod, *S.D.* | 8 | 8 | 0 | 0 | 48 |
| Lofton, James, *Buff.* | 8 | 0 | 8 | 0 | 48 |
| Butts, Marion, *S.D.* | 7 | 6 | 1 | 0 | 42 |
| Jeffires, Haywood, *Hou.* | 7 | 0 | 7 | 0 | 42 |
| Beebe, Don, *Buff.* | 6 | 0 | 6 | 0 | 36 |
| Brown, Tim, *Raiders* | 6 | 0 | 5 | 1 | 36 |
| Elway, John, *Den.* | 6 | 6 | 0 | 0 | 36 |
| Green, Eric, *Pitt.* | 6 | 0 | 6 | 0 | 36 |
| Barnett, Tim, *K.C.* | 5 | 0 | 5 | 0 | 30 |
| Burkett, Chris, *Jets* | 5 | 0 | 4 | 1 | 30 |
| Davis, Kenneth, *Buff.* | 5 | 4 | 1 | 0 | 30 |
| Duper, Mark, *Mia.* | 5 | 0 | 5 | 0 | 30 |
| Givins, Ernest, *Hou.* | 5 | 0 | 5 | 0 | 30 |
| Hester, Jessie, *Ind.* | 5 | 0 | 5 | 0 | 30 |
| Horton, Ethan, *Raiders* | 5 | 0 | 5 | 0 | 30 |
| Moore, Rob, *Jets* | 5 | 0 | 5 | 0 | 30 |
| Stone, Dwight, *Pitt.* | 5 | 0 | 5 | 0 | 30 |
| Williams, John L., *Sea.* | 5 | 4 | 1 | 0 | 30 |

# AFC KICKOFF RETURNERS

| | No | Yards | Ave | Long | TD |
|---|---|---|---|---|---|
| Lewis, Nate, *S.D.* | 23 | 578 | 25.1 | t95 | 1 |
| Martin, Sammy, *N.E.-Ind.* | 20 | 483 | 24.2 | 38 | 0 |
| Loville, Derek, *Sea.* | 18 | 412 | 22.9 | 50 | 0 |
| Warren, Chris, *Sea.* | 35 | 792 | 22.6 | 55 | 0 |
| Williams, Harvey, *K.C.* | 24 | 524 | 21.8 | 76 | 0 |
| Vaughn, Jon, *N.E.* | 34 | 717 | 21.1 | t99 | 1 |
| Mathis, Terance, *Jets* | 29 | 599 | 20.7 | 50 | 0 |
| Edwards, Al, *Buff.* | 31 | 623 | 20.1 | t91 | 1 |
| Woodson, Rod, *Pitt.* | 44 | 880 | 20.0 | 47 | 0 |
| Elder, Donnie, *S.D.* | 27 | 535 | 19.8 | 42 | 0 |
| Pinkett, Allen, *Hou.* | 26 | 508 | 19.5 | 41 | 0 |
| Craver, Aaron, *Mia.* | 32 | 615 | 19.2 | 49 | 0 |
| Verdin, Clarence, *Ind.* | 36 | 689 | 19.1 | t88 | 1 |
| Holland, Jamie, *Raiders* | 22 | 421 | 19.1 | 27 | 0 |
| Montgomery, Alton, *Den.* | 26 | 488 | 18.8 | 55 | 0 |
| Morris, Joe, *Clev.* | 18 | 310 | 17.2 | 36 | 0 |
| Graddy, Sam, *Raiders* | 22 | 373 | 17.0 | 37 | 0 |
| Metcalf, Eric, *Clev.* | 23 | 351 | 15.3 | 24 | 0 |

t = touchdown
Leader based on average return, minimum 18 returns

*Mark Clayton returned to his best form with 12 touchdown receptions.*

# AFC PUNTERS

| | No | Yards | Long | Ave | TB | Blk | Opp Ret | Ret Yds | In 20 | Net Ave |
|---|---|---|---|---|---|---|---|---|---|---|
| Roby, Reggie, *Mia.* | 54 | 2466 | 64 | 45.7 | 7 | 1 | 29 | 324 | 17 | 36.4 |
| Gossett, Jeff, *Raiders* | 67 | 2961 | 61 | 44.2 | 2 | 0 | 41 | 341 | 26 | 38.5 |
| Montgomery, Greg, *Hou.* | 48 | 2105 | 60 | 43.9 | 4 | 2 | 28 | 183 | 13 | 36.8 |
| Johnson, Lee, *Cin.* | 64 | 2795 | 62 | 43.7 | 6 | 0 | 38 | 456 | 15 | 34.7 |
| Tuten, Rick, *Sea.* | 49 | 2106 | 60 | 43.0 | 3 | 0 | 29 | 239 | 8 | 36.9 |
| Stark, Rohn, *Ind.* | 82 | 3492 | 65 | 42.6 | 6 | 0 | 47 | 516 | 14 | 34.8 |
| Hansen, Brian, *Clev.* | 80 | 3397 | 65 | 42.5 | 6 | 0 | 40 | 388 | 20 | 36.1 |
| Horan, Mike, *Den.* | 72 | 3012 | 71 | 41.8 | 8 | 1 | 28 | 170 | 24 | 36.7 |
| Stryzinski, Dan, *Pitt.* | 74 | 2996 | 63 | 40.5 | 3 | 1 | 29 | 210 | 10 | 36.3 |
| Barker, Bryan, *K.C.* | 57 | 2303 | 57 | 40.4 | 6 | 0 | 27 | 190 | 11 | 35.0 |
| Kidd, John, *S.D.* | 76 | 3064 | 60 | 40.3 | 6 | 1 | 32 | 267 | 22 | 34.8 |
| McCarthy, Shawn, *N.E.* | 66 | 2650 | 93 | 40.2 | 3 | 2 | 26 | 163 | 17 | 35.7 |
| Aguiar, Louie, *Jets* | 64 | 2521 | 61 | 39.4 | 7 | 0 | 29 | 164 | 14 | 34.6 |
| Mohr, Chris, *Buff.* | 54 | 2085 | 58 | 38.6 | 4 | 0 | 15 | 53 | 12 | 36.1 |

Leader based on gross average, minimum 40 punts

# AFC SACKERS

| | No |
|---|---|
| Fuller, William, *Hou.* | 15.0 |
| Fletcher, Simon, *Den.* | 13.5 |
| Thomas, Derrick, *K.C.* | 13.5 |
| Townsend, Greg, *Raiders* | 13.0 |
| Smith, Anthony, *Raiders* | 10.5 |
| Croel, Mike, *Den.* | 10.0 |
| Jones, Sean, *Hou.* | 10.0 |
| Lageman, Jeff, *Jets* | 10.0 |
| Porter, Rufus, *Sea.* | 10.0 |
| Bennett, Cornelius, *Buff.* | 9.0 |
| Mecklenburg, Karl, *Den.* | 9.0 |
| O'Neal, Leslie, *S.D.* | 9.0 |
| Williams, Jerrol, *Pitt.* | 9.0 |
| Perry, Michael Dean, *Clev.* | 8.5 |
| Tippett, Andre, *N.E.* | 8.5 |
| Lloyd, Greg, *Pitt.* | 8.0 |
| Smith, Neil, *K.C.* | 8.0 |
| Byrd, Dennis, *Jets* | 7.0 |
| Childress, Ray, *Hou.* | 7.0 |
| Cross, Jeff, *Mia.* | 7.0 |
| Seau, Junior, *S.D.* | 7.0 |
| Willis, Keith, *Pitt.* | 7.0 |
| Davis, Scott, *Raiders* | 6.5 |
| Kennedy, Cortez, *Sea.* | 6.5 |
| Matthews, Clay, *Clev.* | 6.5 |
| Green, Jacob, *Sea.* | 6.0 |
| Washington, Marvin, *Jets* | 6.0 |
| Wright, Jeff, *Buff.* | 6.0 |
| Griggs, David, *Mia.* | 5.5 |
| Grossman, Burt, *S.D.* | 5.5 |
| Bickett, Duane, *Ind.* | 5.0 |
| Hand, Jon, *Ind.* | 5.0 |
| Holmes, Ron, *Den.* | 5.0 |
| Junior, E.J., *Mia.* | 5.0 |
| Klingbeil, Chuck, *Mia.* | 5.0 |
| Martin, Chris, *K.C.* | 5.0 |
| Thompson, Donnell, *Ind.* | 5.0 |
| Krumrie, Tim, *Cin.* | 4.0 |
| Maas, Bill, *K.C.* | 4.0 |
| Stubbs, Danny, *Dall.-Cin.* | 4.0 |
| Talley, Darryl, *Buff.* | 4.0 |
| Turner, T.J., *Mia.* | 4.0 |
| Veris, Garin, *N.E.* | 4.0 |
| Kragen, Greg, *Den.* | 3.5 |
| Williams, Brent, *N.E.* | 3.5 |

# AFC INTERCEPTORS

| | No | Yards | Ave | Long | TD |
|---|---|---|---|---|---|
| Lott, Ronnie, *Raiders* | 8 | 52 | 6.5 | 27 | 0 |
| Dishman, Cris, *Hou.* | 6 | 61 | 10.2 | 43 | 0 |
| Byrd, Gill, *S.D.* | 6 | 48 | 8.0 | 22 | 0 |
| Odomes, Nate, *Buff.* | 5 | 120 | 24.0 | 48 | 1 |
| Atwater, Steve, *Den.* | 5 | 104 | 20.8 | 49 | 0 |
| Oliver, Louis, *Mia.* | 5 | 80 | 16.0 | 37 | 0 |
| Smith, Dennis, *Den.* | 5 | 60 | 12.0 | 39 | 0 |
| Robinson, Eugene, *Sea.* | 5 | 56 | 11.2 | 27 | 0 |
| Talley, Darryl, *Buff.* | 5 | 45 | 9.0 | 13 | 0 |
| Washington, Lionel, *Raiders* | 5 | 22 | 4.4 | 16 | 0 |
| Harper, Dwayne, *Sea.* | 4 | 84 | 21.0 | 43 | 0 |
| Braxton, Tyrone, *Den.* | 4 | 55 | 13.8 | t52 | 1 |
| Everett, Thomas, *Pitt.* | 4 | 53 | 13.3 | 27 | 0 |
| Brim, Michael, *Jets* | 4 | 52 | 13.0 | 24 | 0 |
| Fulcher, David, *Cin.* | 4 | 51 | 12.8 | t27 | 1 |
| Baylor, John, *Ind.* | 4 | 50 | 12.5 | 32 | 0 |
| Cherry, Deron, *K.C.* | 4 | 31 | 7.8 | 16 | 0 |
| Jackson, Kirby, *Buff.* | 4 | 31 | 7.8 | 15 | 0 |
| McDowell, Bubba, *Hou.* | 4 | 31 | 7.8 | 23 | 0 |
| Orlando, Bo, *Hou.* | 4 | 18 | 4.5 | 18 | 0 |
| McMillan, Erik, *Jets* | 3 | 168 | 56.0 | t83 | 2 |
| Lathon, Lamar, *Hou.* | 3 | 77 | 25.7 | t52 | 1 |
| Woodson, Rod, *Pitt.* | 3 | 72 | 24.0 | 41 | 0 |
| Blackmon, Robert, *Sea.* | 3 | 59 | 19.7 | 29 | 0 |
| Shelton, Richard, *Pitt.* | 3 | 57 | 19.0 | t57 | 1 |
| Prior, Mike, *Ind.* | 3 | 50 | 16.7 | 37 | 0 |
| Pearson, J.C., *K.C.* | 3 | 43 | 14.3 | 43 | 0 |
| Hasty, James, *Jets* | 3 | 39 | 13.0 | 39 | 0 |
| Dimry, Charles, *Den.* | 3 | 35 | 11.7 | t26 | 1 |
| Carrington, Darren, *S.D.* | 3 | 30 | 10.0 | 19 | 0 |
| Daniel, Eugene, *Ind.* | 3 | 22 | 7.3 | 12 | 0 |
| Smith, Leonard, *Buff.* | 3 | 22 | 7.3 | 22 | 0 |
| Hurst, Maurice, *N.E.* | 3 | 21 | 7.0 | 21 | 0 |
| Lewis, Albert, *K.C.* | 3 | 21 | 7.0 | 21 | 0 |
| Braggs, Stephen, *Clev.* | 3 | 15 | 5.0 | 15 | 0 |
| Thomas, Eric, *Cin.* | 3 | 0 | 0.0 | 0 | 0 |

t = touchdown

# AFC PUNT RETURNERS

| | No | FC | Yards | Ave | Long | TD |
|---|---|---|---|---|---|---|
| Woodson, Rod, *Pitt.* | 28 | 12 | 320 | 11.4 | 40 | 0 |
| Brown, Tim, *Raiders* | 29 | 10 | 330 | 11.4 | t75 | 1 |
| Taylor, Kitrick, *S.D.* | 28 | 18 | 269 | 9.6 | 48 | 0 |
| Warren, Chris, *Sea.* | 32 | 19 | 298 | 9.3 | t59 | 1 |
| Miller, Scott, *Mia.* | 28 | 10 | 248 | 8.9 | 32 | 0 |
| Henderson, Jerome, *N.E.* | 27 | 10 | 201 | 7.4 | 39 | 0 |
| Johnson, Vance, *Den.* | 24 | 14 | 174 | 7.3 | 20 | 0 |
| Mathis, Terance, *Jets* | 23 | 10 | 157 | 6.8 | 25 | 0 |
| Stradford, Troy, *K.C.* | 22 | 4 | 150 | 6.8 | 18 | 0 |
| Slaughter, Webster, *Clev.* | 17 | 3 | 112 | 6.6 | 17 | 0 |
| Verdin, Clarence, *Ind.* | 25 | 10 | 165 | 6.6 | 22 | 0 |
| Coleman, Patrick, *Hou.* | 22 | 8 | 138 | 6.3 | 24 | 0 |

t = touchdown
Leader based on average return, minimum 17 returns

*LEFT: William Fuller had his best season so far to lead the conference in sacks.*

*RIGHT: Cris Dishman intercepted six passes and defensed another 23 to earn All-Pro honours in 1991.*

# BUFFALO BILLS

**Address** One Bills Drive, Orchard Park, New York 14127.
**Stadium** Rich Stadium, Orchard Park.
 *Capacity* 80,290 *Playing Surface* AstroTurf.
**Team Colours** Royal Blue, Scarlet Red, and White.
**Head Coach** Marv Levy – 7th year; 12th NFL.
**Championships** Division 1980,'88,'89,'90,'91;
 AFL 1964,'65; Conference 1990,'91.
**History** AFL 1960-69, AFC 1970-

For the past two years the Bills have ruled the AFC. In 1991 they set nine club records and equalled one. Over the last four seasons they lead the NFL in scoring and, with 47 victories, rank second only to San Francisco's 48. Alarmingly, however, they slumped to 27th in the NFL for total defense, unwillingly confirming the old adage, 'Offense wins games but defense wins championships.'

Defensive players were selected in rounds two to five of the 1992 draft but there's little doubt that the problems lay entirely with the league's premier defensive end, Bruce Smith, whose injuries meant that he was hardly a factor. On most downs, the whole effort is built around Smith's fearsome rush from the right side, forcing opponents to use double coverage and leaving themselves vulnerable to attack by any one of several impact players. The good news is that Smith is ready for 1992, which should ease the pressure on nose tackle Jeff Wright and defensive left end Leon Seals. And it is healthy that there will be heat from another direction in the improving Phil Hansen and high-round draftees James Patton and Frank Kmet.

The extra freedom will be felt also at linebacker, where the quartet of Darryl Talley, Carlton Bailey, Shane Conlan and the mercurial Cornelius Bennett should once again dominate. Collectively, Talley, Conlan and Bennett have gathered eight Pro Bowl selections in the past four years while Bailey made great strides in his first year as a starter after displacing Ray Bentley. The foursome did play outstandingly well last year – Talley even tied for the team lead with five interceptions – but it still needs the edge that Smith can generate.

There are no weaknesses in the secondary, and though strong safety Leonard Smith is entering his tenth year, there is no suggestion that backup Dwight Drane is ready to take over, while draftee Matt Darby will need time to settle.

However, former first-round draftees James Williams and Henry Jones are ready to make their bids for playing time at cornerback, where the incumbents are Nate Odomes and Kirby Jackson. At free safety, Mark Kelso is the model of reliability.

The signing of Steve Christie under Plan B means that placekicker Scott Norwood faces a battle in camp. There's little to choose between the two and, if only for his experience with the team, Norwood may just hang on to his job. Punter Chris Mohr had a modest gross average but he was the only AFC punter to set up more fair catches than returns last year.

'High powered' hardly begins to describe an offense which often puts the game away before half time. It can score at any time from any position in a bewildering variety of ways. And behind the starters there are those who, given the opportunity, could easily start elsewhere. Running back Kenneth Davis is one such player but he has to settle for picking up the scraps left by the brilliant Thurman Thomas, who led all AFC rushers by the margin of 370 yards and logged the 12th-highest dual-purpose yardage total in NFL history. Thomas was one of several Bills players to disappoint in Super Bowl XXVI and suffered the indignity of being unable to find his helmet for the opening play. Starting fullback Carwell Gardner is another who has to bide his time.

At wide receiver, Don Beebe carves out great swathes of territory – against Pittsburgh he caught ten passes for 112 yards and four touchdowns, the latter equalling the club record – but he has to wait his turn behind two 1,000-yard receivers, James Lofton and Andre Reed. Lofton has the all-time receiving yardage record at his mercy (he needs 55 yards to go beyond Steve Largent's 13,089) and is hurtling towards the Pro Football Hall of Fame. Then there is Jim Kelly, the strong-armed AFC passing leader, who, sadly, reserved one of his worst days for Super Bowl XXVI. He'll send that memory on its way in double-quick time.

One area which perhaps needs attention is the offensive line, and for this, help came in the shape of top draftee tackle John Fina. However, on opening day Will Wolford and Howard Ballard will be manning the tackle positions with Jim Ritcher and John Davis at guard, and All-Pro Kent Hull at center.

**1992 Draft**

| Round | Name | Pos. | Ht. | Wt. | College |
|---|---|---|---|---|---|
| 1. | Fina, John | T | 6-6 | 281 | Arizona |
| 2. | Patton, James | NT | 6-3 | 276 | Texas |
| 3. | Goganious, Keith | LB | 6-2 | 237 | Penn State |
| 4. | Kmet, Frank | DE | 6-3 | 289 | Purdue |
| 5. | Darby, Matt | S | 6-1 | 200 | UCLA |
| 6. | Turner, Nate | TE | 6-1 | 241 | Nebraska |
| 7. | Schulz, Kurt | S | 5-11 | 205 | Eastern Washington |
| 8. | Humphries, Leonard | CB | 5-8 | 172 | Penn State |
| 9. | Walsh, Chris | WR | 6-0 | 182 | Stanford |
| 10. | Rose, Barry | WR | 5-10 | 183 | Stevens Point, Wis. |
| 11. | Marrow, Vince | TE | 6-3 | 249 | Toledo |
| 12. | Rodgers, Matt | QB | 6-2 | 221 | Iowa |

## VETERAN ROSTER

| No. | Name | Pos. | Ht. | Wt. | NFL Year | College |
|---|---|---|---|---|---|---|
| 54 | Bailey, Carlton | LB | 6-3 | 235 | 5 | North Carolina |
| | Baldinger, Brian | G-C | 6-4 | 278 | 10 | Duke |
| 92 | Baldinger, Gary | NT | 6-3 | 270 | 6 | Wake Forest |
| 75 | Ballard, Howard | T | 6-6 | 325 | 5 | Alabama A&M |
| 82 | Beebe, Don | WR | 5-11 | 183 | 4 | Chadron State, Neb. |
| 97 | Bennett, Cornelius | LB | 6-2 | 236 | 6 | Alabama |
| 64 | Brennan, Mike | T | 6-5 | 282 | 3 | Notre Dame |
| | Brownlow, Darrick | LB | 5-10 | 237 | 2 | Illinois |
| | Christie, Steve | K | 6-0 | 185 | 3 | William & Mary |
| 58 | Conlan, Shane | LB | 6-3 | 230 | 6 | Penn State |
| 65 | Davis, John | G | 6-4 | 310 | 6 | Georgia Tech |
| 23 | Davis, Kenneth | RB | 5-10 | 209 | 7 | Texas Christian |
| 45 | Drane, Dwight | S | 6-2 | 205 | 7 | Oklahoma |
| 85 | Edwards, Al | WR | 5-8 | 171 | 3 | Northwestern State, La. |
| | Fairs, Eric | LB | 6-3 | 244 | 7 | Memphis State |
| 59 | Frerotte, Mitch | G | 6-3 | 285 | 4 | Penn State |
| 33 | Fuller, Eddie | RB | 5-9 | 201 | 2 | Louisiana State |
| 35 | Gardner, Carwell | RB | 6-2 | 232 | 3 | Louisville |
| 99 | Garner, Hal | LB | 6-4 | 235 | 6 | Utah State |
| 7 | Gilbert, Gale | QB | 6-3 | 210 | 5 | California |
| 68 | Hackemack, Ken | T | 6-9 | 309 | 1 | Texas |
| 26 | Hale, Chris | CB | 5-7 | 165 | 4 | Southern California |
| 90 | Hansen, Phil | DE | 6-5 | 258 | 2 | North Dakota State |
| 27 | Hicks, Clifford | CB | 5-10 | 188 | 6 | Oregon |
| 67 | Hull, Kent | C | 6-5 | 275 | 7 | Mississippi State |
| 47 | Jackson, Kirby | CB | 5-10 | 180 | 6 | Mississippi State |
| 20 | Jones, Henry | CB | 6-0 | 197 | 2 | Illinois |
| 12 | Kelly, Jim | QB | 6-3 | 218 | 7 | Miami |
| 38 | Kelso, Mark | S | 5-11 | 185 | 7 | William & Mary |
| 81 | Lamb, Brad | WR | 5-10 | 171 | 1 | Anderson, Ind. |
| 63 | Lingner, Adam | C | 6-4 | 263 | 10 | Illinois |
| 73 | Lodish, Mike | NT | 6-3 | 265 | 3 | UCLA |
| 80 | Lofton, James | WR | 6-3 | 190 | 15 | Stanford |
| 55 | Maddox, Mark | LB | 6-1 | 220 | 1 | Northern Michigan |
| 84 | McKeller, Keith | TE | 6-4 | 245 | 5 | Jacksonville State |
| 88 | Metzelaars, Pete | TE | 6-7 | 250 | 11 | Wabash |
| 9 | Mohr, Chris | P | 6-5 | 215 | 3 | Alabama |
| 41 | Mueller, Jamie | RB | 6-1 | 224 | 5 | Benedictine |
| 11 | Norwood, Scott | K | 6-0 | 207 | 8 | James Madison |
| 37 | Odomes, Nate | CB | 5-10 | 188 | 6 | Wisconsin |
| 74 | Parker, Glenn | T | 6-5 | 301 | 3 | Arizona |
| 28 | Paterra, Greg | RB | 5-11 | 220 | 3 | Slippery Rock |
| 53 | Patton, Marvcus | LB | 6-2 | 226 | 3 | UCLA |
| 94 | Pike, Mark | DE | 6-4 | 272 | 6 | Georgia Tech |
| 83 | Reed, Andre | WR | 6-1 | 190 | 8 | Kutztown State |
| 14 | Reich, Frank | QB | 6-4 | 210 | 8 | Maryland |
| 51 | Ritcher, Jim | G | 6-3 | 273 | 13 | North Carolina State |
| 96 | Seals, Leon | DE | 6-5 | 270 | 6 | Jackson State |
| 78 | Smith, Bruce | DE | 6-4 | 275 | 8 | Virginia Tech |
| 46 | Smith, Leonard | S | 5-11 | 202 | 10 | McNeese State |
| 79 | Staysniak, Joe | T | 6-5 | 298 | 2 | Ohio State |
| 56 | Talley, Darryl | LB | 6-4 | 235 | 10 | West Virginia |
| 89 | Tasker, Steve | WR-KR | 5-9 | 183 | 8 | Northwestern |
| 21 | Taylor, Brian | CB | 5-10 | 195 | 3 | Oregon State |
| | Thomas, Ed | TE | 6-3 | 245 | 3 | Houston |
| 34 | Thomas, Thurman | RB | 5-10 | 198 | 5 | Oklahoma State |
| | Williams, Chris | NT | 6-3 | 304 | 2 | American International |
| 31 | Williams, James | CB | 5-10 | 172 | 3 | Fresno State |
| 69 | Wolford, Will | T | 6-5 | 295 | 7 | Vanderbilt |
| 91 | Wright, Jeff | NT | 6-3 | 270 | 5 | Central Missouri State |

*ABOVE RIGHT: Andre Reed is the Bills' all-time leading receiver.*

**1992 SCHEDULE OF GAMES**

**September**

| | | |
|---|---|---|
| 6 | LOS ANGELES RAMS | 1:00 |
| 13 | at San Francisco | 1:00 |
| 20 | INDIANAPOLIS | 8:00 |
| 27 | at New England | 1:00 |

**October**

| | | |
|---|---|---|
| 4 | MIAMI | 1:00 |
| 11 | at Los Angeles Raiders | 1:00 |
| 18 | Open Date | |
| 26 | at New York Jets (Mon.) | 9:00 |

**November**

| | | |
|---|---|---|
| 1 | NEW ENGLAND | 1:00 |
| 8 | PITTSBURGH | 4:00 |
| 16 | at Miami (Mon.) | 9:00 |
| 22 | ATLANTA | 1:00 |
| 29 | at Indianapolis | 4:00 |

**December**

| | | |
|---|---|---|
| 6 | NEW YORK JETS | 1:00 |
| 12 | DENVER (Sat.) | 12:30 |
| 20 | at New Orleans | 12:00 |
| 27 | at Houston | 7:00 |

# INDIANAPOLIS COLTS

**Address** P.O. Box 535000, Indianapolis, Indiana 46253.

**Stadium** Hoosier Dome, Indianapolis.

*Capacity* 60,129 *Playing Surface* AstroTurf.

**Team Colours** Royal Blue and White.

**Head Coach** Ted Marchibroda – 1st year; 6th NFL.

**Championships** Division 1970,'75,'76,'77,'87;
Conference 1970; NFL 1958,'59,'68;
Super Bowl 1970.

**History** NFL 1953-69, AFC 1970-.
(Until 1984, they were known as the Baltimore Colts.
A team of the same name played in the AAFC, from
1947 to 1949, and in the NFL in 1950, at the end of
which they went out of business.)

Head coach Ted Marchibroda returns to the Colts, with whom he enjoyed some successes over the period 1975-79, and brings new hope to a club which solved a nagging problem by trading running back Eric Dickerson to the Raiders and reinforced the defense with the top two picks overall in the collegiate draft.

With Dickerson's departure went the Colts' one player of all-time class, but he had been unsettled and it is not out of the question that Albert Bentley, who missed almost the entire 1991 season through injury, will blossom now that he is to be the focus of the rushing game. The obvious backup will be Ken Clark, an honest player who saw action last year, with Anthony Johnson in the competition following an eye injury which forced him on to the injured reserve list for the final seven games of the season. Tim Manoa is pencilled in as the premier blocker but Marchibroda promises to use a variety of sets, with one or two running backs and even sending the backs out wide in multiple receiver formations.

The primary wide receivers will be Bill Brooks and Jessie Hester. Both men have great speed and developed well as a partnership in 1991, when they became only the third pair in team history in which each player caught 60 or more passes. Clarence Verdin, who is also an excellent dual-purpose kick returner, offers electrifying pace as the third receiver, while former Cleveland starter Reggie Langhorne was a valuable Plan-B signing.

So much depends on the rehabilitation of the offensive line which, in 1991, was ravaged to the extent that the team needed to use 15 players in ten different interior line formations. When healthy, the line could be a powerful unit with Kevin Call and either Irv Pankey or Zefross Moss at tackle, Randy Dixon and Plan-B signing Ron Solt at guard, and former Pro Bowler Ray Donaldson at center. However, the tight end position may be a problem, as youngsters Tim Bruton and Kerry Cash vie with Bob Mrosko for duties which may place the emphasis on blocking.

Given any kind of protection, quarterback Jeff George can direct the offense with great authority. George has unquestioned talent and polish, the latter which has survived through two difficult learning years. He may be ready to light up a few scoreboards.

The Colts did not disguise their intentions in the draft when they selected Steve Emtman, who was the best defensive lineman available, and the ferocious Quentin Coryatt, who joins a group of linebackers which represents the strength of the defense. The Colts intend switching to a four-man defensive line to use the formidable Emtman at tackle, where he will partner one of Travis Davis and Tony Siragusa, with fourth-round draftee Anthony McCoy expected to compete as the season wears on. There is class at defensive end in the shape of former first-round pick Jon Hand but the retirement of Donnell Thompson is a blow. There is just the possibility that he will return, failing which, Sam Clancy and Mel Agee will fill in even though neither is an every-down player.

Those linebackers really are tough, with club-leading tackler Jeff Herrod at the inside spot and Duane Bickett, who came second, to his right. Shortly behind Bickett in the contact list came left inside linebacker Scott Radecic, who had a career-best total of 117 tackles but may lose his starting job. It is not clear just how the Colts will use Coryatt – that will be settled some time in August – but it is by no means certain that former Pro Bowler Chip Banks is ready to step aside at left linebacker. He may even be spurred to his best by the competition.

At defensive back, the club is comfortable without threatening drama and the loss of Keith Taylor has left the unit a little thin. The senior veterans at cornerback are Eugene Daniel and Chris Goode, with Michael Ball and Mike Prior at safety. But second-round draftee Ashley Ambrose comes with a terrific reputation for the big play and must be brought into action.

Rohn Stark, a former Pro Bowler, is now well established as the Colts' punter, but placekicker Dean Biasucci is coming off a sub-par season. However, he has no obvious challenger and the Colts may feel that anyone who can land 14 career field goals of 50 yards or better deserves a little consideration.

*RIGHT: A healthy offensive line could help Jeff
George to put the sparkle back into the Colts'
offense.*

## 1992 SCHEDULE OF GAMES

### September

| | | |
|---|---|---|
| 6 | CLEVELAND | 12:00 |
| 13 | HOUSTON | 3:00 |
| 20 | at Buffalo | 8:00 |
| 27 | Open Date | |

### October

| | | |
|---|---|---|
| 4 | at Tampa Bay | 1:00 |
| 11 | NEW YORK JETS | 3:00 |
| 18 | SAN DIEGO | 12:00 |
| 25 | at Miami | 4:00 |

### November

| | | |
|---|---|---|
| 1 | at San Diego | 1:00 |
| 8 | MIAMI | 1:00 |
| 15 | NEW ENGLAND | 1:00 |
| 22 | at Pittsburgh | 1:00 |
| 29 | BUFFALO | 4:00 |

### December

| | | |
|---|---|---|
| 6 | at New England | 1:00 |
| 13 | at New York Jets | 1:00 |
| 20 | PHOENIX | 1:00 |
| 27 | at Cincinnati | 1:00 |

## 1992 Draft

| Round | Name | Pos. | Ht. | Wt. | College |
|---|---|---|---|---|---|
| 1. | Emtman, Steve | DT | 6-3 | 294 | Washington |
| 1. | Coryatt, Quentin | LB | 6-3 | 237 | Texas A&M |
| 2. | Ambrose, Ashley | CB-KR | 5-10 | 177 | Mississippi Valley State |
| 4. | Culver, Rodney | RB | 5-9 | 221 | Notre Dame |
| 4. | McCoy, Tony | NT | 6-1 | 280 | Florida |
| 5. | Toy, Maury | RB | 6-0 | 231 | UCLA |
| 6. | Habersham, Shoun | WR | 5-10 | 177 | Tennessee-Chattanooga |
| 7. | Steele, Derek | DE | 6-3 | 267 | Maryland |
| 8. | Belser, Jason | S | 5-8 | 182 | Oklahoma |
| 8. | Humphrey, Ronald | RB | 5-10 | 201 | Mississippi Valley State |
| 9. | Miller, Eddie | WR | 5-11 | 185 | South Carolina |
| 10. | Grant, Steve | LB | 6-0 | 225 | West Virginia |
| 12. | Brandon, Mike | DE | 6-4 | 296 | Florida |

## VETERAN ROSTER

| No. | Name | Pos. | Ht. | Wt. | NFL Year | College |
|---|---|---|---|---|---|---|
| 90 | Agee, Mel | DE | 6-5 | 290 | 2 | Illinois |
| 31 | Ball, Michael | S | 6-0 | 220 | 5 | Southern |
| 51 | Banks, Chip | LB | 6-4 | 254 | 10 | Southern California |
| 36 | Baylor, John | CB | 6-0 | 203 | 4 | Southern Mississippi |
| 20 | Bentley, Albert | RB | 5-11 | 217 | 7 | Miami |
| 4 | Biasucci, Dean | K | 6-0 | 190 | 8 | Western Carolina |
| 50 | Bickett, Duane | LB | 6-5 | 251 | 8 | Southern California |
| 80 | Brooks, Bill | WR | 6-0 | 189 | 7 | Boston University |
| | Bruton, Tim | TE | 6-3 | 252 | 1 | Missouri |
| 71 | Call, Kevin | T | 6-7 | 308 | 9 | Colorado State |
| 88 | Cash, Kerry | TE | 6-4 | 247 | 2 | Texas |
| 76 | Clancy, Sam | DE | 6-7 | 300 | 9 | Pittsburgh |
| 32 | Clark, Ken | RB | 5-9 | 204 | 3 | Nebraska |
| 38 | Daniel, Eugene | CB | 5-11 | 188 | 9 | Louisiana State |
| 95 | Davis, Travis | NT | 6-2 | 283 | 3 | Michigan State |
| 69 | Dixon, Randy | G | 6-3 | 302 | 6 | Pittsburgh |
| 53 | Donaldson, Ray | C | 6-3 | 300 | 13 | Georgia |
| 64 | Garalczyk, Mark | DL | 6-6 | 281 | 3 | Western Michigan |
| 11 | George, Jeff | QB | 6-4 | 221 | 3 | Illinois |
| 37 | Goode, Chris | CB | 6-0 | 196 | 6 | Alabama |
| 26 | Grant, Alan | CB | 5-10 | 187 | 3 | Stanford |
| 78 | Hand, Jon | DE | 6-7 | 301 | 7 | Alabama |
| 9 | Herrmann, Mark | QB | 6-4 | 220 | 11 | Purdue |
| 54 | Herrod, Jeff | LB | 6-0 | 246 | 5 | Mississippi |
| 84 | Hester, Jessie | WR | 5-11 | 172 | 7 | Florida State |
| 25 | Holloway, Cornell | CB | 5-11 | 182 | 3 | Pittsburgh |
| 1 | Huffman, Darvell | WR | 5-8 | 158 | 2 | Boston University |
| 23 | Johnson, Anthony | RB | 6-0 | 222 | 3 | Notre Dame |
| 85 | Langhorne, Reggie | WR | 6-2 | 205 | 8 | Elizabeth City State |
| 44 | Manoa, Tim | RB | 6-1 | 245 | 5 | Penn State |
| 86 | Martin, Sammy | WR-KR | 5-11 | 175 | 5 | Louisiana State |
| 63 | Matich, Trevor | C-T-G | 6-4 | 297 | 8 | Brigham Young |
| 42 | McCloughan, Dave | DB | 6-1 | 180 | 2 | Colorado |
| 96 | McDonald, Quintus | LB | 6-3 | 263 | 4 | Penn State |
| 73 | Moss, Zefross | T | 6-6 | 338 | 4 | Alabama State |
| 81 | Mrosko, Bob | TE | 6-5 | 260 | 4 | Penn State |
| 75 | Pankey, Irv | T | 6-5 | 295 | 12 | Penn State |
| 39 | Prior, Mike | S | 6-0 | 210 | 7 | Illinois State |
| 97 | Radecic, Scott | LB | 6-3 | 236 | 9 | Penn State |
| 74 | Schultz, William | T | 6-5 | 305 | 3 | Southern California |
| 65 | Shoulders, Darin | G | 6-3 | 288 | 2 | Tulane |
| 98 | Siragusa, Tony | NT | 6-3 | 303 | 3 | Pittsburgh |
| 66 | Solt, Ron | G | 6-3 | 275 | 8 | Maryland |
| 3 | Stark, Rohn | P | 6-3 | 203 | 11 | Florida State |
| 68 | Tomberlin, Pat | G | 6-2 | 310 | 2 | Florida State |
| 10 | Trudeau, Jack | QB | 6-3 | 219 | 7 | Illinois |
| 7 | Tupa, Tom | QB | 6-4 | 215 | 5 | Ohio State |
| 58 | Vanderbeek, Matt | LB | 6-3 | 258 | 3 | Michigan State |
| 72 | Vander Poel, Mark | T | 6-7 | 303 | 2 | Colorado |
| 83 | Verdin, Clarence | WR-PR | 5-8 | 162 | 7 | Southwestern Louisiana |
| 92 | Walker, Tony | LB | 6-3 | 235 | 3 | Southeast Missouri St. |
| 93 | Zander, Carl | LB | 6-2 | 235 | 8 | Tennessee |

# MIAMI DOLPHINS

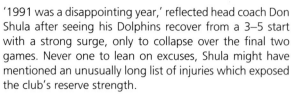

**Address** Joe Robbie Stadium, 2269 N.W. 199th Street, Miami, Florida 33056.

**Stadium** Joe Robbie Stadium, Miami.
*Capacity* 73,000 *Playing Surface* Grass (PAT).

**Team Colours** Aqua, Coral, and White.

**Head Coach** Don Shula – 23rd year; 30th NFL.

**Championships** Division 1971,'72,'73,'74,'79,'81, '83,'84,'85; Conference 1971,'72,'73,'82,'84; Super Bowl 1972,'73.

**History** AFL 1966-69, AFC 1970-

'1991 was a disappointing year,' reflected head coach Don Shula after seeing his Dolphins recover from a 3–5 start with a strong surge, only to collapse over the final two games. Never one to lean on excuses, Shula might have mentioned an unusually long list of injuries which exposed the club's reserve strength.

But he can be optimistic about the 1992 campaign when, as usual, the prime force will be quarterback Dan Marino. It was in just his second pro year that the brash Marino shredded most of the NFL single-season passing records. Operating in offenses which emphasise the passing game, others have begun to chip away at his marks but, with 44 touchdown passes in 1986, only Marino himself has come close to matching his 48 of that phenomenal 1984 campaign. Entering his tenth year, Marino is the team leader around whom everything could happen.

Last year, the offensive line was expected to re-establish traditional Miami authority, but the best-laid plans were disrupted by injuries to young stars Richmond Webb and Keith Sims. Both Jeff Uhlenhake and Harry Galbreath signed late and took time to reach match fitness, leaving right tackle Mark Dennis as the one player to enjoy a trouble-free season. This quintet is expected to resume with the pairing of Webb and Sims regaining its dominance on the left side. Last year, two-time Pro Bowl tight end Ferrell Edmunds was hardly a factor following his late signing and subsequent injuries. Again, a healthy Edmunds could give the offense a major boost.

The 1991 season saw a return to form of the pairing of wide receivers Mark Duper and Mark Clayton, when,

*LEFT: Pro Bowl linebacker John Offerdahl.*

| 1992 SCHEDULE OF GAMES | September | |
|---|---|---|
| | 6 NEW ENGLAND | 4:00 |
| | 14 at Cleveland (Mon.) | 9:00 |
| | 20 LOS ANGELES RAMS | 4:00 |
| | 27 at Seattle | 1:00 |
| | October | |
| | 4 at Buffalo | 1:00 |
| | 11 ATLANTA | 1:00 |
| | 18 Open Date | |
| | 25 INDIANAPOLIS | 4:00 |
| | November | |
| | 1 at New York Jets | 1:00 |
| | 8 at Indianapolis | 1:00 |
| | 16 BUFFALO (Mon.) | 9:00 |
| | 22 HOUSTON | 1:00 |
| | 29 at New Orleans | 12:00 |
| | December | |
| | 6 at San Francisco | 1:00 |
| | 14 LOS ANGELES RAIDERS (Mon.) | 9:00 |
| | 20 NEW YORK JETS | 8:00 |
| | 27 at New England | 1:00 |

for the third time as a partnership, Clayton and Duper each gained over 1,000 yards pass receiving. They offer every prospect of continuing at top pace, ahead of the exciting Tony Martin. Former Detroit starter Robert Clark, who was signed as a Plan-B free agent, is a reliable backup.

One key ingredient missing from Shula's teams for well over a decade has been consistent power at running back. Not since Delvin Williams in 1978 has there been a 1,000-yard rusher. First-round draftee from 1989, Sammie Smith, was expected to solve the problem but could not elevate his game. Mark Higgs, a 1990 Plan-B signing from Philadelphia, had emerged as the potential spearhead, but he seems certain to step aside for Bobby Humphrey, who came to Miami from Denver in a straight swap for Smith. Humphrey rushed for over 1,000 yards in each of 1989 and 1990 but was barely a factor last year following a contractual dispute. For Miami, he could be a godsend.

The defense, too, did not escape its injury problems, with right inside linebacker John Offerdahl and strong safety Jarvis Williams missing a total of 15 games. John Grimsley, who was expected to stiffen the defense at left inside linebacker after being acquired in a preseason trade with Houston, missed the entire year with a severe knee injury. Without doubt the returning veteran will help enormously, with Cliff Odom in the shuffle for an inside position. Also, the club expects much from the draft, which brought both cornerback Troy Vincent and blitzing outside linebacker Marco Coleman in round one, defensive tackle Eddie Blake in the second round and defensive end Larry Webster in the third.

Coleman could be a major factor, either as a starter or in the rôle of extra pass rusher, in a group which lacked penetration. Last year, T.J. Turner and Alfred Oglesby were alternated at defensive end and nose tackle, but Turner will open the season on the left side with Oglesby starting out at nose tackle, though pressed by Chuck Klingbeil, Blake and Shawn Lee. Jeff Cross secures the right side. At outside linebacker, Coleman will press the fiery Bryan Cox and David Griggs.

The secondary is strong in the middle, with the hard-tackling Louis Oliver at free safety and Williams

regaining his spot from Bobby Harden. Vincent appears likely to start immediately, probably displacing left corner-back Vestee Jackson, with J.B. Brown appearing to be more secure on the right side.

Miami can expect continued quality in its kicking game, with Reggie Roby having recovered from his Achilles tendon problems and placekicker Pete Stoyanovich coming off a season in which he set a club record with 121 points.

## 1992 Draft

| Round | Name | Pos. | Ht. | Wt. | College |
|---|---|---|---|---|---|
| 1. | Vincent, Troy | CB-PR | 6-0 | 191 | Wisconsin |
| 1. | Coleman, Marco | LB | 6-2 | 259 | Georgia Tech |
| 2. | Blake, Eddie | DT-G | 6-3 | 321 | Auburn |
| 3. | Webster, Larry | DT | 6-5 | 285 | Maryland |
| 4. | Hollier, Dwight | LB | 6-2 | 242 | North Carolina |
| 5. | Perez, Christopher | T | 6-5 | 285 | Kansas |
| 6. | Collins, Roosevelt | LB | 6-3 | 235 | Texas Christian |
| 7. | Moore, Dave | TE | 6-2 | 242 | Pittsburgh |
| 8. | Powell, Andre | LB | 6-2 | 242 | Penn State |
| 9. | Tellington, Tony | DB | 5-11 | 191 | Youngstown State |
| 10. | Spears, Raoul | RB | 6-1 | 234 | Southern California |
| 11. | Miles, Lee | WR | 5-6 | 156 | Baylor |
| 11. | Barsotti, Mark | QB | 6-1 | 205 | Fresno State |
| 12. | Biggins, Milton | TE | 6-0 | 269 | Western Kentucky |
| 12. | Bell, Kameno | RB | 5-11 | 225 | Illinois |

## VETERAN ROSTER

| No. | Name | Pos. | Ht. | Wt. | NFL Year | College |
|---|---|---|---|---|---|---|
| 40 | Alexander, Bruce | CB | 5-9 | 169 | 3 | Stephen F. Austin |
| 86 | Banks, Fred | WR | 5-10 | 185 | 7 | Liberty |
| 84 | Baty, Greg | TE | 6-5 | 240 | 5 | Stanford |
| 53 | Bolcar, Ned | LB | 6-1 | 235 | 3 | Notre Dame |
| 37 | Brown, J.B. | CB | 6-0 | 192 | 4 | Maryland |
| 81 | Clark, Robert | WR | 5-11 | 173 | 5 | North Carolina Central |
| 83 | Clayton, Mark | WR | 5-9 | 185 | 10 | Louisville |
| 50 | Cooper, Louis | LB | 6-2 | 238 | 8 | Western Carolina |
| 51 | Cox, Bryan | LB | 6-3 | 235 | 2 | Western Illinois |
| 34 | Craver, Aaron | RB | 5-11 | 215 | 2 | Fresno State |
| 91 | Cross, Jeff | DE | 6-4 | 272 | 5 | Missouri |
| 65 | Dellenbach, Jeff | T-C | 6-6 | 285 | 8 | Wisconsin |
| 74 | Dennis, Mark | T | 6-6 | 295 | 6 | Illinois |
| 75 | Downing, Tim | DE | 6-5 | 260 | 1 | Washington State |
| 85 | Duper, Mark | WR | 5-9 | 192 | 11 | Northwestern State, La. |
| 80 | Edmunds, Ferrell | TE | 6-6 | 254 | 5 | Maryland |
| 62 | Galbreath, Harry | G | 6-1 | 275 | 5 | Tennessee |
| 35 | Glenn, Kerry | CB | 5-9 | 178 | 6 | Minnesota |
| 42 | Green, Chris | CB | 5-11 | 188 | 2 | Illinois |
| 92 | Griggs, David | LB | 6-3 | 248 | 4 | Virginia |
| 59 | Grimsley, John | LB | 6-2 | 238 | 8 | Kentucky |
| 45 | Harden, Bobby | S | 6-0 | 192 | 2 | Miami |
| 21 | Higgs, Mark | RB-KR | 5-7 | 195 | 5 | Kentucky |
| 29 | Hobley, Liffort | S | 6-0 | 202 | 6 | Louisiana State |
|  | Humphrey, Bobby | RB | 6-1 | 201 | 4 | Alabama |
| 48 | Iaquaniello, Mike | S | 6-3 | 208 | 2 | Michigan State |
| 24 | Jackson, Vestee | CB | 6-0 | 186 | 7 | Washington |
| 11 | Jensen, Jim | WR-RB | 6-4 | 224 | 12 | Boston University |
| 90 | Jones, Brian | LB | 6-1 | 240 | 2 | Texas |
| 54 | Junior, E.J. | LB | 6-3 | 242 | 12 | Alabama |
| 99 | Klingbeil, Chuck | NT | 6-1 | 260 | 2 | Northern Michigan |
| 98 | Lee, Shawn | NT | 6-2 | 285 | 5 | North Alabama |
| 13 | Marino, Dan | QB | 6-4 | 224 | 10 | Pittsburgh |
| 89 | Martin, Tony | WR | 6-0 | 180 | 3 | Mesa, Colorado |
| 28 | McGruder, Michael | CB | 5-11 | 190 | 2 | Kent State |
| 82 | Miller, Scott | WR | 5-10 | 179 | 2 | UCLA |
| 19 | Mitchell, Scott | QB | 6-6 | 230 | 1 | Utah |
| 77 | Nichols, Gerald | NT | 6-2 | 260 | 6 | Florida State |
| 93 | Odom, Cliff | LB | 6-2 | 243 | 12 | Texas-Arlington |
| 56 | Offerdahl, John | LB | 6-3 | 238 | 7 | Western Michigan |
| 96 | Oglesby, Alfred | DE-NT | 6-3 | 278 | 3 | Houston |
| 25 | Oliver, Louis | S | 6-2 | 226 | 4 | Florida |
| 49 | Paige, Tony | RB | 5-10 | 235 | 9 | Virginia Tech |
| 23 | Ray, Pat | CB | 5-10 | 180 | 1 | Missouri |
| 4 | Roby, Reggie | P | 6-2 | 246 | 10 | Iowa |
| 22 | Saxon, James | RB | 5-11 | 234 | 4 | San Jose State |
| 9 | Secules, Scott | QB | 6-3 | 220 | 5 | Virginia |
| 69 | Sims, Keith | G | 6-2 | 305 | 3 | Iowa State |
| 30 | Smith, Don | RB | 5-11 | 200 | 4 | Mississippi State |
| 10 | Stoyanovich, Pete | K | 5-10 | 185 | 4 | Indiana |
| 67 | Swoopes, Pat | NT | 6-3 | 277 | 4 | Mississippi State |
| 95 | Turner, T.J. | DE | 6-4 | 280 | 7 | Houston |
| 63 | Uhlenhake, Jeff | C | 6-3 | 284 | 4 | Ohio State |
| 78 | Webb, Richmond | T | 6-6 | 298 | 3 | Texas A&M |
| 60 | Weidner, Bert | C | 6-3 | 284 | 3 | Kent State |
| 61 | Williams, Gene | G | 6-2 | 308 | 2 | Iowa State |
| 26 | Williams, Jarvis | S | 5-11 | 200 | 5 | Florida |
| 87 | Williams, Mike | WR | 5-10 | 177 | 2 | Northeastern |

# NEW ENGLAND PATRIOTS

**Address** Foxboro Stadium, Route 1, Foxboro,
Mass. 02035.
**Stadium** Foxboro Stadium, Foxboro.
*Capacity* 60,794 *Playing Surface* Grass.
**Team Colours** Red, White, and Blue.
**Head Coach** Dick MacPherson — 2nd year.
**Championships** Division 1978, '86; Conference 1985.
**History** AFL 1960-69, AFC 1970-
(Until 1971, they were known as the Boston Patriots.)

*A re-enthused Irving Fryar is coming off a banner campaign in 1991.*

Without question, the inspirational leadership of new head coach Dick MacPherson was the key factor in the beginnings of a comeback which saw the Patriots improve from 1–15 in 1990 to 6–10.

One of his changes saw the installation of Hugh Millen in place of Tom Hodson at quarterback, and he responded with exciting wins over Houston, Minnesota, Buffalo and the Colts. Millen still has much progress to make but this young man, who surprisingly was discarded by the Rams and saw little action with Atlanta, may turn out to be a winner.

In 1991, MacPherson used his premier option to draft right tackle Pat Harlow, who was in for all 977 offensive snaps and gives the line a player with the potential to match the dominance of Pro Bowl left tackle Bruce Armstrong. The strength is enhanced further by the arrival of top draftee Eugene Chung, who will start at left guard if Harlow's return from offseason back surgery is not delayed. Elsewhere, Calvin Stephens will battle with former Cleveland, San Diego and New Orleans starter Larry Williams for the right guard position with Gene Chilton continuing at center. The line enjoyed blocking for 1991 rookie running back Leonard Russell, who exceeded all expectations as he rushed for 959 yards and earned All-Rookie honours. Jon Vaughn was another pleasant surprise, bringing great speed both to the offensive backfield and as a kickoff returner. Disappointingly, however, John Stephens was still unable to rediscover the penetration of his 1988 rookie season.

MacPherson's influence was felt no greater than at wide receiver, where Irving Fryar, who was the first pick overall in the 1984 draft, went over the 1,000-yard mark for the first time in his eight years with the club. The Patriots hope that Hart Lee Dykes, who, like Fryar, was a first-round pick, can return from injury but, in his year-long absence, Greg McMurtry used his opportunities to show every sign of developing into a top-class performer. Michael Timpson offers the option of burning speed.

Not since Russ Francis at his best in the late 1970s has New England had a tight end of all-league stature. However, while Marv Cook is not yet the complete tight end that Francis was, he is far more prolific and is coming off a year in which he led all NFL tight ends and the Patriots with 82 catches.

A defensive ranking of 26th does not do justice to a competitive group which throws down a solid challenge with its three-man front. Nose tackle Tim Goad bears the initial brunt, with Brent Williams at defensive right end

**1992 Draft**

| Round | Name | Pos. | Ht. | Wt. | College |
|---|---|---|---|---|---|
| 1. | Chung, Eugene | T | 6-4 | 295 | Virginia Tech |
| 2. | Smith, Rod | CB | 5-11 | 187 | Notre Dame |
| 3. | Collins, Todd | LB | 6-2 | 242 | Carson-Newman |
| 3. | Turner, Kevin | RB | 6-0 | 224 | Alabama |
| 4. | Lambert, Dion | CB | 6-0 | 185 | UCLA |
| 4. | Anderson, Darren | CB | 5-10 | 180 | Toledo |
| 5. | Sabb, Dwayne | LB | 6-4 | 248 | New Hampshire |
| 6. | Boyd, Tracy | G | 6-4 | 296 | Elizabeth City State |
| 7. | Hawkins, Wayne | WR | 5-10 | 186 | Southwest State, Minn. |
| 7. | Gray, Jim | NT | 6-2 | 285 | West Virginia |
| 8. | Lockwood, Scott | RB | 5-10 | 200 | Southern California |
| 8. | Gash, Sam | RB | 5-11 | 224 | Penn State |
| 9. | Dixon, David | NT | 6-5 | 348 | Arizona State |
| 10. | Baur, Turner | TE | 6-4 | 247 | Stanford |
| 10. | Gordon, Steve | C | 6-3 | 279 | California |
| 11. | Petko, Mike | LB | 6-2 | 232 | Nebraska |
| 12. | Baysinger, Freeman | WR | 5-9 | 179 | Humboldt State |

**VETERAN ROSTER**

| No. | Name | Pos. | Ht. | Wt. | NFL Year | College |
|---|---|---|---|---|---|---|
| 92 | Agnew, Ray | DE | 6-3 | 272 | 3 | North Carolina State |
| 39 | Allen, Marvin | RB | 5-10 | 208 | 5 | Tulane |
| 78 | Armstrong, Bruce | T | 6-4 | 284 | 6 | Louisville |
| 8 | Baumann, Charlie | K | 6-1 | 203 | 2 | West Virginia |
| | Bowles, Scott | T | 6-5 | 280 | 1 | North Texas State |
| 59 | Brown, Vincent | LB | 6-2 | 245 | 5 | Mississippi Valley State |
| 63 | Chilton, Gene | C | 6-3 | 286 | 5 | Texas |
| | Clark, Reggie | LB | 6-2 | 226 | 1 | North Carolina |
| 87 | Coates, Ben | TE | 6-4 | 245 | 2 | Livingstone |
| 85 | Cook, Marv | TE | 6-4 | 234 | 4 | Iowa |
| 88 | Dykes, Hart Lee | WR | 6-4 | 218 | 3 | Oklahoma State |
| 80 | Fryar, Irving | WR | 6-0 | 200 | 9 | Nebraska |
| 91 | Gannon, Chris | DE | 6-6 | 260 | 4 | Southwestern Louisiana |
| 72 | Goad, Tim | NT | 6-3 | 280 | 5 | North Carolina |
| 41 | Gordon, Tim | S | 6-0 | 188 | 6 | Tulsa |
| 77 | Harlow, Pat | T | 6-6 | 290 | 2 | Southern California |
| 36 | Henderson, Jerome | CB | 5-10 | 189 | 2 | Clemson |
| 60 | Hobby, Marion | DE | 6-4 | 277 | 3 | Tennessee |
| 13 | Hodson, Tom | QB | 6-3 | 195 | 3 | Louisiana State |
| 99 | Howard, David | LB | 6-1 | 230 | 8 | Long Beach State |
| 45 | Hunter, Ivy Joe | RB | 6-1 | 248 | 4 | Kentucky |
| 37 | Hurst, Maurice | CB | 5-10 | 185 | 4 | Southern |
| 50 | Jarostchuk, Ilia | LB | 6-3 | 245 | 5 | New Hampshire |
| | Johnson, Alex | WR | 5-9 | 167 | 2 | Miami |
| 26 | Key, David | CB | 5-10 | 198 | 2 | Michigan |
| 51 | Lockhart, Eugene | LB | 6-2 | 233 | 9 | Houston |
| 11 | McCarthy, Shawn | P | 6-6 | 227 | 2 | Purdue |
| | McGovern, Rob | LB | 6-2 | 223 | 4 | Holy Cross |
| 86 | McMurtry, Greg | WR | 6-2 | 207 | 3 | Michigan |
| 7 | Millen, Hugh | QB | 6-5 | 216 | 5 | Washington |
| 10 | Murphy, Mike | WR | 5-9 | 163 | 1 | Southwest Texas State |
| 27 | Pool, David | CB | 5-9 | 182 | 3 | Carson-Newman |
| 71 | Rakoczy, Gregg | C-G | 6-5 | 280 | 6 | Miami |
| | Redding, Reggie | T | 6-3 | 290 | 2 | Cal State-Fullerton |
| 52 | Rembert, Johnny | LB | 6-3 | 234 | 10 | Clemson |
| | Robbins, Randy | S | 6-2 | 189 | 9 | Arizona |
| 32 | Russell, Leonard | RB | 6-2 | 235 | 2 | Arizona State |
| 55 | Singleton, Chris | LB | 6-2 | 247 | 3 | Arizona |
| 66 | Smerlas, Fred | NT | 6-4 | 291 | 14 | Boston College |
| 68 | Stephens, Calvin | G | 6-2 | 285 | 1 | South Carolina |
| 44 | Stephens, John | RB | 6-1 | 215 | 5 | Northwestern State, La. |
| 53 | Tardits, Richard | LB | 6-2 | 235 | 2 | Georgia |
| 83 | Timpson, Michael | WR | 5-10 | 175 | 3 | Penn State |
| 56 | Tippett, Andre | LB | 6-3 | 241 | 10 | Iowa |
| 24 | Vaughn, Jon | RB | 5-9 | 203 | 2 | Michigan |
| 90 | Veris, Garin | DE | 6-4 | 255 | 7 | Stanford |
| 21 | Washington, M. | CB | 5-9 | 187 | 3 | Texas A&M |
| 96 | Williams, Brent | DE | 6-4 | 275 | 7 | Toledo |
| | Williams, Larry | G | 6-5 | 294 | 5 | Notre Dame |
| 16 | Zolak, Scott | QB | 6-5 | 222 | 2 | Maryland |

and Garin Veris sharing the left end position with 1990 first-round pick Ray Agnew. A broken hand early in the season meant that Agnew started slowly and he did not progress as anticipated. However, there was a great performance from Vincent Brown, who earned club MVP honours starting at right inside linebacker. Brown is partnered on the inside by former Cowboys favourite Eugene (Hitting Machine) Lockhart. Though never likely to regain his best of the mid-1980s, when he had 35 sacks in a two-year period, former All-Pro outside linebacker Andre Tippett made further progress following an injury which forced him to miss the entire 1989 campaign. For Tippett, 8.5 sacks is small change but it was good enough to lead the team and he will be striving even more in 1992. At right outside linebacker, 1990 first-round pick Chris Singleton starts and, although taking more time than the Patriots would like, he is making good steady progress.

The Patriots could not afford the loss of three starters from a defensive secondary which now has to be considered the weakest of the three units. Only right corner-back Maurice Hurst, who led the team with three interceptions, remains. It means that high draftee Rodney Smith will have to start on the left side with Tim Gordon assuming seniority at free safety and former Denver backup Randy Robbins at strong safety. If the plans do not work out, New England must hope for early contributions from draftees Dion Lambert and Darren Anderson.

Charlie Baumann, who arrived off waivers in November, should continue as the placekicker. He missed a couple of easy field goals but was successful on all five in the range 40-49 yards. Punter Shawn McCarthy is nothing special but, entering camp, he has no obvious competition.

# NEW YORK JETS

**Address** 1000 Fulton Avenue, Hempstead, New York 11550.

**Stadium** Giants Stadium, East Rutherford, N.J. *Capacity* 76,891 *Playing Surface* AstroTurf.

**Team Colours** Kelly Green and White.

**Head Coach** Bruce Coslet – 3rd year.

**Championships** AFL 1968; Super Bowl 1968.

**History** AFL 1960-69, AFC 1970-

(Until 1963, they were known as the New York Titans.)

Benefiting enormously from both minimal injuries and a level of stability which saw only one permanent change from the opening-day starting lineups, the Jets fought their way into the playoffs as a wild card. And the signs are that they will be more competitive in 1992.

While reflecting on his good fortune, head coach Bruce Coslet openly declares the need for impact players and he may have found one in first-round draftee Johnny Mitchell, a pass receiving tight end who has been compared to the prolific Keith Jackson of Philadelphia. And Mitchell must help out in an area which has been bolstered by Plan-B signing Pat Beach. Otherwise, there is no obvious need for personnel changes, beginning with an offensive line which now has top quality even amongst the reserves. At center, Jim Sweeney ranks alongside the league's best while right guard Dwayne White confirmed the 1990 form which saw him develop to the extent that former first-round pick Dave Cadigan is left to battle with Mike Haight for the other guard position. Two solid tackles, Irv Eatman and Jeff Criswell, complete the lineup.

At quarterback, Ken O'Brien has few, if any, weaknesses. He's not likely to murder the opposition but he showed his consistency by becoming the first in club history to pass for over 3,000 yards in four seasons. For the reserve position, Troy Taylor battles Browning Nagle. Reliability is the keynote also at wide receiver, and it is only the Jets' conservative use of starters Al Toon and Rob Moore which limits their averages to around 14 yards per catch. Last year, Toon had 74 receptions to lead the club, ahead of Moore's 70. Playing with great exuberance and sparkle, backups Terance Mathis and Chris Burkett fit into the system well in addition to starring on special teams. Here, Mathis returns

both kickoffs and punts while Burkett, unusually, ranked second in tackles behind a defensive player, Erik McMillan, impressing his teammates who voted him the club's MVP.

If there is a relative need, it may be for explosiveness at running back. There is no questioning the commitment of starters Blair Thomas and Brad Baxter, while backups Freeman McNeil and Johnny Hector are first class. Indeed, McNeil is a former first-round draftee who has been selected to three Pro Bowls. But Thomas has not yet come through as a major running back and, for that reason, he has to be considered a current disappointment.

Defensively, the Jets have firmed up as, among others, Jeff Lageman started to produce in his second year following the conversion from outside linebacker to defensive right end. He led the team with ten sacks, ahead of starting right tackle Dennis Byrd and defensive left end Marvin Washington. Scott Mersereau is solid at left defensive tackle. The package allows little opportunity for backups Bill Pickel, Paul Frase and Mark Gunn to show their paces. At left linebacker, Mo Lewis was a revelation, earning selection to most All-Rookie teams while Kyle Clifton and Joe Kelly have given away little over the years. However, in the search for impact players, the Jets picked linebackers with three of their first six options in the 1992 draft.

It was in the secondary that the one new starter, Mike Brim, emerged. Brim displaced Tony Stargell at left cornerback and led the team with four interceptions. At free safety, Lonnie Young stayed ahead of the enigmatic Erik McMillan, who nonetheless was an important part of the Dime defense and underlined his value on special teams. Primed for action at strong safety, Brian Washington cemented his authority with 107 tackles to rank second in

| 1992 SCHEDULE OF GAMES | September | |
|---|---|---|
| | 6 at Atlanta | 1:00 |
| | 13 at Pittsburgh | 4:00 |
| | 20 SAN FRANCISCO | 1:00 |
| | 27 at Los Angeles Rams | 1:00 |
| | October | |
| | 4 NEW ENGLAND | 8:00 |
| | 11 at Indianapolis | 3:00 |
| | 18 Open Date | |
| | 26 BUFFALO (Mon.) | 9:00 |
| | November | |
| | 1 MIAMI | 1:00 |
| | 8 at Denver | 2:00 |
| | 15 CINCINNATI | 1:00 |
| | 22 at New England | 4:00 |
| | 29 KANSAS CITY | 1:00 |
| | December | |
| | 6 at Buffalo | 1:00 |
| | 13 INDIANAPOLIS | 1:00 |
| | 20 at Miami | 8:00 |
| | 26 NEW ORLEANS (Sat.) | 12:30 |

*1992 is a season of decision for Blair Thomas.*

### 1992 Draft

| Round | Name | Pos. | Ht. | Wt. | College |
|---|---|---|---|---|---|
| 1. | Mitchell, Johnny | TE | 6-2 | 258 | Nebraska |
| 2. | Barber, Kurt | LB | 6-3 | 243 | Southern California |
| 3. | Malamala, Siupeli | T | 6-5 | 313 | Washington |
| 4. | Coleman, Keo | LB | 6-0 | 252 | Mississippi State |
| 5. | Dixon, Cal | C | 6-3 | 276 | Florida |
| 6. | Cadrez, Glenn | LB | 6-2 | 238 | Houston |
| 6. | Blake, Jeff | QB | 5-11 | 202 | East Carolina |
| 8. | Brownlee, Vincent | WR | 5-11 | 195 | Mississippi |
| 10. | Johnson, Mario | DT | 6-3 | 300 | Missouri |
| 11. | Boles, Eric | WR | 6-3 | 204 | Central Washington |

### VETERAN ROSTER

| No. | Name | Pos. | Ht. | Wt. | NFL Year | College |
|---|---|---|---|---|---|---|
| 4 | Aguiar, Louie | P | 6-2 | 200 | 2 | Utah State |
| 2 | Allegre, Raul | K | 5-10 | 167 | 9 | Texas |
| 30 | Baxter, Brad | RB | 6-1 | 235 | 3 | Alabama State |
|  | Beach, Pat | TE | 6-4 | 249 | 10 | Washington State |
| 80 | Boyer, Mark | TE | 6-4 | 242 | 8 | Southern California |
| 43 | Brim, Michael | CB | 6-0 | 192 | 5 | Virginia Union |
| 29 | Brown, A.B. | RB | 5-9 | 215 | 3 | West Virginia |
| 87 | Burkett, Chris | WR | 6-4 | 200 | 8 | Jackson State |
| 90 | Byrd, Dennis | DT | 6-5 | 266 | 4 | Tulsa |
| 66 | Cadigan, Dave | G | 6-4 | 285 | 5 | Southern California |
|  | Carpenter, Rob | WR | 6-2 | 215 | 2 | Syracuse |
|  | Chaffey, Pat | RB | 6-1 | 218 | 2 | Oregon State |
| 59 | Clifton, Kyle | LB | 6-4 | 236 | 9 | Texas Christian |
| 69 | Criswell, Jeff | T | 6-7 | 291 | 6 | Graceland |
| 89 | Dawkins, Dale | WR | 6-1 | 190 | 3 | Miami |
| 84 | Dressel, Chris | TE | 6-4 | 239 | 9 | Stanford |
| 62 | Duffy, Roger | C | 6-3 | 285 | 3 | Penn State |
| 75 | Eatman, Irv | T | 6-7 | 298 | 7 | UCLA |
| 44 | Egu, Patrick | RB | 5-11 | 206 | 2 | Nevada-Reno |
|  | Fishback, Joe | S | 5-11 | 198 | 2 | Carson-Newman |
| 91 | Frase, Paul | DE-DT | 6-5 | 270 | 4 | Syracuse |
|  | Gardner, Donnie | DE | 6-3 | 260 | 2 | Kentucky |
| 76 | Goetz, Chris | G | 6-2 | 272 | 1 | Pittsburgh |
| 96 | Gunn, Mark | DE | 6-5 | 292 | 2 | Pittsburgh |
| 79 | Haight, Mike | G-T | 6-4 | 291 | 7 | Iowa |
|  | Hart, Roy | DT | 6-0 | 285 | 3 | South Carolina |
| 40 | Hasty, James | CB | 6-0 | 201 | 5 | Washington State |
| 34 | Hector, Johnny | RB | 5-11 | 214 | 10 | Texas A&M |
| 55 | Houston, Bobby | LB | 6-2 | 235 | 2 | North Carolina State |
| 95 | Johnson, Troy | LB | 6-2 | 236 | 5 | Oklahoma |
| 58 | Kelly, Joe | LB | 6-2 | 235 | 7 | Washington |
| 82 | Kelly, Pat | TE | 6-6 | 252 | 4 | Syracuse |
| 25 | Kors, R.J. | S | 6-0 | 195 | 2 | Cal State-Long Beach |
| 56 | Lageman, Jeff | DE | 6-5 | 266 | 4 | Virginia |
| 5 | Leahy, Pat | K | 6-0 | 200 | 19 | St Louis |
| 57 | Lewis, Mo | LB | 6-3 | 240 | 2 | Georgia |
| 81 | Mathis, Terance | WR-KR | 5-10 | 170 | 3 | New Mexico |
| 22 | McMillan, Erik | S | 6-2 | 200 | 5 | Missouri |
| 24 | McNeil, Freeman | RB | 5-11 | 208 | 12 | UCLA |
| 94 | Mersereau, Scott | DT | 6-3 | 275 | 6 | Southern Connecticut |
| 72 | Miller, Brett | T | 6-7 | 286 | 10 | Iowa |
| 85 | Moore, Rob | WR | 6-3 | 205 | 3 | Syracuse |
| 51 | Mott, Joe | LB | 6-4 | 234 | 3 | Iowa |
| 8 | Nagle, Browning | QB | 6-3 | 225 | 2 | Louisville |
| 7 | O'Brien, Ken | QB | 6-4 | 212 | 10 | Cal-Davis |
| 21 | Odegard, Don Boyd | CB | 6-0 | 180 | 3 | Nevada-Las Vegas |
| 71 | Pickel, Bill | DT | 6-5 | 265 | 10 | Rutgers |
| 20 | Price, Dennis | CB | 6-1 | 175 | 3 | UCLA |
| 45 | Stargell, Tony | CB | 5-11 | 180 | 3 | Tennessee State |
|  | Staurovsky, Jason | K | 5-9 | 170 | 5 | Tulsa |
| 53 | Sweeney, Jim | C | 6-4 | 286 | 9 | Pittsburgh |
| 11 | Taylor, Troy | QB | 6-4 | 200 | 3 | California |
| 32 | Thomas, Blair | RB | 5-10 | 195 | 3 | Penn State |
| 88 | Toon, Al | WR | 6-4 | 205 | 8 | Wisconsin |
|  | Turner, Marcus | DB | 6-0 | 190 | 4 | UCLA |
| 48 | Washington, Brian | S | 6-1 | 212 | 4 | Nebraska |
| 97 | Washington, Marvin | DE-DT | 6-6 | 272 | 4 | Idaho |
| 86 | Whisenhunt, Ken | TE | 6-3 | 240 | 6 | Georgia Tech |
| 67 | White, Dwayne | G | 6-2 | 305 | 3 | Alcorn State |
| 31 | Young, Lonnie | S | 6-1 | 192 | 8 | Michigan State |

the club behind Clifton's 146. Completing the quartet, right cornerback James Hasty could have received no better compliment than that offered by Buffalo wide receiver James Lofton, who said, 'Hasty may be the best cover guy in the NFL. He silenced Andre Reed.' Reed added his respect when he admitted, 'I voted for him for the Pro Bowl. He's one of the best four or five in the league. It's a shame no one knows it.'

There could be a change at placekicker, equivalent to knocking down the Statue of Liberty, with either Raul Allegre or Plan-B signing Jason Staurovsky likely to displace 18-year veteran Pat Leahy. Punter Louie Aguiar could use a few extra yards but he is valued for his deep kickoffs.

# CINCINNATI BENGALS

**Address** 200 Riverfront Stadium, Cincinnati, Ohio 45202.

**Stadium** Riverfront Stadium, Cincinnati.
 *Capacity* 60,389 *Playing Surface* AstroTurf-8.

**Team Colours** Black, Orange, and White.

**Head Coach** David Shula – 1st year.

**Championships** Division 1970,'73,'81,'88,'90; Conference 1981,'88.

**History** AFL 1968-69, AFC 1970-

The late Paul Brown used to say, 'If a championship quarterback is there, get him whatever the needs elsewhere.' New head coach David Shula perhaps had this in mind when he picked David Klingler with the first of his two options in round one. Klingler has every talent you'd need and is lucky that, with Boomer Esiason still the unquestioned starter, he'll be given time to settle in. Esiason is coming off two modest campaigns after having led the AFC in 1989. If the Bengals are to make strides, the eight-year veteran simply must offer the kind of service which saw wide receiver Eddie Brown catch 53 passes for 1,273 yards and nine touchdowns (1988) and the other starter, Tim McGee, excel with 65 receptions for 1,211 yards and eight touchdowns (1989). The starting partnership should continue but Reggie Rembert, who saw limited action in his first season of availability, and second-round draftee Carl Pickens, may offer a degree of variety which keeps opponents guessing. Those same opponents will know that they have to make plans for tight end Rodney Holman, who has been a classy receiver for several years and it is this level of play which has kept Eric Kattus in a backup rôle.

The Bengals have no real worries over an offensive line which has been anchored for twelve seasons by eleven-time Pro Bowler and perennial All-Pro left tackle Anthony Munoz. Joe Walter is a very sound right tackle and there is dependability in right guard Ken Moyer. The loss of normal starting left guard Bruce Reimers means that former center Bruce Kozerski will remain at left guard, where he subbed for the injured Reimers in the latter part of the 1991 campaign, with Mike Arthur being given a full term at center. The Bengals were hoping to bring Arthur, a 1991 fifth-round draftee, along slowly. But he showed exceptional

maturity when called into emergency action in early December.

There are great hopes at running back, where the rapid development of Harold Green has in part compensated for the anticipated release of the injured Ickey Woods, though, with the latter in mind, it was surprising that the Bengals allowed James Brooks to depart as a free agent. In nine starts, Green thrashed for 731 yards at a fine average of 4.6 per carry. He will be supported by Eric Ball, who hopes to return from injury, and former Seattle heavyweight Derrick Fenner, who pounded for 859 yards at an average of four yards per carry in 1990 but was used only sparingly last year.

New defensive coordinator Ron Lynn loves to emphasize the pass rush, and he may just find a way of springing James

*A young head coach will look to Anthony Munoz for on-the-field leadership to set Cincinnati on the road back.*

Francis and Alfred Williams. First-round picks in 1990 and 1991 respectively, they are outside linebackers of immense potential. The defensive line has the tough, penetrative Tim Krumrie at nose tackle, with Alonzo Mitz and David Grant probably continuing in the end positions. However, with sacks in mind, Lynn will want to bring in Danny Stubbs and the largely untried Lamar Rogers to rush the passer as much as possible. For the second line of defense against the run, Cincinnati has Leo Barker and Kevin Walker, the latter who is favoured over former Bills starter Ray Bentley to replace the departed Carl Zander. Just behind these two and waiting to pounce is one of the league's most telling hitters in David Fulcher, a strong safety with a linebacker's mentality. The feeling among the scouts is that Fulcher slipped a little after three straight Pro Bowl selections but he still led the team in tackles (95), interceptions (4) and fumbles recovered (4), tying for first place in fumbles forced (3). If first-round draftee Darryl Williams is able to start at free safety immediately, it will release Rickey Dixon to compete with Wayne Haddix for the spot at left cornerback. In addition, former Tampa Bay first-round pick Rod Jones could be a factor if he can recover from an arm injury. Right corner-back Eric Thomas is excellent and under no challenge for his place.

There are few more valuable placekickers in the league than Jim Breech, who is entering his 14th NFL campaign. Punter Lee Johnson has just had his best year, ranking sixth in the NFL for gross average, and brings the added value of being able to drive kickoffs into the end zone. Reserve cornerback Mitchell Price subsidized his earnings by returning punts and ripped off the AFC's longest with a 78-yarder for a touchdown.

## 1992 Draft

| Round | Name | Pos. | Ht. | Wt. | College |
|---|---|---|---|---|---|
| 1. | Klingler, David | QB | 6-2 | 205 | Houston |
| 1. | Williams, Darryl | S | 6-0 | 191 | Miami |
| 2. | Pickens, Carl | WR | 6-2 | 206 | Tennessee |
| 3. | Wheeler, Leonard | CB | 5-11 | 189 | Troy State |
| 4. | McDonald, Ricardo | LB | 6-1 | 230 | Pittsburgh |
| 5. | Thompson, Craig | TE | 6-2 | 245 | North Carolina A&T |
| 6. | Burns, Chris | DT | 6-4 | 281 | Middle Tennessee State |
| 7. | Olberding, Lance | T | 6-6 | 300 | Iowa |
| 8. | Nix, Roosevelt | DE | 6-6 | 305 | Central State, Ohio |
| 9. | Miles, Ostell | RB | 5-11 | 236 | Houston |
| 10. | Smith, Horace | DB | 5-10 | 183 | Oregon Tech |
| 11. | Earle, John | T | 6-5 | 290 | Western Illinois |
| 12. | Shaw, Eric | LB | 6-3 | 236 | Louisiana Tech |

## VETERAN ROSTER

| No. | Name | Pos. | Ht. | Wt. | NFL Year | College |
|---|---|---|---|---|---|---|
| 65 | Arthur, Mike | C | 6-3 | 271 | 2 | Texas A&M |
| 42 | Ball, Eric | RB | 6-2 | 214 | 4 | UCLA |
| 86 | Barber, Mike | WR | 5-11 | 172 | 4 | Marshall |
| 53 | Barker, Leo | LB | 6-2 | 230 | 9 | New Mexico State |
| 35 | Bennett, Antoine | CB | 5-11 | 185 | 2 | Florida A&M |
|  | Bentley, Ray | LB | 6-2 | 235 | 7 | Central Michigan |
| 3 | Breech, Jim | K | 5-6 | 161 | 14 | California |
| 81 | Brown, Eddie | WR | 6-0 | 185 | 8 | Miami |
| 27 | Bussey, Barney | S | 6-0 | 210 | 7 | South Carolina State |
| 38 | Dingle, Mike | RB | 6-2 | 240 | 2 | South Carolina |
| 29 | Dixon, Rickey | S | 5-11 | 191 | 5 | Oklahoma |
| 7 | Esiason, Boomer | QB | 6-5 | 220 | 9 | Maryland |
|  | Fenner, Derrick | RB | 6-3 | 228 | 4 | North Carolina |
| 50 | Francis, James | LB | 6-5 | 252 | 3 | Baylor |
| 33 | Fulcher, David | S | 6-3 | 238 | 7 | Arizona State |
| 89 | Garrett, Shane | WR | 5-11 | 185 | 2 | Texas A&M |
| 58 | Gordon, Alex | LB | 6-5 | 245 | 6 | Cincinnati |
| 98 | Grant, David | DE | 6-5 | 278 | 5 | West Virginia |
| 28 | Green, Harold | RB | 6-2 | 222 | 3 | South Carolina |
| 45 | Haddix, Wayne | CB | 6-1 | 205 | 5 | Liberty |
| 12 | Hollas, Donald | QB | 6-3 | 215 | 2 | Rice |
| 82 | Holman, Rodney | TE | 6-3 | 238 | 11 | Tulane |
| 11 | Johnson, Lee | P | 6-2 | 200 | 8 | Brigham Young |
| 25 | Jones, Rod | CB | 6-0 | 185 | 7 | Southern Methodist |
| 70 | Jones, Scott | T | 6-6 | 280 | 4 | Washington |
| 84 | Kattus, Eric | TE | 6-5 | 251 | 7 | Michigan |
|  | Kirk, Randy | LB | 6-1 | 218 | 4 | San Diego State |
| 64 | Kozerski, Bruce | C | 6-4 | 287 | 9 | Holy Cross |
| 69 | Krumrie, Tim | NT | 6-2 | 274 | 10 | Wisconsin |
| 85 | McGee, Tim | WR | 5-10 | 183 | 7 | Tennessee |
|  | Melander, Jon | T | 6-7 | 280 | 2 | Minnesota |
| 99 | Mitz, Alonzo | DE | 6-4 | 278 | 6 | Florida |
| 73 | Moyer, Ken | G | 6-7 | 297 | 4 | Toledo |
| 78 | Munoz, Anthony | T | 6-6 | 284 | 13 | Southern California |
| 32 | Price, Mitchell | CB-PR | 5-9 | 181 | 3 | Tulane |
| 88 | Rembert, Reggie | WR | 6-5 | 200 | 2 | West Virginia |
| 87 | Riggs, Jim | TE | 6-5 | 245 | 6 | Clemson |
| 79 | Rogers, Lamar | DE | 6-4 | 292 | 2 | Auburn |
| 76 | Scrafford, Kirk | T | 6-6 | 255 | 3 | Montana |
| 97 | Stewart, Andrew | DE | 6-5 | 265 | 2 | Cincinnati |
| 67 | Stubbs, Daniel | DE | 6-4 | 264 | 5 | Miami |
| 20 | Taylor, Craig | RB | 6-0 | 228 | 4 | West Virginia |
| 22 | Thomas, Eric | CB | 5-11 | 181 | 6 | Tulane |
| 96 | Tuatagaloa, Natu | DE | 6-4 | 274 | 4 | California |
| 34 | Vinson, Fernandus | S | 5-10 | 197 | 2 | North Carolina State |
| 59 | Walker, Kevin | LB | 6-3 | 244 | 5 | Maryland |
| 63 | Walter, Joe | T | 6-7 | 292 | 8 | Texas Tech |
| 51 | White, Leon | LB | 6-3 | 242 | 7 | Brigham Young |
| 4 | Wilhelm, Erik | QB | 6-3 | 217 | 4 | Oregon State |
| 94 | Williams, Alfred | LB | 6-6 | 240 | 2 | Colorado |
| 60 | Withycombe, Mike | T | 6-5 | 310 | 4 | Fresno State |

## 1992 SCHEDULE OF GAMES

**September**

| | | |
|---|---|---|
| 6 | at Seattle | 1:00 |
| 13 | LOS ANGELES RAIDERS | 1:00 |
| 20 | at Green Bay | 12:00 |
| 27 | MINNESOTA | 1:00 |

**October**

| | | |
|---|---|---|
| 4 | Open Date | |
| 11 | HOUSTON | 4:00 |
| 19 | at Pittsburgh (Mon.) | 9:00 |
| 25 | at Houston | 12:00 |

**November**

| | | |
|---|---|---|
| 1 | CLEVELAND | 4:00 |
| 8 | at Chicago | 7:00 |
| 15 | at New York Jets | 1:00 |
| 22 | DETROIT | 1:00 |
| 29 | PITTSBURGH | 1:00 |

**December**

| | | |
|---|---|---|
| 6 | at Cleveland | 1:00 |
| 13 | at San Diego | 1:00 |
| 20 | NEW ENGLAND | 1:00 |
| 27 | INDIANAPOLIS | 1:00 |

# CLEVELAND BROWNS

**Address** Tower B, Cleveland Stadium, Cleveland, Ohio 44114.

**Stadium** Cleveland Stadium, Cleveland.
*Capacity* 80,098 *Playing Surface* Grass.

**Team Colours** Seal Brown, Orange, and White.

**Head Coach** Bill Belichick – 2nd year.

**Championships** Division 1971, '80, '85, '86, '87, '89; AAFC 1946, '47, '48, '49; NFL 1950, '54, '55, '64.

**History** AAFC 1946-49, NFL 1950-69, AFC 1970-

Cleveland is a football hotbed and the Browns should always be respected. The latter has been no less true following the arrival of head coach Bill Belichick, who has given a sense of purpose to a modest squad. In the 1992 draft, Belichick chose developmental players, not many of whom are likely to start immediately. However, in Plan-B free agent signings James Brooks, Jamie Holland and Pete Holohan, he found veterans who could make an instant contri-

bution. Certainly, Brooks and Holohan will give the club a little breathing space to bring along the younger players.

The 1991 Browns were far more competitive than most scouts anticipated as, despite using several inexperienced starters and simply making do in some areas, Belichick saw his team lose seven games by a total of just 24 points. He does have classy performers, not least in quarterback Bernie Kosar, whose outward aloofness disguises an intense desire to make Cleveland a winner. Before the age of 27, Kosar had led the Browns to four division titles and three AFC Championship Games but for two years his priority has been to survive. Even so, last year, he was the fifth-ranked NFL passer, along the way setting a new all-time record with 308 passing attempts without an interception. The arrival of Holland should make up for the loss of Reggie Langhorne and, on balance, gives the Browns speed to complement the all-round skills of Webster Slaughter at wide receiver. Again, Holohan offers a classy receiving option from the tight end position.

Even including top draftee Tommy Vardell and with the suspicion that Eric Metcalf may not progress, the Browns look ponderous at running back but there's the possibility of sparkle in the feet of Brooks, who may wish to make a point when Cleveland meets his former clubs San Diego and Cincinnati (twice). Brooks could share time with Leroy Hoard at halfback with Kevin Mack continuing ahead of Lee Rouson at fullback. Vardell will be groomed as the future fullback.

The offensive line is a mixture of youth and experience and, surprisingly, was not reinforced, either through the draft or Plan B. Tony Jones and Dan Fike start at tackle, with guards John Rienstra and Ed King flanking Mike Baab. As a rookie King made great progress, fully justifying his second-round draft status. As the senior backup at both guard and tackle, Paul Farren is vastly experienced, having started 84 of the 87 games for which he was available between 1985 and 1991.

Belichick's youth policy was evident on the defensive line, where two rookies, end Pio Sagapolutele and left tackle James Jones, and second-year defensive right end Rob Burnett settled in alongside the outstanding All-Pro, Michael Dean Perry. Of the backups, Ernie Logan and John Thornton were rookies and Anthony Pleasant was in only his second year. The collective effort did not frighten the opposition but, as a group, they held up well under pressure.

There is dependability at linebacker, where 14-year veteran Clay Matthews shows few signs of slowing. David Brandon is steady at left linebacker and Richard Brown hung on in the middle spot, but the return of a fully fit Mike Johnson is of critical importance. Entering the 1991 season, Johnson had led the team in tackles for four consecutive years but his campaign ended with a foot injury in September.

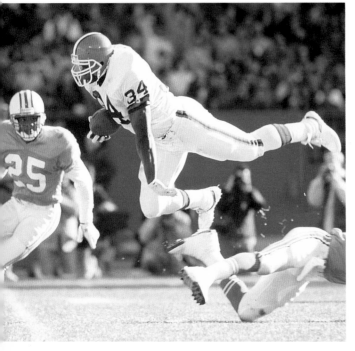

*Kevin Mack leads the Browns' power-based running game.*

For the secondary, Cleveland may have found a future All-Pro in safety Eric Turner. After making a late start to his rookie campaign, Turner came in for the second half and was little short of sensational. He's worth the price of admission. Alongside Turner, left cornerback Frank Minnifield continues, sometimes excellent and always challenging, right cornerback Randy Hilliard stood up to the pressure in his first year as a starter and right safety Vince Newsome had a great year, coming second on the team in tackles.

Changes to the kicking game are not expected, with placekicker Matt Stover and punter Brian Hansen continuing. However, for when the opposition mounts its returns, the Browns signed Plan-B free agent Ron Wolfley, who had been selected to four Pro Bowls as the leader of the Cardinals' special-teams tacklers but, surprisingly, was left unprotected.

## 1992 SCHEDULE OF GAMES

### September

| | | |
|---|---|---|
| 6 | at Indianapolis | 12:00 |
| 14 | MIAMI (Mon.) | 9:00 |
| 20 | at Los Angeles Raiders | 1:00 |
| 27 | DENVER | 1:00 |

### October

| | | |
|---|---|---|
| 4 | Open Date | |
| 11 | PITTSBURGH | 1:00 |
| 18 | GREEN BAY | 1:00 |
| 25 | at New England | 4:00 |

### November

| | | |
|---|---|---|
| 1 | at Cincinnati | 4:00 |
| 8 | at Houston | 12:00 |
| 15 | SAN DIEGO | 1:00 |
| 22 | at Minnesota | 12:00 |
| 29 | CHICAGO | 1:00 |

### December

| | | |
|---|---|---|
| 6 | CINCINNATI | 1:00 |
| 13 | at Detroit | 1:00 |
| 20 | HOUSTON | 1:00 |
| 27 | at Pittsburgh | 1:00 |

## 1992 Draft

| Round | Name | Pos. | Ht. | Wt. | College |
|---|---|---|---|---|---|
| 1. | Vardell, Tommy | RB | 6-1 | 238 | Stanford |
| 2. | Rowe, Patrick | WR | 6-0 | 191 | San Diego State |
| 3. | Johnson, Bill | DT | 6-3 | 302 | Michigan State |
| 3. | Dixon, Gerald | LB | 6-2 | 250 | South Carolina |
| 6. | Smith, Rico | WR | 5-11 | 186 | Colorado |
| 6. | Williams, George | DT | 6-2 | 315 | Notre Dame |
| 7. | Jones, Selwyn | CB | 5-11 | 182 | Colorado State |
| 9. | Hill, Tim | CB | 5-7 | 170 | Kansas |
| 10. | Lowe, Marcus | NT | 6-2 | 308 | Baylor |
| 11. | Olobia, Augustin | WR | 5-11 | 190 | Washington State |
| 12. | McCant, Keithen | QB | 6-3 | 203 | Nebraska |
| 12. | Simpson, Tim | C-G | 6-1 | 301 | Illinois |

## VETERAN ROSTER

| No. | Name | Pos. | Ht. | Wt. | NFL Year | College |
|---|---|---|---|---|---|---|
| 61 | Baab, Mike | C | 6-4 | 275 | 11 | Texas |
| 24 | Baldwin, Randy | RB | 5-10 | 216 | 2 | Mississippi |
| 37 | Barnett, Harlon | S | 5-11 | 200 | 3 | Michigan State |
| 42 | Berry, Latin | CB | 5-10 | 196 | 3 | Oregon |
| 36 | Braggs, Stephen | S | 5-9 | 180 | 6 | Texas |
| 58 | Brandon, David | LB | 6-4 | 230 | 5 | Memphis State |
| | Brooks, James | RB | 5-10 | 182 | 12 | Auburn |
| 52 | Brown, Richard | LB | 6-3 | 240 | 5 | San Diego State |
| 90 | Burnett, Rob | DE | 6-4 | 270 | 3 | Syracuse |
| 71 | Burton, Leonard | C | 6-3 | 277 | 5 | South Carolina |
| | Childress, Freddie | G | 6-4 | 333 | 2 | Arkansas |
| 26 | Clayborn, Raymond | CB | 6-1 | 190 | 15 | Texas |
| 99 | Cooks, Johnie | LB | 6-4 | 251 | 11 | Mississippi State |
| 27 | Douglas, Derrick | RB | 5-10 | 222 | 2 | Louisiana Tech |
| 74 | Farren, Paul | T-G | 6-6 | 270 | 10 | Boston University |
| 53 | Figaro, Cedric | LB | 6-3 | 255 | 5 | Notre Dame |
| 69 | Fike, Dan | T-G | 6-7 | 285 | 8 | Florida |
| 13 | Francis, Jeff | QB | 6-4 | 225 | 1 | Tennessee |
| 81 | Galbraith, Scott | TE | 6-3 | 260 | 3 | Southern California |
| 8 | Greenfield, Brian | P | 5-11 | 227 | 1 | Pittsburgh |
| | Hampton, Alonzo | DB | 5-10 | 195 | 3 | Pittsburgh |
| 11 | Hansen, Brian | P | 6-4 | 220 | 8 | Sioux Falls |
| 23 | Harper, Mark | CB | 5-9 | 185 | 6 | Alcorn State |
| 38 | Harris, Odie | DB | 6-0 | 190 | 5 | Sam Houston State |
| 39 | Hilliard, Randy | CB | 5-11 | 160 | 3 | Northwestern State, La. |
| 33 | Hoard, Leroy | RB | 5-11 | 230 | 3 | Michigan |
| | Holland, Jamie | WR | 6-1 | 195 | 6 | Ohio State |
| | Holohan, Pete | TE | 6-4 | 247 | 12 | Notre Dame |
| 41 | Jackson, Alfred | CB | 6-0 | 180 | 4 | San Diego State |
| 1 | Jackson, Michael | WR | 6-4 | 195 | 2 | Southern Mississippi |
| 40 | James, Lynn | WR | 6-0 | 190 | 3 | Arizona State |
| 59 | Johnson, Mike | LB | 6-1 | 230 | 7 | Virginia Tech |
| 96 | Jones, James | DT | 6-2 | 294 | 2 | Northern Iowa |
| 66 | Jones, Tony | T | 6-5 | 290 | 5 | Western Carolina |
| 48 | Kinchen, Brian | TE | 6-2 | 232 | 4 | Louisiana State |
| 68 | King, Ed | G | 6-4 | 303 | 2 | Auburn |
| 19 | Kosar, Bernie | QB | 6-5 | 215 | 8 | Miami |
| 97 | Logan, Ernie | DL | 6-3 | 271 | 2 | East Carolina |
| 34 | Mack, Kevin | RB | 6-0 | 230 | 8 | Clemson |
| 57 | Matthews, Clay | LB | 6-2 | 245 | 15 | Southern California |
| | McCardell, Keenan | WR | 6-1 | 185 | 1 | Nevada-Las Vegas |
| 49 | McGonnigal, Bruce | TE | 6-4 | 230 | 2 | Virginia |
| 21 | Metcalf, Eric | RB | 5-10 | 190 | 4 | Texas |
| 31 | Minnifield, Frank | CB | 5-9 | 180 | 9 | Louisville |
| | Moore, Stevon | S | 5-11 | 204 | 2 | Mississippi |
| 20 | Morris, Joe | RB | 5-7 | 195 | 10 | Syracuse |
| | Moss, Anthony | LB | 6-4 | 240 | 1 | Florida State |
| 22 | Newsome, Vince | S | 6-1 | 185 | 10 | Washington |
| | Perkins, Bruce | RB | 6-2 | 230 | 3 | Arizona State |
| 92 | Perry, Michael Dean | DT | 6-1 | 285 | 5 | Clemson |
| 17 | Philcox, Todd | QB | 6-4 | 225 | 3 | Syracuse |
| 98 | Pleasant, Anthony | DE | 6-5 | 258 | 3 | Tennessee State |
| 70 | Rienstra, John | G | 6-5 | 275 | 7 | Temple |
| 44 | Rouson, Lee | TE-RB | 6-1 | 222 | 8 | Colorado |
| 75 | Sagapolutele, Pio | DT | 6-6 | 297 | 2 | San Diego State |
| 28 | Shavers, Tyrone | WR | 6-3 | 210 | 1 | Lamar |
| 84 | Slaughter, Webster | WR | 6-1 | 170 | 7 | San Diego State |
| 3 | Stover, Matt | K | 5-11 | 178 | 2 | Louisiana State |
| | Taylor, Terry | CB | 5-10 | 191 | 8 | Southern Illinois |
| 67 | Thome, Chris | C | 6-4 | 280 | 2 | Minnesota |
| 91 | Thornton, John | DT | 6-3 | 303 | 2 | Cincinnati |
| 85 | Tillman, Lawyer | WR | 6-5 | 230 | 2 | Auburn |
| 65 | Trumbull, Rick | T | 6-6 | 300 | 2 | Missouri |
| 29 | Turner, Eric | S | 6-1 | 207 | 2 | UCLA |
| 50 | Waiters, Van | LB | 6-4 | 250 | 5 | Indiana |
| 93 | Wise, Mike | DE | 6-7 | 270 | 6 | California-Davis |
| | Wolfley, Ron | RB | 6-0 | 230 | 8 | West Virginia |
| 78 | Woods, Rob | T | 6-5 | 295 | 2 | Arizona |
| | Zackery, Tony | S | 6-2 | 195 | 2 | Washington |

# HOUSTON OILERS

**Address** 6910 Fannin Street, Houston, Texas 77030.
**Stadium** Astrodome, Houston.
  *Capacity* 60,502 *Playing Surface* AstroTurf-8.
**Team Colours** Columbia Blue, Scarlet, and White.
**Head Coach** Jack Pardee – 3rd year; 9th NFL.
**Championships** Division 1991; AFL 1960,'61.
**History** AFL 1960-69, AFC 1970-

There seems little more that the Houston Oilers can do to be successful. A well-coached 1991 squad with no obvious weaknesses was strolling through the divisional playoff game against Denver when lightning, in the form of John Elway, struck. From being in a position of control, the Oilers suddenly were beaten. Perhaps they needed a little luck.

The key player in the Oilers' demanding 'Run 'n Shoot' offense is quarterback Warren Moon, and it is perhaps one benefit of having spent six seasons in the wide-open Canadian Football League that the nine-year NFL veteran has developed the system to a fine art. When Moon is on song the offense is a thing of beauty and, inevitably with four wide receivers on parade, he has begun to gather impressive single-season and career passing totals. Reserve quarterback Cody Carlson has taken time to learn the system but he has put the practice sessions to good use and, should he be needed, he could keep the engine ticking over if not perhaps firing on all cylinders.

Houston wide receivers are always likely to catch lots of passes and, for the second straight year, Haywood Jeffires led the AFC in both catches and receiving yardage. He has lost his best partner in Drew Hill, who mysteriously was not protected under Plan B, but the starting quartet of Jeffires, Ernest Givins, Curtis Duncan and one of Leonard Harris and Plan-B signing Jeff Query, is expected to maintain the standard of excellence.

The one weakness of the 'Run 'n Shoot' was that if it didn't work to perfection, Houston did not have many variations to offer by way of a rushing game. This aspect has received attention during the offseason and, should

the coaches need to shift the emphasis, in Lorenzo White they have one of the league's better running backs as the spearhead. As his reserve, Gary Brown has made excellent progress, to the extent that the Oilers felt able to trade away Allen Pinkett, who is a player of high class. Former Oiler Spencer Tillman was a sensible signing via Plan B.

The whole process is set up by one of the league's finest offensive lines, led by guards Mike Munchak and Doug Dawson with the peerless Bruce Matthews at center. David Williams has developed quickly into a genuine starter while Don Maggs has established his authority in the crucial position of left tackle. There could hardly be a better pair of reserves than Dean Steinkuhler and John Flannery.

The process of building defensive strength which began under Jerry Glanville accelerated as the Oilers switched to a 4-3 defense. It has brought the best out of defensive ends William Fuller, who led the AFC in 1991 with 15 sacks, and Sean Jones, who had ten. Versatile Pro Bowler Ray Childress has proved to be equally effective at defensive tackle in partnership with the aggressive Doug Smith.

Intensity extends into the linebacking trio, where the hard-nosed Al Smith jams the middle. Even though exiting on passing downs, Smith was the leading tackler for the second year in a row. To his left, Lamar Lathon, who was a 1990 first-round pick, made tremendous progress in his second year while, on the right, a return to top quality is expected of Johnny Meads, who started slowly in 1991 following a contract dispute.

At strong safety, Bubba McDowell is the player that most NFL teams covet. A shuddering tackler who bravely bears the pain, McDowell is a fine pass defender, with four interceptions last year, and has an instinct for being around when there's a fumble to recover. His partner at free safety, Bo Orlando, also intercepted four passes in his first year as a starter. The corners could hardly be in better hands, literally, than those of Cris Dishman and Richard Johnson. Last year Dishman tied for second place in the NFL with six interceptions while, in 1990, Johnson led the AFC with eight. The worry is that Johnson, whose 1991 campaign was marred by injury, may not rediscover his best form. Accordingly, former Rams starter and Pro Bowl MVP Jerry Gray was picked up when, surprisingly, he was left unprotected under Plan B.

The kicking game is sound. Al Del Greco took over from the disappointing Ian Howfield in mid-season and has the strength to land 50-yard field goals. Interestingly, Del Greco's arrival coincided with an improvement by punter Greg Montgomery, who brought finesse and controlled direction to the strength of his punts.

## 1992 Draft

| Round | Name | Pos. | Ht. | Wt. | College |
|---|---|---|---|---|---|
| 2. | Robinson, Eddie | LB | 6-1 | 239 | Alabama State |
| 3. | Harris, Corey | RB-WR | 5-11 | 195 | Vanderbilt |
| 4. | Mooney, Mike | T | 6-6 | 333 | Georgia Tech |
| 5. | Bowden, Joe | LB | 5-11 | 227 | Oklahoma |
| 5. | Brown, Tony | CB | 5-9 | 183 | Fresno State |
| 5. | Roberts, Tim | DT | 6-5 | 305 | Southern Mississippi |
| 6. | Bailey, Mario | WR | 5-9 | 162 | Washington |
| 7. | Turner, Elbert | WR | 5-11 | 165 | Illinois |
| 8. | Richardson, Bucky | QB | 6-1 | 220 | Texas A&M |
| 9. | Daffney, Bernard | T | 6-5 | 317 | Tennessee |
| 10. | Johnson, Dion | WR-KR | 5-7 | 164 | East Carolina |
| 11. | Davis, Anthony | LB | 6-0 | 231 | Utah |
| 12. | Wood, Joe | K | 6-1 | 202 | Air Force |

## VETERAN ROSTER

| No. | Name | Pos. | Ht. | Wt. | NFL Year | College |
|---|---|---|---|---|---|---|
| 76 | Alm, Jeff | DT | 6-6 | 269 | 3 | Notre Dame |
| 33 | Brown, Gary | RB | 5-11 | 224 | 2 | Penn State |
| 14 | Carlson, Cody | QB | 6-3 | 202 | 6 | Baylor |
| 79 | Childress, Ray | DT-DE | 6-6 | 272 | 8 | Texas A&M |
| 87 | Coleman, Pat | WR | 5-7 | 173 | 2 | Mississippi |
| 66 | Dawson, Doug | C-G | 6-3 | 288 | 5 | Texas |
| 3 | Del Greco, Al | K | 5-10 | 200 | 9 | Auburn |
| 28 | Dishman, Cris | CB | 6-0 | 178 | 5 | Purdue |
| 77 | Donnalley, Kevin | T | 6-5 | 290 | 2 | North Carolina |
| 38 | Dumas, Mike | S | 5-11 | 178 | 2 | Indiana |
| 80 | Duncan, Curtis | WR | 5-11 | 184 | 6 | Northwestern |
| 55 | Flannery, John | G-C | 6-3 | 304 | 2 | Syracuse |
| 95 | Fuller, William | DE | 6-3 | 274 | 7 | North Carolina |
| 81 | Givins, Ernest | WR | 5-9 | 172 | 7 | Louisville |
| 93 | Graf, Rick | LB | 6-5 | 244 | 6 | Wisconsin |
| 21 | Gray, Jerry | CB | 6-0 | 185 | 8 | Texas |
| 83 | Harris, Leonard | WR-KR | 5-8 | 162 | 7 | Texas Tech |
| 24 | Jackson, Steve | CB | 5-8 | 182 | 2 | Purdue |
| 84 | Jeffires, Haywood | WR | 6-2 | 201 | 6 | North Carolina State |
| 23 | Johnson, Richard | CB | 6-1 | 195 | 8 | Wisconsin |
| 96 | Jones, Sean | DE | 6-7 | 264 | 9 | Northeastern |
| 30 | Jones, Victor | RB | 5-8 | 212 | 3 | Louisiana State |
| 56 | Kozak, Scott | LB | 6-3 | 222 | 4 | Oregon |
| 57 | Lathon, Lamar | LB | 6-3 | 250 | 3 | Houston |
| 29 | Lewis, Darryll | CB | 5-9 | 188 | 2 | Arizona |
| 78 | Maggs, Don | T | 6-5 | 290 | 6 | Tulane |
| 74 | Matthews, Bruce | C-G | 6-5 | 291 | 10 | Southern California |
| 25 | McDowell, Bubba | S | 6-1 | 198 | 4 | Miami |
| 91 | Meads, Johnny | LB | 6-2 | 226 | 9 | Nicholls State |
| 94 | Montgomery, Glenn | DT | 6-0 | 272 | 4 | Houston |
| 9 | Montgomery, Greg | P | 6-4 | 215 | 5 | Michigan State |
| 1 | Moon, Warren | QB | 6-3 | 212 | 9 | Washington |
| 63 | Munchak, Mike | G | 6-3 | 284 | 11 | Penn State |
| 64 | Norgard, Erik | C-G | 6-1 | 278 | 2 | Colorado |
| 26 | Orlando, Bo | S | 5-10 | 180 | 3 | West Virginia |
| 72 | Peguese, Willis | DE | 6-4 | 273 | 3 | Miami |
| 89 | Query, Jeff | WR-PR | 6-0 | 165 | 4 | Millikin |
| 31 | Robertson, Marcus | S | 5-11 | 197 | 2 | Iowa |
| 53 | Seale, Eugene | LB | 5-10 | 253 | 6 | Lamar |
| 10 | Slack, Reggie | QB | 6-1 | 221 | 2 | Auburn |
| 54 | Smith, Al | LB | 6-1 | 251 | 6 | Utah State |
| 99 | Smith, Doug | DT | 6-6 | 309 | 8 | Auburn |
| 70 | Steinkuhler, Dean | T | 6-3 | 287 | 9 | Nebraska |
| 32 | Tillman, Spencer | RB | 5-11 | 206 | 6 | Oklahoma |
| 44 | White, Lorenzo | RB | 5-11 | 222 | 5 | Michigan State |
| 73 | Williams, David | T | 6-5 | 292 | 4 | Florida |
| 97 | Williams, Lee | DE | 6-6 | 271 | 9 | Bethune-Cookman |

*ABOVE: The 35-year-old Warren Moon improves with age.*

**1992 SCHEDULE OF GAMES**

**September**

| | | |
|---|---|---|
| 6 | PITTSBURGH | 12:00 |
| 13 | at Indianapolis | 3:00 |
| 20 | KANSAS CITY | 12:00 |
| 27 | SAN DIEGO | 12:00 |

**October**

| | | |
|---|---|---|
| 4 | Open Date | |
| 11 | at Cincinnati | 4:00 |
| 18 | at Denver | 2:00 |
| 25 | CINCINNATI | 12:00 |

**November**

| | | |
|---|---|---|
| 1 | at Pittsburgh | 1:00 |
| 8 | CLEVELAND | 12:00 |
| 15 | at Minnesota | 12:00 |
| 22 | at Miami | 1:00 |
| 26 | at Detroit (Thanksgiving) | 12:30 |

**December**

| | | |
|---|---|---|
| 7 | CHICAGO (Mon.) | 8:00 |
| 13 | GREEN BAY | 7:00 |
| 20 | at Cleveland | 1:00 |
| 27 | BUFFALO | 7:00 |

# PITTSBURGH STEELERS

**Address** Three Rivers Stadium, 300 Stadium Circle, Pittsburgh, Pennsylvania 15212.

**Stadium** Three Rivers Stadium, Pittsburgh.
*Capacity* 59,492 *Playing Surface* AstroTurf.

**Team Colours** Black and Gold.

**Head Coach** Bill Cowher – 1st year.

**Championships** Division 1972,'74,'75,'76,'77,'78, '79,'83,'84; Conference 1974,'75,'78,'79; Super Bowl 1974,'75,'78,'79.

**History** NFL 1933-69, AFC 1970-
(Until 1940, they were known as the Pittsburgh Pirates.)

In a series of forthright statements, new head coach Bill Cowher has identified as many weaknesses as strengths in the squad that he inherits and it was with frankness rather than mischievous encouragement that he announced that many positions are open to competition.

He is perfectly satisfied with the depth in the key area of quarterback but sees Neil O'Donnell as being just ahead of the more experienced Bubby Brister for the starting position, the pragmatic reason being that Brister is coming off knee surgery which will delay his return until the beginning of camp. Both men had eight starts in 1991 and it will not be to Brister's advantage that he has been inconsistent for some time and still carries the burden of not having tumbled to the passing offense installed by the departed Joe Walton.

There will be a major shift on offense, trading traditional Pittsburgh finesse and guile for greater application of power play. With this philosophy comes the need to beef up the offensive line and it arrived on the hoof in round one with the selection of Leon Searcy. The chances are that last year's regulars, Tunch Ilkin, John Jackson, Dermontti Dawson and Carlton Haselrig, will start the season though the position of left guard, a revolving door last year as Cowher observed, will be won in a camp battle featuring Searcy, Tom Ricketts, Ariel Solomon and Plan-B free agent Duval Love.

If Ricketts has been a disappointment as the second of two 1989 first-round picks, the premier selection, Tim

Worley, has been a disaster. His attitude was poor and he will miss the entire season under suspension for violating the league's substance abuse policy. It is such a pity, for a player of his size and potential could have been perfect for a club which wishes to emphasize an uncomplicated power-rushing game. As it is, the burden falls on the shoulders of Merril Hoge, whom Cowher feels lacks inherent talent but is versatile and productive through sheer determination. He's the kind of player that any coach would value. He'll start, probably in tandem with Barry Foster, whose 1991 campaign was marred by a recurring ankle injury but who can present problems with his low, ground-hog style of running. As a shock trooper, Warren Williams can prise open holes with his slashing style.

Turning to the passing game, there is an ever-present deep threat in starters Louis Lipps and, particularly, Dwight Stone, whose five touchdown scores in 1991 covered 89, 65, 57, 43 and 40 yards. Of the backups, Jeff Graham and the less-polished Ernie Mills will see increased playing time. One area of unquestioned strength is the tight end position, where the huge Eric Green is future All-Pro material and the slightly smaller Adrian Cooper adjusted quickly after playing mostly in a run-oriented offense in college.

The 1992 defensive roster would not rank among the club's historic best and it is difficult to imagine an early return to par. Entering camp, Cowher has not identified a preferred formation, intending rather to put the talent to its best use. Of the more prominent defensive linemen, Gerald Williams is steady but Aaron Jones has been slow to develop and Donald Evans has been discarded by both the Rams and Philadelphia. Draftee nose tackle Joel Steed could be useful against the run but the pass rush is likely to come from the

| 1992 SCHEDULE OF GAMES | | |
|---|---|---|
| **September** | | |
| 6 | at Houston | 12:00 |
| 13 | NEW YORK JETS | 4:00 |
| 20 | at San Diego | 1:00 |
| 27 | at Green Bay | 3:00 |
| **October** | | |
| 4 | Open Date | |
| 11 | at Cleveland | 1:00 |
| 19 | CINCINNATI (Mon.) | 9:00 |
| 25 | at Kansas City | 6:30 |
| **November** | | |
| 1 | HOUSTON | 1:00 |
| 8 | at Buffalo | 4:00 |
| 15 | DETROIT | 1:00 |
| 22 | INDIANAPOLIS | 1:00 |
| 29 | at Cincinnati | 1:00 |
| **December** | | |
| 6 | SEATTLE | 1:00 |
| 13 | at Chicago | 12:00 |
| 20 | MINNESOTA | 1:00 |
| 27 | CLEVELAND | 1:00 |

| Round | Name | Pos. | Ht. | Wt. | College |
|---|---|---|---|---|---|
| 1. | Searcy, Leon | T-G | 6-3 | 296 | Miami |
| 2. | Kirkland, Levon | LB | 6-0 | 240 | Clemson |
| 3. | Steed, Joel | NT | 6-2 | 281 | Colorado |
| 4. | Davenport, Charles | WR | 6-3 | 206 | North Carolina State |
| 5. | Haller, Alan | CB | 5-10 | 177 | Michigan State |
| 7. | Campbell, Russ | TE | 6-5 | 252 | Kansas State |
| 7. | Graham, Scottie | RB | 5-8 | 222 | Ohio State |
| 8. | Perry, Darren | S | 5-10 | 190 | Penn State |
| 8. | Ismail, Hesham | G | 6-2 | 293 | Florida |
| 8. | Williams, Nate | DT | 6-2 | 285 | Mississippi State |
| 9. | Webster, Elnardo | LB | 6-2 | 248 | Rutgers |
| 10. | Saunders, Mike | RB | 5-10 | 203 | Iowa |
| 11. | Gammon, Kendall | G | 6-4 | 272 | Pittsburg, Kansas |
| 12. | Benton, Cornelius | QB | 6-3 | 209 | Connecticut |

## VETERAN ROSTER

| No. | Name | Pos. | Ht. | Wt. | NFL Year | College |
|---|---|---|---|---|---|---|
| 1 | Anderson, Gary | K | 5-11 | 179 | 11 | Syracuse |
| 60 | Blankenship, Brian | G-C | 6-1 | 280 | 6 | Nebraska |
| 6 | Brister, Bubby | QB | 6-3 | 217 | 7 | Northeast Louisiana |
| 61 | Caliguire, Dean | G-C | 6-2 | 280 | 2 | Pittsburgh |
|  | Clayton, Stan | G | 6-3 | 265 | 5 | Penn State |
| 87 | Cooper, Adrian | TE | 6-5 | 259 | 2 | Oklahoma |
| 64 | Davidson, Kenny | DE | 6-5 | 264 | 3 | Louisiana State |
| 63 | Dawson, Dermontti | C | 6-2 | 275 | 5 | Kentucky |
| 76 | Dingman, Dean | G | 6-2 | 270 | 1 | Michigan |
|  | Drummond, Robert | RB | 6-1 | 205 | 4 | Syracuse |
| 66 | Evans, Donald | DE | 6-2 | 258 | 4 | Winston-Salem State |
| 27 | Everett, Thomas | S | 5-9 | 183 | 6 | Baylor |
| 29 | Foster, Barry | RB | 5-10 | 218 | 3 | Arkansas |
|  | Gibson, Tom | DE | 6-8 | 275 | 4 | Northern Arizona |
| 81 | Graham, Jeff | WR | 6-1 | 195 | 2 | Ohio State |
| 86 | Green, Eric | TE | 6-5 | 280 | 3 | Liberty |
| 22 | Griffin, Larry | S | 6-0 | 202 | 7 | North Carolina |
| 77 | Haselrig, Carlton | G | 6-1 | 295 | 3 | Pitt-Johnstown |
| 53 | Hinkle, Bryan | LB | 6-2 | 224 | 11 | Oregon |
| 33 | Hoge, Merril | RB | 6-2 | 222 | 6 | Idaho State |
| 62 | Ilkin, Tunch | T | 6-3 | 273 | 13 | Indiana State |
| 65 | Jackson, John | T | 6-6 | 289 | 5 | Eastern Kentucky |
|  | Jaworski, Matt | LB | 6-1 | 226 | 2 | Colgate |
| 44 | Johnson, David | CB | 6-0 | 181 | 4 | Kentucky |
| 97 | Jones, Aaron | DE | 6-5 | 257 | 5 | Eastern Kentucky |
| 25 | Jones, Gary | S | 6-1 | 208 | 3 | Texas A&M |
| 37 | Lake, Carnell | S | 6-1 | 207 | 4 | UCLA |
| 83 | Lipps, Louis | WR | 5-10 | 185 | 9 | Southern Mississippi |
| 50 | Little, David | LB | 6-1 | 236 | 12 | Florida |
| 95 | Lloyd, Greg | LB | 6-2 | 223 | 5 | Fort Valley State |
| 67 | Love, Duval | G | 6-3 | 287 | 8 | UCLA |
| 89 | Mills, Ernie | WR | 5-11 | 178 | 2 | Florida |
| 84 | Mularkey, Mike | TE | 6-4 | 240 | 10 | Florida |
| 54 | Nickerson, Hardy | LB | 6-2 | 227 | 6 | California |
| 14 | O'Donnell, Neil | QB | 6-3 | 223 | 3 | Maryland |
| 55 | Olsavsky, Jerry | LB | 6-1 | 219 | 4 | Pittsburgh |
| 90 | Richardson, Huey | LB | 6-5 | 233 | 2 | Florida |
| 71 | Ricketts, Tom | G-T | 6-5 | 288 | 4 | Pittsburgh |
| 3 | Royals, Mark | P | 6-5 | 215 | 3 | Appalachian State |
| 24 | Shelton, Richard | CB | 5-9 | 196 | 3 | Liberty |
|  | Smagala, Stan | S | 5-10 | 184 | 3 | Notre Dame |
| 41 | Smith, Kevin | S | 5-11 | 204 | 2 | Rhode Island |
| 69 | Solomon, Ariel | T | 6-5 | 271 | 2 | Colorado |
| 20 | Stone, Dwight | WR-RB | 6-0 | 190 | 6 | Middle Tennessee State |
| 11 | Strom, Rick | QB | 6-2 | 197 | 4 | Georgia Tech |
| 73 | Strzelczyk, Justin | T | 6-5 | 297 | 3 | Maine |
| 34 | Thompson, Leroy | RB | 5-10 | 215 | 2 | Penn State |
| 91 | Veasey, Craig | DE | 6-2 | 285 | 3 | Houston |
| 43 | Vincent, Shawn | CB | 5-10 | 180 | 2 | Akron |
| 23 | Walker, Sammy | CB | 5-11 | 197 | 2 | Texas Tech |
| 98 | Williams, Gerald | NT | 6-3 | 282 | 7 | Auburn |
| 57 | Williams, Jerrol | LB | 6-5 | 237 | 4 | Purdue |
| 42 | Williams, Warren | RB | 6-0 | 213 | 5 | Miami |
| 26 | Woodson, Rod | CB-KR | 6-0 | 197 | 6 | Purdue |

*Rod Woodson will hope to rebound from a sub-par 1991 campaign.*

outside linebacker positions, led by specialist Jerrol Williams. In the regular starting positions, the incumbent quartet of Hardy Nickerson, David Little, Bryan Hinkle and Greg Lloyd is set to continue for a fourth straight year, though Levon Kirkland was not drafted in round two to be a bench-warmer.

The secondary should be a strength but, again, will need to rebound from a sub-par campaign. David Johnson is a solid left cornerback but, at the right cornerback position, the highly acclaimed Rod Woodson slipped a little below his best. Free safety Thomas Everett is regarded as one of the league's most telling tacklers but he is exposed by the long pass. The other safety, Carnell Lake, is now seen as the more effective of the inside pairing.

Kicker Gary Anderson has been ranked with the best for most of his ten pro seasons. He is joined by Plan-B signing Mark Royals, who takes over the vacant position of punter and will hold for Anderson on shots at goal.

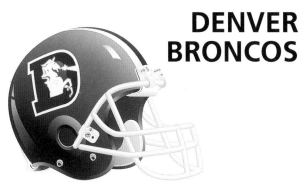

# DENVER BRONCOS

**Address** 13655 Broncos Parkway, Englewood, Colorado 80112.

**Stadium** Denver Mile High Stadium.
*Capacity* 76,273 *Playing Surface* Grass (PAT).

**Team Colours** Orange, Royal Blue, and White.

**Head Coach** Dan Reeves – 12th year.

**Championships** Division 1977,'78,'84,'86,'87,'89,'91; Conference 1977,'86,'87,'89.

**History** AFL 1960-69, AFC 1970-

We should not have been surprised that Denver went from last place in 1990 to first place, earning a bye for the first-round playoffs by having the AFC's second-best regular-season record. And it was hardly a shock when John Elway rallied the Broncos for an unlikely win against Houston, before losing narrowly to Buffalo in the AFC Championship Game. If anything, they look a little stronger in 1992.

One reason is the arrival of Sammie Smith, who came as a straight swap with Miami in return for Bobby Humphrey. Smith may not have Humphrey's speed but, whereas Humphrey was unsettled, Smith will be anxious to make a point. He is not likely to start but he can ease the burden on Gaston Green, who has silenced a few doubters with his 1,000-yard rushing campaign, and it means that the Broncos can threaten from the running back position on every down. Greg Lewis was another pleasant surprise and gives the club fine depth.

Elway, of course, is the nerve centre of the Denver offense and his importance, coupled with the retirement of long-time backup Gary Kubiak, moved the team to seek both emergency veteran experience and youth for the long term. Accordingly, Steve Pelluer was signed under Plan B and Tommy Maddox came in the first round of the draft. Elway's job may be a little easier in the coming season for, in addition to the arrival of Smith at running back, he will now have a fine pass receiving tight end in Plan-B acquisition Robert Awalt, who is another wishing to show his former clubs, Phoenix and the Cowboys, what he could have done if featured. Currently, as much for his blocking as his pass receiving, the starting tight end is Clarence Kay, but he has had his disagreements with the club and may concede

seniority to Awalt. Elway's main targets will be wide receivers Mark Jackson, who was leading the club before an injury, and Mike Young. Together with last year's promising rookie, Derek Russell, Vance Johnson will vie for playing time in yet another area that is likely to be stronger.

If Denver has a weakness it is on the offensive line, where the power of left tackle Gerald Perry, whose trade to the Rams brought Green to Denver, was missed. Elbert Crawford has arrived via Plan B and, together with Crawford Ker, will challenge Doug Widell at right guard. Otherwise the lineup will have Ken Lanier at right tackle, Sean Farrell at left guard, Keith Kartz at center and the pairing of Jeff Davidson and Harvey Salem rotating at left tackle.

Several factors, notably a surprise resurgence by both inside linebacker Karl Mecklenburg and strong safety Dennis Smith, but mostly a superb rookie debut by outside linebacker Mike Croel, meant that Denver emerged as the AFC's best defense. Gradually, Warren Powers took over from Alphonso Carreker at defensive left end to operate with nose tackle Greg Kragen and right end Ron Holmes. The feeling is that Kenny Walker and second-round draftee Shane Dronett can develop into starting defensive ends. With the line bearing the brunt of the rush, it was the linebackers who collared the quarterback, with Simon Fletcher (13.5), Croel (10) and Mecklenburg (9) the leading sackers. There is no suggestion that Mecklenburg is slowing but he will be pressed by the ambitious Keith Traylor, who is waiting for his chance. At the left inside spot, Michael Brooks continues to reward the club for its faith in his complete rehabilitation from a college injury in 1986.

Even though seemingly at the peak of his powers, Dennis Smith has been around since 1981 and 1992 is projected by

| 1992 SCHEDULE OF GAMES | September | |
|---|---|---|
| | 6 LOS ANGELES RAIDERS | 6:00 |
| | 13 SAN DIEGO | 2:00 |
| | 20 at Philadelphia | 1:00 |
| | 27 at Cleveland | 1:00 |
| | October | |
| | 4 KANSAS CITY | 2:00 |
| | 12 at Washington (Mon.) | 9:00 |
| | 18 HOUSTON | 2:00 |
| | 25 at San Diego | 1:00 |
| | November | |
| | 1 Open Date | |
| | 8 NEW YORK JETS | 2:00 |
| | 15 NEW YORK GIANTS | 6:00 |
| | 22 at Los Angeles Raiders | 1:00 |
| | 30 at Seattle (Mon.) | 6:00 |
| | December | |
| | 6 DALLAS | 2:00 |
| | 12 at Buffalo (Sat.) | 12:30 |
| | 20 SEATTLE | 2:00 |
| | 27 at Kansas City | 12:00 |

| Round | Name | Pos. | Ht. | Wt. | College |
|---|---|---|---|---|---|
| 1. | Maddox, Tommy | QB | 6-3 | 195 | UCLA |
| 2. | Dronett, Shane | DE | 6-5 | 273 | Texas |
| 4. | Johnson, Chuck | G | 6-3 | 280 | Texas |
| 5. | Robinson, Frank | CB | 5-10 | 175 | Boise State |
| 7. | Geater, Ron | DE | 6-5 | 275 | Iowa |
| 7. | Johnson; Jim | T | 6-4 | 301 | Michigan State |
| 7. | Bostick, Jon | WR | 6-0 | 191 | Nebraska |
| 8. | Lockridge, Dietrich | G | 6-2 | 325 | Jackson State |
| 9. | Oliver, Muhammad | CB | 5-10 | 172 | Oregon |
| 10. | Meeks, Bob | C | 6-1 | 286 | Auburn |
| 11. | Tillman, Cedric | WR | 6-3 | 190 | Alcorn State |
| 12. | Granby, John | DB | 6-2 | 203 | Virginia Tech |

**VETERAN ROSTER**

| No. | Name | Pos. | Ht. | Wt. | NFL Year | College |
|---|---|---|---|---|---|---|
| 27 | Atwater, Steve | S | 6-3 | 213 | 4 | Arkansas |
|  | Awalt, Robert | TE | 6-5 | 245 | 6 | San Diego State |
| 34 | Braxton, Tyrone | CB | 5-11 | 185 | 6 | North Dakota State |
| 56 | Brooks, Michael | LB | 6-1 | 235 | 6 | Louisiana State |
|  | Crawford, Elbert | G | 6-3 | 280 | 3 | Arkansas |
| 51 | Croel, Mike | LB | 6-3 | 231 | 2 | Nebraska |
| 62 | Davidson, Jeff | G | 6-5 | 309 | 3 | Ohio State |
| 29 | Dimry, Charles | CB | 6-0 | 175 | 5 | Nevada-Las Vegas |
| 7 | Elway, John | QB | 6-3 | 215 | 10 | Stanford |
| 63 | Farrell, Sean | G | 6-3 | 260 | 11 | Penn State |
| 73 | Fletcher, Simon | LB | 6-5 | 240 | 8 | Houston |
| 28 | Green, Gaston | RB | 5-11 | 192 | 5 | UCLA |
| 93 | Haliburton, Ronnie | LB | 6-4 | 230 | 3 | Louisiana State |
| 24 | Henderson, Wymon | CB | 5-9 | 186 | 6 | Nevada-Las Vegas |
| 90 | Holmes, Ron | DE | 6-4 | 265 | 8 | Washington |
| 2 | Horan, Mike | P | 5-11 | 190 | 9 | Cal State-Long Beach |
| 80 | Jackson, Mark | WR | 5-9 | 180 | 7 | Purdue |
| 86 | Johnson, Barry | WR | 6-2 | 197 | 2 | Maryland |
| 89 | Johnson, Reggie | TE | 6-2 | 256 | 2 | Florida State |
| 82 | Johnson, Vance | WR | 5-11 | 185 | 8 | Arizona |
| 72 | Kartz, Keith | C | 6-4 | 270 | 6 | California |
| 88 | Kay, Clarence | TE | 6-2 | 237 | 9 | Georgia |
| 68 | Ker, Crawford | G | 6-3 | 283 | 8 | Florida |
| 71 | Kragen, Greg | NT | 6-3 | 265 | 8 | Utah State |
| 21 | Lang, Le-Lo | CB | 5-11 | 185 | 3 | Washington |
| 76 | Lanier, Ken | T | 6-3 | 290 | 12 | Florida State |
| 41 | Lewis, Greg | RB | 5-10 | 214 | 2 | Washington |
| 59 | Lucas, Tim | LB | 6-3 | 230 | 6 | California |
| 77 | Mecklenburg, Karl | LB | 6-3 | 240 | 10 | Minnesota |
| 52 | Mills, Jeff | LB | 6-3 | 238 | 3 | Nebraska |
| 22 | Montgomery, Alton | S | 6-0 | 195 | 3 | Houston |
| 12 | Moore, Shawn | QB | 6-2 | 214 | 2 | Virginia |
| 57 | Murray, Mark | LB | 6-2 | 240 | 2 | Florida |
|  | Pelluer, Steve | QB | 6-4 | 212 | 9 | Washington |
| 33 | Perryman, Robert | RB | 6-2 | 233 | 6 | Michigan |
|  | Pollack, Frank | T-G | 6-5 | 285 | 3 | Northern Arizona |
| 91 | Powers, Warren | DE | 6-6 | 287 | 4 | Maryland |
| 38 | Rivers, Reggie | RB | 6-1 | 215 | 2 | Southwest Texas State |
| 85 | Russell, Derek | WR | 6-0 | 179 | 2 | Arkansas |
| 74 | Salem, Harvey | T | 6-6 | 289 | 10 | California |
| 30 | Sewell, Steve | RB-WR | 6-3 | 210 | 8 | Oklahoma |
| 81 | Sharpe, Shannon | TE-WR | 6-2 | 225 | 3 | Savannah State |
| 49 | Smith, Dennis | S | 6-3 | 200 | 12 | Southern California |
|  | Smith, Sammie | RB | 6-2 | 230 | 4 | Florida State |
| 70 | Sochia, Brian | NT | 6-3 | 278 | 10 | N.W. Oklahoma |
| 60 | Subis, Nick | T-G | 6-4 | 278 | 2 | San Diego State |
| 54 | Traylor, Keith | LB | 6-2 | 260 | 2 | Central State, Okla. |
| 9 | Treadwell, David | K | 6-1 | 175 | 4 | Clemson |
| 96 | Walker, Kenny | DE | 6-3 | 246 | 2 | Nebraska |
| 79 | Widell, Dave | G-C | 6-6 | 292 | 5 | Boston College |
| 67 | Widell, Doug | G | 6-4 | 287 | 4 | Boston College |
| 83 | Young, Michael | WR | 6-1 | 183 | 8 | UCLA |

him to be his final campaign. The Broncos will miss this five-time Pro Bowler who controls the centre of the field as much by influence as athleticism. Steve Atwater is widely regarded as the finest free safety in the AFC and, with Smith, shared the club lead for interceptions (5). Atwater has been a Pro Bowler after the last two of his three NFL years. Tyrone Braxton and Wymon Henderson are two solid cornerbacks but the reserve strength is modest and it is a disappointment that Alton Montgomery, who can cover at both safety and cornerback, has not developed as expected.

Punter Mike Horan is steady enough and has learned the subtleties of charting the atmospheric layers of Mile High Stadium. However, David Treadwell is coming off a sub-par season, culminating in field goal misses of 47, 42 and 37 yards in the AFC title game against Buffalo when one would have earned a tie. He should be given the chance to atone.

*ABOVE: Linebacker Simon Fletcher led the Broncos in sacks for the fourth consecutive season.*

# KANSAS CITY CHIEFS

**Address** One Arrowhead Drive, Kansas City, Missouri 64129.

**Stadium** Arrowhead Stadium, Kansas City. *Capacity* 78,067 *Playing Surface* AstroTurf-8.

**Team Colours** Red, Gold, and White.

**Head Coach** Marty Schottenheimer – 4th year; 9th NFL.

**Championships** Division 1971; AFL 1962, '66, '69; Super Bowl 1969.

**History** AFL 1960-69, AFC 1970- (Until 1963, they were known as the Dallas Texans.)

The Chiefs have reached the playoffs as a wild card in each of the last two seasons. They enter 1992 strongly fancied to bid for the division title.

While the defense is certainly not a sleeping partner, most of the optimism surrounds the offense where Kansas City has three genuine starters for the running back positions. The system is triggered by a primeval force surging out of the backfield as either of the two heavyweights, Christian Okoye and Barry Word, comes bursting through the line of scrimmage. It means that a defender always comes away with bruises and obliges opponents to gang-tackle most of the time. With the softening-up process complete, the mercurial Harvey Williams is on hand to dodge and scythe his way through the open spaces. Last year, this combination gave the Chiefs the NFL's third-best rushing attack and it is reasonable to feel that only the modesty of the passing offense prevented their challenging the Broncos more effectively. Sadly, the deep passing game disappeared with the loss of top wide receiver Stephone Paige, who, in 1985, set the NFL single-game receiving yardage record of 309. Paige played just two games and, in his absence, the combination of Robb Thomas and Tim Barnett could not make up the shortfall. Encouragingly, Barnett showed good style as a rookie and should be a key element as the third receiver behind the starting pair of Paige and Thomas. Tight end Jonathan Hayes has been a good servant for seven years but, with a single-season best of 22 receptions in 1988, he has never been a big-time receiver.

*Former nose tackle Bill Maas is starting his third season at defensive end.*

| 1992 SCHEDULE OF GAMES | | |
|---|---|---|
| **September** | | |
| 6 at San Diego | | 1:00 |
| 13 SEATTLE | | 12:00 |
| 20 at Houston | | 12:00 |
| 28 LOS ANGELES RAIDERS (Mon.) | | 8:00 |
| **October** | | |
| 4 at Denver | | 2:00 |
| 11 PHILADELPHIA | | 12:00 |
| 18 at Dallas | | 12:00 |
| 25 PITTSBURGH | | 6:30 |
| **November** | | |
| 1 Open Date | | |
| 8 SAN DIEGO | | 3:00 |
| 15 WASHINGTON | | 12:00 |
| 22 at Seattle | | 5:00 |
| 29 at New York Jets | | 1:00 |
| **December** | | |
| 6 at Los Angeles Raiders | | 1:00 |
| 13 NEW ENGLAND | | 12:00 |
| 19 at New York Giants (Sat.) | | 12:30 |
| 27 DENVER | | 12:00 |

However, there could be an improvement with the acquisition of free agent Mike Dyal, who made great progress as a Raiders rookie in 1989 before fading from the picture with an injury early in 1990.

For the quarterback position, Seattle eight-year starter Dave Krieg has been signed as a free agent. A battler who knows his way around the AFC West, Krieg could add a degree of variety and initiative not yet revealed by Mark Vlasic, who was left exposed by the loss of Steve DeBerg to free agency. It is most likely that Krieg will start and, at least, will be fun to watch. Draftee Matt Blundin represents the long-term future. Krieg will certainly be given better protection than he received in Seattle by an offensive line of immense security. With John Alt, Dave Szott, Tim Grunhard and Dave Lutz in place, the only doubt surrounds the right tackle spot. Here, Derrick Graham replaced Rich Baldinger late in 1991 but he may be pressed by Joe Valerio, who may have progressed well enough in the World League to earn his chance.

On defense, there are few worries and, again, there is great stability in most areas. The line will be unchanged, with defensive ends Neil Smith and Bill Maas flanking the powerful nose tackle, Dan Saleaumua. Smith, a first-round draftee for whom Kansas City traded up in 1988, led the trio with eight sacks. But the real devastation comes from the right outside linebacker position in the form of Derrick Thomas, who has had 43.5 sacks over his three pro years. Another former first-round pick, Percy Snow, is expected to resume at left inside linebacker, partnering the fearsome Dino Hackett. Currently, Chris Martin holds off his challengers for the spot at left outside linebacker and he should retain his status, despite the obvious improvement shown by Lonnie Marts.

For how long Kansas City can assume excellence in the secondary no one can be certain. In the cornerback positions, Pro Bowlers Albert Lewis and Kevin Ross have ruled as a pairing ever since 1984 except for when injuries intervened. Thankfully, these have been very few but a big one, that dreadful posterior cruciate ligament damage, hit Lewis last season and his return to top speed is far from certain. In his absence, Jayice Pearson did well enough, intercepting three passes. Free safety Deron Cherry has been starting since 1983 and is a six-time Pro Bowler. While he could manage another season at the top, the Chiefs felt it prudent to draft Dale Carter as his successor. At strong safety, Kevin Porter should hold off the challenge of Martin Bayless.

For the special teams, help has arrived in the form of free agent signing Bennie Thompson, who was the Pro Bowl specialist on kick coverage. He also offers reserve strength at defensive back. As usual, Nick Lowery is expected to handle the job of placekicker with great composure, but punter Bryan Barker could use a little more distance with his efforts.

## 1992 Draft

| Round | Name | Pos. | Ht. | Wt. | College |
|---|---|---|---|---|---|
| 1. | Carter, Dale | S | 6-0 | 188 | Tennessee |
| 2. | Blundin, Matt | QB | 6-6 | 228 | Virginia |
| 4. | Evans, Mike | DE | 6-3 | 266 | Michigan |
| 6. | Smith, Tony | WR | 6-1 | 189 | Notre Dame |
| 7. | Anderson, Erick | LB | 6-1 | 241 | Michigan |
| 8.. | Jennings, Jim | G | 6-2 | 270 | San Diego State |
| 9. | Leeuwenburg, Jay | C | 6-2 | 279 | Colorado |
| 10. | Ostroski, Jerry | G | 6-3 | 316 | Tulsa |
| 11. | Rigby, Doug | DE | 6-5 | 288 | Wyoming |
| 12. | Williams, Corey | DB | 5-10 | 182 | Oklahoma State |

## VETERAN ROSTER

| No. | Name | Pos. | Ht. | Wt. | NFL Year | College |
|---|---|---|---|---|---|---|
| 76 | Alt, John | T | 6-8 | 296 | 9 | Iowa |
| 38 | Anders, Kimble | RB | 5-11 | 219 | 2 | Houston |
| | Anderson, Herbie | DB | 5-9 | 183 | 1 | Texas A&I |
| 77 | Baldinger, Rich | T-G | 6-4 | 293 | 11 | Wake Forest |
| 4 | Barker, Bryan | P | 6-1 | 187 | 3 | Santa Clara |
| 82 | Barnett, Tim | WR | 6-1 | 209 | 2 | Jackson State |
| | Bayless, Martin | S | 6-2 | 212 | 9 | Bowling Green |
| 40 | Bell, Billy | CB | 5-10 | 170 | 3 | Lamar |
| 88 | Birden, J.J. | WR | 5-9 | 170 | 3 | Oregon |
| | Cash, Keith | TE | 6-4 | 235 | 2 | Texas |
| 20 | Cherry, Deron | S | 5-11 | 203 | 12 | Rutgers |
| 71 | Dohring, Tom | T | 6-6 | 290 | 1 | Michigan |
| | Dyal, Mike | TE | 6-2 | 235 | 3 | Texas A&I |
| 39 | Everett, Eric | CB | 5-10 | 170 | 5 | Texas Tech |
| 74 | Graham, Derrick | T | 6-4 | 306 | 3 | Appalachian State |
| 98 | Griffin, Leonard | DE | 6-4 | 278 | 7 | Grambling |
| 61 | Grunhard, Tim | C | 6-2 | 299 | 3 | Notre Dame |
| 56 | Hackett, Dino | LB | 6-3 | 230 | 7 | Appalachian State |
| | Hagy, John | S | 6-0 | 190 | 4 | Texas |
| | Hargain, Tony | WR | 6-0 | 188 | 1 | Oregon |
| 86 | Harry, Emile | WR | 5-11 | 180 | 6 | Stanford |
| 85 | Hayes, Jonathan | TE | 6-5 | 248 | 8 | Iowa |
| | Irvin, Ray | CB | 5-11 | 176 | 1 | Central Florida |
| 43 | Jones, Bill | RB | 5-11 | 227 | 3 | Southwest Texas State |
| 80 | Jones, Fred | WR | 5-9 | 182 | 3 | Grambling |
| | Krieg, Dave | QB | 6-1 | 192 | 13 | Milton |
| 29 | Lewis, Albert | CB | 6-2 | 195 | 10 | Grambling |
| | Lewis, Tahaun | DB | 5-10 | 175 | 1 | Nebraska |
| 8 | Lowery, Nick | K | 6-4 | 205 | 13 | Dartmouth |
| 72 | Lutz, David | G-T | 6-6 | 305 | 10 | Georgia Tech |
| 63 | Maas, Bill | DE | 6-5 | 275 | 9 | Pittsburgh |
| 57 | Martin, Chris | LB | 6-2 | 241 | 10 | Auburn |
| 51 | Marts, Lonnie | LB | 6-1 | 243 | 2 | Tulane |
| 48 | McNair, Todd | RB | 6-1 | 197 | 4 | Temple |
| 42 | Mincy, Charles | DB | 5-11 | 187 | 1 | Washington |
| 30 | Mitchell, Stump | RB | 5-9 | 194 | 10 | Citadel |
| 35 | Okoye, Christian | RB | 6-1 | 260 | 6 | Azusa Pacific |
| 83 | Paige, Stephone | WR | 6-2 | 188 | 10 | Fresno State |
| 24 | Pearson, Jayice | CB | 5-11 | 185 | 7 | Washington |
| 27 | Porter, Kevin | S | 5-10 | 214 | 5 | Auburn |
| 55 | Randle, Ervin | LB | 6-1 | 250 | 8 | Baylor |
| 52 | Rogers, Tracy | LB | 6-2 | 241 | 3 | Fresno State |
| 31 | Ross, Kevin | CB | 5-9 | 182 | 9 | Temple |
| 97 | Saleaumua, Dan | NT | 6-0 | 295 | 6 | Arizona State |
| 54 | Simien, Tracy | LB | 6-1 | 245 | 2 | Texas Christian |
| 95 | Sims, Tom | NT | 6-2 | 285 | 2 | Pittsburgh |
| 90 | Smith, Neil | DE | 6-4 | 275 | 5 | Nebraska |
| 59 | Snow, Percy | LB | 6-2 | 244 | 2 | Michigan State |
| 25 | Stradford, Troy | RB | 5-9 | 195 | 6 | Boston College |
| 79 | Szott, David | G | 6-4 | 275 | 3 | Penn State |
| 58 | Thomas, Derrick | LB | 6-3 | 236 | 4 | Alabama |
| 81 | Thomas, Robb | WR | 5-11 | 175 | 4 | Oregon State |
| | Thompson, Bennie | S | 6-0 | 200 | 3 | Grambling |
| 73 | Valerio, Joe | T | 6-5 | 293 | 2 | Pennsylvania |
| 13 | Vlasic, Mark | QB | 6-3 | 205 | 5 | Iowa |
| 44 | Williams, Harvey | RB | 6-2 | 222 | 2 | Louisiana State |
| 23 | Word, Barry | RB | 6-2 | 242 | 4 | Virginia |

# LOS ANGELES RAIDERS

**Address** 332 Center Street, El Segundo,
California 90245.

**Stadium** Los Angeles Memorial Coliseum.
*Capacity* 92,488 *Playing Surface* Grass.

**Team Colours** Silver and Black.

**Head Coach** Art Shell – 4th year.

**Championships** Division 1970,'72,'73,'74,'75,'76,
'83,'85,'90; Conference 1976,'80,'83; AFL 1967;
Super Bowl 1976,'80,'83.

**History** AFL 1960-69, AFC 1970-
(Until 1982, they were known as the Oakland Raiders.)

The Raiders still have a few problems to solve but there can be little doubt that, as usual, they will contend for a title.

Never one to miss the opportunity to pick up 'name' players who have been either unsuccessful with other clubs or simply are disgruntled, Raiders owner Al Davis has signed Aundray Bruce, who was the first pick overall in the 1988 draft but never lived up to that reputation with Atlanta. The Falcons even tried him out at tight end last season. Another linebacker, Anthony Bell, was the fifth pick overall in 1986, and while he started for Phoenix he never developed into a superstar. Dave Waymer, who was essentially a 12-year starting defensive back with New Orleans and San Francisco and has 48 career interceptions, was another veteran acquisition under Plan B.

And then there is Eric Dickerson. On his day, the former Rams and Colts player can be the most destructive running back in football but his career has been dogged by disputes. Depending on your point of view, with the Raiders either everyone has an ego or no one has. Dickerson will fit in and might tear up the gridiron just for the hell of it.

Each new member of the squad has a rôle to play but none will be involved in the most critical position of all, namely at quarterback, where the strong-armed Jay Schroeder is challenged by the young but highly talented Todd Marinovich. Most scouts would favour Schroeder's experience but the chances are that the Raiders will opt for the potential of raw talent. Marinovich did look composed as the starter for the Raiders' final two outings of last year. In addition to the long passing game, the quarterback will have to use finesse in servicing a collection of thoroughbred wide receivers in Willie Gault, Mervyn Fernandez, Tim Brown and Sam Graddy. The Raiders re-acquired Mike Alexander, who does not have top-class speed but may squeeze on to the roster for his excellent hands. At the tight end position, Ethan Horton can explode for his big days while the club is highly impressed with backup Andrew Glover.

Much as the Raiders love the deep passing game, they have always respected the value of power at running back. The plan was that, as Marcus Allen eased out graciously, the bruising Nick Bell would come to the fore, with Steve Smith established as the blocking fullback. Now that Dickerson has appeared on the scene, there will be a scramble for playing time. The loss of Roger Craig may have avoided a log jam.

One area of uncertainty in recent years has been the offensive line, which always seems to be one class player short. Draftee tackle Greg Skrepenak should fill that need but not immediately. It means that the starting lineup will remain intact with Bruce Wilkerson and Steve Wright at tackle, Steve Wisniewski and Max Montoya at guard and Don Mosebar at center. Problems arise when one of the starters is injured.

*LEFT: Howie Long, the senior player on the Raiders squad, would love to end his illustrious career with a second Super Bowl ring.*

## 1992 SCHEDULE OF GAMES

### September
| | | |
|---|---|---|
| 6 | at Denver | 6:00 |
| 13 | at Cincinnati | 1:00 |
| 20 | CLEVELAND | 1:00 |
| 28 | at Kansas City (Mon.) | 8:00 |

### October
| | | |
|---|---|---|
| 4 | NEW YORK GIANTS | 1:00 |
| 11 | BUFFALO | 1:00 |
| 18 | at Seattle | 1:00 |
| 25 | DALLAS | 1:00 |

### November
| | | |
|---|---|---|
| 1 | Open Date | |
| 8 | at Philadelphia | 1:00 |
| 15 | SEATTLE | 1:00 |
| 22 | DENVER | 1:00 |
| 29 | at San Diego | 5:00 |

### December
| | | |
|---|---|---|
| 6 | KANSAS CITY | 1:00 |
| 14 | at Miami (Mon.) | 9:00 |
| 20 | SAN DIEGO | 1:00 |
| 26 | at Washington (Sat.) | 4:00 |

## 1992 Draft

| Round | Name | Pos. | Ht. | Wt. | College |
|---|---|---|---|---|---|
| 1. | McGlockton, Ch. | DT | 6-3 | 337 | Clemson |
| 2. | Skrepenak, Greg | T | 6-6 | 316 | Michigan |
| 5. | Hoskins, Derrick | S | 6-2 | 201 | Southern Mississippi |
| 6. | Rowell, Tony | C | 6-4 | 277 | Florida |
| 7. | Cotton, Curtis | DB | 5-11 | 209 | Nebraska |
| 7. | Smith, Kevin | RB | 6-3 | 262 | UCLA |
| 10. | White, Alberto | LB | 6-3 | 234 | Texas Southern |
| 12. | Roth, Tom | G | 6-5 | 296 | Southern Illinois |

## VETERAN ROSTER

| No. | Name | Pos. | Ht. | Wt. | NFL Year | College |
|---|---|---|---|---|---|---|
| | Alexander, Mike | WR | 6-3 | 185 | 3 | Penn State |
| 32 | Allen, Marcus | RB | 6-2 | 210 | 11 | Southern California |
| 33 | Anderson, Eddie | S | 6-1 | 210 | 7 | Fort Valley State |
| | Bell, Anthony | LB | 6-3 | 235 | 7 | Michigan State |
| 38 | Bell, Nick | RB | 6-2 | 255 | 2 | Iowa |
| 54 | Benson, Tom | LB | 6-2 | 240 | 9 | Oklahoma |
| | Brown, Ron | WR-KR | 5-11 | 185 | 9 | Arizona State |
| 81 | Brown, Tim | WR-KR | 6-0 | 190 | 4 | Notre Dame |
| | Bruce, Aundray | LB | 6-5 | 250 | 5 | Auburn |
| 70 | Davis, Scott | DT | 6-7 | 275 | 5 | Illinois |
| | Dickerson, Eric | RB | 6-3 | 224 | 10 | Southern Methodist |
| 46 | Dorn, Torin | CB | 6-0 | 190 | 3 | North Carolina |
| | Ellison, Bernard | CB | 6-0 | 192 | 1 | Nevada-Reno |
| 50 | Ellison, Riki | LB | 6-2 | 225 | 9 | Southern California |
| 11 | Evans, Vince | QB | 6-2 | 210 | 13 | Southern California |
| 86 | Fernandez, Mervyn | WR | 6-3 | 200 | 6 | San Jose State |
| 73 | FitzPatrick, James | T | 6-7 | 320 | 7 | Southern California |
| 83 | Gault, Willie | WR | 6-1 | 175 | 10 | Tennessee |
| 87 | Glover, Andrew | TE | 6-6 | 240 | 2 | Grambling |
| 79 | Golic, Bob | DT | 6-2 | 275 | 13 | Notre Dame |
| 7 | Gossett, Jeff | P | 6-2 | 195 | 11 | Eastern Illinois |
| 85 | Graddy, Sam | WR | 5-10 | 175 | 5 | Tennessee |
| 60 | Graves, Rory | T | 6-6 | 295 | 5 | Ohio State |
| 74 | Harrison, Nolan | DT | 6-5 | 285 | 2 | Indiana |
| 88 | Horton, Ethan | TE | 6-4 | 240 | 6 | North Carolina |
| 18 | Jaeger, Jeff | K | 5-11 | 195 | 5 | Washington |
| 58 | Jimerson, A.J. | DE | 6-3 | 235 | 3 | Norfolk State |
| | Jones, David | WR | 6-2 | 217 | 1 | Delaware State |
| 52 | Jones, Mike | LB | 6-1 | 225 | 2 | Missouri |
| 25 | Land, Dan | S | 6-0 | 195 | 4 | Albany State |
| 75 | Long, Howie | DE | 6-5 | 270 | 12 | Villanova |
| 42 | Lott, Ronnie | S | 6-0 | 205 | 12 | Southern California |
| 12 | Marinovich, Todd | QB | 6-4 | 215 | 2 | Southern California |
| 41 | McCallum, Napoleon | RB | 6-2 | 225 | 4 | Navy |
| 36 | McDaniel, Terry | CB | 5-10 | 180 | 4 | Tennessee |
| 77 | McElroy, Reggie | T | 6-6 | 290 | 10 | West Texas State |
| 65 | Montoya, Max | G | 6-5 | 290 | 14 | UCLA |
| 72 | Mosebar, Don | C | 6-6 | 285 | 10 | Southern California |
| 99 | Moss, Winston | LB | 6-3 | 240 | 6 | Miami |
| 31 | Mueller, Vance | RB | 6-0 | 225 | 7 | Occidental |
| | Noga, Niko | LB | 6-1 | 235 | 9 | Hawaii |
| 71 | Patten, Joel | T | 6-7 | 290 | 8 | Duke |
| 43 | Patterson, Elvis | S | 5-11 | 195 | 9 | Kansas |
| 13 | Schroeder, Jay | QB | 6-4 | 215 | 9 | UCLA |
| | Seale, Sam | CB | 5-9 | 185 | 9 | Western State, Colo. |
| 94 | Smith, Anthony | DE | 6-3 | 270 | 2 | Arizona |
| 35 | Smith, Steve | RB | 6-1 | 240 | 6 | Penn State |
| 93 | Townsend, Greg | DE | 6-3 | 265 | 10 | Texas Christian |
| 67 | Turk, Dan | C | 6-4 | 270 | 7 | Wisconsin |
| 51 | Wallace, Aaron | LB | 6-3 | 235 | 3 | Texas A&M |
| 48 | Washington, Lionel | CB | 6-0 | 185 | 10 | Tulane |
| | Waymer, Dave | S | 6-1 | 188 | 13 | Notre Dame |
| 68 | Wilkerson, Bruce | T | 6-5 | 295 | 6 | Tennessee |
| 76 | Wisniewski, Steve | G | 6-4 | 285 | 4 | Penn State |
| 66 | Wright, Steve | T | 6-6 | 280 | 10 | Northern Iowa |

The defensive line is an area of perennial Raiders strength, particularly at the end positions. They didn't need another but draftee Chester McGlockton, who may be a more athletic version of Chicago's William Perry, was too good to overlook. He joins a group containing Pro Bowlers Greg Townsend and Howie Long, Nolan Harrison and Anthony Smith, the latter who reminds some scouts of the great Deacon Jones and is on course for All-Pro status. As Smith develops, Long may move inside to play tackle more often in partnership with Scott Davis.

Linebacking is a relative weakness though there's no shortage of venom in the likes of Riki Ellison, Winston Moss and Tom Benson, while Aaron Wallace has shown himself to be a murderous pass rusher. It is in this group that Bell and Bruce have the chance to make an impact.

There may be a spot for Waymer in the secondary, though he will not displace strong safety Ronnie Lott, who has had a Hall of Fame career and still has another couple of seasons left in him. Waymer could share time with free safety Eddie Anderson. The cornerbacks, Terry McDaniel and Lionel Washington, are steady enough without reaching the heights of former Raiders stars such as Lester Hayes and Mike Haynes.

Los Angeles may have the best special teams in football, not only in placekicker Jeff Jaeger and punter Jeff Gossett, two current Pro Bowlers, but also in Pro Bowl kick returner Tim Brown who is at his best when circling under a punt.

# SAN DIEGO CHARGERS

**Address** San Diego Jack Murphy Stadium, P.O. Box 609609, San Diego, California 92160-9609.

**Stadium** San Diego Jack Murphy Stadium.
*Capacity* 60,835 *Playing Surface* Grass.

**Team Colours** Navy Blue, White, and Gold.

**Head Coach** Bobby Ross – 1st year.

**Championships** Division 1979,'80,'81; AFL 1963.

**History** AFL 1960-69, AFC 1970-

(For 1960 only, they were known as the Los Angeles Chargers.)

*25-year-old John Friesz continues to hone his passing skills in the heat of NFL action.*

Since their last winning campaign, the Chargers have laboured through three 6–10 seasons and, last year, sunk to 4–12. It is their lot to play in a division which is gathering strength after a few lean years but, under new head coach Bobby Ross and with the prospect of an improved defense, they might hope for better in 1992.

A great deal rests on the showing of quarterback John Friesz, who earned the starting job over Billy Joe Tolliver in the second half of a 1991 preseason game against the Raiders. Friesz subsequently struggled but the club persevered with him and it would appear that 1992 will again see him gaining on-the-job experience. A young quarterback is always helped if he can turn to reliability at running back and this should be there in the shape of Marion Butts. A huge specimen, Butts is a steam hammer and, like those relics of our industrial past, he needs time to gather momentum. When he does, defenders perish on the anvil. Over his three years since arriving as a seventh-round draft pick, Butts has slammed for 4.4 yards per carry and, simply, needs to be featured to give of his best. With linebackers gathering in the collective effort to handle him, the fringes are available for exploitation by Rod Bernstine, who is listed as an H-back but is equally well identified as a long-striding outside runner. Bernstine, too, is hungry for yardage after having been unsuccessful as a tight end in his early years.

Last season, the one-two combination gave San Diego the second-best rushing game in the entire NFL but, alone,

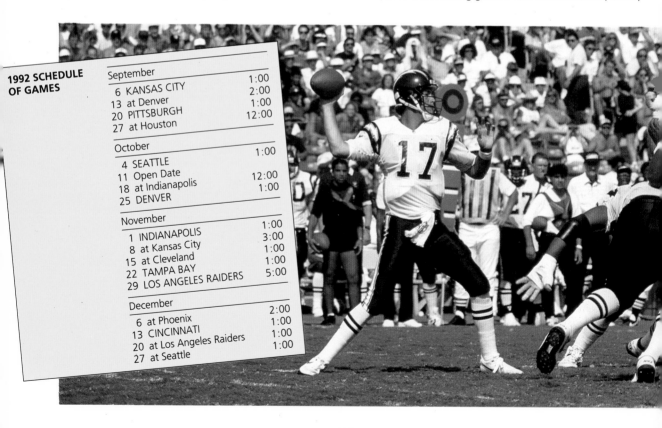

it can not finish off opponents. It means that the passing game, for which this club was once so feared, must resurface. For this, the Chargers have a true burner in wide receiver Anthony Miller, but he is coming off a campaign in which he was only barely more productive than his starting partner, Nate Lewis, with the two gaining only 1,203 yards in total. The spice for the mixture came from dual-purpose back Ronnie Harmon, who led the team with 59 catches, but a deep threat must emerge. The prospect of this, together with a helping of potential excitement, comes with third-round draftee Ray Ethridge. But there is need for a contribution from the tight end position, where Derrick Walker and Craig McEwen will compete.

The young offensive line is solid and improving steadily. Last year, the combination of Harry Swayne, Eric Moten, Courtney Hall, David Richards and Broderick Thompson gave up a respectable 35 sacks and opened up some running lanes.

The prospects for improvement lie on defense, where there is an embarrassment of talent for what is projected to be a change to the 4-3 formation. Leslie O'Neal and Junior Seau could start in the defensive end positions, with Burt Grossman and either Joe Phillips or George Thornton at tackle. The line would be at its best when turned loose to rush the passer, with the linebacking trio of Billy Ray Smith, Gary Plummer and Henry Rolling responsible primarily for pass coverage and run defense. The arrangement may depend on the speed with which top draftee defensive end Chris Mims settles in. Some scouts feel that Seau's range and instincts are put to their best use at linebacker, where he has the time to read and react as distinct from forcing a play from the end position. O'Neal started out as a defensive end before dropping back to outside linebacker during his rehabilitation from a severe knee injury suffered in late November 1986. He has confirmed his return by leading the Chargers in sacks for three consecutive years.

For the secondary, San Diego has true veteran class in left cornerback Gill Byrd, who raised his interception total to 27 over the past four seasons with a club-leading six. Free safety Stanley Richard was a 1991 first-round draft pick and is just beginning to live up to that status. However, both cornerback Sam Seale and strong safety Martin Bayless were lost to Plan-B free agency, meaning that draftee cornerback Marquez Pope will battle Cedric Mack, while former Pittsburgh starter Delton Hall has been brought in to compete with Anthony Shelton.

Outstanding kickoff returning by Lewis usually gives San Diego decent field position and placekicker John Carney needs only to develop a little more accuracy to complement his power. As a stimulus, draftee Carlos Huerta came in the 12th round. Accepting placement in lieu of distance, the club seems to be satisfied with punter John Kidd.

**1992 Draft**

| Round | Name | Pos. | Ht. | Wt. | College |
|---|---|---|---|---|---|
| 1. | Mims, Chris | DE | 6-4 | 281 | Tennessee |
| 2. | Pope, Marquez | S | 5-9 | 188 | Fresno State |
| 3. | Ethridge, Ray | WR | 5-10 | 180 | Pasadena City |
| 5. | Whitley, Curtis | C | 6-1 | 288 | Clemson |
| 5. | Little, Kevin | LB | 6-2 | 251 | North Carolina A&T |
| 5. | Jonassen, Eric | T | 6-5 | 310 | Bloomsburg, Pa. |
| 6. | White, Reggie | DT | 6-4 | 292 | North Carolina A&T |
| 7. | May, Deems | TE | 6-4 | 250 | North Carolina |
| 8. | Fuller, James | S | 5-11 | 205 | Portland State |
| 9. | Barnes, Johnnie | WR | 5-10 | 181 | Hampton |
| 10. | Paul, Arthur | DT | 6-4 | 300 | Arizona State |
| 11. | McAfee, Keith | RB | 6-0 | 218 | Texas A&M |
| 12. | Huerta, Carlos | K | 5-6 | 172 | Miami |

**VETERAN ROSTER**

| No. | Name | Pos. | Ht. | Wt. | NFL Year | College |
|---|---|---|---|---|---|---|
| 52 | Anno, Sam | LB | 6-2 | 235 | 6 | Southern California |
| 95 | Benson, Mitchell | NT | 6-4 | 300 | 4 | Texas Christian |
| 82 | Bernstine, Rod | RB | 6-3 | 238 | 6 | Texas A&M |
| 32 | Bieniemy, Eric | RB | 5-7 | 210 | 2 | Colorado |
| 37 | Blaylock, Anthony | CB | 5-11 | 190 | 5 | Winston-Salem State |
| 35 | Butts, Marion | RB | 6-1 | 248 | 4 | Florida State |
| 22 | Byrd, Gill | CB | 5-11 | 198 | 10 | San Jose State |
| 3 | Carney, John | K | 5-11 | 170 | 4 | Notre Dame |
| 29 | Carrington, Darren | S | 6-2 | 200 | 4 | Northern Arizona |
| 59 | Clark, Greg | LB | 6-0 | 232 | 5 | Arizona State |
| 28 | Elder, Donnie | CB-KR | 5-9 | 178 | 7 | Memphis State |
| 26 | Fields, Floyd | S | 6-0 | 208 | 2 | Arizona State |
| 27 | Frank, Donald | CB | 6-0 | 192 | 3 | Winston-Salem State |
| 17 | Friesz, John | QB | 6-4 | 218 | 2 | Idaho |
| 16 | Gagliano, Bob | QB | 6-3 | 205 | 6 | Utah State |
| 67 | Goeas, Leo | T | 6-4 | 292 | 3 | Hawaii |
| 7 | Graham, Jeff | QB | 6-5 | 215 | 2 | Long Beach State |
|  | Grayson, David | LB | 6-3 | 230 | 5 | Fresno State |
| 92 | Grossman, Burt | DE | 6-4 | 255 | 4 | Pittsburgh |
| 53 | Hall, Courtney | C | 6-2 | 281 | 4 | Rice |
|  | Hall, Delton | CB | 6-1 | 204 | 6 | Clemson |
| 33 | Harmon, Ronnie | RB | 5-11 | 207 | 7 | Iowa |
| 34 | Hendrickson, Steve | H-B | 6-0 | 258 | 4 | California |
|  | Jackson, Cedric | RB | 5-11 | 229 | 2 | Texas Christian |
| 80 | Jefferson, Shawn | WR | 5-11 | 172 | 2 | Central Florida |
|  | Joelson, Greg | DE | 6-3 | 270 | 2 | Arizona State |
| 21 | Kelson, Derrick | DB | 6-0 | 187 | 1 | Purdue |
| 10 | Kidd, John | P | 6-3 | 208 | 9 | Northwestern |
| 81 | Lewis, Nate | WR | 5-11 | 198 | 3 | Oregon Tech |
| 47 | Mack, Cedric | CB | 5-11 | 190 | 10 | Baylor |
|  | Marve, Eugene | LB | 6-2 | 240 | 11 | Saginaw Valley State |
| 31 | McEwen, Craig | H-B | 6-1 | 226 | 6 | Utah |
| 83 | Miller, Anthony | WR | 5-11 | 189 | 5 | Tennessee |
| 77 | Moten, Eric | G | 6-2 | 306 | 2 | Michigan State |
| 91 | O'Neal, Leslie | LB | 6-4 | 259 | 6 | Oklahoma State |
|  | Parrish, James | T | 6-5 | 292 | 1 | Temple |
| 75 | Phillips, Joe | NT | 6-5 | 315 | 7 | Southern Methodist |
| 50 | Plummer, Gary | LB | 6-2 | 244 | 7 | California |
|  | Price, Terry | DE | 6-4 | 272 | 2 | Texas A&M |
| 24 | Richard, Stanley | S | 6-2 | 197 | 2 | Texas |
| 65 | Richards, David | G-T | 6-5 | 310 | 5 | UCLA |
| 57 | Rolling, Henry | LB | 6-2 | 225 | 5 | Nevada-Reno |
| 55 | Seau, Junior | LB | 6-3 | 250 | 3 | Southern California |
| 23 | Shelton, Anthony | S | 6-1 | 195 | 3 | Tennessee State |
| 54 | Smith, Billy Ray | LB | 6-3 | 236 | 10 | Arkansas |
| 72 | Swayne, Harry | T | 6-5 | 290 | 6 | Rutgers |
| 56 | Thaxton, Galand | LB | 6-1 | 240 | 3 | Wyoming |
| 84 | Thigpen, Yancey | WR | 6-1 | 208 | 2 | Winston-Salem State |
| 76 | Thompson, Broderick | G-T | 6-5 | 295 | 8 | Kansas |
| 93 | Thornton, George | DT | 6-3 | 300 | 2 | Alabama |
|  | Vanhorse, Sean | CB | 5-10 | 180 | 1 | Howard |
| 89 | Walker, Derrick | TE | 6-1 | 250 | 3 | Michigan |
| 87 | Young, Duane | TE | 6-1 | 276 | 2 | Michigan State |
| 70 | Zandofsky, Mike | G | 6-2 | 285 | 4 | Washington |

# SEATTLE SEAHAWKS

**Address** 11220 N.E. 53rd Street, Kirkland,
Washington 98033.
**Stadium** Kingdome, Seattle.
*Capacity* 64,984 *Playing Surface* AstroTurf.
**Team Colours** Blue, Green, and Silver.
**Head Coach** Tom Flores – 1st year; 10th NFL.
**Championships** Division 1988.
**History** NFC 1976, AFC 1977-

There will be a change of style in Seattle, where former Raiders head coach Tom Flores adds this rôle to his responsibilities as president/general manager following the departure of Chuck Knox to the Rams. Filling gaps through the Plan-B system and the draft, Flores should keep the Seahawks competitive.

The major decision surrounds the position of starting quarterback, made vacant by the departure of Dave Krieg. The job will go to either Kelly Stouffer or Dan McGwire, with the latter probably ahead if only because Stouffer has not been able to use his previous opportunities to effect. It will take time for the new man to settle in and it is of critical importance that he is surrounded by solid veteran experience.

The club took a chance by trading for Rueben Mayes, who was selected to two Pro Bowls with New Orleans but whose career was thought to have been ruined by injury. Still, the Seahawks were sufficiently confident that they gave up a fourth-round draft option to find a potential game-breaker who could start at halfback in partnership with fullback John L. Williams. Through the years, Williams has been an excellent receiver while chipping in with solid rushing and bone-jarring blocking. James Jones would become the reserve in both positions.

Seattle wide receivers have always produced the goods and Brian Blades has done well after taking over from the incomparable Steve Largent. Blades' starting partner will be Tommy Kane, who has a similar style and is not seriously challenged for his seniority. But there will be a change at tight end, where Travis McNeal takes over from stalwart Mike Tice who was lost to Plan-B free agency. McNeal had

come through as the better receiver and could just blossom.

Gradually, the offensive line has been coming together and it received a major boost with the drafting of Ray Roberts, who is expected to start immediately at left tackle, with 1989 first-round draftee Andy Heck switching to the right side. Edwin Bailey is expected to resume at left guard following injury and the club is optimistic that Grant Feasel will be back at center, after missing the end of last season with a knee problem. Bryan Millard completes the lineup at right guard.

A trade brought defensive tackle Keith Millard from Minnesota. Millard also has had serious injuries but, if he could just reproduce the form of his Pro Bowl campaigns (1988-89), with Cortez Kennedy at defensive right tackle, he could generate a force to wreck any offensive interior. Time seems not to diminish the power of defensive end Jacob Green, who raised his sack total to 97.5 since 1982 when records first were kept. Completing the four-man line, Tony Woods has not yet made the impact expected of a former first-round draftee though he did tie for the team lead with four fumbles recovered.

There are impact players at outside linebacker, where Terry Wooden was the team-leading tackler and Rufus Porter led the club with ten sacks and was unlucky not to earn a third Pro Bowl selection. Draftee outside linebacker Bobby Spitulski is a typical Seahawk, all enthusiasm and terrific work ethic, and he may be switched to play inside, offering a challenge to incumbent Darren Comeaux. This becomes more likely if Dave Wyman, who is another obvious candidate for the middle position, does not return to his best.

One area of unquestioned reliability is the secondary,

| 1992 SCHEDULE OF GAMES | September | |
|---|---|---|
| | 6 CINCINNATI | 1:00 |
| | 13 at Kansas City | 12:00 |
| | 20 at New England | 1:00 |
| | 27 MIAMI | 1:00 |
| | October | |
| | 4 at San Diego | 1:00 |
| | 11 at Dallas | 12:00 |
| | 18 LOS ANGELES RAIDERS | 1:00 |
| | 25 at New York Giants | 1:00 |
| | November | |
| | 1 Open Date | |
| | 8 WASHINGTON | 1:00 |
| | 15 at Los Angeles Raiders | 1:00 |
| | 22 KANSAS CITY | 5:00 |
| | 30 DENVER (Mon.) | 6:00 |
| | December | |
| | 6 at Pittsburgh | 1:00 |
| | 13 PHILADELPHIA | 1:00 |
| | 20 at Denver | 2:00 |
| | 27 SAN DIEGO | 1:00 |

where the starting lineup will have Dwayne Harper and Patrick Hunter at cornerback with Robert Blackmon and Eugene Robinson manning the safety positions. Harper in particular has taken great strides, throwing his lightweight frame around and hounding pass receivers. He came second to Robinson on the team with four interceptions. For the backup spots, the Seahawks have Washington's 1987 second-round pick, Brian Davis, James Jefferson and the best kind of veteran savvy in Nesby Glasgow.

Placekicker John Kasay took over from Norm Johnson and surprised a few of Johnson's fans by keeping his nerve at times of pressure. He set a new club record with 25 field goals in 31 attempts, hitting 13 in a row to equal the team record. Rick Tuten takes advantage of playing indoors for much of the time, last year delivering his accurate punts at a 43-yard average.

*Dwayne Harper is a three-year starter at left cornerback.*

## 1992 Draft

| Round | Name | Pos. | Ht. | Wt. | College |
|---|---|---|---|---|---|
| 1. | Roberts, Ray | T | 6-5 | 304 | Virginia |
| 3. | Spitulski, Bobby | LB | 6-2 | 235 | Central Florida |
| 5. | Dandridge, Gary | S | 6-0 | 213 | Appalachian State |
| 6. | Bates, Michael | WR-KR | 5-9 | 191 | Arizona |
| 7. | Frier, Mike | DT | 6-3 | 280 | Appalachian State |
| 8. | Shamsid-Deen, M. | RB | 5-10 | 195 | Tennessee-Chattanooga |
| 9. | Stayner, Larry | TE | 6-5 | 248 | Boise State |
| 10. | Hamlet, Anthony | DE | 6-3 | 264 | Miami |
| 11. | Rongen, Kris | G | 6-4 | 286 | Washington |
| 12. | Fraley, Chico | LB | 6-1 | 216 | Washington |
| 12. | MacNeill, John | DE | 6-5 | 272 | Michigan State |

## VETERAN ROSTER

| No. | Name | Pos. | Ht. | Wt. | NFL Year | College |
|---|---|---|---|---|---|---|
| 65 | Bailey, Edwin | G | 6-4 | 284 | 12 | South Carolina State |
| 25 | Blackmon, Robert | S | 6-0 | 197 | 3 | Baylor |
| 89 | Blades, Brian | WR | 5-11 | 189 | 5 | Miami |
| 60 | Blados, Brian | G-T | 6-3 | 296 | 9 | North Carolina |
| 64 | Brilz, Darrick | G-C | 6-3 | 287 | 6 | Oregon State |
| 77 | Bryant, Jeff | DT | 6-5 | 281 | 11 | Clemson |
| 59 | Cain, Joe | LB | 6-1 | 233 | 4 | Oregon Tech |
| 84 | Clark, Louis | WR | 6-0 | 198 | 6 | Mississippi State |
| 53 | Comeaux, Darren | LB | 6-1 | 239 | 11 | Arizona State |
| 51 | Cotton, Marcus | LB | 6-3 | 233 | 5 | Southern California |
| 88 | Daniels, David | WR | 6-1 | 190 | 2 | Penn State |
| 34 | Davis, Brian | CB | 6-2 | 187 | 6 | Nebraska |
| 23 | Davis, Harlan | CB | 6-0 | 191 | 1 | Tennessee |
| 33 | Dodge, Dedrick | S | 6-2 | 184 | 2 | Florida State |
| 54 | Feasel, Grant | C | 6-7 | 283 | 8 | Abilene Christian |
| 18 | Gelbaugh, Stan | QB | 6-3 | 207 | 5 | Maryland |
| 22 | Glasgow, Nesby | S | 5-10 | 187 | 14 | Washington |
| 79 | Green, Jacob | DE | 6-3 | 263 | 13 | Texas A&M |
| 29 | Harper, Dwayne | CB | 5-11 | 174 | 5 | South Carolina State |
| 78 | Hayes, Eric | DT | 6-3 | 297 | 3 | Florida State |
| 66 | Heck, Andy | T | 6-6 | 289 | 4 | Notre Dame |
| 16 | Hilger, Rusty | QB | 6-4 | 209 | 7 | Oklahoma State |
| 76 | Hitchcock, Bill | T | 6-6 | 291 | 2 | Purdue |
| 27 | Hunter, Patrick | CB | 5-11 | 186 | 7 | Nevada-Reno |
| 20 | Jefferson, James | CB | 6-1 | 199 | 4 | Texas A&I |
| 43 | Johnson, Tracy | RB | 6-0 | 230 | 4 | Clemson |
| 30 | Jones, James | RB | 6-2 | 232 | 10 | Florida |
| 83 | Junkin, Trey | TE | 6-2 | 237 | 10 | Louisiana Tech |
| 81 | Kane, Tommy | WR | 5-11 | 181 | 5 | Syracuse |
| 4 | Kasay, John | K | 5-10 | 189 | 2 | Georgia |
| 96 | Kennedy, Cortez | DT | 6-3 | 293 | 3 | Miami |
| 63 | Lee, Ronnie | T | 6-3 | 296 | 14 | Baylor |
| 62 | Leggett, Brad | C | 6-4 | 270 | 2 | Southern California |
| 36 | Mayes, Rueben | RB | 5-11 | 200 | 5 | Washington State |
| 26 | McElroy, Vann | S | 6-2 | 199 | 10 | Baylor |
| 10 | McGwire, Dan | QB | 6-8 | 243 | 2 | San Diego State |
| 86 | McNeal, Travis | TE | 6-3 | 244 | 4 | Tennessee-Chattanooga |
| 71 | Millard, Bryan | G | 6-5 | 277 | 9 | Texas |
| 75 | Millard, Keith | DT | 6-5 | 263 | 7 | Washington State |
| 72 | Nash, Joe | DT | 6-3 | 278 | 11 | Boston College |
| 58 | Newbill, Richard | LB | 6-1 | 240 | 2 | Miami |
| 21 | Oliphant, Mike | WR | 5-9 | 171 | 3 | Puget Sound |
| 97 | Porter, Rufus | LB | 6-1 | 227 | 5 | Southern |
| 41 | Robinson, Eugene | S | 6-0 | 191 | 8 | Colgate |
| 70 | Sinclair, Michael | DE | 6-4 | 250 | 1 | Eastern New Mexico |
| 94 | Stephens, Rod | LB | 6-1 | 237 | 4 | Georgia Tech |
| 11 | Stouffer, Kelly | QB | 6-3 | 214 | 4 | Colorado State |
| 85 | Thomas, Doug | WR | 5-10 | 178 | 2 | Clemson |
| 56 | Tofflemire, Joe | C | 6-2 | 273 | 3 | Arizona |
| 14 | Tuten, Rick | P | 6-2 | 218 | 4 | Florida State |
| 42 | Warren, Chris | RB | 6-2 | 225 | 3 | Ferrum |
| 74 | Wheat, Warren | G | 6-6 | 286 | 3 | Brigham Young |
| 32 | Williams, John L. | RB | 5-11 | 231 | 7 | Florida |
| 90 | Wooden, Terry | LB | 6-3 | 236 | 3 | Syracuse |
| 57 | Woods, Tony | DE | 6-4 | 269 | 6 | Pittsburgh |
| 92 | Wyman, David | LB | 6-2 | 248 | 6 | Stanford |

# CHAPTER SIX

# NATIONAL FOOTBALL CONFERENCE

## TEAM RANKINGS

| | OFFENSE | | | | | | DEFENSE | | | | | |
| | Total Yds. | Rushing | Passing | Points For | No. Intercepted | No. Sacked | Total Yds. | Rushing | Passing | Points Against | Interceptions | Sacks |
|---|---|---|---|---|---|---|---|---|---|---|---|---|
| Atlanta | 3 | 9 | 3 | 3 | 11 | 8 | 14 | 12 | 12 | 11 | =4 | 11 |
| Chicago | 6 | 4 | 7 | 8 | =7 | 5 | 4 | 7 | 6 | 5 | =6 | 5 |
| Dallas | 4 | 7 | 5 | 4 | =3 | 10 | 12 | 6 | 13 | 9 | =10 | 13 |
| Detroit | 9 | 5 | 11 | 6 | =7 | 4 | 10 | 10 | 11 | 6 | =4 | 10 |
| Green Bay | 11 | 12 | 8 | 11 | 9 | =12 | 7 | 5 | 10 | 10 | 9 | 4 |
| L.A. Rams | 10 | 14 | 4 | 12 | 10 | 7 | 13 | 8 | 14 | 14 | =13 | 14 |
| Minnesota | 5 | 1 | 10 | 7 | 6 | 6 | 9 | 11 | 9 | 8 | =6 | 8 |
| New Orleans | 7 | 8 | 6 | 5 | 5 | 2 | 2 | 2 | 2 | 1 | 1 | =2 |
| N.Y. Giants | 8 | 2 | 12 | 10 | 1 | 9 | 6 | 9 | 4 | 7 | =10 | 7 |
| Philadelphia | 12 | 11 | 9 | 9 | 13 | =12 | 1 | 1 | 1 | =3 | 3 | 1 |
| Phoenix | 14 | 13 | 13 | 14 | 12 | 11 | 11 | 14 | 5 | 12 | =6 | 12 |
| San Francisco | 1 | 6 | 1 | 2 | =3 | 3 | 5 | 4 | 8 | 2 | =10 | 9 |
| Tampa Bay | 13 | 10 | 14 | 13 | 14 | 14 | 8 | 13 | 3 | 13 | =13 | 6 |
| Washington | 2 | 3 | 2 | 1 | 2 | 1 | 3 | 3 | 7 | =3 | 2 | =2 |

## NFC PASSERS

| | Att | Comp | % Comp | Yards | Ave Gain | TD | % TD | Long | Int | % Int | Rating Points |
|---|---|---|---|---|---|---|---|---|---|---|---|
| Young, Steve, *S.F.* | 279 | 180 | 64.5 | 2517 | 9.02 | 17 | 6.1 | t97 | 8 | 2.9 | 101.8 |
| Rypien, Mark, *Wash.* | 421 | 249 | 59.1 | 3564 | 8.47 | 28 | 6.7 | t82 | 11 | 2.6 | 97.9 |
| Bono, Steve, *S.F.* | 237 | 141 | 59.5 | 1617 | 6.82 | 11 | 4.6 | 78 | 4 | 1.7 | 88.5 |
| Aikman, Troy, *Dall.* | 363 | 237 | 65.3 | 2754 | 7.59 | 11 | 3.0 | 61 | 10 | 2.8 | 86.7 |
| Hostetler, Jeff, *Giants* | 285 | 179 | 62.8 | 2032 | 7.13 | 5 | 1.8 | 55 | 4 | 1.4 | 84.1 |
| Gannon, Rich, *Minn.* | 354 | 211 | 59.6 | 2166 | 6.12 | 12 | 3.4 | 50 | 6 | 1.7 | 81.5 |
| Miller, Chris, *Atl.* | 413 | 220 | 53.3 | 3103 | 7.51 | 26 | 6.3 | t80 | 18 | 4.4 | 80.6 |
| McMahon, Jim, *Phil.* | 311 | 187 | 60.1 | 2239 | 7.20 | 12 | 3.9 | t75 | 11 | 3.5 | 80.3 |
| Walsh, Steve, *N.O.* | 255 | 141 | 55.3 | 1638 | 6.42 | 11 | 4.3 | 41 | 6 | 2.4 | 79.5 |
| Hebert, Bobby, *N.O.* | 248 | 149 | 60.1 | 1676 | 6.76 | 9 | 3.6 | t65 | 8 | 3.2 | 79.0 |
| Harbaugh, Jim, *Chi.* | 478 | 275 | 57.5 | 3121 | 6.53 | 15 | 3.1 | t84 | 16 | 3.3 | 73.7 |
| Tomczak, Mike, *G.B.* | 238 | 128 | 53.8 | 1490 | 6.26 | 11 | 4.6 | t75 | 9 | 3.8 | 72.6 |
| Kramer, Erik, *Det.* | 265 | 136 | 51.3 | 1635 | 6.17 | 11 | 4.2 | t73 | 8 | 3.0 | 71.8 |
| Everett, Jim, *Rams* | 490 | 277 | 56.5 | 3438 | 7.02 | 11 | 2.2 | 78 | 20 | 4.1 | 68.9 |
| Tupa, Tom, *Phoe.* | 315 | 165 | 52.4 | 2053 | 6.52 | 6 | 1.9 | t62 | 13 | 4.1 | 62.0 |
| Majkowski, Don, *G.B.* | 226 | 115 | 50.9 | 1362 | 6.03 | 3 | 1.3 | 39 | 8 | 3.5 | 59.3 |
| Testaverde, Vinny, *T.B.* | 326 | 166 | 50.9 | 1994 | 6.12 | 8 | 2.5 | t87 | 15 | 4.6 | 59.0 |
| Kemp, Jeff, *Sea.-Phil.* | 295 | 151 | 51.2 | 1753 | 5.94 | 9 | 3.1 | 57 | 17 | 5.8 | 55.7 |
| **Non-qualifiers** | | | | | | | | | | | |
| Simms, Phil, *Giants* | 141 | 82 | 58.2 | 993 | 7.04 | 8 | 5.7 | 38 | 4 | 2.8 | 87.0 |
| Kiel, Blair, *G.B.* | 50 | 29 | 58.0 | 361 | 7.22 | 3 | 6.0 | 35 | 2 | 4.0 | 83.8 |
| Beuerlein, Steve, *Dall.* | 137 | 68 | 49.6 | 909 | 6.64 | 5 | 3.6 | t66 | 2 | 1.5 | 77.2 |
| Tolliver, Billy Joe, *Atl.* | 82 | 40 | 48.8 | 531 | 6.48 | 4 | 4.9 | t75 | 2 | 2.4 | 75.8 |
| Peete, Rodney, *Det.* | 194 | 116 | 59.8 | 1339 | 6.90 | 5 | 2.6 | t68 | 9 | 4.6 | 69.9 |
| Wilson, Wade, *Minn.* | 122 | 72 | 59.0 | 825 | 6.76 | 3 | 2.5 | t46 | 10 | 8.2 | 53.5 |

t = touchdown          Leader based on rating points, minimum 224 attempts

# NFC RECEIVERS – Most Receptions

| | No | Yards | Ave | Long | TD |
|---|---|---|---|---|---|
| Irvin, Michael, *Dall.* | 93 | 1523 | 16.4 | t66 | 8 |
| Rison, Andre, *Atl.* | 81 | 976 | 12.0 | t39 | 12 |
| Rice, Jerry, *S.F.* | 80 | 1206 | 15.1 | t73 | 14 |
| Carter, Cris, *Minn.* | 72 | 962 | 13.4 | 50 | 5 |
| Monk, Art, *Wash.* | 71 | 1049 | 14.8 | t64 | 8 |
| Clark, Gary, *Wash.* | 70 | 1340 | 19.1 | t82 | 10 |
| Sharpe, Sterling, *G.B.* | 69 | 961 | 13.9 | t58 | 4 |
| Martin, Eric, *N.O.* | 66 | 803 | 12.2 | 30 | 4 |
| Ellard, Henry, *Rams* | 64 | 1052 | 16.4 | 38 | 3 |
| Taylor, John, *S.F.* | 64 | 1011 | 15.8 | t97 | 9 |
| Turner, Floyd, *N.O.* | 64 | 927 | 14.5 | t65 | 8 |
| Barnett, Fred, *Phil.* | 62 | 948 | 15.3 | t75 | 4 |
| Byars, Keith, *Phil.* | 62 | 564 | 9.1 | 37 | 3 |
| Jones, Ernie, *Phoe.* | 61 | 957 | 15.7 | 53 | 4 |
| Davis, Wendell, *Chi.* | 61 | 945 | 15.5 | t75 | 6 |
| Novacek, Jay, *Dall.* | 59 | 664 | 11.3 | 49 | 4 |
| Jordan, Steve, *Minn.* | 57 | 638 | 11.2 | 25 | 2 |
| Dawsey, Lawrence, *T.B.* | 55 | 818 | 14.9 | t65 | 3 |
| Proehl, Ricky, *Phoe.* | 55 | 766 | 13.9 | t62 | 2 |
| Delpino, Robert, *Rams* | 55 | 617 | 11.2 | 78 | 1 |
| Waddle, Tom, *Chi.* | 55 | 599 | 10.9 | t37 | 3 |
| Perriman, Brett, *Det.* | 52 | 668 | 12.8 | 42 | 1 |
| Ingram, Mark, *Giants* | 51 | 824 | 16.2 | 41 | 3 |
| Carter, Anthony, *Minn.* | 51 | 553 | 10.8 | t46 | 5 |
| Haynes, Michael, *Atl.* | 50 | 1122 | 22.4 | t80 | 11 |
| Pritchard, Mike, *Atl.* | 50 | 624 | 12.5 | 29 | 2 |
| Meggett, Dave, *Giants* | 50 | 412 | 8.2 | 22 | 3 |

t = touchdown

# NFC RECEIVERS – Most Yards

| | Yards | No | Ave | Long | TD |
|---|---|---|---|---|---|
| Irvin, Michael, *Dall.* | 1523 | 93 | 16.4 | t66 | 8 |
| Clark, Gary, *Wash.* | 1340 | 70 | 19.1 | t82 | 10 |
| Rice, Jerry, *S.F.* | 1206 | 80 | 15.1 | t73 | 14 |
| Haynes, Michael, *Atl.* | 1122 | 50 | 22.4 | t80 | 11 |
| Ellard, Henry, *Rams* | 1052 | 64 | 16.4 | 38 | 3 |
| Monk, Art, *Wash.* | 1049 | 71 | 14.8 | t64 | 8 |
| Taylor, John, *S.F.* | 1011 | 64 | 15.8 | t97 | 9 |
| Rison, Andre, *Atl.* | 976 | 81 | 12.0 | t39 | 12 |
| Carter, Cris, *Minn.* | 962 | 72 | 13.4 | 50 | 5 |
| Sharpe, Sterling, *G.B.* | 961 | 69 | 13.9 | t58 | 4 |
| Jones, Ernie, *Phoe.* | 957 | 61 | 15.7 | 53 | 4 |
| Barnett, Fred, *Phil.* | 948 | 62 | 15.3 | t75 | 4 |
| Davis, Wendell, *Chi.* | 945 | 61 | 15.5 | t75 | 6 |
| Turner, Floyd, *N.O.* | 927 | 64 | 14.5 | t65 | 8 |
| Ingram, Mark, *Giants* | 824 | 51 | 16.2 | 41 | 3 |
| Dawsey, Lawrence, *T.B.* | 818 | 55 | 14.9 | t65 | 3 |
| Martin, Eric, *N.O.* | 803 | 66 | 12.2 | 30 | 4 |
| Proehl, Ricky, *Phoe.* | 766 | 55 | 13.9 | t62 | 2 |
| Carrier, Mark, *T.B.* | 698 | 47 | 14.9 | 35 | 2 |
| Perriman, Brett, *Det.* | 668 | 52 | 12.8 | 42 | 1 |
| Novacek, Jay, *Dall.* | 664 | 59 | 11.3 | 49 | 4 |
| Clark, Robert, *Det.* | 640 | 47 | 13.6 | t68 | 6 |
| Jordan, Steve, *Minn.* | 638 | 57 | 11.2 | 25 | 2 |
| Pritchard, Mike, *Atl.* | 624 | 50 | 12.5 | 29 | 2 |
| Delpino, Robert, *Rams* | 617 | 55 | 11.2 | 78 | 1 |
| Waddle, Tom, *Chi.* | 599 | 55 | 10.9 | t37 | 3 |
| Green, Willie, *Det.* | 592 | 39 | 15.2 | t73 | 7 |

t = touchdown

*Michael Irvin led the NFC in receptions and yardage.*

# NFC RUSHERS

| | Att | Yards | Ave | Long | TD |
|---|---|---|---|---|---|
| Smith, Emmitt, *Dall.* | 365 | 1563 | 4.3 | t75 | 12 |
| Sanders, Barry, *Det.* | 342 | 1548 | 4.5 | t69 | 16 |
| Hampton, Rodney, *Giants* | 256 | 1059 | 4.1 | 44 | 10 |
| Byner, Earnest, *Wash.* | 274 | 1048 | 3.8 | 32 | 5 |
| Walker, Herschel, *Minn.* | 198 | 825 | 4.2 | t71 | 10 |
| Cobb, Reggie, *T.B.* | 196 | 752 | 3.8 | t59 | 7 |
| Anderson, Neal, *Chi.* | 210 | 747 | 3.6 | t42 | 6 |
| Delpino, Robert, *Rams* | 214 | 688 | 3.2 | 36 | 9 |
| Ervins, Ricky, *Wash.* | 145 | 680 | 4.7 | t65 | 3 |
| Johnson, Johnny, *Phoe.* | 196 | 666 | 3.4 | 21 | 4 |
| Allen, Terry, *Minn.* | 120 | 563 | 4.7 | t55 | 2 |
| Henderson, Keith, *S.F.* | 137 | 561 | 4.1 | 25 | 2 |
| McAfee, Fred, *N.O.* | 109 | 494 | 4.5 | 34 | 2 |
| Fenerty, Gill, *N.O.* | 139 | 477 | 3.4 | 54 | 3 |
| Thompson, Darrell, *G.B.* | 141 | 471 | 3.3 | t40 | 1 |
| Broussard, Steve, *Atl.* | 99 | 449 | 4.5 | 36 | 4 |
| Joseph, James, *Phil.* | 135 | 440 | 3.3 | 24 | 3 |
| Young, Steve, *S.F.* | 66 | 415 | 6.3 | 21 | 4 |
| Muster, Brad, *Chi.* | 90 | 412 | 4.6 | 24 | 6 |
| Byars, Keith, *Phil.* | 94 | 383 | 4.1 | 28 | 1 |
| Carter, Dexter, *S.F.* | 85 | 379 | 4.5 | t53 | 2 |
| Thompson, Anthony, *Phoe.* | 126 | 376 | 3.0 | 22 | 1 |
| Rozier, Mike, *Hou.-Atl.* | 96 | 361 | 3.8 | 19 | 0 |
| Pegram, Erric, *Atl.* | 101 | 349 | 3.5 | 34 | 1 |
| Harbaugh, Jim, *Chi.* | 70 | 338 | 4.8 | 20 | 2 |
| Woodside, Keith, *G.B.* | 84 | 326 | 3.9 | 29 | 1 |
| Tillman, Lewis, *Giants* | 65 | 287 | 4.4 | 17 | 1 |
| Sherman, Heath, *Phil.* | 106 | 279 | 2.6 | 12 | 0 |
| Hostetler, Jeff, *Giants* | 42 | 273 | 6.5 | t47 | 2 |
| Anderson, Gary, *T.B.* | 72 | 263 | 3.7 | t64 | 1 |
| Heyward, Craig, *N.O.* | 76 | 260 | 3.4 | 15 | 4 |
| Hilliard, Dalton, *N.O.* | 79 | 252 | 3.2 | t65 | 4 |
| Riggs, Gerald, *Wash.* | 78 | 248 | 3.2 | 32 | 11 |
| Gary, Cleveland, *Rams* | 68 | 245 | 3.6 | 14 | 1 |
| Sydney, Harry, *S.F.* | 57 | 245 | 4.3 | 32 | 5 |
| Workman, Vince, *G.B.* | 71 | 237 | 3.3 | t30 | 7 |
| Gannon, Rich, *Minn.* | 43 | 236 | 5.5 | 42 | 2 |
| Miller, Chris, *Atl.* | 32 | 229 | 7.2 | 20 | 0 |
| Green, Mark, *Chi.* | 61 | 217 | 3.6 | 18 | 3 |
| Nelson, Darrin, *Minn.* | 28 | 210 | 7.5 | 29 | 2 |
| Rathman, Tom, *S.F.* | 63 | 183 | 2.9 | 16 | 6 |
| Kemp, Jeff, *Sea.-Phil.* | 38 | 179 | 4.7 | 18 | 0 |
| Dupree, Marcus, *Rams* | 49 | 179 | 3.7 | 24 | 1 |
| Wilson, Robert, *T.B.* | 42 | 179 | 4.3 | 20 | 0 |
| Meggett, Dave, *Giants* | 29 | 153 | 5.3 | t30 | 1 |
| Jordan, Buford, *N.O.* | 47 | 150 | 3.2 | 25 | 2 |
| Anderson, Ottis, *Giants* | 53 | 141 | 2.7 | 9 | 1 |
| Chaffey, Pat, *Atl.* | 29 | 127 | 4.4 | 27 | 1 |
| Jones, Keith, *Atl.* | 35 | 126 | 3.6 | 14 | 0 |
| Peete, Rodney, *Det.* | 25 | 125 | 5.0 | 26 | 2 |
| Sanders, Thomas, *Phil.* | 54 | 122 | 2.3 | 16 | 1 |
| Anderson, Alfred, *Minn.* | 26 | 118 | 4.5 | 19 | 1 |
| Carter, Anthony, *Minn.* | 13 | 117 | 9.0 | 32 | 1 |
| Chandler, Chris, *T.B.-Phoe.* | 26 | 111 | 4.3 | 12 | 0 |
| Carthon, Maurice, *Giants* | 32 | 109 | 3.4 | 10 | 0 |
| Majkowski, Don, *G.B.* | 25 | 108 | 4.3 | 15 | 2 |
| Testaverde, Vinny, *T.B.* | 32 | 101 | 3.2 | 19 | 0 |
| Rice, Allen, *Minn.* | 30 | 100 | 3.3 | 21 | 0 |

t = touchdown

# NFC SCORING – Touchdowns

| | TD | TDR | TDP | TDM | PTS |
|---|---|---|---|---|---|
| Sanders, Barry, *Det.* | 17 | 16 | 1 | 0 | 102 |
| Rice, Jerry, *S.F.* | 14 | 0 | 14 | 0 | 84 |
| Smith, Emmitt, *Dall.* | 13 | 12 | 1 | 0 | 78 |
| Rison, Andre, *Atl.* | 12 | 0 | 12 | 0 | 72 |
| Haynes, Michael, *Atl.* | 11 | 0 | 11 | 0 | 66 |
| Riggs, Gerald, *Wash.* | 11 | 11 | 0 | 0 | 66 |
| Workman, Vince, *G.B.* | 11 | 7 | 4 | 0 | 66 |
| Clark, Gary, *Wash.* | 10 | 0 | 10 | 0 | 60 |
| Delpino, Robert, *Rams* | 10 | 9 | 1 | 0 | 60 |
| Hampton, Rodney, *Giants* | 10 | 10 | 0 | 0 | 60 |
| Walker, Herschel, *Minn.* | 10 | 10 | 0 | 0 | 60 |
| Anderson, Neal, *Chi.* | 9 | 6 | 3 | 0 | 54 |
| Taylor, John, *S.F.* | 9 | 0 | 9 | 0 | 54 |
| Irvin, Michael, *Dall.* | 8 | 0 | 8 | 0 | 48 |
| Monk, Art, *Wash.* | 8 | 0 | 8 | 0 | 48 |
| Turner, Floyd, *N.O.* | 8 | 0 | 8 | 0 | 48 |
| Cobb, Reggie, *T.B.* | 7 | 7 | 0 | 0 | 42 |
| Green, Willie, *Det.* | 7 | 0 | 7 | 0 | 42 |
| Muster, Brad, *Chi.* | 7 | 6 | 1 | 0 | 42 |
| Sydney, Harry, *S.F.* | 7 | 5 | 2 | 0 | 42 |
| Carter, Anthony, *Minn.* | 6 | 1 | 5 | 0 | 36 |
| Clark, Robert, *Det.* | 6 | 0 | 6 | 0 | 36 |
| Davis, Wendell, *Chi.* | 6 | 0 | 6 | 0 | 36 |
| Johnson, Johnny, *Phoe.* | 6 | 4 | 2 | 0 | 36 |
| Rathman, Tom, *S.F.* | 6 | 6 | 0 | 0 | 36 |
| Sanders, Ricky, *Wash.* | 6 | 1 | 5 | 0 | 36 |

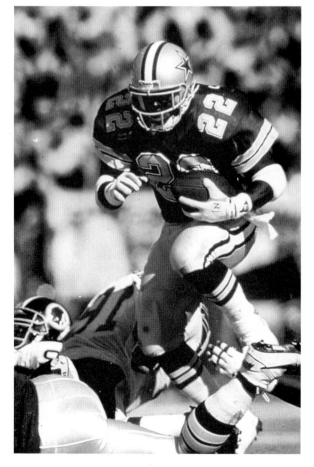

*Emmitt Smith won the NFL rushing title in just his second season.*

## NFC Scoring – Kickers

| | XP | XPA | FG | FGA | PTS |
|---|---|---|---|---|---|
| Lohmiller, Chip, *Wash.* | 56 | 56 | 31 | 43 | 149 |
| Willis, Ken, *Dall.* | 37 | 37 | 27 | 39 | 118 |
| Andersen, Morten, *N.O.* | 38 | 38 | 25 | 32 | 113 |
| Ruzek, Roger, *Phil.* | 27 | 29 | 28 | 33 | 111 |
| Murray, Eddie, *Det.* | 40 | 40 | 19 | 28 | 97 |
| Johnson, Norm, *Atl.* | 38 | 39 | 19 | 23 | 95 |
| Cofer, Mike, *S.F.* | 49 | 50 | 14 | 28 | 91 |
| Bahr, Matt, *Giants* | 24 | 25 | 22 | 29 | 90 |
| Butler, Kevin, *Chi.* | 32 | 34 | 19 | 29 | 89 |
| Jacke, Chris, *G.B.* | 31 | 31 | 18 | 24 | 85 |
| Reveiz, Fuad, *Minn.* | 34 | 35 | 17 | 24 | 85 |
| Davis, Greg, *Phoe.* | 19 | 19 | 21 | 30 | 82 |
| Zendejas, Tony, *Rams* | 25 | 26 | 17 | 17 | 76 |
| Christie, Steve, *T.B.* | 22 | 22 | 15 | 20 | 67 |
| Daluiso, Brad, *Atl.* | 2 | 2 | 2 | 3 | 8 |

## NFC Kickoff Returners

| | No | Yards | Ave | Long | TD |
|---|---|---|---|---|---|
| Gray, Mel, *Det.* | 36 | 929 | 25.8 | 71 | 0 |
| Wright, Alexander, *Dall.* | 21 | 514 | 24.5 | t102 | 1 |
| Wilson, Charles, *G.B.* | 23 | 522 | 22.7 | t82 | 1 |
| Carter, Dexter, *S.F.* | 37 | 839 | 22.7 | t98 | 1 |
| Sanders, Deion, *Atl.* | 26 | 576 | 22.2 | t100 | 1 |
| Dixon, James, *Dall.* | 18 | 398 | 22.1 | 39 | 0 |
| Nelson, Darrin, *Minn.* | 31 | 682 | 22.0 | 50 | 0 |
| Meggett, Dave, *Giants* | 25 | 514 | 20.6 | 42 | 0 |
| Mitchell, Brian, *Wash.* | 29 | 583 | 20.1 | 35 | 0 |
| Turner, Vernon, *Rams* | 24 | 457 | 19.0 | 36 | 0 |
| Anderson, Gary, *T.B.* | 34 | 643 | 18.9 | 39 | 0 |
| Atkins, Gene, *N.O.* | 20 | 368 | 18.4 | 27 | 0 |
| Harris, Rod, *Phil.* | 28 | 473 | 16.9 | 33 | 0 |

t = touchdown
Leader based on average return, minimum 18 returns

*Mel Gray is the first player to lead the league both in punt and kickoff returns.*

# NFC PUNTERS

| | No | Yards | Long | Ave | TB | Blk | Opp Ret | Ret Yds | In 20 | Net Ave |
|---|---|---|---|---|---|---|---|---|---|---|
| Newsome, Harry, *Minn.* | 68 | 3095 | 65 | 45.5 | 10 | 0 | 42 | 426 | 17 | 36.3 |
| Camarillo, Rich, *Phoe.* | 76 | 3445 | 60 | 45.3 | 7 | 1 | 48 | 313 | 19 | 38.9 |
| Barnhardt, Tommy, *N.O.* | 86 | 3743 | 61 | 43.5 | 10 | 1 | 50 | 470 | 20 | 35.3 |
| Landeta, Sean, *Giants* | 64 | 2768 | 61 | 43.3 | 8 | 0 | 35 | 350 | 16 | 35.3 |
| Fulhage, Scott, *Atl.* | 81 | 3470 | 60 | 42.8 | 6 | 0 | 45 | 387 | 21 | 36.6 |
| Saxon, Mike, *Dall.* | 57 | 2426 | 64 | 42.6 | 5 | 0 | 28 | 231 | 16 | 36.8 |
| Feagles, Jeff, *Phil.* | 87 | 3640 | 77 | 41.8 | 11 | 1 | 42 | 431 | 29 | 34.0 |
| Arnold, Jim, *Det.* | 75 | 3092 | 63 | 41.2 | 5 | 0 | 35 | 340 | 27 | 35.4 |
| Buford, Maury, *Chi.* | 69 | 2814 | 64 | 40.8 | 8 | 1 | 28 | 205 | 13 | 35.0 |
| McJulien, Paul, *G.B.* | 86 | 3473 | 62 | 40.4 | 7 | 0 | 35 | 375 | 22 | 34.4 |
| Royals, Mark, *T.B.* | 84 | 3389 | 56 | 40.3 | 6 | 0 | 49 | 559 | 22 | 32.3 |
| Goodburn, Kelly, *Wash.* | 52 | 2070 | 61 | 39.8 | 3 | 3 | 31 | 190 | 16 | 33.1 |
| Prokop, Joe, *S.F.* | 40 | 1541 | 58 | 38.5 | 1 | 0 | 21 | 138 | 8 | 34.6 |
| Hatcher, Dale, *Rams* | 63 | 2403 | 52 | 38.1 | 5 | 0 | 29 | 231 | 16 | 32.9 |

Leader based on gross average, minimum 40 punts

# NFC SACKERS

| | No |
|---|---|
| Swilling, Pat, *N.O.* | 17.0 |
| White, Reggie, *Phil.* | 15.0 |
| Bennett, Tony, *G.B.* | 13.0 |
| Simmons, Clyde, *Phil.* | 13.0 |
| Jackson, Rickey, *N.O.* | 11.5 |
| Mann, Charles, *Wash.* | 11.5 |
| Marshall, Leonard, *Giants* | 11.0 |
| Thomas, Broderick, *T.B.* | 11.0 |
| Dent, Richard, *Chi.* | 10.5 |
| Randle, John, *Minn.* | 9.5 |
| Brown, Jerome, *Phil.* | 9.0 |
| Harvey, Ken, *Phoe.* | 9.0 |
| McMichael, Steve, *Chi.* | 9.0 |
| Roper, John, *Chi.* | 8.0 |
| Thomas, Henry, *Minn.* | 8.0 |
| Paup, Bryce, *G.B.* | 7.5 |
| Doleman, Chris, *Minn.* | 7.0 |
| Haley, Charles, *S.F.* | 7.0 |
| Nunn, Freddie Joe, *Phoe.* | 7.0 |
| Roberts, Larry, *S.F.* | 7.0 |
| Taylor, Lawrence, *Giants* | 7.0 |
| Tolbert, Tony, *Dall.* | 7.0 |
| Warren, Frank, *N.O.* | 7.0 |
| Johnson, Pepper, *Giants* | 6.5 |
| Joyner, Seth, *Phil.* | 6.5 |
| Manley, Dexter, *T.B.* | 6.5 |
| Stokes, Fred, *Wash.* | 6.5 |
| Hunter, Jeff, *Det.* | 6.0 |
| Marshall, Wilber, *Wash.* | 5.5 |
| Owens, Dan, *Det.* | 5.5 |
| Perry, William, *Chi.* | 5.5 |
| Green, Tim, *Atl.* | 5.0 |
| McCants, Keith, *T.B.* | 5.0 |
| Newton, Tim, *T.B.* | 5.0 |
| Archambeau, Lester, *G.B.* | 4.5 |
| Geathers, James, *Wash.* | 4.5 |
| Maryland, Russell, *Dall.* | 4.5 |
| Wilson, Bobby, *Wash.* | 4.5 |
| Banks, Carl, *Giants* | 4.0 |
| Brown, Robert, *G.B.* | 4.0 |
| Jamison, George, *Det.* | 4.0 |
| Jeffcoat, Jim, *Dall.* | 4.0 |
| Jordan, Brian, *Atl.* | 4.0 |
| Swann, Eric, *Phoe.* | 4.0 |

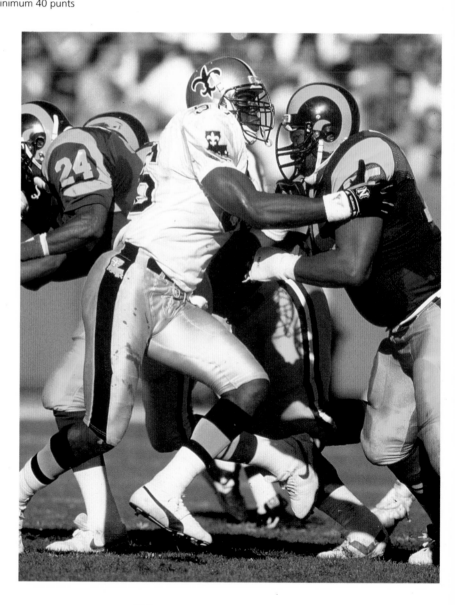

# NFC PUNT RETURNERS

| | No | FC | Yards | Ave | Long | TD |
|---|---|---|---|---|---|---|
| Gray, Mel, *Det.* | 25 | 14 | 385 | 15.4 | t78 | 1 |
| Mitchell, Brian, *Wash.* | 45 | 21 | 600 | 13.3 | t69 | 2 |
| Martin, Kelvin, *Dall.* | 21 | 8 | 244 | 11.6 | t85 | 1 |
| Meggett, Dave, *Giants* | 28 | 9 | 287 | 10.3 | t70 | 1 |
| Drewrey, Willie, *T.B.* | 38 | 15 | 360 | 9.5 | 33 | 0 |
| Sikahema, Vai, *Phoe.* | 26 | 4 | 239 | 9.2 | 62 | 0 |
| Turner, Vernon, *Rams* | 23 | 4 | 201 | 8.7 | 29 | 0 |
| Taylor, John, *S.F.* | 31 | 14 | 267 | 8.6 | 24 | 0 |
| Buck, Vince, *N.O.* | 31 | 13 | 260 | 8.4 | 52 | 0 |
| Sanders, Deion, *Atl.* | 21 | 9 | 170 | 8.1 | 23 | 0 |
| Jackson, John, *Phoe.* | 31 | 3 | 244 | 7.9 | 19 | 0 |
| Harris, Rod, *Phil.* | 53 | 9 | 416 | 7.8 | 40 | 0 |
| Bailey, Johnny, *Chi.* | 36 | 11 | 281 | 7.8 | 37 | 0 |
| Lewis, Leo, *Minn.* | 30 | 15 | 225 | 7.5 | 44 | 0 |

t = touchdown
Leader based on average return, minimum 20 returns

# NFC INTERCEPTORS

| | No | Yards | Ave | Long | TD |
|---|---|---|---|---|---|
| Crockett, Ray, *Det.* | 6 | 141 | 23.5 | t96 | 1 |
| Sanders, Deion, *Atl.* | 6 | 119 | 19.8 | t55 | 1 |
| Williams, Aeneas, *Phoe.* | 6 | 60 | 10.0 | 32 | 0 |
| McKyer, Tim, *Atl.* | 6 | 24 | 4.0 | 24 | 0 |
| Atkins, Gene, *N.O.* | 5 | 198 | 39.6 | 79 | 0 |
| Browner, Joey, *Minn.* | 5 | 97 | 19.4 | 45 | 0 |
| Marshall, Wilber, *Wash.* | 5 | 75 | 15.0 | t54 | 1 |
| Green, Darrell, *Wash.* | 5 | 47 | 9.4 | 24 | 0 |
| McDonald, Tim, *Phoe.* | 5 | 36 | 7.2 | 13 | 0 |
| Hopkins, Wes, *Phil.* | 5 | 26 | 5.2 | 14 | 0 |
| Allen, Eric, *Phil.* | 5 | 20 | 4.0 | 8 | 0 |
| Buck, Vince, *N.O.* | 5 | 12 | 2.4 | 12 | 0 |
| Collins, Mark, *Giants* | 4 | 77 | 19.3 | 41 | 0 |
| Waymer, Dave, *S.F.* | 4 | 77 | 19.3 | 42 | 0 |
| Stinson, Lemuel, *Chi.* | 4 | 69 | 17.3 | t34 | 1 |
| Edwards, Brad, *Wash.* | 4 | 52 | 13.0 | 27 | 0 |
| Glenn, Vencie, *N.O.* | 4 | 35 | 8.8 | 18 | 0 |
| Taylor, Terry, *Det.* | 4 | 26 | 6.5 | 23 | 0 |
| Walls, Everson, *Giants* | 4 | 7 | 1.8 | 5 | 0 |
| McMillian, Audrey, *Minn.* | 4 | 5 | 1.3 | 3 | 0 |
| Holt, Issiac, *Dall.* | 4 | 2 | 0.5 | 2 | 0 |
| Rutland, Reggie, *Minn.* | 3 | 104 | 34.7 | t97 | 1 |
| Gray, Jerry, *Rams* | 3 | 83 | 27.7 | t59 | 1 |
| Cecil, Chuck, *G.B.* | 3 | 76 | 25.3 | 32 | 0 |
| Jones, Reggie, *N.O.* | 3 | 61 | 20.3 | 51 | 0 |
| Lynch, Lorenzo, *Phoe.* | 3 | 59 | 19.7 | t35 | 1 |
| Cook, Toi, *N.O.* | 3 | 54 | 18.0 | 22 | 0 |
| Jamison, George, *Det.* | 3 | 52 | 17.3 | 19 | 0 |
| Joyner, Seth, *Phil.* | 3 | 41 | 13.7 | 41 | 0 |
| Maxie, Brett, *N.O.* | 3 | 33 | 11.0 | t31 | 1 |
| Mayhew, Martin, *Wash.* | 3 | 31 | 10.3 | t31 | 1 |
| Miano, Rich, *Phil.* | 3 | 30 | 10.0 | 18 | 0 |
| Murphy, Mark, *G.B.* | 3 | 27 | 9.0 | 16 | 0 |
| Henley, Darryl, *Rams* | 3 | 22 | 7.3 | 22 | 0 |
| Covington, Tony, *T.B.* | 3 | 21 | 7.0 | 18 | 0 |
| Paul, Markus, *Chi.* | 3 | 21 | 7.0 | 10 | 0 |
| Butler, LeRoy, *G.B.* | 3 | 6 | 2.0 | 6 | 0 |

t = touchdown

*LEFT: Pat Swilling terrorized quarterbacks all year.*

*RIGHT: Ray Crockett came to the fore in his third pro campaign.*

# DALLAS COWBOYS

**Address** Cowboys Center, One Cowboys Parkway, Irving, Texas 75063.
**Stadium** Texas Stadium, Irving.
*Capacity* 65,024 *Playing Surface* Texas Turf.
**Team Colours** Royal Blue, Metallic Silver Blue, and White.
**Head Coach** Jimmy Johnson – 4th year.
**Championships** Division 1970,'71,'73,'76,'77,'78, '79,'81,'85; Conference 1970,'71,'75,'77,'78; Super Bowl 1971,'77.
**History** NFL 1960-69, NFC 1970-

*Quarterback Troy Aikman runs the Cowboys' exciting offense.*

The Cowboys are only part of the way along the road to greatness and yet they still won a playoff game. They have abundant talent in many areas but there were weaknesses on the offensive line, at linebacker and in the secondary. It was for these units that priority was given in the draft, using up eight of their first nine options. And it is a measure of the wealth of picks which the club had collected by shrewd trading that all eight draftees came in the first five rounds. The one luxury item was wide receiver Jimmy Smith, whom they must have seen as being just too good to overlook, for he certainly was not needed by a team which can field Alvin Harper, Alexander Wright, Kelvin Martin and the NFL leader in receiving yardage, Michael Irvin. In his fourth pro year, the speedy University of Miami product caught 93 passes for 1,523 yards and eight touchdowns.

Underlining the quality of the receiving corps, tight end Jay Novacek was the NFC leader at his position. Novacek is not known for his blocking and, while Alfredo Roberts can take up that rôle, the offensive line could use a little more help. Currently, the starters are Mark Tuinei, Kevin Gogan, Mark Stepnoski, John Gesek and Nate Newton. It is a decent unit but needed an upgrade which the draftees may not be able to offer immediately.

Whatever its failings, the line did create enough opportunities for Emmitt Smith to blaze his way to the NFL rushing title by a margin of 15 yards over Detroit ace Barry Sanders. Smith can do everything and removed any remaining doubts over his ability to go the distance with his 75-yard run for one of his 12 touchdowns in that category. The rest, with Daryl Johnston the starting fullback, exist to serve Smith.

Another shrewd trade brought former Raiders quarterback Steve Beuerlein, who was seen as a backup but showed his worth when starting four regular-season games after Troy Aikman was injured. But Aikman is the man. A superior athlete with great powers of leadership, Aikman has had his share of injuries and disappointments in his first three pro years, and he must now be ready to go out and destroy opponents.

An ample supply of top-class players for the defensive line means that the Cowboys do not struggle at all when one or two starters need a rest. Currently, Tony Tolbert and Jim Jeffcoat are at defensive end, with Tony Casillas and Russell Maryland in the tackle positions. Behind them lie former first-round pick Danny Noonan and Jimmie Jones, the latter available as a fine pass rusher when Jeffcoat

## 1992 SCHEDULE OF GAMES

### September
|     |                          |       |
| --- | ------------------------ | ----- |
| 7   | WASHINGTON (Mon.)        | 8:00  |
| 13  | at New York Giants       | 1:00  |
| 20  | PHOENIX                  | 3:00  |
| 27  | Open Date                |       |

### October
|     |                          |       |
| --- | ------------------------ | ----- |
| 5   | at Philadelphia (Mon.)   | 9:00  |
| 11  | SEATTLE                  | 12:00 |
| 18  | KANSAS CITY              | 12:00 |
| 25  | at Los Angeles Raiders   | 1:00  |

### November
|     |                          |       |
| --- | ------------------------ | ----- |
| 1   | PHILADELPHIA             | 3:00  |
| 8   | at Detroit               | 1:00  |
| 15  | LOS ANGELES RAMS         | 12:00 |
| 22  | at Phoenix               | 2:00  |
| 26  | NEW YORK GIANTS (Thanksgiving) | 3:00 |

### December
|     |                          |       |
| --- | ------------------------ | ----- |
| 6   | at Denver                | 2:00  |
| 13  | at Washington            | 1:00  |
| 21  | at Atlanta               | 9:00  |
| 27  | CHICAGO                  | 3:00  |

## 1992 Draft

| Round | Name              | Pos. | Ht.   | Wt. | College          |
| ----- | ----------------- | ---- | ----- | --- | ---------------- |
| 1.    | Smith, Kevin      | CB   | 5-10  | 173 | Texas A&M        |
| 1.    | Jones, Robert     | LB   | 6-1   | 236 | East Carolina    |
| 2.    | Smith, Jimmy      | WR   | 6-0   | 200 | Jackson State    |
| 2.    | Woodson, Darren   | S    | 6-1   | 219 | Arizona State    |
| 3.    | Holmes, Clayton   | CB   | 5-10  | 178 | Carson-Newman    |
| 3.    | Brown, James      | T    | 6-6   | 325 | Virginia State   |
| 4.    | Myslinski, Tom    | G-C  | 6-2   | 293 | Tennessee        |
| 5.    | Briggs, Greg      | S    | 6-2   | 209 | Texas Southern   |
| 5.    | Milstead, Rod     | G    | 6-1   | 290 | Delaware State   |
| 6.    | Wacasey, Fallon   | TE   | 6-7   | 245 | Tulsa            |
| 9.    | Kirtman, Nate     | DB   | 6-0   | 187 | Pomona-Pitzer    |
| 9.    | Hall, Chris       | CB   | 6-2   | 186 | East Carolina    |
| 10.   | Terry, John       | G    | 6-3   | 285 | Livingstone      |
| 11.   | Daniel, Tim       | WR   | 5-11  | 186 | Florida A&M      |
| 12.   | Harris, Don       | DB   | 5-11  | 198 | Texas Tech       |

## VETERAN ROSTER

| No. | Name              | Pos.  | Ht.   | Wt. | NFL Year | College               |
| --- | ----------------- | ----- | ----- | --- | -------- | --------------------- |
| 34  | Agee, Tommie      | RB    | 6-0   | 225 | 5        | Auburn                |
| 8   | Aikman, Troy      | QB    | 6-4   | 222 | 4        | UCLA                  |
| 36  | Albritton, Vince  | S     | 6-2   | 216 | 9        | Washington            |
| 40  | Bates, Bill       | S     | 6-1   | 205 | 10       | Tennessee             |
| 7   | Beuerlein, Steve  | QB    | 6-2   | 209 | 4        | Notre Dame            |
| 46  | Blake, Ricky      | RB    | 6-2   | 244 | 2        | Alabama A&M           |
| 32  | Brooks, Michael   | S     | 6-0   | 189 | 2        | North Carolina State  |
| 24  | Brown, Larry      | CB    | 5-11  | 182 | 2        | Texas Christian       |
| 75  | Casillas, Tony    | DT    | 6-3   | 277 | 7        | Oklahoma              |
| 59  | Clark, Bernard    | LB    | 6-2   | 248 | 3        | Miami                 |
| 93  | Cooper, Reggie    | LB    | 6-2   | 215 | 2        | Nebraska              |
| 65  | Cornish, Frank    | C-G   | 6-4   | 289 | 3        | UCLA                  |
| 5   | Daluiso, Brad     | K     | 6-2   | 208 | 2        | UCLA                  |
| 58  | Edwards, Dixon    | LB    | 6-1   | 224 | 2        | Michigan State        |
| 29  | Gant, Kenneth     | CB    | 5-11  | 188 | 3        | Albany State          |
| 63  | Gesek, John       | G     | 6-5   | 279 | 6        | Cal State-Sacramento  |
| 66  | Gogan, Kevin      | G-T   | 6-7   | 317 | 6        | Washington            |
| 80  | Harper, Alvin     | WR    | 6-3   | 203 | 2        | Tennessee             |
| 94  | Harris, Kevin     | DE    | 6-5   | 251 | 1        | Texas Southern        |
| 70  | Hellestrae, Dale  | G-C   | 6-5   | 285 | 6        | Southern Methodist    |
| 90  | Hill, Tony        | DE    | 6-6   | 242 | 2        | Tennessee-Chattanooga |
| 30  | Holt, Issiac      | CB    | 6-2   | 201 | 8        | Alcorn State          |
| 20  | Horton, Ray       | S     | 5-11  | 190 | 10       | Washington            |
| 88  | Irvin, Michael    | WR    | 6-2   | 199 | 5        | Miami                 |
| 77  | Jeffcoat, Jim     | DE    | 6-5   | 274 | 10       | Arizona State         |
| 48  | Johnston, Daryl   | RB    | 6-2   | 236 | 4        | Syracuse              |
| 97  | Jones, Jimmie     | DT    | 6-4   | 276 | 3        | Miami                 |
| 9   | Kupp, Craig       | QB    | 6-4   | 215 | 2        | Pacific Lutheran      |
| 78  | Lett, Leon        | DL    | 6-6   | 287 | 2        | Emporia State         |
| 21  | Lewis, Garry      | CB    | 5-11  | 185 | 3        | Alcorn State          |
| 83  | Martin, Kelvin    | WR    | 5-9   | 162 | 6        | Boston College        |
| 67  | Maryland, Russell | DT    | 6-1   | 277 | 2        | Miami                 |
| 25  | Mitchell, Brian   | CB    | 5-9   | 164 | 2        | Brigham Young         |
| 98  | Myles, Godfrey    | LB    | 6-1   | 241 | 2        | Florida               |
| 61  | Newton, Nate      | T     | 6-3   | 332 | 7        | Florida A&M           |
| 73  | Noonan, Danny     | DT    | 6-4   | 275 | 6        | Nebraska              |
| 51  | Norton, Ken       | LB    | 6-2   | 238 | 5        | UCLA                  |
| 84  | Novacek, Jay      | TE    | 6-4   | 231 | 8        | Wyoming               |
| 52  | Pruitt, Mickey    | LB    | 6-1   | 218 | 5        | Colorado              |
| 27  | Richards, Curvin  | RB    | 5-9   | 195 | 1        | Pittsburgh            |
| 87  | Roberts, Alfredo  | TE    | 6-3   | 252 | 5        | Miami                 |
| 4   | Saxon, Mike       | P     | 6-3   | 202 | 8        | San Diego State       |
| 82  | Shepard, Derrick  | WR-PR | 5-10  | 183 | 5        | Oklahoma              |
| 22  | Smith, Emmitt     | RB    | 5-9   | 203 | 3        | Florida               |
| 57  | Smith, Vinson     | LB    | 6-2   | 231 | 4        | East Carolina         |
| 53  | Stepnoski, Mark   | C-G   | 6-2   | 269 | 4        | Pittsburgh            |
| 92  | Tolbert, Tony     | DE    | 6-6   | 265 | 4        | Texas-El Paso         |
| 71  | Tuinei, Mark      | T     | 6-5   | 299 | 10       | Hawaii                |
| 76  | Veingrad, Alan    | G-T   | 6-5   | 280 | 6        | East Texas State      |
| 37  | Washington, James | S     | 6-1   | 197 | 5        | UCLA                  |
| 79  | Williams, Erik    | T     | 6-6   | 319 | 2        | Central State, Ohio   |
| 23  | Williams, Robert  | CB    | 5-10  | 190 | 6        | Baylor                |
| 81  | Wright, Alexander | WR    | 6-0   | 190 | 3        | Auburn                |
|     | Zimmerman, Jeff   | G     | 6-3   | 332 | 5        | Florida               |

begins to slow. Appearing out of the blue, literally, Chad Hennings, who was an 11th-round pick in 1988, has joined the club after serving his time in the US Air Force. Had he moved straight into the NFL, Hennings was projected as a future All-Pro. He'll certainly be in excellent physical shape and the mind goes back to Hall-of-Fame quarterback Roger Staubach, who joined Dallas in similar circumstances.

At linebacker, however, a vulnerable spot has been overlooked in the rebuilding process. It is in the middle position, which became vacant by the Plan-B loss of both Jack Del Rio and his backup, Darrick Brownlow. A sequence of moves could solve the problem, with Vinson Smith moving inside, where he would compete with draftee Robert Jones, allowing 1991 second-round pick Dixon Edwards to move up to the weakside spot. Ken Norton, now as famous as his dad, the former heavyweight boxer, mans the strong side.

There could be changes in as many as three positions in the secondary with the introduction of seven draftees. Issiac Holt should remain at left cornerback but Kevin Smith may start immediately on the right side. One of current starting safeties Ray Horton and James Washington could feel the heat from draftee Darren Woodson and former starter Vince Albritton, if the latter can recover from an injury which forced him to miss all but six games last year.

Dallas lost a good placekicker, Ken Willis, to Plan-B free agency. His replacement, Brad Daluiso, is largely untried on field goals but was signed by Buffalo specifically for his ability to kick off deep and was on the Bills' Super Bowl squad. There may be others in the competition come the preseason. The punting duties are safe in the hands of Mike Saxon, who averaged a steady 42.6 yards last year.

# NEW YORK GIANTS

Feature running back Rodney Hampton.

**Address** Giants Stadium, East Rutherford,
New Jersey 07073.

**Stadium** Giants Stadium, East Rutherford, N.J.
*Capacity* 77,311 *Playing Surface* AstroTurf.

**Team Colours** Blue, Red, and White.

**Head Coach** Ray Handley – 2nd year.

**Championships** Division 1986,'89,'90; Conference
1986,'90; NFL 1927,'34,'38,'56; Super Bowl 1986,'90.

**History** NFL 1925-69, NFC 1970-

Following their hard-won victory over Buffalo in Super Bowl XXV, the Giants laboured through the 1991 campaign, never winning more than three games in a row, and they need to regroup if they are to contend in a division which will be no less competitive in 1992.

Head coach Ray Handley had a difficult job, taking over from Bill Parcells in mid-May, and never was able to stamp his own style on the team. He has begun preparations for his second year by identifying the starting quarterback as Jeff Hostetler, thus removing a potential controversy involving long-time starter Phil Simms. There is little doubt that Simms is the better passer and he is vastly more experienced, but Hostetler's all-round sharpness gives him the advantage.

The offense at least does have one key ingredient in running back Rodney Hampton, who would expect to rush for 1,000 yards in a season, always with the distinct possibility of breaking for a long play. Behind Hampton, though, there is not much by way of excitement, unless Dave Meggett can reproduce the form of his first two NFL seasons when he was considered one of the most elusive players in the game. 1991 first-round pick Jarrod Bunch assumes the fullback duties from Maurice Carthon, who has been released.

If the Giants are to shed themselves of their predictable, ball-control style, the passing offense will have to expand. There is no doubting the big-play potential of Mark Ingram and Stephen Baker but they have not caught as many passes as other starting partnerships around the NFL, and there will be no bonus yardage from Odessa Turner, who has been lost under Plan B. However, there is the possibility of a greater contribution from the tight end position, an area which the club was desperate to improve as it drafted Derek Brown and Aaron Pierce with its first and third options respectively. That New York spent heavily for rookies is surprising since the incumbent, Howard Cross, has shown flashes, catching his 20 passes at a good average of 14.2 yards.

Brown, who has terrific hands, is also a solid blocker, though again the Giants weren't short of talent for the offensive line. Indeed, the quintet of John Elliott, William Roberts, Bart Oates, Eric Moore and Doug Riesenberg is better than most groups in the league. Backups Brian Williams, who can play either guard or center, and Bob Kratch were 1989 first- and third-round draft picks respectively.

One area on which Handley can rely is the defense, which is packed with high-class talent and extensive experience. Few coaches wouldn't wish to have Lawrence Taylor, Pepper Johnson, Gary Reasons and Carl Banks as their starting linebackers. Taylor has begun to slow but he can never be ignored in any gameplan. He did enough in the 1980s to confirm his place in history as the best ever to play the outside linebacker position, and skills such as he possesses simply do not disappear overnight. If he is beyond his prime, there is compensation in that Johnson is just coming to the boil. The three-man line, too, is a formidable unit, with the immensely strong Erik Howard at nose tackle, flanked by Eric Dorsey and club-leading sacker Leonard Marshall.

Perhaps the secondary could use a little speed, and in draftee Phillippi Sparks there is all of that and more. He delivers a hammer-blow tackle and, if he can adjust quickly to the demands of the NFL, he will start at cornerback. Mark Collins underlined his mettle as a tackler by coming third on the team, which is unusual for a cornerback and almost unthinkable on a Giants squad with so many hitters. Patrolling the middle of the field, the fourth-year pairing of safeties Myron Guyton and Greg Jackson improves with each campaign.

Throughout the defense, though, there begins to appear a shortage of reserves and this was recognized when, other than the tight ends, defensive players were picked in the top seven rounds.

When it comes to booting the ball, New York is well off, with a two-time Pro Bowler, Sean Landeta, punting and the unflappable Matt Bahr as placekicker. For seven years, Landeta has been remarkably consistent, falling below 42.7 yards only in his injury-shortened 1988 campaign. He averages 43.4 over his career. Bahr, of course, is the one who trundles on to the field with the clock winding down and the game on the line. He doesn't have great range but his kicks usually split the uprights.

## 1992 Draft

| Round | Name | Pos. | Ht. | Wt. | College |
|---|---|---|---|---|---|
| 1. | Brown, Derek | TE | 6-5 | 252 | Notre Dame |
| 2. | Sparks, Phillippi | DB | 5-11 | 186 | Arizona State |
| 3. | Pierce, Aaron | TE | 6-5 | 246 | Washington |
| 4. | Hamilton, Keith | DT | 6-5 | 279 | Pittsburgh |
| 5. | Wright, Michael | DB | 6-0 | 184 | Washington State |
| 6. | Dillard, Stacey | DT | 6-4 | 289 | Oklahoma |
| 7. | Widmer, Corey | NT | 6-3 | 273 | Montana State |
| 8. | Graham, Kent | QB | 6-4 | 230 | Ohio State |
| 9. | Prior, Anthony | DB | 5-10 | 184 | Washington State |
| 10. | Rooks, George | NT | 6-3 | 275 | Syracuse |
| 11. | Singleton, Nate | WR | 5-11 | 185 | Grambling |
| 12. | Swann, Charles | WR | 6-0 | 187 | Indiana State |

## VETERAN ROSTER

| No. | Name | Pos. | Ht. | Wt. | NFL Year | College |
|---|---|---|---|---|---|---|
| 51 | Abrams, Bobby | LB | 6-3 | 230 | 3 | Michigan |
|  | Amsler, Greg | RB | 6-3 | 232 | 1 | Tennessee |
| 24 | Anderson, Ottis | RB | 6-2 | 225 | 14 | Miami |
| 9 | Bahr, Matt | K | 5-10 | 175 | 14 | Penn State |
| 85 | Baker, Stephen | WR | 5-8 | 160 | 6 | Fresno State |
| 58 | Banks, Carl | LB | 6-4 | 235 | 9 | Michigan State |
| 46 | Brown, Roger | CB | 6-0 | 196 | 3 | Virginia Tech |
| 33 | Bunch, Jarrod | RB | 6-2 | 248 | 2 | Michigan |
| 62 | Butler, Jay | T | 6-7 | 306 | 1 | Bucknell |
|  | Calloway, Chris | WR | 5-10 | 190 | 3 | Michigan |
|  | Carlson, Jeff | QB | 6-3 | 215 | 3 | Weber State |
| 44 | Carthon, Maurice | RB | 6-1 | 225 | 8 | Arkansas State |
| 6 | Cavanaugh, Matt | QB | 6-2 | 210 | 15 | Pittsburgh |
| 25 | Collins, Mark | CB | 5-10 | 190 | 7 | Cal State-Fullerton |
| 87 | Cross, Howard | TE | 6-5 | 245 | 4 | Alabama |
| 99 | DeOssie, Steve | LB | 6-2 | 248 | 9 | Boston College |
| 77 | Dorsey, Eric | DE | 6-5 | 280 | 7 | Notre Dame |
| 76 | Elliott, John | T | 6-7 | 305 | 5 | Michigan |
| 93 | Fox, Mike | DE | 6-6 | 275 | 3 | West Virginia |
| 29 | Guyton, Myron | S | 6-1 | 205 | 4 | Eastern Kentucky |
|  | Hamilton, Millard | WR | 5-10 | 185 | 1 | Clark, Georgia |
| 27 | Hampton, Rodney | RB | 5-11 | 215 | 3 | Georgia |
| 15 | Hostetler, Jeff | QB | 6-3 | 212 | 8 | West Virginia |
| 74 | Howard, Erik | NT | 6-4 | 268 | 7 | Washington State |
| 82 | Ingram, Mark | WR | 5-10 | 188 | 6 | Michigan State |
| 47 | Jackson, Greg | S | 6-1 | 200 | 4 | Louisiana State |
| 79 | James, Clint | DE | 6-6 | 270 | 1 | Louisiana State |
| 52 | Johnson, Pepper | LB | 6-3 | 248 | 7 | Ohio State |
| 68 | Jones, Clarence | T | 6-6 | 280 | 2 | Maryland |
| 49 | Kaumeyer, Thom | S | 5-11 | 190 | 2 | Oregon |
| 61 | Kratch, Bob | G | 6-3 | 288 | 4 | Iowa |
| 5 | Landeta, Sean | P | 6-0 | 210 | 7 | Towson State |
| 70 | Marshall, Leonard | DE | 6-3 | 285 | 10 | Louisiana State |
| 81 | McCaffrey, Ed | WR | 6-5 | 215 | 2 | Stanford |
| 96 | McGhee, Kanavis | LB | 6-4 | 257 | 2 | Colorado |
| 38 | McGriggs, Lamar | DB | 6-3 | 210 | 2 | Western Illinois |
| 30 | Meggett, Dave | RB-KR | 5-7 | 180 | 4 | Towson State |
| 57 | Miller, Corey | LB | 6-2 | 255 | 2 | South Carolina |
| 60 | Moore, Eric | G | 6-5 | 290 | 5 | Indiana |
| 84 | Mowatt, Zeke | TE | 6-3 | 240 | 9 | Florida State |
| 65 | Oates, Bart | C | 6-3 | 265 | 8 | Brigham Young |
| 12 | Perez, Mike | QB | 6-1 | 210 | 2 | San Jose State |
| 55 | Reasons, Gary | LB | 6-4 | 234 | 9 | Northwestern State, La. |
|  | Reynolds, Ed | LB | 6-5 | 242 | 10 | Virginia |
| 72 | Riesenberg, Doug | T | 6-5 | 275 | 6 | California |
| 66 | Roberts, William | G | 6-5 | 280 | 8 | Ohio State |
| 11 | Simms, Phil | QB | 6-3 | 214 | 13 | Morehead State |
| 18 | Taylor, Greg | WR | 5-8 | 163 | 1 | Auburn |
| 56 | Taylor, Lawrence | LB | 6-3 | 243 | 12 | North Carolina |
| 21 | Thompson, Reyna | CB | 6-0 | 193 | 7 | Baylor |
| 34 | Tillman, Lewis | RB | 6-0 | 195 | 4 | Jackson State |
| 28 | Walls, Everson | CB | 6-1 | 194 | 12 | Grambling |
| 73 | Washington, John | DE | 6-4 | 275 | 7 | Oklahoma State |
| 59 | Williams, Brian | C-G | 6-5 | 300 | 4 | Minnesota |
| 23 | Williams, Perry | CB | 6-2 | 203 | 9 | North Carolina State |

## 1992 SCHEDULE OF GAMES

**September**

| | | |
|---|---|---|
| 6 | SAN FRANCISCO | 4:00 |
| 13 | DALLAS | 1:00 |
| 21 | at Chicago (Mon.) | 8:00 |
| 27 | Open Date | |

**October**

| | | |
|---|---|---|
| 4 | at Los Angeles Raiders | 1:00 |
| 11 | PHOENIX | 1:00 |
| 18 | at Los Angeles Rams | 1:00 |
| 25 | SEATTLE | 1:00 |

**November**

| | | |
|---|---|---|
| 1 | at Washington | 8:00 |
| 8 | GREEN BAY | 1:00 |
| 15 | at Denver | 6:00 |
| 22 | PHILADELPHIA | 1:00 |
| 26 | at Dallas (Thanksgiving) | 3:00 |

**December**

| | | |
|---|---|---|
| 6 | WASHINGTON | 4:00 |
| 12 | at Phoenix (Sat.) | 2:00 |
| 19 | KANSAS CITY (Sat.) | 12:30 |
| 27 | at Philadelphia | 1:00 |

# PHILADELPHIA EAGLES

**Address** Veterans Stadium, Broad St. and Pattison Ave., Philadelphia, Pennsylvania 19148.

**Stadium** Veterans Stadium, Philadelphia.
*Capacity* 65,356 *Playing Surface* AstroTurf-8.

**Team Colours** Kelly Green, Silver, and White.

**Head Coach** Rich Kotite – 2nd year.

**Championships** Division 1980,'88; Conference 1980; NFL 1948,'49,'60.

**History** NFL 1933-69, NFC 1970-

It was one of the surprises of the 1991 season that Philadelphia was able to remain competitive to the end after losing quarterback Randall Cunningham in the early stages of the opening game. The offense turned up just often enough but the defense was outstanding over the long haul and truly earned the ranking of NFL's best.

The four-man defensive line of Reggie White, the late Jerome Brown, Mike Pitts and Clyde Simmons was the most feared in the game. White, Brown and Simmons formed the starting trio in the Pro Bowl, where a three-man line is mandatory. Collectively, the foursome logged 39 sacks, a total which was better than those of 18 NFL teams, as its contribution to the Eagles' league-leading 55. The unremitting pressure mounted by these exponents of terror is supported with no less determination by the linebacking trio of Seth Joyner, Byron Evans and William Thomas. Joyner has been a good one for some time but he attended his first Pro Bowl only last year. The emergence of Thomas, a rookie, was a major shock. A fourth-rounder, he weighs a mere 218 pounds, yet he hits like a train and has outstanding range. With the Plan-B departure of Jessie Small, whom Thomas displaced at right linebacker, Britt Hager becomes the senior backup but he is happier in the middle spot and there could be a shortage of depth for the outsides.

'The defensive backs; I love 'em,' says defensive coordinator Bud Carson of a unit in which Andre Waters starts at strong safety, Wes Hopkins in the free rôle, and which has the pairing of Eric Allen and Ben Smith at cornerback. Waters led the team in tackles for the third time in his career. Sadly, Smith suffered a serious knee injury in November and may not be ready until October. If Smith's future is in doubt, he may take heart from the example of Hopkins, whose career was thought to be over in 1986, but he has fought back to the verge of Pro Bowl quality. In Smith's absence, Izel Jenkins stepped in smoothly. All three backups, John Booty, Rich Miano and 1991 second-round draftee Jesse Campbell were protected under Plan B.

The return of Cunningham, who is described as being ahead of schedule and will be back to his best by the season opener, also means the return of the Eagles' best rusher. In addition to having a bazooka arm, Cunningham is the only quarterback in league history to have led his team in rushing for four straight years. In his absence, Jim McMahon and Jeff Kemp did their best but courage is no substitute for the brilliance which will return with Cunningham. His wide receivers, who did well last year despite being put 'on hold', may be ready to enter a higher orbit. The starters are Fred Barnett and Calvin Williams but veteran Roy Green cannot be excluded from the group of backups which will make its contributions. Added to these, Philadelphia has one of the NFC's best pass receiving tight ends in Keith Jackson, and the best coming out of the backfield in the shape of running back Keith Byars.

Excluding Cunningham, the Eagles do have a shortage of both class and variety at running back, where James Joseph, Heath Sherman and Thomas Sanders will compete to start in partnership with Byars. Second-round draftee Siran Stacy has good vision and moves but hardly shapes up as a franchise back. One explanation for the lack of productivity in rushing for some time has been the weakness of the offen-

| 1992 SCHEDULE OF GAMES | September | |
|---|---|---|
| | 6 NEW ORLEANS | 1:00 |
| | 13 at Phoenix | 5:00 |
| | 20 DENVER | 1:00 |
| | 27 Open Date | |
| | October | |
| | 5 DALLAS (Mon.) | 9:00 |
| | 11 at Kansas City | 12:00 |
| | 18 at Washington | 1:00 |
| | 25 PHOENIX | 1:00 |
| | November | |
| | 1 at Dallas | 3:00 |
| | 8 LOS ANGELES RAIDERS | 1:00 |
| | 15 vs Green Bay at Milwaukee | 12:00 |
| | 22 at New York Giants | 1:00 |
| | 29 at San Francisco | 1:00 |
| | December | |
| | 6 MINNESOTA | 1:00 |
| | 13 at Seattle | 1:00 |
| | 20 WASHINGTON | 1:00 |
| | 27 NEW YORK GIANTS | 1:00 |

sive line. The unit wasn't helped last year by many injuries which forced constant readjustment of personnel. The most probable lineup will have Ron Heller and Antone Davis at tackle, Dennis McKnight and Rob Selby in the guard positions and David Alexander at center. But several players, including John Hudson, Daryle Smith, Cecil Gray and Mike Schad, will be tried in camp. Overall, it is a talented group of individuals, well-known names, who have been high draft picks or, perhaps, were respected when playing for other clubs. Even allowing for injuries, the Eagles have struggled for too long seeking the correct formula.

Punter Jeff Feagles seems to have settled down well. His gross average of 41.8 yards is acceptable though new special teams coach Larry Pasquale will look for improvement in a punt coverage team which allowed opponents room to run in 1991. Having failed on only three of 30 field goal attempts inside 50 yards, placekicker Roger Ruzek is alongside the very best in the NFL.

### 1992 Draft

| Round | Name | Pos. | Ht. | Wt. | College |
|---|---|---|---|---|---|
| 2. | Stacy, Siran | RB | 5-11 | 203 | Alabama |
| 3. | Jeter, Tommy | DT | 6-5 | 282 | Texas |
| 4. | Brooks, Tony | RB | 6-0 | 230 | Notre Dame |
| 4. | Weldon, Casey | QB | 6-0 | 200 | Florida State |
| 5. | Barlow, Corey | DB | 5-9 | 182 | Auburn |
| 6. | Sydner, Jeff | WR-KR | 5-6 | 177 | Hawaii |
| 7. | Boatwright, William | G | 6-2 | 307 | Virginia Tech |
| 8. | Bullough, Chuck | LB | 6-1 | 226 | Michigan State |
| 9. | Bartley, Ephesians | LB | 6-2 | 220 | Florida |
| 10. | McMillian, Mark | CB | 5-8 | 165 | Alabama |
| 11. | Tudors, Pumpy | P | 5-8 | 197 | Tennessee-Chattanooga |
| 12. | Houston, Brandon | T | 6-4 | 292 | Oklahoma |

*Ben Smith (26) has speed and can hit.*

### VETERAN ROSTER

| No. | Name | Pos. | Ht. | Wt. | NFL Year | College |
|---|---|---|---|---|---|---|
| 72 | Alexander, David | C | 6-3 | 275 | 6 | Tulsa |
| 21 | Allen, Eric | CB | 5-10 | 180 | 5 | Arizona State |
| 18 | Archer, David | QB | 6-2 | 208 | 8 | Iowa State |
| 86 | Barnett, Fred | WR | 6-0 | 199 | 3 | Arkansas State |
| 65 | Bingham, Guy | C | 6-3 | 260 | 13 | Montana |
| 42 | Booty, John | CB | 6-0 | 180 | 5 | Texas Christian |
| 67 | Bruhin, John | G | 6-3 | 285 | 5 | Tennessee · |
| 41 | Byars, Keith | RB | 6-1 | 238 | 7 | Ohio State |
| 37 | Campbell, Jesse | S | 6-1 | 215 | 1 | North Carolina State |
|  | Conlin, Chris | G-T | 6-4 | 290 | 4 | Penn State |
| 12 | Cunningham, Randall | QB | 6-4 | 205 | 7 | Nevada-Las Vegas |
| 78 | Davis, Antone | T | 6-4 | 325 | 2 | Tennessee |
| 84 | Dixon, Floyd | WR | 5-9 | 170 | 7 | Stephen F. Austin |
| 56 | Evans, Byron | LB | 6-2 | 235 | 6 | Arizona |
| 5 | Feagles, Jeff | P | 6-1 | 205 | 5 | Miami |
| 95 | Flores, Mike | DE | 6-3 | 256 | 2 | Louisville |
| 61 | Floyd, Eric | G-T | 6-5 | 310 | 3 | Auburn |
| 8 | Goebel, Brad | QB | 6-3 | 198 | 2 | Baylor |
| 90 | Golic, Mike | DT | 6-5 | 275 | 7 | Notre Dame |
| 71 | Gray, Cecil | T | 6-4 | 275 | 2 | North Carolina |
| 81 | Green, Roy | WR | 6-1 | 195 | 14 | Henderson State |
| 54 | Hager, Britt | LB | 6-1 | 225 | 4 | Texas |
| 91 | Harmon, Andy | DE | 6-4 | 265 | 2 | Kent State |
| 80 | Harris, Rod | WR | 5-10 | 185 | 4 | Texas A&M |
| 73 | Heller, Ron | T | 6-6 | 280 | 9 | Penn State |
| 48 | Hopkins, Wes | S | 6-1 | 215 | 9 | Southern Methodist |
| 76 | Hudson, John | G-C | 6-2 | 275 | 2 | Auburn |
| 88 | Jackson, Keith | TE | 6-2 | 250 | 5 | Oklahoma |
| 83 | Jackson, Kenny | WR | 6-0 | 180 | 9 | Penn State |
| 46 | Jenkins, Izel | CB | 5-10 | 190 | 5 | North Carolina State |
| 87 | Johnson, Maurice | TE | 6-2 | 243 | 2 | Temple |
| 32 | Joseph, James | RB | 6-0 | 222 | 2 | Auburn |
| 59 | Joyner, Seth | LB | 6-2 | 235 | 7 | Texas-El Paso |
| 16 | Kemp, Jeff | QB | 6-0 | 201 | 12 | Dartmouth |
| 84 | Kovell, Paul | TE | 6-2 | 233 | 1 | Indiana, Pa. |
| 57 | Kowalkowski, Scott | LB | 6-2 | 228 | 2 | Notre Dame |
| 62 | McKnight, Dennis | C-G | 6-3 | 280 | 10 | Drake |
| 9 | McMahon, Jim | QB | 6-1 | 195 | 11 | Brigham Young |
| 38 | Miano, Rich | DB | 6-1 | 200 | 7 | Hawaii |
| 35 | Mitchell, Chris | DB | 6-1 | 197 | 1 | Mississippi |
| 25 | Overton, Don | RB | 6-2 | 221 | 3 | Fairmont State |
| 74 | Pitts, Mike | DT | 6-5 | 280 | 10 | Alabama |
| 55 | Rose, Ken | LB | 6-1 | 215 | 6 | Nevada-Las Vegas |
| 7 | Ruzek, Roger | K | 6-1 | 200 | 6 | Weber State |
| 45 | Sanders, Thomas | RB | 5-11 | 202 | 8 | Texas A&M |
| 79 | Schad, Mike | G | 6-5 | 290 | 4 | Queens, Canada |
| 75 | Selby, Ron | T-G | 6-3 | 286 | 2 | Auburn |
| 23 | Sherman, Heath | RB-KR | 6-0 | 205 | 4 | Texas A&I |
| 82 | Shuler, Mickey | TE | 6-3 | 230 | 15 | Penn State |
| 22 | Sikahema, Vai | RB-KR | 5-9 | 191 | 7 | Brigham Young |
| 96 | Simmons, Clyde | DE | 6-6 | 280 | 7 | Western Carolina |
| 26 | Smith, Ben | CB | 5-11 | 185 | 3 | Georgia |
| 63 | Smith, Daryle | T | 6-5 | 276 | 6 | Tennessee |
| 30 | Smith, Otis | CB | 5-11 | 184 | 2 | Missouri |
| 51 | Thomas, William | LB | 6-2 | 219 | 2 | Texas A&M |
| 20 | Waters, Andre | S | 5-11 | 200 | 9 | Cheyney State |
| 92 | White, Reggie | DE | 6-5 | 285 | 8 | Tennessee |
| 89 | Williams, Calvin | WR | 5-11 | 190 | 3 | Purdue |

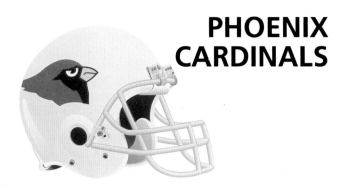

# PHOENIX CARDINALS

**Address** P.O. Box 888, Phoenix, Arizona 85001-0888.
**Stadium** Sun Devil Stadium, Tempe.
   *Capacity* 72,608 *Playing Surface* Grass.
**Team Colours** Cardinal Red, Black, and White.
**Head Coach** Joe Bugel – 3rd year.
**Championships** Division 1974, '75; NFL 1925, '47.
**History** NFL 1920-69, NFC 1970-
   (They were known as the Chicago Cardinals until 1960,
   when they moved to St Louis. In 1988, the franchise,
   still under the same ownership, was transferred to
   Phoenix.)

The Cardinals have some leeway to make up if they are to compete for a title and it will be seen as success if they reach par.

Last season's setbacks began on August 21 when starting quarterback Timm Rosenbach was lost for the season with a knee injury suffered in non-contact drills. Tom Tupa, Chris Chandler and Stan Gelbaugh, the latter of Monarchs fame, attempted to fill the void but none was able to kick-start an offense which did not score a touchdown in five games and produced only one in seven other contests, while being shut out twice for the first time since 1955. The club scored fewer than ten points seven times, had only six rushing touchdowns to set an unenviable club-record low, and only four times as a team did they rush for over 100 yards in a game. Clearly, the return of a healthy Rosenbach is critical, not least for his feisty team leadership. Failing this, second-round draftee Tony Sacca is hardly likely to come in and run the show.

At running back, both Johnny Johnson and Anthony Thompson disappointed following promising rookie seasons. Johnson slipped from 926 rushing yards as a rookie to a modest 666 yards. Thompson could manage only 376. However, the so-called sophomore jinx is not unusual in pro football and is often followed by a significant upturn. In an effort to maximize the yield from their talent, the Cardinals freely switch formations, sometimes using three wide receivers and, at other times, an H-back who is essentially a mobile tight end. However, only very rarely do they have two running backs on the field at the same time.

Without question, the three senior wide receivers, Ernie Jones, Ricky Proehl and Randal Hill, have enormous potential and it makes sense to bring them into action as much as possible. Jones came to the fore in 1991 and flirted with his first 1,000-yards-receiving campaign, falling short by just 43 as he led the club. Proehl's first two campaigns promise much while Hill was a 1991 first-round draftee of Miami who came to Phoenix in a trade.

The variety at the tight end position comes in the form of Walter Reeves, who is an out-and-out blocker, with Tim Jorden the more likely to catch passes from the H-back position. Jorden takes on greater responsibility following the loss of Ron Wolfley under Plan B. Wolfley was a tough blocker and could be missed by an offensive line which must take some of the blame for the team's poor offensive output. It was hoped that Joe Wolf could step up at left guard following the trade of Derek Kennard to New Orleans, but he was slowed by a shoulder injury, forcing the Cardinals to rotate Vernice Smith and Willie Williams in that

## 1992 Draft

| Round | Name | Pos. | Ht. | Wt. | College |
|---|---|---|---|---|---|
| 2. | Sacca, Tony | QB | 6-4 | 234 | Penn State |
| 3. | Cunningham, Ed | C | 6-2 | 292 | Washington |
| 4. | Christy, Jeff | T | 6-3 | 290 | Pittsburgh |
| 4. | Bankston, Michael | NT | 6-1 | 284 | Sam Houston State |
| 6. | Brauninger, Brian | T | 6-5 | 287 | Oklahoma |
| 7. | Ware, Derek | TE | 6-2 | 245 | Central State, Ok. |
| 8. | Blount, Eric | WR | 5-11 | 185 | North Carolina |
| 9. | Henson, David | NT | 6-1 | 265 | Central Arkansas |
| 9. | Williams, Tyrone | WR | 6-5 | 208 | Western Ontario |
| 10. | Yarbrough, Reggie | RB | 6-1 | 212 | Cal State-Fullerton |
| 11. | Baxley, Rob | T | 6-4 | 286 | Iowa |
| 12. | Wilson, Lance | NT | 6-3 | 282 | Texas |

## VETERAN ROSTER

| No. | Name | Pos. | Ht. | Wt. | NFL Year | College |
|---|---|---|---|---|---|---|
|  | Bailey, Johnny | RB-KR | 5-8 | 180 | 3 | Texas A&I |
| 54 | Braxton, David | LB | 6-2 | 230 | 4 | Wake Forest |
| 33 | Brown, Ivory Lee | RB | 6-2 | 230 | 1 | Arkansas-Pine Bluff |
| 16 | Camarillo, Rich | P | 5-11 | 195 | 12 | Washington |
| 37 | Centers, Larry | RB | 6-0 | 200 | 3 | Stephen F. Austin |
| 17 | Chandler, Chris | QB | 6-4 | 220 | 5 | Washington |
| 93 | Coleman, Sidney | LB | 6-2 | 250 | 5 | Southern Mississippi |
| 48 | Davis, Dexter | CB | 5-10 | 190 | 2 | Clemson |
| 5 | Davis, Greg | K | 6-0 | 200 | 6 | Citadel |
| 22 | Duerson, Dave | S | 6-1 | 208 | 10 | Notre Dame |
| 83 | Edwards, Anthony | WR | 5-9 | 190 | 4 | New Mexico Highlands |
|  | Eilers, Pat | S | 5-11 | 192 | 3 | Notre Dame |
| 94 | Faulkner, Jeff | DE | 6-4 | 305 | 4 | Southern |
| 56 | Harvey, Ken | LB | 6-3 | 230 | 5 | California |
| 58 | Hill, Eric | LB | 6-2 | 250 | 4 | Louisiana State |
| 81 | Hill, Randal | WR | 5-10 | 177 | 2 | Miami |
| 97 | Hyche, Steve | LB | 6-2 | 226 | 3 | Livingston |
| 80 | Jackson, John | WR | 6-0 | 183 | 3 | Southern California |
| 53 | Jax, Garth | LB | 6-3 | 240 | 7 | Florida State |
| 39 | Johnson, Johnny | RB | 6-3 | 220 | 3 | San Jose State |
| 86 | Jones, Ernie | WR | 6-0 | 200 | 5 | Indiana |
| 55 | Jones, Jock | LB | 6-2 | 227 | 3 | Virginia Tech |
| 75 | Jones, Mike | DE | 6-4 | 285 | 2 | North Carolina State |
| 85 | Jorden, Tim | TE | 6-2 | 235 | 3 | Indiana |
| 57 | Kauahi, Kani | C | 6-2 | 274 | 10 | Hawaii |
| 51 | Lewis, Bill | C | 6-6 | 290 | 7 | Nebraska |
| 42 | Lofton, Steve | CB | 5-9 | 180 | 2 | Texas A&M |
| 29 | Lynch, Lorenzo | CB | 5-10 | 200 | 5 | Cal State-Sacramento |
| 40 | Massey, Robert | CB | 5-10 | 185 | 4 | North Carolina Central |
|  | May, Mark | G-T | 6-6 | 296 | 11 | Pittsburgh |
| 46 | McDonald, Tim | S | 6-2 | 215 | 6 | Southern California |
| 50 | Nunn, Freddie Joe | LB | 6-4 | 250 | 8 | Mississippi |
| 76 | Patterson, Craig | DT | 6-4 | 317 | 3 | Brigham Young |
| 87 | Proehl, Ricky | WR | 6-0 | 190 | 3 | Wake Forest |
| 89 | Reeves, Walter | TE | 6-3 | 266 | 4 | Auburn |
|  | Rolle, Butch | TE | 6-3 | 245 | 7 | Michigan State |
| 3 | Rosenbach, Timm | QB | 6-1 | 210 | 3 | Washington State |
| 67 | Sharpe, Luis | T | 6-5 | 295 | 11 | UCLA |
|  | Small, Jessie | LB | 6-3 | 240 | 4 | Eastern Kentucky |
| 61 | Smith, Lance | G | 6-2 | 290 | 8 | Louisiana State |
| 69 | Smith, Vernice | G-T | 6-2 | 298 | 3 | Florida A&M |
| 90 | Stowe, Tyronne | LB | 6-1 | 249 | 6 | Rutgers |
| 98 | Swann, Eric | DE | 6-4 | 310 | 2 | None |
| 27 | Taylor, Jay | CB | 5-9 | 175 | 4 | San Jose State |
| 34 | Thompson, Anthony | RB | 5-11 | 210 | 3 | Indiana |
|  | Villa, Danny | T | 6-5 | 305 | 6 | Arizona State |
| 66 | Wahler, Jim | DT | 6-3 | 275 | 4 | UCLA |
| 35 | Williams, Aeneas | CB | 5-11 | 187 | 2 | Southern |
| 60 | Williams, Willie | T-TE | 6-6 | 300 | 2 | Louisiana State |
| 68 | Wolf, Joe | G | 6-5 | 295 | 4 | Boston College |
| 38 | Zordich, Michael | S | 6-0 | 200 | 6 | Penn State |

*LEFT: Tim McDonald is a one-man defense for the Cardinals.*

position. There's a gap to fill at right tackle but, elsewhere, Luis Sharpe, Lance Smith and Bill Lewis are up to par. The draft brought center Ed Cunningham in the third round while Mark May and Danny Villa were veteran acquisitions, but the signs are that it will be a patchwork outfit which slogs its way through the season.

Defensively, the Cardinals rely on star individuals and there is a sprinkling of those, with strong safety Tim McDonald being the brightest light. Defensing passes, forcing fumbles, leading the team in solo tackles and the rest, McDonald is often a one-man wrecking crew and, deservedly, went to his second Pro Bowl. At outside linebacker, Ken Harvey and Freddie Joe Nunn give everything and do have their excellent games. Phoenix needed a little luck and in the 1991 draft they came up with a real find in cornerback Aeneas Williams, who defensed 17 passes and led the team with six interceptions to earn All-Rookie honours. There is just the possibility that they may have found another premier player in defensive end Eric Swann, 'the Big Beefaroni' as he was affectionately termed by head coach Joe Bugel. Drafted after playing only semi-pro football, Swann's rookie campaign was marred by a preseason knee injury. But he did come through to have four sacks as a specialist pass rusher and offers every hope of becoming a player of the highest class.

The Cardinals can always rely on Rich Camarillo to salvage something out of modest field position. Last year he went to the Pro Bowl for the third time after averaging 45.3 yards on 76 punts. Placekicker Greg Davis also rose to the occasion in 1991, being one of only six players of his breed in the NFL not to miss a field goal from 40 yards or less, and twice equalling the team record with 52-yard field goals.

### 1992 SCHEDULE OF GAMES

**September**

| | | |
|---|---|---|
| 6 | at Tampa Bay | 4:00 |
| 13 | PHILADELPHIA | 5:00 |
| 20 | at Dallas | 3:00 |
| 27 | Open Date | |

**October**

| | | |
|---|---|---|
| 4 | WASHINGTON | 1:00 |
| 11 | at New York Giants | 1:00 |
| 18 | NEW ORLEANS | 1:00 |
| 25 | at Philadelphia | 1:00 |

**November**

| | | |
|---|---|---|
| 1 | SAN FRANCISCO | 2:00 |
| 8 | at Los Angeles Rams | 1:00 |
| 15 | at Atlanta | 1:00 |
| 22 | DALLAS | 2:00 |
| 29 | at Washington | 1:00 |

**December**

| | | |
|---|---|---|
| 6 | SAN DIEGO | 2:00 |
| 12 | NEW YORK GIANTS (Sat.) | 2:00 |
| 20 | at Indianapolis | 1:00 |
| 27 | TAMPA BAY | 2:00 |

# WASHINGTON REDSKINS

**Address** Redskin Park, P.O. Box 17247, Dulles
International Airport, Washington, D.C. 20041.

**Stadium** Robert F. Kennedy Stadium, Washington.
*Capacity* 55,683 *Playing Surface* Grass.

**Team Colours** Burgundy and Gold.

**Head Coach** Joe Gibbs – 12th year.

**Championships** Division 1972,'83,'84,'87,'91;
Conference 1972,'82,'83,'87,'91; NFL 1937,'42;
Super Bowl 1982,'87,'91.

**History** NFL 1932-69, NFC 1970-
(Originally named the Boston Braves for the 1932
season only, they were renamed the Boston Redskins
until, in 1937, they moved to Washington.)

Super Bowl champions always look invincible entering the following campaign but the 1991 Washington Redskins were almost superhuman. And with an essentially unchanged starting lineup, and reserve strength improved by the addition of Heisman Trophy winner Desmond Howard, the task facing their opponents becomes frightening. More than just murdering the AFC's best team, the Redskins truly rank amongst history's great clubs.

Their two defeats came by a total of just five points as they became only the sixth team to record 17 or more wins in a single season. Their 12-game winning streak was the eighth-longest in NFL annals as they set a team record with 11 consecutive wins at RFK Stadium. There are many more individual superlatives sprinkled around a squad which sent eight players to the Pro Bowl, but the most telling statistic was generated by the offensive line, which allowed a league-low nine quarterback sacks. In addition, it escorted the runners to a league-leading 21 rushing touchdowns.

There is ample backup for starters Jim Lachey, Raleigh McKenzie, Jeff Bostic, Mark Schlereth and Joe Jacoby, but fresh talent came from the draft in the form of Paul Siever, who will compensate for the retirement of Russ Grimm. Such is the class of the Redskins' starting trio of wide receivers that the glamour pick in the entire draft, Howard, may not see much action as a rookie. The silky-smooth Art Monk, who holds the single-season reception record of

106, is within 19 catches of setting a new career record. Gary Clark is always expected to break the 1,000-yard barrier and if Ricky Sanders is coming off a modest campaign by Washington standards, he can always step up a gear. With running back Earnest Byner chipping in with a clutch of receptions, Washington can afford the luxury of a pure blocker, Don Warren, at tight end.

As a rusher, Byner led the team but his heir apparent, Ricky Ervins, is ready to take over. Byner and Ervins are used singly at running back with Gerald Riggs coming on both for short-yardage plays and to hammer into the end zone. Such a galaxy of talent needs a great quarterback and in Mark Rypien the Redskins have a tough competitor with a rifle arm and a quick brain. Over the final seven regular-season games, Rypien was peerless as he passed for 17 touchdowns with just three interceptions. Not once in 19 games did a Washington quarterback throw an interception in his own half.

On defense, while other great teams might 'dominate', 'wreck' or 'destroy', the Redskins 'swarm'. Thirteen different players made contributions to the 'Skins' 50 sacks while another dozen individuals had at least one interception in the team total of 27. Defensive end Charles Mann was the sack leader with 11.5, while linebacker Wilber Marshall tied with cornerback Darrell Green for the team lead with five interceptions. Green, who is the NFL's premier player in his position, also defensed a huge 21 passes.

There is unremitting brawling, spoiling pressure brought to bear by the four-man defensive line of Mann, Eric Williams, Tim Johnson and Fred Stokes. A step behind them, Marshall and Andre Collins deliver the pincer blows from the outside positions and Matt Millen did his usual job of stuffing the run. However, the inspirational Millen, who has also earned Super Bowl winner's rings with the Raiders and San Francisco, has retired. Kurt Gouveia will step up. In the secondary, safeties Brad Edwards and Danny Copeland, and cornerback Martin Mayhew all were signed as Plan-B free agents, confirming the judgement of the scouts. That all three have prospered in the Washington system says something about the professional skill of former Kansas City all-star and now Redskins defensive backs coach Emmitt Thomas. The fourth and best-known member of the group, right cornerback Green, usually wins the title of 'NFL's Fastest Man' and has added the title of 'World's Fastest Athlete'.

Not often do the Redskins need help to win games from their placekicker but, in Chip Lohmiller, they have one of the best. Now and then, he hits a hot streak when distance seems not to be a factor. It is a measure of a good team when its punter doesn't have very many attempts and Washington had the NFC low of 55. Punting more for position than distance, Kelly Goodburn had a modest gross average but no one is complaining.

*Jim Lachey is a favourite with 'Hog' fans.*

## 1992 Draft

| Round | Name | Pos. | Ht. | Wt. | College |
|---|---|---|---|---|---|
| 1. | Howard, Desmond | WR-KR | 5-9 | 184 | Michigan |
| 2. | Collins, Shane | DE | 6-2 | 269 | Arizona State |
| 3. | Siever, Paul | G | 6-5 | 295 | Penn State |
| 4. | Hakel, Chris | QB | 6-2 | 231 | William & Mary |
| 6. | Rowe, Ray | TE | 6-2 | 247 | San Diego State |
| 7. | Holmes, Calvin | CB | 5-8 | 183 | Southern California |
| 8. | Moore, Darryl | G | 6-2 | 282 | Texas-El Paso |
| 9. | Powell, Boone | LB | 6-3 | 229 | Texas |
| 10. | Barker, Tony | LB | 6-3 | 225 | Rice |
| 11. | Smith, Terry | WR | 5-8 | 157 | Penn State |
| 12. | Elliott, Matt | C | 6-2 | 274 | Michigan |

## VETERAN ROSTER

| No. | Name | Pos. | Ht. | Wt. | NFL Year | College |
|---|---|---|---|---|---|---|
| 61 | Adickes, Mark | G | 6-4 | 285 | 7 | Baylor |
| 53 | Bostic, Jeff | C | 6-2 | 278 | 13 | Clemson |
| 82 | Brandes, John | TE | 6-2 | 250 | 6 | Cameron, Oklahoma |
| 67 | Brown, Ray | T | 6-5 | 310 | 5 | Arkansas State |
| 99 | Buck, Jason | DE | 6-5 | 264 | 6 | Brigham Young |
| 21 | Byner, Earnest | RB | 5-10 | 218 | 9 | East Carolina |
| 50 | Caldwell, Ravin | LB | 6-3 | 240 | 6 | Arkansas |
| 84 | Clark, Gary | WR | 5-9 | 173 | 8 | James Madison |
| 51 | Coleman, Monte | LB | 6-2 | 245 | 14 | Central Arkansas |
| 55 | Collins, Andre | LB | 6-1 | 233 | 3 | Penn State |
| 12 | Conklin, Cary | QB | 6-4 | 223 | 1 | Washington |
| 26 | Copeland, Danny | S | 6-2 | 213 | 4 | Eastern Kentucky |
| 27 | Edwards, Brad | S | 6-2 | 207 | 5 | South Carolina |
| 64 | Elewonibi, Mo | T | 6-4 | 310 | 1 | Brigham Young |
| 32 | Ervins, Ricky | RB | 5-7 | 200 | 2 | Southern California |
| | Gabbard, Steve | T | 6-3 | 293 | 2 | Florida State |
| 97 | Geathers, James | DE | 6-7 | 289 | 8 | Wichita State |
| 2 | Goodburn, Kelly | P | 6-2 | 199 | 6 | Emporia State |
| 54 | Gouveia, Kurt | LB | 6-1 | 228 | 6 | Brigham Young |
| 28 | Green, Darrell | CB | 5-8 | 170 | 10 | Texas A&I |
| 36 | Gulledge, David | S | 6-1 | 203 | 1 | Jacksonville State |
| | Hinkle, George | DT | 6-5 | 269 | 5 | Arizona |
| 34 | Hoage, Terry | S | 6-3 | 206 | 9 | Georgia |
| 86 | Hobbs, Stephen | WR | 5-11 | 200 | 3 | North Alabama |
| 16 | Humphries, Stan | QB | 6-2 | 224 | 3 | Northeast Louisiana |
| 66 | Jacoby, Joe | T | 6-6 | 314 | 12 | Louisville |
| 88 | Jenkins, Jason | TE | 6-2 | 234 | 2 | Rutgers |
| 47 | Johnson, Anthony | CB | 5-8 | 170 | 4 | Southwest Texas State |
| 80 | Johnson, Joe | WR | 5-8 | 170 | 3 | Notre Dame |
| 45 | Johnson, Sidney | CB | 5-9 | 175 | 4 | California |
| 78 | Johnson, Tim | DT | 6-3 | 283 | 6 | Penn State |
| 74 | Koch, Markus | DE | 6-5 | 260 | 7 | Boise State |
| 79 | Lachey, Jim | T | 6-6 | 294 | 8 | Ohio State |
| 8 | Lohmiller, Chip | K | 6-3 | 210 | 5 | Minnesota |
| 71 | Mann, Charles | DE | 6-6 | 272 | 10 | Nevada-Reno |
| 58 | Marshall, Wilber | LB | 6-1 | 231 | 9 | Florida |
| 35 | Mayhew, Martin | CB | 5-8 | 172 | 4 | Florida State |
| 20 | Mays, Alvoid | CB | 5-9 | 180 | 3 | West Virginia |
| 63 | McKenzie, Raleigh | G | 6-2 | 279 | 8 | Tennessee |
| 87 | Middleton, Ron | TE | 6-2 | 270 | 6 | Auburn |
| 30 | Mitchell, Brian | RB-KR | 5-10 | 209 | 3 | Southwestern Louisiana |
| 81 | Monk, Art | WR | 6-3 | 210 | 13 | Syracuse |
| 89 | Orr, Terry | TE | 6-2 | 235 | 7 | Texas |
| 37 | Riggs, Gerald | RB | 6-1 | 240 | 11 | Arizona State |
| 10 | Rutledge, Jeff | QB | 6-1 | 193 | 14 | Alabama |
| 11 | Rypien, Mark | QB | 6-4 | 234 | 5 | Washington State |
| 83 | Sanders, Ricky | WR | 5-11 | 180 | 7 | Southwest Texas State |
| 69 | Schlereth, Mark | G | 6-3 | 283 | 4 | Idaho |
| 23 | Settle, John | RB | 5-9 | 213 | 5 | Appalachian State |
| 76 | Simmons, Ed | T | 6-5 | 300 | 6 | Eastern Washington |
| 60 | Stokes, Fred | DE | 6-3 | 274 | 6 | Georgia Southern |
| 31 | Vaughn, Clarence | S | 6-0 | 202 | 5 | Northern Illinois |
| 40 | Walton, Alvin | S | 6-0 | 180 | 7 | Kansas |
| 85 | Warren, Don | TE | 6-4 | 242 | 14 | San Diego State |
| | Wilkins, Gary | TE | 6-2 | 248 | 5 | Georgia Tech |
| 75 | Williams, Eric | DT | 6-4 | 290 | 9 | Washington State |
| | Willis, Keith | DE | 6-1 | 260 | 10 | Northeastern |
| 94 | Wilson, Bobby | DT | 6-2 | 283 | 2 | Michigan State |

# CHICAGO BEARS

**Address** Halas Hall, 250 N. Washington, Lake Forest, Illinois 60045.

**Stadium** Soldier Field, Chicago.
*Capacity* 66,946 *Playing Surface* Grass.

**Team Colours** Navy Blue, Orange, and White.

**Head Coach** Mike Ditka – 11th year.

**Championships** Division 1984, '85, '86, '87, '88, '90; Conference 1985; NFL 1921, '32, '33, '40, '41, '43, '46, '63; Super Bowl 1985.

**History** NFL 1920-69, NFC 1970-
(Before 1922, they were known as firstly the Decatur Staleys and then the Chicago Staleys.)

*Jim Harbaugh set club records for passing attempts (478) and completions (275) last season.*

Never one to diguise his feelings, head coach Mike Ditka said, 'You have to run the football to win in the NFL. The people who think they are going to throw it every down aren't going to win. The people who believe you can win by passing the football, the media and the experts, are fools.'

He might have pointed to the difficulties last year when only rarely did the Bears have their top two running backs, Neal Anderson and Brad Muster, free from hamstring injuries. Typical Chicago players that they are, both men battled on anyway but their lack of full effectiveness was the key factor in Chicago's inability to convert good scoring positions into game-winning points. Anderson is a genuine top-class back with limitless courage while Muster has a real burst of speed. Both men are fully fit to resume as the main focus of the offense.

Not for some time have the Bears had greatness at wide receiver and that still is the case, although Wendell Davis does have decent moves and good hands, while Tom Waddle is a terrific battler. The offense really does need the speed and physical presence of Ron Morris to force opponents into respecting the passing game. However, Morris has been troubled with a knee problem and played in only three games last year. Should he not regain his full powers, the need grows for a higher level of productivity from the tight end position. Here, Jim Thornton has seniority over Keith Jennings but, thus far, neither man has shown much by way of big-play potential.

At the quarterback position, Chicago has calm authority in Jim Harbaugh, who was the first Bear to start all 16 regular-season games since Vince Evans in 1981. Last season, he set club records for attempts and completions, falling short of the yardage best by 55. Behind Harbaugh, Peter Tom Willis is being eased into the action slowly but has impressed on his few opportunities and enjoys Ditka's confidence.

On the offensive line, Chicago has had to face up to not having All-Pro left tackle Jim Covert, who has lost his battle with injuries. Stan Thomas was his obvious replacement but, following his injury setback after seven games as the starter, John Wojciechowski stood in and held his place when Thomas had regained fitness. It may be that Thomas settles in at right tackle as Keith Van Horne eases out, but no one is saying that the 11-year veteran is yet ready to concede his seniority. On the other hand, high draftee Troy Auzenne could be Van Horne's eventual replacement. The interior trio of two fine guards, Mark Bortz and Tom Thayer, and All-Pro center Jay Hilgenberg give the Bears a combination of range, guile and power from which to launch the offense.

## 1992 SCHEDULE OF GAMES

### September
| | | |
|---|---|---|
| 6 | DETROIT | 12:00 |
| 13 | at New Orleans | 12:00 |
| 21 | NEW YORK GIANTS (Mon.) | 8:00 |
| 27 | ATLANTA | 12:00 |

### October
| | | |
|---|---|---|
| 4 | at Minnesota | 12:00 |
| 11 | Open Date | |
| 18 | TAMPA BAY | 12:00 |
| 25 | at Green Bay | 12:00 |

### November
| | | |
|---|---|---|
| 2 | MINNESOTA (Mon.) | 8:00 |
| 8 | CINCINNATI | 7:00 |
| 15 | at Tampa Bay | 4:00 |
| 22 | GREEN BAY | 12:00 |
| 29 | at Cleveland | 1:00 |

### December
| | | |
|---|---|---|
| 7 | at Houston (Mon.) | 8:00 |
| 13 | PITTSBURGH | 12:00 |
| 20 | at Detroit | 4:00 |
| 27 | at Dallas | 3:00 |

## 1992 Draft

| Round | Name | Pos. | Ht. | Wt. | College |
|---|---|---|---|---|---|
| 1. | Spellman, Alonzo | DE | 6-4 | 280 | Ohio State |
| 2. | Auzenne, Troy | T | 6-7 | 282 | California |
| 3. | Lincoln, Jeremy | CB | 5-10 | 180 | Tennessee |
| 4. | Furrer, Will | QB | 6-2 | 208 | Virginia Tech |
| 5. | Harrison, Todd | TE | 6-3 | 260 | North Carolina State |
| 6. | Berry, Mark | CB | 5-11 | 180 | Texas |
| 7. | Brown, John | WR | 6-1 | 199 | Houston |
| 9. | Jurkovic, Mirko | G | 6-2 | 283 | Notre Dame |
| 10. | Fisher, Nikki | RB | 5-10 | 227 | Virginia |
| 11. | Age, Louis | T | 6-7 | 334 | Southwestern Louisiana |
| 12. | Wilson, Chris | LB | 6-0 | 229 | Oklahoma |

## VETERAN ROSTER

| No. | Name | Pos. | Ht. | Wt. | NFL Year | College |
|---|---|---|---|---|---|---|
| 35 | Anderson, Neal | RB | 5-11 | 210 | 7 | Florida |
| 93 | Armstrong, Trace | DE | 6-4 | 259 | 4 | Florida |
| 62 | Bortz, Mark | G | 6-6 | 272 | 10 | Iowa |
| 8 | Buford, Maury | P | 6-0 | 198 | 11 | Texas Tech |
| 6 | Butler, Kevin | K | 6-1 | 190 | 8 | Georgia |
| 20 | Carrier, Mark | S | 6-1 | 180 | 3 | Southern California |
| 54 | Cox, Ron | LB | 6-2 | 242 | 3 | Fresno State |
| 82 | Davis, Wendell | WR | 5-11 | 188 | 5 | Louisiana State |
| 95 | Dent, Richard | DE | 6-5 | 268 | 10 | Tennessee State |
| 37 | Douglass, Maurice | DB | 5-11 | 200 | 7 | Kentucky |
| | Fain, Richard | CB | 5-10 | 183 | 2 | Florida |
| 67 | Fontenot, Jerry | G | 6-3 | 272 | 4 | Texas A&M |
| 17 | Gardocki, Chris | P-K | 6-1 | 194 | 2 | Clemson |
| 23 | Gayle, Shaun | S | 5-11 | 194 | 9 | Ohio State |
| 29 | Gentry, Dennis | WR-KR | 5-8 | 180 | 11 | Baylor |
| 31 | Green, Mark | RB | 5-11 | 184 | 4 | Notre Dame |
| 4 | Harbaugh, Jim | QB | 6-3 | 220 | 6 | Michigan |
| 63 | Hilgenberg, Jay | C | 6-3 | 260 | 12 | Iowa |
| 85 | Jennings, Keith | TE | 6-4 | 251 | 2 | Clemson |
| 53 | Jones, Dante | LB | 6-1 | 236 | 5 | Oklahoma |
| 88 | Kozlowski, Glen | WR | 6-1 | 205 | 6 | Brigham Young |
| 70 | Kumerow, Eric | DE-DT | 6-7 | 260 | 4 | Ohio State |
| 33 | Lewis, Darren | RB | 5-10 | 219 | 2 | Texas A&M |
| 65 | Long, Stacy | G | 6-1 | 294 | 1 | Clemson |
| 46 | Lott, James | CB | 5-9 | 181 | 1 | Clemson |
| 26 | Mangum, John | CB | 5-10 | 173 | 3 | Alabama |
| 75 | Mattes, Ron | T | 6-6 | 300 | 6 | Virginia |
| 76 | McMichael, Steve | DT | 6-2 | 268 | 13 | Texas |
| 81 | Morgan, Anthony | WR | 6-1 | 195 | 2 | Tennessee |
| 84 | Morris, Ron | WR | 6-1 | 195 | 6 | Southern Methodist |
| 51 | Morrissey, Jim | LB | 6-3 | 227 | 8 | Michigan State |
| 25 | Muster, Brad | RB | 6-3 | 231 | 5 | Stanford |
| 36 | Paul, Markus | S | 6-2 | 199 | 4 | Syracuse |
| 72 | Perry, William | DT | 6-2 | 360 | 8 | Clemson |
| 59 | Rivera, Ron | LB | 6-3 | 240 | 9 | California |
| | Rodenhauser, Mark | C | 6-5 | 283 | 5 | Illinois State |
| 55 | Roper, John | LB | 6-1 | 228 | 4 | Texas A&M |
| 30 | Rouse, James | RB | 6-0 | 220 | 3 | Arkansas |
| 96 | Ryan, Tim | DE | 6-4 | 268 | 3 | Southern California |
| 50 | Singletary, Mike | LB | 6-0 | 230 | 12 | Baylor |
| | Smith, Quintin | WR | 5-10 | 172 | 2 | Kansas |
| 32 | Stinson, Lemuel | CB | 5-9 | 159 | 5 | Texas Tech |
| 58 | Stonebreaker, Mike | LB | 6-0 | 226 | 2 | Notre Dame |
| 49 | Tate, David | S | 6-0 | 177 | 5 | Colorado |
| 57 | Thayer, Tom | G | 6-4 | 270 | 8 | Notre Dame |
| 60 | Thomas, Stan | T | 6-5 | 302 | 2 | Texas |
| 80 | Thornton, James | TE | 6-2 | 242 | 5 | Cal State-Fullerton |
| 78 | Van Horne, Keith | T | 6-6 | 283 | 12 | Southern California |
| 87 | Waddle, Tom | WR | 6-0 | 181 | 4 | Boston College |
| 71 | Williams, James | DE | 6-7 | 305 | 2 | Cheyney State |
| 10 | Willis, Peter Tom | QB | 6-2 | 188 | 3 | Florida State |
| 73 | Wojciechowski, John | G | 6-4 | 270 | 6 | Michigan State |
| 21 | Woolford, Donnell | CB | 5-9 | 187 | 4 | Clemson |
| 83 | Wright, Eric | WR | 6-0 | 197 | 1 | Stephen F. Austin |
| 97 | Zorich, Chris | DT | 6-1 | 267 | 2 | Notre Dame |

The Bears never give away much on defense, starting with one of the best four-man lines in football and on, through the heart of the linebacking trio, to a pair of excellent safeties. On the line, to the trio of highly respected players, Richard Dent, William Perry and Steve McMichael, must now be added the name of Trace Armstrong, who has started for the past three seasons. As usual, Ditka will complain about Perry's refusal to shed blubber but the immense defensive tackle compensates with unexpected athleticism. First-round draftee Alonzo Spellman may be eased in as a specialist pass rusher.

Playing to the left of the incomparable Mike Singletary at linebacker, John Roper came fifth on the team in tackles, and third with eight sacks, in his first full year as the starter. At right linebacker, Jim Morrissey came in when starter Ron Rivera was injured and held his spot even when Rivera was ready to return. That position will see a battle in camp. The secondary has come together around the play of Pro Bowl free safety Mark Carrier, with strong safety Shaun Gayle edging into the NFC squad as an injury replacement. The pairing of Lemuel Stinson and Donnell Woolford has settled in comfortably at cornerback, while in Markus Paul, David Tate and Maurice Douglass, there is excellent depth.

Kevin Butler is coming off a campaign in which he missed two extra points and was only 69 per cent successful on field goals inside 50 yards. He has been a good one but he may have opened the door for Chris Gardocki, a 1991 third-round draftee, who spent most of the season on injured reserve but has a strong leg which the club finds useful for kickoffs. It may be a reminder to Maury Buford, who too had a modest campaign, that Gardocki can also punt.

# DETROIT LIONS

**Address** Pontiac Silverdome, 1200 Featherstone Road,
Pontiac, Michigan 48342.
**Stadium** Pontiac Silverdome.
*Capacity* 80,500 *Playing Surface* AstroTurf.
**Team Colours** Honolulu Blue and Silver.
**Head Coach** Wayne Fontes – 5th year.
**Championships** Division 1983,'91;
NFL 1935,'52,'53,'57.
**History** NFL 1930-69, NFC 1970-
(Until 1934, they were known as the Portsmouth
(Ohio) Spartans.)

No one expected the Lions to be a contender in 1991 and
yet they reached the conference title game for the first time
in their history. Head coach Wayne Fontes has a blend of
solid veterans and all-league stars with which to renew his
bid.

The Lions were well beaten by Washington in the NFC
Championship Game and yet the story could have been
different but for Detroit's injuries in key positions. One such
was on the offensive line, with normal starting right tackle
Eric Sanders unavailable. He will resume, with Pro Bowler
Lomas Brown at left tackle, Ken Dallafior in one guard position and Kevin Glover at center. It is not the best line in pro
football but it's not the weakest either. Sanders' replacement, rookie Scott Conover, came through his baptism of
fire well singed without being reduced to ashes. The
problem is a lack of depth, and the health of veteran
Dallafior is a concern for next season.

Fontes has a most difficult choice at quarterback. Rodney
Peete is the senior man, as much a fine football player as a
smart quarterback who runs the system well. Erik Kramer
was Peete's injury replacement for the last eight games and,
after two losses, he reeled off six straight wins to clinch the
division title before, in the playoffs, utterly destroying
Dallas. Peete is the more versatile but Kramer has a more
cultivated arm. The third contender, 1989 Heisman Trophy
winner Andre Ware, is an athlete of prodigious talent but
has not yet been able to unravel the subtleties of NFL football. Detroit uses four wide receivers almost permanently,
with Willie Green as an outside receiver and the pairing of
Brett Perriman and Mike Farr manning the inside lanes.
Following the Plan-B loss of Robert Clark, 1991 first-round
pick Herman Moore will step in wide to the right.

*Chris Spielman (54) has been to the last three Pro Bowls.*

The jewel in the crown is Barry Sanders, a running back
who transfixes linebackers, terrorizes defensive backs
and leaves defensive linemen lumbering in confusion. He
induces yawning gaps with a Payton-like feint in his own
backfield. Though statistically a touch behind the Cowboys'
Emmitt Smith last year and without the receiving productivity of Buffalo's Thurman Thomas, Sanders still is regarded
by most scouts as the NFL's best back. There is a possibility

that Detroit may adjust the emphasis this year to make better use of his abilities.

Defensively, the Lions usually put opponents under pressure without tearing away at the flesh, but there has been a gradual sharpening of teeth with the arrival of first-round draftee defensive ends Kelvin Pritchett and Robert Porcher in each of the last two years. They will be groomed to offer a pass rush with Pritchett seeing increased action after a learning campaign. For the moment, the starting trio will have Marc Spindler and Dan Owens at defensive end with Pro Bowler Jerry Ball expected to return fully fit at nose tackle. Behind them, at linebacker, there is good speed and toughness in George Jamison, Chris Spielman and Dennis Gibson, but the sparkle will return with Michael Cofer if he can come back after missing most of last year with an injury. In his absence, Tracy Hayworth started in all but two games, including the playoffs, but draftee Tracy Scroggins is seen as Cofer's heir. Spielman, the team-leading tackler, and Cofer are Pro Bowlers.

The secondary is particulary tough, focusing around Pro Bowl free safety Bennie Blades, who is starting to control the middle of the field with great authority. Strong safety William White is excellent against the run and is developing as a zone defender. At left cornerback, Ray Crockett was a revelation with six interceptions in only his third campaign, while at right cornerback Melvin Jenkins proved to be a tremendous Plan-B signing. Sheldon White gives some cover but there is a shortage of depth.

There will almost certainly be a change in the kicking department, where draftee Jason Hanson will challenge both Eddie Murray and Jim Arnold. Murray is under the greater pressure but Hanson will need to rediscover his form of the 1990 season if he is to displace one of the best veterans of the past decade. Returning kickoffs and punts is a Lions forte, with Pro Bowler Mel Gray having become the first player in history to lead the NFL in both categories in the same season. Sensibly, Detroit also likes to use its starting defensive players on special teams, whereas most clubs use backups and youngsters who need the experience.

## VETERAN ROSTER

| No. | Name | Pos. | Ht. | Wt. | NFL Year | College |
|---|---|---|---|---|---|---|
| 6 | Arnold, Jim | P | 6-3 | 211 | 10 | Vanderbilt |
| 93 | Ball, Jerry | NT | 6-1 | 298 | 6 | Southern Methodist |
| 40 | Barrett, Reggie | WR | 6-3 | 215 | 2 | Texas-El Paso |
| 36 | Blades, Bennie | S | 6-1 | 221 | 5 | Miami |
| 66 | Bouwens, Shawn | G | 6-4 | 290 | 3 | Nebraska-Wesleyan |
| 75 | Brown, Lomas | T | 6-4 | 287 | 8 | Florida |
| 87 | Campbell, Jeff | WR | 5-8 | 167 | 3 | Colorado |
| 50 | Caston, Toby | LB | 6-1 | 243 | 6 | Louisiana State |
| 55 | Cofer, Michael | LB | 6-5 | 244 | 10 | Tennessee |
| 21 | Colon, Harry | S | 5-11 | 203 | 2 | Missouri |
| 76 | Conover, Scott | T | 6-4 | 285 | 2 | Purdue |
| 39 | Crockett, Ray | CB | 5-9 | 181 | 4 | Baylor |
| 67 | Dallafior, Ken | G-C | 6-4 | 285 | 8 | Minnesota |
| 42 | Dozier, D.J. | RB | 6-0 | 205 | 6 | Penn State |
| 81 | Farr, Mike | WR | 5-10 | 192 | 3 | UCLA |
| 98 | Gibson, Dennis | LB | 6-2. | 243 | 6 | Iowa State |
| 53 | Glover, Kevin | C-G | 6-2 | 282 | 8 | Maryland |
| 23 | Gray, Mel | WR-KR | 5-9 | 162 | 7 | Purdue |
| 86 | Green, Willie | WR | 6-2 | 179 | 2 | Mississippi |
| 99 | Hayworth, Tracy | LB-DE | 6-3 | 260 | 3 | Tennessee |
| 97 | Hunter, Jeff | DE | 6-5 | 285 | 3 | Albany State |
| 58 | Jamison, George | LB | 6-1 | 228 | 6 | Cincinnati |
| 24 | Jenkins, Melvin | CB | 5-10 | 173 | 6 | Cincinnati |
| 48 | Johnson, Jimmie | TE | 6-2 | 248 | 4 | Howard |
| 57 | Jones, Victor | LB | 6-2 | 250 | 5 | Virginia Tech |
| 12 | Kramer, Erik | QB | 6-1 | 195 | 3 | North Carolina State |
| 89 | Little, David | TE | 6-2 | 226 | 9 | Middle Tennessee State |
| 16 | Long, Chuck | QB | 6-4 | 217 | 6 | Iowa |
| 83 | Matthews, Aubrey | WR | 5-7 | 165 | 6 | Delta State |
| 79 | Milburn, Darryl | DE | 6-3 | 260 | 2 | Grambling |
| 84 | Moore, Herman | WR | 6-3 | 205 | 2 | Virginia |
| 3 | Murray, Eddie | K | 5-10 | 180 | 13 | Tulane |
| 90 | Owens, Dan | DE | 6-3 | 280 | 3 | Southern California |
| 77 | Paris, Bubba | T | 6-6 | 315 | 10 | Michigan |
| 9 | Peete, Rodney | QB | 6-0 | 193 | 4 | Southern California |
| 80 | Perriman, Brett | WR | 5-9 | 180 | 5 | Miami |
| 96 | Pete, Lawrence | NT | 6-0 | 295 | 4 | Nebraska |
| 94 | Pritchett, Kelvin | DE | 6-2 | 281 | 2 | Mississippi |
| 20 | Sanders, Barry | RB | 5-8 | 203 | 4 | Oklahoma State |
| 64 | Sanders, Eric | T-G | 6-7 | 286 | 12 | Nevada-Reno |
| 38 | Scott, Kevin | CB | 5-9 | 175 | 2 | Stanford |
| 54 | Spielman, Chris | LB | 6-0 | 247 | 5 | Ohio State |
| 92 | Spindler, Marc | DE | 6-5 | 290 | 3 | Pittsburgh |
| 46 | Tennell, Derek | TE | 6-5 | 270 | 6 | UCLA |
| 11 | Ware, Andre | QB | 6-2 | 205 | 3 | Houston |
| 27 | Welch, Herb | S | 5-11 | 180 | 7 | UCLA |
| 25 | White, Sheldon | CB | 5-11 | 188 | 5 | Miami, Ohio |
| 35 | White, William | S | 5-10 | 191 | 5 | Ohio State |

---

**1992 SCHEDULE OF GAMES**

**September**

| | | |
|---|---|---|
| 6 | at Chicago | 12:00 |
| 13 | MINNESOTA | 1:00 |
| 20 | at Washington | 4:00 |
| 27 | TAMPA BAY | 1:00 |

**October**

| | | |
|---|---|---|
| 4 | NEW ORLEANS | 1:00 |
| 11 | Open Date | |
| 15 | at Minnesota (Thurs.) | 6:30 |
| 25 | at Tampa Bay | 1:00 |

**November**

| | | |
|---|---|---|
| 1 | GREEN BAY | 1:00 |
| 8 | DALLAS | 1:00 |
| 15 | at Pittsburgh | 1:00 |
| 22 | at Cincinnati | 1:00 |
| 26 | HOUSTON (Thanksgiving) | 12:30 |

**December**

| | | |
|---|---|---|
| 6 | vs Green Bay at Milwaukee | 12:00 |
| 13 | CLEVELAND | 1:00 |
| 20 | CHICAGO | 4:00 |
| 28 | at San Francisco (Mon.) | 6:00 |

**1992 Draft**

| Round | Name | Pos. | Ht. | Wt. | College |
|---|---|---|---|---|---|
| 1. | Porcher, Robert | DE | 6-3 | 283 | South Carolina State |
| 2. | Scroggins, Tracy | LB | 6-2 | 255 | Tulsa |
| 2. | Hanson, Jason | K-P | 5-11 | 183 | Washington State |
| 3. | McLemore, Thomas | TE | 6-5 | 248 | Southern |
| 6. | Tharpe, Larry | T | 6-4 | 299 | Tennessee State |
| 8. | Clay, Willie | CB | 5-9 | 184 | Georgia Tech |
| 11. | Tillison, Ed | RB | 5-10 | 224 | Northwest Missouri St. |

# GREEN BAY PACKERS

**Address** 1265 Lombardi Avenue, P.O. Box 10628,
Green Bay, Wisconsin 54307-0628.

**Stadia** Lambeau Field, Green Bay, and Milwaukee
County Stadium, Milwaukee.
*Capacity* (Lambeau Field) 59,543, (Milwaukee County
Stadium) 56,051. *Playing Surfaces* Grass, both stadia.

**Team Colours** Dark Green, Gold, and White.

**Head Coach** Mike Holmgren – 1st year.

**Championships** Division 1972; NFL 1929,'30,'31,
'36,'39,'44,'61,'62,'65,'66,'67;
Super Bowl 1966,'67.

**History** NFL 1921-69, NFC 1970-

New head coach Mike Holmgren brings all the style and panache gathered over six seasons with San Francisco and even managed to attract two 49ers assistants, Ray Rhodes and Sherman Lewis, as he makes a start in regenerating the Green Bay machine.

Crucial to his efforts is the health of quarterback Don Majkowski, whose star was on the rise in 1989 before a contractual dispute and injuries brought him back to earth. All the necessary surgery to his passing shoulder has been successful but the form didn't return and the feeling is that common sense rest and recuperation may be what's needed. Reserve Mike Tomczak is a decent sort who can go out and win games but he does not seem to have staying power. Also involved in the planning is Brett Favre, for whom Green Bay sent a first-round draft option to Atlanta in a trade. Favre has not yet completed a pass in the NFL but he was considered by many scouts to have at least as much potential as any of the 1992 draftees.

It was uncertainty at the quarterback position which saw wide receiver Sterling Sharpe have the poorest campaign of his four-year career. His return to the top is crucial to the Packers' hopes for he is their one offensive player of all-league quality. His starting partner will be Perry Kemp but Holmgren has trawled the wide oceans for available prospects, which include Sanjay Beach, whom he coached at San Francisco, Kitrick Taylor and draftee Robert Brooks. Last year, a decent yield came from the running back position, with Vince Workman drifting out of the backfield for 46 catches.

In his primary rôle, Workman also was a fair third running

back and did crack the end zone a club-leading seven times but, like the rest, he showed little open-field sparkle in a team effort which averaged only 3.6 yards per carry. The power should come from Darrell Thompson with Keith Woodside offering the penetration, but it hasn't worked out like that so far. It may be a pointer that draftees Edgar Bennett and Dexter McNabb are solid fullbacks with a knack for catching passes.

The offensive line is coming together, though taking more time to gel than expected following the excitement of the 1989 draft which brought right tackle Tony Mandarich. Described by some scouts as the most dominating player available, in any position, Mandarich has progressed slowly but he does now start, with Ken Ruettgers resuming at left tackle after an injury, Rich Moran and Ron Hallstrom in the guard positions and James Campen at center. Without question, new arrivals Tootie Robbins and Dave Viaene upgrade a unit which can always rely on the league's best blocking tight end, Ed West, who continues to obliterate linebackers with great consistency.

Hidden away among the moderate statistics is one which shows Green Bay conceding fewer rushing yards per game than at any time since 1940. And only Philadelphia allowed less than Green Bay's average of 3.38 yards per rush. That's the kind of platform on which a coach can build and, for this, another couple of top pass rushers might do the trick. Last year, right outside linebacker Tony Bennett led the team with 13 sacks while Bryce Paup reeled off 7.5 in four games before the opposition realized that here was a player to watch. The three-man line found a solid core in 1991 draftee nose tackle Esera Tuaolo, with Matt Brock and

| 1992 SCHEDULE OF GAMES | September | |
|---|---|---|
| | 6 MINNESOTA | 12:00 |
| | 13 at Tampa Bay | 1:00 |
| | 20 CINCINNATI | 12:00 |
| | 27 PITTSBURGH | 3:00 |
| | October | |
| | 4 at Atlanta | 1:00 |
| | 11 Open Date | |
| | 18 at Cleveland | 1:00 |
| | 25 CHICAGO | 12:00 |
| | November | |
| | 1 at Detroit | 1:00 |
| | 8 at New York Giants | 1:00 |
| | 15 PHILADELPHIA at Milwaukee | 12:00 |
| | 22 at Chicago | 12:00 |
| | 29 TAMPA BAY at Milwaukee | 12:00 |
| | December | |
| | 6 DETROIT at Milwaukee | 12:00 |
| | 13 at Houston | 7:00 |
| | 20 LOS ANGELES RAMS | 12:00 |
| | 27 at Minnesota | 12:00 |

Can Don Majkowski recapture his form of 1989?

Robert Brown at defensive end. Another defensive end, Shawn Patterson, was missed after being injured in late November and his return will be welcomed.

Cementing the defense against the run at inside linebacker, the pairing of Brian Noble and Johnny Holland is coming off an exceptionally good year while left outside linebacker Scott Stephen did not look out of place. However, Stephen is expected to come under pressure from second-round draftee Mark D'Onofrio. The secondary was given priority in the draft in the shape of first-rounder Terrell Buckley. The plan is that Buckley will start at right cornerback with Vinnie Clark on the other side, meaning that former starting cornerback LeRoy Butler can challenge free safety Chuck Cecil. Even so, Cecil did form a good run-stuffing partnership with strong safety Mark Murphy and will not easily give up his seniority.

Third-year placekicker Chris Jacke is not much better than par but he does have a powerful leg and always might land the big one. Paul McJulien never makes any headlines but he goes about his job of punter with care and precision.

### 1992 Draft

| Round | Name | Pos. | Ht. | Wt. | College |
|---|---|---|---|---|---|
| 1. | Buckley, Terrell | CB | 5-9 | 174 | Florida State |
| 2. | D'Onofrio, Mark | LB | 6-2 | 236 | Penn State |
| 3. | Brooks, Robert | WR | 6-0 | 175 | South Carolina |
| 4. | Bennett, Edgar | RB | 5-11 | 208 | Florida State |
| 5. | McNabb, Dexter | RB | 6-1 | 238 | Florida |
| 5. | McKay, Orlando | WR | 5-10 | 175 | Washington |
| 6. | Chmura, Mark | TE | 6-5 | 235 | Boston College |
| 7. | Holder, Christopher | WR-KR | 5-11 | 185 | Tuskegee |
| 9. | Detmer, Ty | QB | 5-11 | 179 | Brigham Young |
| 9. | Bradley, Shazzon | NT | 6-1 | 274 | Tennessee |
| 10. | Oberg, Andrew | T | 6-6 | 300 | North Carolina |
| 11. | Mokwuah, Gabe | LB | 6-1 | 248 | American International |
| 12. | Collins, Brett | LB | 6-2 | 236 | Washington |

### VETERAN ROSTER

| No. | Name | Pos. | Ht. | Wt. | NFL Year | College |
|---|---|---|---|---|---|---|
| 74 | Archambeau, Lester | DE | 6-4 | 271 | 3 | Stanford |
| 67 | Ard, Billy | G | 6-3 | 273 | 12 | Wake Forest |
| 32 | Avery, Steve | RB | 6-1 | 225 | 1 | Northern Michigan |
| | Beach, Sanjay | WR | 6-1 | 190 | 2 | Colorado State |
| 90 | Bennett, Tony | LB | 6-2 | 233 | 3 | Mississippi |
| | Billups, Lewis | CB | 5-11 | 182 | 7 | North Alabama |
| | Brady, Jeff | LB | 6-1 | 224 | 2 | Kentucky |
| 62 | Brock, Matt | DE | 6-5 | 285 | 3 | Oregon |
| 93 | Brown, Robert | DE | 6-3 | 270 | 11 | Virginia Tech |
| 36 | Butler, LeRoy | CB | 6-0 | 192 | 3 | Florida State |
| 63 | Campen, James | C | 6-3 | 275 | 6 | Tulane |
| 26 | Cecil, Chuck | S | 6-0 | 188 | 5 | Arizona |
| 78 | Cheek, Louis | T | 6-6 | 295 | 5 | Texas A&M |
| 25 | Clark, Vinnie | CB | 6-0 | 194 | 2 | Ohio State |
| | Conover, Frank | DT | 6-5 | 317 | 2 | Syracuse |
| 99 | Davey, Don | DE | 6-3 | 273 | 2 | Wisconsin |
| 42 | Dean, Walter | RB | 5-9 | 211 | 2 | Grambling |
| 56 | Dent, Burnell | LB | 6-1 | 234 | 7 | Tulane |
| | Favre, Brett | QB | 6-2 | 220 | 2 | Southern Mississippi |
| 21 | Fuller, Joe | CB | 5-11 | 181 | 3 | Northern Iowa |
| 58 | Garten, Joe | C-G | 6-2 | 286 | 1 | Colorado |
| 65 | Hallstrom, Ron | G | 6-6 | 297 | 11 | Iowa |
| 80 | Harris, Jackie | TE | 6-3 | 243 | 3 | Northeast Louisiana |
| 24 | Hauck, Tim | S | 5-11 | 181 | 3 | Montana |
| 50 | Holland, Johnny | LB | 6-2 | 232 | 6 | Texas A&M |
| 44 | Holmes, Jerry | CB | 6-2 | 176 | 11 | West Virginia |
| 13 | Jacke, Chris | K | 6-0 | 197 | 4 | Texas-El Paso |
| 92 | Jurkovic, John | NT | 6-2 | 297 | 2 | Eastern Illinois |
| 81 | Kemp, Perry | WR | 5-11 | 165 | 6 | California, Pa. |
| 59 | Larson, Kurt | LB | 6-4 | 241 | 4 | Michigan State |
| 7 | Majkowski, Don | QB | 6-2 | 206 | 6 | Virginia |
| 77 | Mandarich, Tony | T | 6-5 | 298 | 4 | Michigan State |
| | McDonald, Mike | LB | 6-1 | 240 | 8 | Southern California |
| 16 | McJulien, Paul | P | 5-10 | 190 | 2 | Jackson State |
| 47 | Mitchell, Roland | CB | 5-11 | 180 | 6 | Texas Tech |
| 57 | Moran, Rich | G | 6-2 | 280 | 8 | San Diego State |
| 37 | Murphy, Mark | S | 6-2 | 209 | 11 | West Liberty |
| 91 | Noble, Brian | LB | 6-4 | 250 | 8 | Arizona State |
| 96 | Patterson, Shawn | DE | 6-4 | 273 | 5 | Arizona State |
| 95 | Paup, Bryce | LB | 6-5 | 247 | 3 | Northern Iowa |
| 64 | Porter, Rapier | TE | 6-3 | 275 | 1 | Arkansas-Pine Bluff |
| 31 | Rice, Allen | RB | 5-10 | 206 | 9 | Baylor |
| | Robbins, Tootie | T | 6-5 | 310 | 11 | East Carolina |
| 75 | Ruettgers, Ken | T | 6-5 | 286 | 8 | Southern California |
| 84 | Sharpe, Sterling | WR | 6-0 | 205 | 5 | South Carolina |
| 68 | Singletary, Reggie | T | 6-3 | 285 | 6 | North Carolina State |
| 54 | Stephen, Scott | LB | 6-2 | 243 | 6 | Arizona State |
| | Taylor, Kitrick | WR-KR | 5-11 | 191 | 5 | Washington State |
| 39 | Thompson, Darrell | RB | 6-0 | 215 | 3 | Minnesota |
| 18 | Tomczak, Mike | QB | 6-1 | 204 | 8 | Ohio State |
| | Townsend, Andre | DE | 6-3 | 265 | 8 | Mississippi |
| 98 | Tuaolo, Esera | NT | 6-2 | 284 | 2 | Oregon State |
| 70 | Uecker, Keith | G-T | 6-5 | 299 | 9 | Auburn |
| | Viaene, Dave | C-T | 6-5 | 300 | 3 | Minnesota-Duluth |
| | Washington, Charles | S | 6-1 | 210 | 4 | Cameron |
| 87 | Weathers, Clarence | WR | 5-9 | 169 | 10 | Delaware State |
| 30 | Webb, Chuck | RB | 5-9 | 201 | 2 | Tennessee |
| 86 | West, Ed | TE | 6-1 | 244 | 9 | Auburn |
| | White, Adrian | S | 6-0 | 200 | 5 | Florida |
| 88 | Wilson, Charles | WR-KR | 5-9 | 178 | 3 | Memphis State |
| | Wilson, Marcus | RB | 6-1 | 205 | 1 | Virginia |
| | Winters, Frank | C | 6-3 | 285 | 6 | Western Illinois |
| 33 | Woodside, Keith | RB | 6-0 | 217 | 5 | Texas A&M |
| 46 | Workman, Vince | RB-KR | 5-10 | 201 | 4 | Ohio State |

# MINNESOTA VIKINGS

**Address** 9520 Viking Drive, Eden Prairie,
Minnesota 55344.
**Stadium** Hubert H. Humphrey Metrodome, Minneapolis.
*Capacity* 63,000 *Playing Surface* AstroTurf.
**Team Colours** Purple, Gold, and White.
**Head Coach** Dennis Green – 1st year.
**Championships** Division 1970,'71,'73,'74,'75,'76,
'77,'78,'80,'89; Conference 1973,'74,'76;
NFL 1969.
**History** NFL 1961-69, NFC 1970-

It has been one of the NFL's mysteries why the Minnesota Vikings have not been as competitive as might be expected of such a collection of quality players. Even small changes under new head coach Dennis Green might do the trick.

Green faces the task of using the multi-talented Herschel Walker, who, some scouts feel, was accepted with reluctance by then head coach Jerry Burns. Despite the enormity of that 1989 trade with Dallas, the Vikings did not adjust to the I-formation, which has seen Walker at his most effective, and, in most senses since joining the Vikings, the former Heisman Trophy winner and NFL leading rusher has been just another solid player. He might even be traded. If he remains with the club, he'll be in partnership with the fast-improving Terry Allen at running back. Alfred Anderson is still worth his spot as a backup, Darrin Nelson has returned following a brief retirement and Roger Craig has been acquired under Plan B.

There is plenty of ability at wide receiver, where Cris Carter has shown the Eagles to be rash when they waived him in 1990. The other starter, Anthony Carter, may have lost a step or two but compensates with inherent class. Leo Lewis and Hassan Jones are speedy backups who fit into the system with ease, while Pro Bowl tight end Steve Jordan, as usual, would be expected to make a·major contribution to the passing game. Jordan is not noted for his blocking and when the offense needs two tight ends, either Brent Novoselsky or Mike Jones comes in. Former Seattle starter Mike Tice was signed under Plan B, meaning that there will be a competition in camp.

One strength over the years has been the offensive line, which will continue intact with Gary Zimmerman and Tim Irwin at tackle, Randall McDaniel and Todd Kalis in the guard positions and Kirk Lowdermilk at center. McDaniel is now a fixture in the Pro Bowl while Zimmerman, too, has been selected three times although failing to catch the eye for the past two years. The unit provides a solid platform for the running game and should continue to give quarterback Rich Gannon good protection as he attempts to confirm his starting status ahead of the more experienced Wade Wilson. Gannon's early opportunities came because of injuries to Wilson, and while he does not look the sort to take a game by the scruff of the neck, he has improved steadily. However, it is more because of his potential than a superiority over Wilson that Gannon will retain preference.

The one weak area on defense is at linebacker where Ray Berry did not look completely comfortable playing in the middle, even though logging 146 tackles in 1991, and Jimmy Williams appeared to be past his best. Mark Dusbabek missed the entire season with an injury. There will be

*Wide receiver Anthony Carter is a seven-year starter for the Vikings.*

## 1992 SCHEDULE OF GAMES

**September**

| | | |
|---|---|---|
| 6 | at Green Bay | 12:00 |
| 13 | at Detroit | 1:00 |
| 20 | TAMPA BAY | 12:00 |
| 27 | at Cincinnati | 1:00 |

**October**

| | | |
|---|---|---|
| 4 | CHICAGO | 12:00 |
| 11 | Open Date | |
| 15 | DETROIT (Thurs.) | 6:30 |
| 25 | WASHINGTON | 12:00 |

**November**

| | | |
|---|---|---|
| 2 | at Chicago (Mon.) | 8:00 |
| 8 | at Tampa Bay | 1:00 |
| 15 | HOUSTON | 12:00 |
| 22 | CLEVELAND | 12:00 |
| 29 | at Los Angeles Rams | 1:00 |

**December**

| | | |
|---|---|---|
| 6 | at Philadelphia | 1:00 |
| 13 | SAN FRANCISCO | 12:00 |
| 20 | at Pittsburgh | 1:00 |
| 27 | GREEN BAY | 12:00 |

### 1992 Draft

| Round | Name | Pos. | Ht. | Wt. | College |
|---|---|---|---|---|---|
| 2. | Harris, Robert | DT | 6-3 | 285 | Southern |
| 4. | Barker, Roy | DT | 6-4 | 292 | North Carolina |
| 5. | McDaniel, Ed | LB | 5-11 | 232 | Clemson |
| 6. | Gaddis, Mike | RB | 6-0 | 217 | Oklahoma |
| 7. | Wilson, David | S | 5-11 | 198 | California |
| 8. | Fisher, Luke | TE | 6-1 | 235 | East Carolina |
| 9. | Johnson, Brad | QB | 6-4 | 218 | Florida State |
| 9. | West, Ronnie | WR-KR | 6-1 | 215 | Pittsburg, Kansas |
| 10. | Culpepper, Brad | DT | 6-1 | 258 | Florida |
| 11. | Evans, Charles | RB | 5-10 | 203 | Clark, Georgia |
| 12. | Randolph, Joe | WR | 5-9 | 158 | Elon |

### VETERAN ROSTER

| No. | Name | Pos. | Ht. | Wt. | NFL Year | College |
|---|---|---|---|---|---|---|
| 72 | Adams, Scott | T | 6-5 | 275 | 1 | Georgia |
| 21 | Allen, Terry | RB | 5-10 | 189 | 2 | Clemson |
| 46 | Anderson, Alfred | RB | 6-1 | 219 | 9 | Baylor |
| 50 | Berry, Ray | LB | 6-2 | 227 | 6 | Baylor |
| 47 | Browner, Joey | S | 6-2 | 231 | 10 | Southern California |
| 53 | Caesar, Ivan | LB | 6-1 | 241 | 2 | Boston College |
| 81 | Carter, Anthony | WR | 5-11 | 176 | 8 | Michigan |
| 80 | Carter, Cris | WR | 6-3 | 198 | 6 | Ohio State |
| 71 | Clarke, Ken | DT | 6-2 | 279 | 15 | Syracuse |
| 33 | Craig, Roger | RB | 6-0 | 215 | 10 | Nebraska |
| 55 | Del Rio, Jack | LB | 6-4 | 240 | 8 | Southern California |
| 56 | Doleman, Chris | DE | 6-5 | 266 | 8 | Pittsburgh |
| 59 | Dusbabek, Mark | LB | 6-3 | 230 | 3 | Minnesota |
| 31 | Fenney, Rick | RB | 6-1 | 233 | 6 | Washington |
| 78 | Freeman, Lorenzo | NT | 6-5 | 319 | 6 | Pittsburgh |
| 16 | Gannon, Rich | QB | 6-3 | 203 | 6 | Delaware |
| 25 | Glenn, Vencie | S | 6-0 | 192 | 7 | Indiana State |
| 74 | Habib, Brian | T | 6-7 | 292 | 4 | Washington |
| 76 | Irwin, Tim | T | 6-7 | 301 | 12 | Tennessee |
| 51 | Jenkins, Carlos | LB | 6-3 | 222 | 2 | Michigan State |
| 84 | Jones, Hassan | WR | 6-0 | 196 | 7 | Florida State |
| 82 | Jones, Mike | TE | 6-3 | 256 | 3 | Texas A&M |
| 83 | Jordan, Steve | TE | 6-4 | 238 | 11 | Brown |
| 69 | Kalis, Todd | G | 6-5 | 285 | 5 | Arizona State |
| 39 | Lee, Carl | CB | 5-11 | 182 | 10 | Marshall |
| 87 | Lewis, Leo | WR | 5-8 | 163 | 12 | Missouri |
| 63 | Lowdermilk, Kirk | C | 6-3 | 270 | 8 | Ohio State |
| 91 | Manusky, Greg | LB | 6-1 | 236 | 5 | Colgate |
| 23 | Mayes, Michael | CB | 5-10 | 179 | 3 | Louisiana State |
| 96 | McClendon, Skip | DE | 6-7 | 287 | 6 | Arizona State |
| 64 | McDaniel, Randall | G | 6-3 | 271 | 5 | Arizona State |
| 26 | McMillian, Audray | CB | 6-0 | 190 | 7 | Houston |
| 57 | Merriweather, Mike | LB | 6-2 | 226 | 10 | Pacific |
| 68 | Morris, Mike | C | 6-5 | 268 | 5 | Northeast Missouri St. |
| 20 | Nelson, Darrin | RB | 5-9 | 180 | 11 | Stanford |
| 18 | Newsome, Harry | P | 6-0 | 189 | 8 | Wake Forest |
| 99 | Noga, Al | DE | 6-1 | 264 | 5 | Hawaii |
| 85 | Novoselsky, Brent | TE | 6-2 | 236 | 5 | Pennsylvania |
| 89 | Obee, Terry | WR | 5-10 | 182 | 1 | Oregon |
| 27 | Parker, Anthony | CB | 5-10 | 178 | 2 | Arizona State |
| 93 | Randle, John | DE | 6-1 | 264 | 3 | Texas A&I |
| 86 | Reed, Jake | WR | 6-3 | 216 | 1 | Grambling |
| 7 | Reveiz, Fuad | K | 5-11 | 225 | 8 | Tennessee |
| 48 | Rutland, Reggie | CB | 6-1 | 191 | 6 | Georgia Tech |
| 12 | Salisbury, Sean | QB | 6-5 | 213 | 4 | Southern California |
| 60 | Schreiber, Adam | C-G | 6-4 | 280 | 9 | Texas |
| 38 | Scott, Todd | CB | 5-10 | 190 | 2 | Southwestern Louisiana |
| 94 | Strauthers, Thomas | DE | 6-4 | 263 | 9 | Jackson State |
| 67 | Teeter, Mike | DT | 6-2 | 269 | 2 | Michigan |
| 97 | Thomas, Henry | DT | 6-2 | 269 | 6 | Louisiana State |
| 87 | Tice, Mike | TE | 6-7 | 249 | 12 | Maryland |
| 34 | Walker, Herschel | RB | 6-1 | 220 | 7 | Georgia |
| 32 | Welborne, Tripp | S | 6-0 | 205 | R | Michigan |
| 41 | Wilcots, Solomon | S | 5-11 | 200 | 6 | Colorado |
| 11 | Wilson, Wade | QB | 6-3 | 205 | 12 | East Texas State |
| 22 | Wright, Felix | S | 6-2 | 197 | 8 | Drake |
| 65 | Zimmerman, Gary | T | 6-6 | 286 | 7 | Oregon |

changes, with Williams having been traded and Jack Del Rio arriving under Plan B. One possibility is that Del Rio will start at middle linebacker, with Mike Merriweather on the right and either Berry or Dusbabek on the left. Merriweather is the one player of authority and led the team with 172 total tackles.

The defensive line, too, has its soft spot in Ken Clarke at left tackle but right tackle Henry Thomas is a bruiser and right end Chris Doleman has been to four Pro Bowls. In only his second year after arriving as a free agent, left end John Randle was a sensation, leading the team with 9.5 sacks ahead of Thomas's eight and Doleman's seven. There's plenty of depth in Al Noga, Thomas Strauthers and second-round draftee Robert Harris.

The secondary slipped a little over the 1991 season but the starters have enough natural ability to rebound. Strong safety Joey Browner, who led the team with five interceptions, missed the trip to the Pro Bowl for the first time in seven years, and left cornerback Carl Lee saw his sequence of selections halted at three. Right cornerback Reggie Rutland made the kind of errors which can be corrected, while free safety Felix Wright, who no longer has big-time speed, nonetheless should continue to prove wrong all those experts who have been writing him off for years. Audray McMillian adds sparkle coming in as the nickel back.

Placekicker Fuad Reveiz is deadly accurate on field goals from inside 40 yards and he made up for longer-range failures with two 50-yard successes. Harry Newsome has proved to be a wise signing as a 1990 Plan-B free agent. With the benefit of punting inside a domed stadium, Newsome's gross average was back up to his 1988 best with an NFC-leading 45.5 yards.

# TAMPA BAY BUCCANEERS

**Address** One Buccaneer Place, Tampa, Florida 33607.
**Stadium** Tampa Stadium, Tampa.
   *Capacity* 74,315 *Playing Surface* Grass.
**Team Colours** Florida Orange, White, and Red.
**Head Coach** Sam Wyche – 1st year; 9th NFL.
**Championships** Division 1979,'81.
**History** AFC 1976, NFC 1977-

It is difficult to avoid the conclusion that Sam Wyche has much to do in his first year as the Buccaneers' head coach.

His primary task is at the nerve centre of the offense, where quarterback Vinny Testaverde, the 1986 Heisman Trophy winner, simply has not yet emerged. Each year he has improved in one or more categories only to slip back in others. Rarely has he looked like taking the opposition apart. Yet even now he has too much raw talent to be discarded and perhaps Wyche, who started at quarterback for the Bengals in their formative period, may have the answer. By way of insurance, Steve DeBerg was signed as a Plan-B free agent. This much-travelled veteran has had the honour of standing in when young players such as John Elway and Joe Montana found the game a little too complex. And back in 1987 when a rookie named Vinny Testaverde found it all too much, it was DeBerg who came in and started eight games. At 37 years old, DeBerg still has a strong arm and the eye of a hawk. Add to these the feeling of annoyance at being shipped around the league and you have all the ingredients of a starter.

Another area in need of improvement is the offensive line, where only left tackle Paul Gruber is of league-wide class. Last year's first-round pick, Charles McRae, could not displace incumbent right tackle Rob Taylor, though perhaps there is satisfaction in the fact that Taylor was stimulated to his best season by the young challenger. The interior trio of guards Tom McHale and Ian Beckles, and center Tony Mayberry needs to develop greater authority and McHale may give way to Bruce Reimers, who was with Wyche at Cincinnati and was signed under Plan B. The return of senior center Randy Grimes from a season-long injury is a plus.

At running back, Gary Anderson has not brought his unquestioned speed to bear and is now a backup to Reggie Cobb, who is a tough competitor but breaks free only occasionally. Fullback Robert Wilson is a fine blocker but, thus far, has not been featured as the ground gainer. The offensive backfield possibly would benefit were opponents forced to respect the passing game and adjust accordingly. As a challenge to the current starting wide receivers, Ricky Nattiel has been acquired in a trade with Denver. He is the elusive sort and could bring a medium-range option to balance the potential deep threat offered by Mark Carrier and Lawrence Dawsey. Second-rounder Courtney Hawkins, who was the Buccaneers' first pick in the draft, will be given every chance to make an early impact. There is class at tight end, where Ron Hall has been on the fringe of all-star selection for the last two years but has suffered from a lack of productivity in others.

On defense there are fewer weaknesses but the line needs the return of a healthy Reuben Davis to start at defensive tackle in the 4-3 formation. Tim Newton should continue alongside Davis with Ray Seals and the fast-developing Keith McCants in the defensive end positions. However, the reserve strength is lean with just Al Chamblee, Rhett Hall and draftee Mark Wheeler available.

The secondary is no more than starter-deep, though cornerbacks Ricky Reynolds and Carl Carter are well respected. Rookie safeties of 1991 Tony Covington and Marty Carter are solid enough but too often are drawn into defense against the run, which is a Tampa Bay weakness, leaving the backfield open for exploitation. Of the three backups, all of which were signed as free agents in previous years, William Frizzell and Darrell Fullington see action in the Buccaneers' nickel package but Roger Jones has been used only sparingly.

One group which will not need much attention is the linebacking trio of Broderick Thomas, Jesse Solomon and Kevin Murphy. Thomas led the team in tackles (174), sacks (11), tackles for loss (10) and forced fumbles (7). In other years, he could have been a Pro Bowler. Solomon came second in tackles while Murphy has fought off more than a few challenges to his starting spot.

Placekicking and punting could have been a difficulty, as both Steve Christie and Mark Royals departed as unprotected free agents. However, by the same process, Ken Willis and Dan Stryzinski have arrived. Willis has had two good seasons as the Cowboys' placekicker and may have the edge on Christie. Similarly, Stryzinski comes after two years with Pittsburgh and, last season, was a touch better than Royals in gross punting average, though this figure depends much upon field position and team philosophy.

*RIGHT: Keith McCants
continues to develop as a
4-3 defensive end.*

## 1992 SCHEDULE OF GAMES

### September
| | | |
|---|---|---|
| 6 | PHOENIX | 4:00 |
| 13 | GREEN BAY | 1:00 |
| 20 | at Minnesota | 12:00 |
| 27 | at Detroit | 1:00 |

### October
| | | |
|---|---|---|
| 4 | INDIANAPOLIS | 1:00 |
| 11 | Open Date | |
| 18 | at Chicago | 12:00 |
| 25 | DETROIT | 1:00 |

### November
| | | |
|---|---|---|
| 1 | at New Orleans | 12:00 |
| 8 | MINNESOTA | 1:00 |
| 15 | CHICAGO | 4:00 |
| 22 | at San Diego | 1:00 |
| 29 | vs Green Bay at Milwaukee | 12:00 |

### December
| | | |
|---|---|---|
| 6 | LOS ANGELES RAMS | 8:00 |
| 13 | ATLANTA | 1:00 |
| 19 | at San Francisco (Sat.) | 1:00 |
| 27 | at Phoenix | 2:00 |

## 1992 Draft

| Round | Name | Pos. | Ht. | Wt. | College |
|---|---|---|---|---|---|
| 2. | Hawkins, Courtney | WR-KR | 5-9 | 183 | Michigan State |
| 3. | Wheeler, Mark | NT | 6-2 | 280 | Texas A&M |
| 3. | Armstrong, Tyji | TE | 6-4 | 257 | Mississippi |
| 4. | Erickson, Craig | QB | 6-1 | 197 | Miami |
| 5. | Green, Rogerick | CB | 5-10 | 173 | Kansas State |
| 5. | Dotson, Santana | DE | 6-4 | 267 | Baylor |
| 6. | Malone, James | LB | 6-2 | 235 | UCLA |
| 7. | Swilling, Ken | LB | 6-2 | 243 | Georgia Tech |
| 8. | McDowell, Anthony | RB | 5-11 | 238 | Texas Tech |
| 8. | Pawlawski, Mike | QB | 6-1 | 204 | California |
| 10. | Alexander, Elijah | LB | 6-1 | 228 | Kansas State |
| 11. | Royster, Mazio | RB | 6-0 | 202 | Southern California |
| 12. | Wilmsmeyer, Klaus | P | 6-1 | 213 | Louisville |

## VETERAN ROSTER

| No. | Name | Pos. | Ht. | Wt. | NFL Year | College |
|---|---|---|---|---|---|---|
| 40 | Anderson, Gary | RB-KR | 6-1 | 190 | 7 | Arkansas |
| 89 | Anderson, Jesse | TE | 6-2 | 245 | 3 | Mississippi State |
| 85 | Anthony, Terry | WR | 6-0 | 200 | 2 | Florida State |
| 62 | Beckles, Ian | G | 6-1 | 295 | 3 | Indiana |
| 53 | Brady, Ed | LB | 6-2 | 236 | 9 | Illinois |
| 47 | Burnette, Reggie | LB | 6-1 | 235 | 2 | Houston |
| 88 | Carrier, Mark | WR | 6-0 | 185 | 6 | Nicholls State |
| 44 | Carter, Carl | CB | 5-11 | 180 | 7 | Texas Tech |
| 23 | Carter, Marty | S | 6-1 | 200 | 2 | Middle Tennessee State |
| 57 | Chamblee, Al | DE-LB | 6-1 | 240 | 2 | Virginia Tech |
| 34 | Cobb, Reggie | RB | 6-0 | 215 | 3 | Tennessee |
| 25 | Covington, Tony | S | 5-11 | 190 | 2 | Virginia |
| 79 | Davis, Reuben | DT | 6-4 | 295 | 5 | North Carolina |
| 80 | Dawsey, Lawrence | WR | 6-0 | 195 | 2 | Florida State |
| 17 | DeBerg, Steve | QB | 6-3 | 217 | 16 | San Jose State |
| 76 | Dill, Scott | G | 6-5 | 285 | 5 | Memphis State |
| 95 | Duckens, Mark | DT | 6-4 | 270 | 3 | Arizona State |
| 87 | Drewrey, Willie | WR-PR | 5-7 | 170 | 8 | West Virginia |
| 33 | Frizzell, William | S | 6-3 | 205 | 9 | North Carolina Central |
| 27 | Fullington, Darrell | S | 6-1 | 195 | 5 | Miami |
| 60 | Grimes, Randy | C | 6-4 | 275 | 9 | Baylor |
| 74 | Gruber, Paul | T | 6-5 | 290 | 5 | Wisconsin |
| 91 | Hall, Rhett | DL | 6-2 | 260 | 2 | California |
| 82 | Hall, Ron | TE | 6-4 | 245 | 6 | Hawaii |
| 36 | Hardy, Robert | RB | 5-10 | 210 | 2 | Carson-Newman |
| 32 | Highsmith, Alonzo | RB | 6-1 | 235 | 6 | Miami |
| 84 | Hill, Bruce | WR | 6-0 | 180 | 6 | Arizona State |
| 62 | Hunter, John | T | 6-8 | 300 | 4 | Brigham Young |
| 28 | Jennings, Stanford | RB-KR | 6-1 | 210 | 9 | Furman |
| 24 | Jones, Roger | CB | 5-9 | 175 | 2 | Tennessee State |
| 41 | King, Joe | CB | 6-2 | 202 | 2 | Oklahoma State |
| 22 | Lilly, Sammy | CB | 5-9 | 178 | 4 | Georgia Tech |
| 24 | Mack, Milton | CB | 5-11 | 182 | 6 | Alcorn State |
| 61 | Mayberry, Tony | C | 6-4 | 285 | 3 | Wake Forest |
| 52 | McCants, Keith | DE | 6-3 | 265 | 3 | Alabama |
| 73 | McHale, Tom | G | 6-4 | 280 | 6 | Cornell |
| 70 | McRae, Charles | T | 6-7 | 290 | 2 | Tennessee |
| 59 | Murphy, Kevin | LB | 6-2 | 235 | 7 | Oklahoma |
| 83 | Nattiel, Ricky | WR | 5-9 | 180 | 6 | Florida |
| 96 | Newton, Tim | DT | 6-0 | 275 | 8 | Florida |
| 66 | Reimers, Bruce | G | 6-7 | 298 | 9 | Iowa State |
| 29 | Reynolds, Ricky | CB | 5-11 | 190 | 6 | Washington State |
| 30 | Robinson, Mark | S | 5-11 | 200 | 8 | Penn State |
| 75 | Rogers, Reggie | DE | 6-6 | 280 | 3 | Washington |
| 64 | Ryan, Tim | G | 6-2 | 280 | 2 | Notre Dame |
| 98 | Seals, Ray | DE | 6-3 | 270 | 3 | None |
| 55 | Solomon, Jesse | LB | 6-0 | 235 | 7 | Florida State |
| 4 | Stryzinski, Dan | P | 6-1 | 189 | 3 | Indiana |
| 72 | Taylor, Rob | T | 6-6 | 290 | 7 | Northwestern |
| 14 | Testaverde, Vinny | QB | 6-5 | 215 | 6 | Miami |
| 51 | Thomas, Broderick | LB | 6-4 | 245 | 4 | Nebraska |
| 58 | Tiggle, Calvin | LB | 6-1 | 235 | 2 | Georgia Tech |
| 54 | Williams, Jimmy | LB | 6-3 | 221 | 11 | Nebraska |
| 1 | Willis, Ken | K | 5-11 | 185 | 3 | Kentucky |
| 20 | Wilson, Robert | RB | 6-0 | 240 | 2 | Texas A&M |

# ATLANTA FALCONS

**Address** Suwanee Road at I-85, Suwanee, Georgia 30174.
**Stadium** Georgia Dome, Atlanta.
*Capacity* 70,500 *Playing Surface* AstroTurf.
**Team Colours** Black, Red, Silver, and White.
**Head Coach** Jerry Glanville – 3rd year; 8th NFL.
**Championships** Division 1980.
**History** NFL 1966-69, NFC 1970-

Had anyone questioned the credibility of the 'new' Atlanta Falcons, the answer was supplied in 1991 with two wins over the 49ers. Head coach Jerry Glanville has the birds of prey soaring and 1992 will tell if they can handle the heady atmosphere of the NFL's upper echelons.

There is no doubting Glanville's powers of inspiration, to which might be added judgement, which saw the club trade away the number one pick overall in the 1990 draft in exchange for Pro Bowl offensive lineman Chris Hinton, future Pro Bowl wide receiver Andre Rison and the Colts' first-round option in 1991, as the major parts of the deal. At a stroke the Falcons were guaranteed the very best in two key areas of the offense but Rison and Hinton may have been even more valuable as seed-crystals. For around them, the rest has developed.

On the offensive line, with Hinton the anchor at right tackle alongside Pro Bowl right guard Bill Fralic, center Jamie Dukes has been given time and space to learn his trade, left guard Houston Hoover has made tremendous progress and 14th-year tackle Mike Kenn allowed just one sack in 531 pass plays. Nonetheless, it made sense to select the magnificent Bob Whitfield, who could secure one of the tackle spots for a decade.

Quarterback Chris Miller was seen as a player with prospects but he is another whose leadership and play have been raised to new heights. In the style of heroes, he rose from his sickbed to rally the team to victory against Green Bay, ending his fifth NFL campaign with a personal-best passer rating of 80.6. Certainly, Miller has an outstanding group of wide receivers in Rison, Michael Haynes, Mike Pritchard and George Thomas. The year 1991 was when Haynes brought the full effects of his moves and great speed to bear as he caught 50 passes at a sensational 22.4-yard average to go over 1,000 yards receiving for the first

time in his four-year career. Mike Pritchard, the rookie who came with the Colts' first-round option, eased into the action with an excellent 50 receptions and threatens to be a great one. Joining Thomas in the competition for the fourth-ranking member of the receiving corps are Plan-B signings Drew Hill and Tony Jones, who were with Glanville in Houston. In 1991, Hill ranked second in the AFC with 90 catches and went over 1,000 yards for the fifth time in his career. More than sheer productivity, Hill could give the Falcons' passing game added subtlety and may turn out to be the Plan-B steal of the season.

At running back, progress has been less dramatic, even disappointing with Steve Broussard being slowed by injuries. There is a solid group available but much rests on draftee Tony Smith, whose stock rose dramatically in the pre-draft scouting combines. If that form is genuine, then Glanville has a player of near 'franchise' quality.

Defensively, the Falcons are less secure but they do have top-class players, particularly in the secondary, where Deion (Prime Time) Sanders and Tim McKyer rate as one of the very best cornerback pairings in the game. When Sanders high-steps into the end zone on one of his returns, some see it as exhibitionism at its most vulgar while others accept it as an exuberant and joyful celebration of athletic achievement. He is a player of prodigious talent and McKyer is not that far behind. McKyer was good enough to start for San Francisco in two Super Bowls and tied with Sanders for the club lead with six interceptions last year. 1991 first-rounder Bruce Pickens is just waiting for his chance. At linebacker, Jessie (The Hammer) Tuggle is the force around which the rest gather. Last year he led the team with 207 tackles. A step in front of Tuggle, rookie nose tackle Moe Gardner filled a need better than most people expected as he started

| 1992 SCHEDULE OF GAMES | | |
|---|---|---|
| **September** | | |
| 6 | NEW YORK JETS | 1:00 |
| 13 | at Washington | 1:00 |
| 20 | NEW ORLEANS | 1:00 |
| 27 | at Chicago | 12:00 |
| **October** | | |
| 4 | GREEN BAY | 1:00 |
| 11 | at Miami | 1:00 |
| 18 | at San Francisco | 1:00 |
| 25 | Open Date | |
| **November** | | |
| 1 | LOS ANGELES RAMS | 1:00 |
| 9 | SAN FRANCISCO (Mon.) | 9:00 |
| 15 | PHOENIX | 1:00 |
| 22 | at Buffalo | 1:00 |
| 29 | NEW ENGLAND | 1:00 |
| **December** | | |
| 3 | at New Orleans (Thurs.) | 7:00 |
| 13 | at Tampa Bay | 1:00 |
| 21 | DALLAS (Mon.) | 9:00 |
| 27 | at Los Angeles Rams | 1:00 |

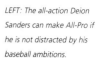

## 1992 Draft

| Round | Name | Pos. | Ht. | Wt. | College |
|---|---|---|---|---|---|
| 1. | Whitfield, Bob | T | 6-5 | 295 | Stanford |
| 1. | Smith, Tony | RB | 6-0 | 214 | Southern Mississippi |
| 2. | Smith, Chuck | LB | 6-2 | 242 | Tennessee |
| 3. | Dinkins, Howard | LB | 6-1 | 221 | Florida State |
| 4. | Smith, Frankie | CB | 5-10 | 180 | Baylor |
| 6. | Ray, Terry | S | 6-0 | 192 | Oklahoma |
| 7. | Paulk, Tim | LB | 6-0 | 230 | Florida |
| 8. | Moore, Derrick | RB | 5-11 | 216 | Northeastern State, Ok. |
| 8. | Dwight, Reggie | TE | 6-3 | 262 | Troy State |
| 9. | Alex, Keith | T | 6-4 | 303 | Texas A&M |
| 10. | Hardy, Darryl | LB | 6-2 | 217 | Tennessee |
| 11. | Jones, Robin | DE | 6-2 | 259 | Baylor |

## VETERAN ROSTER

| No. | Name | Pos. | Ht. | Wt. | NFL Year | College |
|---|---|---|---|---|---|---|
| 72 | Barnett, Oliver | DE | 6-3 | 285 | 3 | Kentucky |
| 34 | Broussard, Steve | RB | 5-7 | 201 | 3 | Washington State |
| 77 | Bryan, Rick | DE | 6-4 | 265 | 8 | Oklahoma |
| 23 | Butler, Bobby | CB | 5-11 | 175 | 12 | Florida State |
| 25 | Case, Scott | S | 6-0 | 188 | 9 | Oklahoma |
| 85 | Collins, Shawn | WR | 6-2 | 204 | 4 | Northern Arizona |
| 56 | Conner, Darion | LB | 6-2 | 250 | 3 | Jackson State |
| 42 | Donaldson, Jeff | S | 6-0 | 190 | 9 | Colorado |
| 64 | Dukes, Jamie | C | 6-1 | 285 | 7 | Florida State |
| 32 | Eaton, Tracey | S | 6-1 | 195 | 5 | Portland State |
| 74 | Epps, Tory | NT | 6-0 | 270 | 3 | Memphis State |
| | Faryniarz, Brett | LB | 6-3 | 232 | 5 | San Diego State |
| | Forde, Brian | LB | 6-3 | 235 | 5 | Washington State |
| | Fortin, Roman | T-C | 6-5 | 290 | 2 | San Diego State |
| 79 | Fralic, Bill | G | 6-5 | 280 | 8 | Pittsburgh |
| 17 | Fulhage, Scott | P | 6-0 | 193 | 6 | Kansas State |
| 76 | Gann, Mike | DE | 6-5 | 270 | 8 | Notre Dame |
| 67 | Gardner, Moe | NT | 6-2 | 258 | 2 | Illinois |
| 99 | Green, Tim | DE | 6-2 | 245 | 7 | Syracuse |
| 81 | Haynes, Michael | WR | 6-0 | 180 | 5 | Northern Arizona |
| | Hill, Drew | WR | 5-9 | 172 | 13 | Georgia Tech |
| 75 | Hinton, Chris | T | 6-4 | 300 | 10 | Northwestern |
| 69 | Hoover, Houston | G | 6-2 | 295 | 5 | Jackson State |
| 9 | Johnson, Norm | K | 6-2 | 203 | 11 | UCLA |
| 38 | Jones, Keith | RB | 6-1 | 210 | 4 | Illinois |
| | Jones, Tony | WR | 5-7 | 139 | 3 | Texas |
| 78 | Kenn, Mike | T | 6-7 | 280 | 15 | Michigan |
| | Kiel, Blair | QB | 6-0 | 203 | 7 | Notre Dame |
| 88 | Le Bel, Harper | TE | 6-4 | 245 | 4 | Colorado State |
| 54 | Lyles, Robert | LB | 6-1 | 230 | 9 | Texas Christian |
| 22 | McKyer, Tim | CB | 6-0 | 174 | 7 | Texas-Arlington |
| 12 | Miller, Chris | QB | 6-2 | 205 | 6 | Oregon |
| | Milling, James | WR | 5-9 | 156 | 3 | Maryland |
| 41 | Pegram, Erric | RB | 5-9 | 188 | 2 | North Texas State |
| 82 | Phillips, Jason | WR | 5-7 | 168 | 4 | Houston |
| 39 | Pickens, Bruce | CB | 5-11 | 190 | 2 | Nebraska |
| 35 | Pritchard, Mike | WR | 5-11 | 180 | 2 | Colorado |
| 59 | Rade, John | LB | 6-1 | 240 | 10 | Boise State |
| 95 | Reid, Michael | LB | 6-2 | 235 | 5 | Wisconsin |
| 80 | Rison, Andre | WR | 6-0 | 188 | 4 | Michigan State |
| 55 | Ruether, Mike | C | 6-4 | 286 | 7 | Texas |
| | Salum, Donnie | LB | 6-1 | 235 | 1 | Arizona |
| 21 | Sanders, Deion | CB-KR | 6-0 | 185 | 4 | Florida State |
| 37 | Shelley, Elbert | S | 5-11 | 185 | 6 | Arkansas State |
| 66 | Sims, Joe | T | 6-3 | 294 | 2 | Nebraska |
| 89 | Thomas, George | WR | 5-9 | 169 | 4 | Nevada-Las Vegas |
| 52 | Tippins, Ken | LB | 6-1 | 230 | 4 | Middle Tennessee State |
| 13 | Tolliver, Billy Joe | QB | 6-1 | 218 | 4 | Texas Tech |
| 58 | Tuggle, Jessie | LB | 5-11 | 230 | 6 | Valdosta State |

in all but three regular-season games. However, there is a lack of venom in the pass pressure, a rôle in which defensive right end Tim Green led the team with just five sacks, and there's not much to fear about a rush defense which ranked 23rd in the league. Second-round draftee Chuck Smith may be the outside pass rusher that the Falcons have been seeking. Another outside linebacker, Brett Faryniarz, is an interesting Plan-B arrival. He started seven games for the Rams last year and could be given a lift by his new environment.

Sensational kickoff and punt returning by Sanders, better-than-average punting by Scott Fulhage and solid placekicking by the much-respected Norm Johnson give the Falcons an edge in special teams play.

# LOS ANGELES RAMS

**Address** 2327 West Lincoln Avenue, Anaheim, California 92801.

**Stadium** Anaheim Stadium, Anaheim.
*Capacity* 69,008 *Playing Surface* Grass.

**Team Colours** Royal Blue, Gold, and White.

**Head Coach** Chuck Knox – 1st year; 20th NFL.

**Championships** Division 1973,'74,'75,'76,'77,'78, '79,'85; Conference 1979; NFL 1945,'51.

**History** NFL 1937-69, NFC 1970-
(Until 1946, they were known as the Cleveland Rams.)

Every new head coach has a great opportunity to start afresh and, while he won't sweep away everything left by his predecessor, Chuck Knox at least is sure to set a different course towards his target.

Knox loves the rushing game and that philosophy always requires an offensive line of substance. There was no major influx of personnel for this unit, through either Plan B or the draft, but a subtle move brought 14-year veteran center Blair Bush. He could even start, enabling one of guard Bern Brostek and center Tom Newberry to shift around to fill the gap left by departed Plan-B free agent right guard Duval Love. Of similar value will be Bush's wisdom as a tutor. With Gerald Perry and the indestructible Jackie Slater in the tackle positions, the line could perform adequately until the next opportunity for reinforcement comes around. The running back position has not developed as anticipated when the Rams gathered in talent as part of the trade which sent Eric Dickerson to the Colts in 1987. Robert Delpino has been tried in several rôles when many scouts felt that he was best used as a pure running back. Perhaps Knox will take the same view, confirming the starting partnership of Delpino and fullback Buford McGee while reshaping the talented Cleveland Gary. Marcus Dupree is working hard to complete his comeback after a 1985 knee injury which was thought to have ended his career. This year may represent his final opportunity.

Delpino catches the ball well, a skill which encouraged previous head coach John Robinson to experiment with him as a receiver and which deferred his installation at running back. Last year Delpino came second in the club with 55 receptions. Henry Ellard was the team leader in what had to rank as a most disappointing year for the rest, with Flipper Anderson being restricted by nagging injuries to only 530 yards and Aaron Cox to 216. Someone has to find a way of igniting a package which truly is explosive – Ellard threatens to go downtown on every play while Anderson holds the NFL single-game receiving record of 336 yards. That responsibility falls to Jim Everett, a quarterback who has slipped over the last two campaigns following his excellent passer rating of 90.6 in 1989. He has looked vulnerable ever since the Rams were smashed 30–3 by the 49ers in the playoffs of that year, and perhaps he needs the kind of inspiration that Knox will bring.

It must be a severe disappointment for the Rams that high options in three successive drafts have been used for the defense yet, although some have become starters, no one has emerged as an impact player. Injuries, too, have been a factor, none more stifling than the back problems suffered by defensive end Bill Hawkins, who started one game in his first two years and had just four tackles in his third. Knox has not yet decided on his formation but he will be seeking to make maximum use of his best defensive player, Kevin Greene, who may be given free range to choose the best left-side spot from which to launch himself. The problem on the right side of the line could be solved if top draftee Sean Gilbert comes through as expected. Defensive tackle Alvin Wright is an honest worker and you'd think that there will be a spot for someone who has started all but three games over the last four years. At linebacker, Larry Kelm and Fred Strickland are the stalwarts without developing an overpowering presence and there is

| 1992 SCHEDULE OF GAMES | September | |
| --- | --- | --- |
| | 6 at Buffalo | 1:00 |
| | 13 NEW ENGLAND | 1:00 |
| | 20 at Miami | 4:00 |
| | 27 NEW YORK JETS | 1:00 |
| | October | |
| | 4 at San Francisco | 1:00 |
| | 11 at New Orleans | 6:30 |
| | 18 NEW YORK GIANTS | 1:00 |
| | 25 Open Date | |
| | November | |
| | 1 at Atlanta | 1:00 |
| | 8 PHOENIX | 1:00 |
| | 15 at Dallas | 12:00 |
| | 22 SAN FRANCISCO | 1:00 |
| | 29 MINNESOTA | 1:00 |
| | December | |
| | 6 at Tampa Bay | 8:00 |
| | 13 NEW ORLEANS | 1:00 |
| | 20 at Green Bay | 12:00 |
| | 27 ATLANTA | 1:00 |

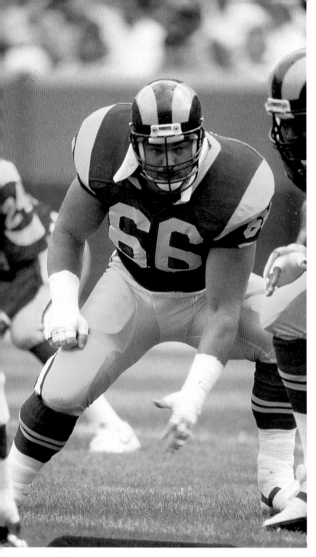

Tom Newberry may move back to guard in 1992.

## 1992 Draft

| Round | Name | Pos. | Ht. | Wt. | College |
|---|---|---|---|---|---|
| 1. | Gilbert, Sean | DE | 6-4 | 315 | Pittsburgh |
| 2. | Israel, Steve | CB-KR | 5-10 | 186 | Pittsburgh |
| 3. | Boutte, Marc | DT | 6-3 | 298 | Louisiana State |
| 3. | Kinchen, Todd | WR-KR | 5-11 | 187 | Louisiana State |
| 4. | Harper, Shawn | T | 6-3 | 290 | Indiana |
| 5. | Crooms, Chris | S | 5-11 | 216 | Texas A&M |
| 6. | Campbell, Joe | RB | 5-8 | 174 | Middle Tennessee State |
| 7. | Ashmore, Darryl | T | 6-6 | 290 | Northwestern |
| 8. | Jones, Ricky | QB | 6-1 | 180 | Alabama State |
| 9. | Rubley, T.J. | QB | 6-2 | 199 | Tulsa |
| 10. | Lester, Tim | RB | 5-9 | 213 | Eastern Kentucky |
| 11. | Townsend, Brian | LB | 6-3 | 235 | Michigan |
| 11. | Thomas, Brian | WR | 6-0 | 190 | Southern |
| 12. | Harris, Kelvin | C | 6-3 | 267 | Miami |

## VETERAN ROSTER

| No. | Name | Pos. | Ht. | Wt. | NFL Year | College |
|---|---|---|---|---|---|---|
| 83 | Anderson, Willie | WR | 6-0 | 175 | 5 | UCLA |
| 28 | Bailey, Robert | CB | 5-9 | 176 | 2 | Miami |
| 61 | Brostek, Bern | G | 6-3 | 300 | 3 | Washington |
| | Bush, Blair | C | 6-3 | 275 | 15 | Washington |
| 59 | Butcher, Paul | LB | 6-0 | 230 | 6 | Wayne State |
| 88 | Carter, Pat | TE | 6-3 | 255 | 5 | Florida State |
| | Chadwick, Jeff | WR | 6-3 | 189 | 10 | Grand Valley State |
| 79 | Charles, Mike | DT | 6-4 | 305 | 10 | Syracuse |
| 84 | Cox, Aaron | WR | 5-10 | 178 | 5 | Arizona State |
| 94 | Crews, Terry | LB | 6-2 | 237 | 2 | Western Michigan |
| 39 | Delpino, Robert | RB | 6-0 | 205 | 5 | Missouri |
| 22 | Dupree, Marcus | RB | 6-2 | 225 | 3 | Oklahoma |
| 80 | Ellard, Henry | WR | 5-11 | 182 | 10 | Fresno State |
| 11 | Everett, Jim | QB | 6-5 | 212 | 7 | Purdue |
| 43 | Gary, Cleveland | RB | 6-0 | 226 | 4 | Miami |
| 91 | Greene, Kevin | LB | 6-3 | 247 | 8 | Auburn |
| 70 | Hawkins, Bill | DE | 6-6 | 266 | 4 | Miami |
| 9 | Helton, Barry | P | 6-3 | 205 | 5 | Colorado |
| 20 | Henley, Darryl | CB-PR | 5-9 | 172 | 4 | UCLA |
| 72 | Jenkins, Robert | T | 6-5 | 285 | 6 | UCLA |
| 86 | Johnson, Damone | TE | 6-4 | 250 | 6 | Cal Poly-SLO |
| 52 | Kelm, Larry | LB | 6-4 | 240 | 6 | Texas A&M |
| 38 | Lang, David | RB | 5-11 | 201 | 2 | Northern Arizona |
| | Loville, Derek | RB-KR | 5-9 | 198 | 3 | Oregon |
| 41 | Lyght, Todd | CB | 6-0 | 186 | 2 | Notre Dame |
| 24 | McGee, Buford | RB | 6-0 | 210 | 9 | Mississippi |
| 71 | Milinichik, Joe | G | 6-5 | 290 | 6 | North Carolina State |
| 66 | Newberry, Tom | C | 6-2 | 285 | 7 | Wisconsin-LaCrosse |
| 26 | Newman, Anthony | S | 6-0 | 199 | 5 | Oregon |
| 14 | Pagel, Mike | QB | 6-2 | 220 | 11 | Arizona State |
| 69 | Pahukoa, Jeff | T-C | 6-2 | 298 | 2 | Washington |
| 64 | Perry, Gerald | T | 6-6 | 305 | 5 | Southern |
| 58 | Phifer, Roman | LB | 6-2 | 230 | 2 | UCLA |
| 95 | Piel, Mike | DT | 6-4 | 270 | 4 | Illinois |
| 87 | Price, Jim | H-B | 6-4 | 247 | 2 | Stanford |
| 18 | Raye, Jimmy | WR | 5-9 | 165 | 1 | San Diego State |
| 97 | Robinson, Gerald | DE | 6-3 | 262 | 5 | Auburn |
| 92 | Rocker, David | DT | 6-4 | 267 | 2 | Auburn |
| 55 | Sanders, Glenell | LB | 6-0 | 224 | 3 | Louisiana Tech |
| | Skow, Jim | DE | 6-3 | 250 | 7 | Nebraska |
| 78 | Slater, Jackie | T | 6-4 | 287 | 17 | Jackson State |
| 56 | Smith, Doug | C | 6-3 | 272 | 15 | Bowling Green |
| 50 | Stams, Frank | LB | 6-2 | 240 | 4 | Notre Dame |
| 23 | Stewart, Michael | S | 6-0 | 199 | 6 | Fresno State |
| 53 | Strickland, Fred | LB | 6-2 | 250 | 5 | Purdue |
| 37 | Terrell, Pat | S | 6-0 | 195 | 3 | Notre Dame |
| 32 | Thompson, Ernie | RB | 5-11 | 230 | 2 | Indiana |
| 82 | Turner, Vernon | WR-PR | 5-8 | 185 | 2 | Carson-Newman |
| 77 | Wilson, Karl | DE | 6-4 | 275 | 6 | Louisiana State |
| 99 | Wright, Alvin | DT | 6-2 | 285 | 7 | Jacksonville State |
| 76 | Young, Robert | DT | 6-6 | 273 | 2 | Mississippi State |
| 10 | Zendejas, Tony | K | 5-8 | 165 | 8 | Nevada-Reno |

a gap to be filled following the departure of Plan-B free agent Brett Faryniarz. It means that Roman Phifer, the 1991 second-round draftee, must come back from injury. Otherwise, with little depth, the Rams may be in a spot of bother.

The secondary will be without Jerry Gray, who has departed under Plan B, but the feeling is that 1991 first-round draftee Todd Lyght needed the space in which to express himself. If Lyght was not an instant success, Darryl Henley improved a great deal last year with 56 tackles and three interceptions. Strong safety Michael Stewart responded with 81 tackles as he, too, began to establish his authority. Free safety Pat Terrell made decent progress in his second year.

Placekicker Tony Zendejas was almost perfect in 1991, missing only one extra point and setting a new NFL record by landing all 17 of his field goal attempts, including a pair of 50-yarders. For the punting duties, Barry Helton, who played for San Francisco in two victorious Super Bowls, took over from Dale Hatcher for the final two games of the season and made a good impression.

# NEW ORLEANS SAINTS

**Address** 1500 Poydras Street, New Orleans, Louisiana 70112.

**Stadium** Louisiana Superdome, New Orleans. *Capacity* 69,065 *Playing Surface* AstroTurf.

**Team Colours** Old Gold, Black, and White.

**Head Coach** Jim Mora – 7th year.

**Championships** Division 1991.

**History** NFL 1967-69, NFC 1970-

Following four consecutive losses, the Saints regrouped for victories over the Raiders and Phoenix to win their first NFC Western division title. It is unusual for a title winner not to boast a 1,000-yard rusher and New Orleans didn't even have one who cracked the 500-yard barrier. Also, they didn't have a 1,000-yard receiver. What they did have was a team effort in which most players contributed significantly. All four of Fred McAfee, Gill Fenerty, Craig Heyward and Dalton Hilliard, each in his own way, can play the halfback position, with Buford Jordan starting at fullback. Hilliard has been troubled with injuries while Heyward's inconsistency has been a worry. It was, then, a pleasant bonus that McAfee, a rookie, looked sprightly in the nine games for which he was available, leading the club in rushing with 494 yards at an average of 4.5.

However, in the search for the ideal formula, the Saints traded for Allen Pinkett and drafted Vaughn Dunbar, a versatile player with decent speed and durability, in the 1992 first round.

Quarterback Bobby Hebert's return after a year out because of a contract dispute was a factor in the club's first title, but there remain doubts in some quarters over his ability to compete in the playoff cauldron. Some scouts also point to the fact that, in all but one game, the Saints led going into the final quarter but let opponents off the hook. Still, he is a favourite down on the bayou and represents the best of the options available to the team. Hebert can count on wide receivers Eric Martin and Floyd Turner to make the most of the service, while Quinn Early proved to be a good Plan-B signing and Wesley Carroll showed some neat touches. The contribution from tight end Hoby Brenner is often overlooked but he has become a dependable pillar.

The offensive line doesn't have any household names but is a solid unit, with Joel Hilgenberg at center, Jim Dombrowski at left guard and right tackle Stan Brock the perennial starters. Richard Cooper stood in well at left tackle and should continue to hold off Kevin Haverdink. By contrast, at right guard Chris Port should step aside for Derek Kennard with Steve Trapilo in the competition if he recovers from injury.

New Orleans ranked second in all three categories of total defense, defense against the run and against the pass. Without question, the strength lies at linebacker, where all four of Rickey Jackson, Sam Mills, Vaughan Johnson and Pat Swilling are Pro Bowlers. Swilling was the NFL leading sacker while, even in his 11th campaign, Jackson still is in his prime. Last year the ferocious outside linebacker had 11.5

*Bobby Hebert (3) runs the controlled New Orleans offense.*

sacks, 59 tackles, forced three fumbles and recovered three. With a combined total of 28.5 sacks, Jackson and Swilling exceeded those of six NFL teams. For much of the season, the secondary was virtually impenetrable with Vince Buck and Toi Cook at cornerback and the pairing of Brett Maxie and Gene Atkins at safety. Atkins, who tied with Buck for the team lead in interceptions, returned his five steals for 198 yards. However, after injuries to both Buck and Cook, the quality fell away and it could be that Buck's neck damage ends his career. Furthermore, backups Milton Mack, Bennie Thompson and Vencie Glenn were lost to free agency. Tyrone Legette, Sean Lumpkin and Kary Vincent came in the top half of the draft but they will need time to settle.

The probable lack of continuity in the secondary places greater importance on a dominance by the front seven, but of this there is every prospect. Wayne Martin, Frank Warren and Jim Wilks form an excellent three-man line, with Renaldo Turnbull progressing steadily as a pass rusher. Robert Goff provides quality depth at nose tackle, while Joel Smeenge, a 1990 third-round pick, is expected to offer an option as a pass rusher.

Placekicker Morten Andersen rarely has a modest year and has been to five Pro Bowls. Tommy Barnhardt is coming off the best of his five NFL campaigns with a punting average of 43.5 yards, good enough for third place in the NFC list. There is a shortage of technique as distinct from speed on kickoff returns, in which Atkins led, averaging just 18.4 yards with a longest of 27 yards. Buck really earned his salary with 31 punt returns at an average of 8.4 yards and this is another area in which he will be missed if his injury is serious.

## 1992 Draft

| Round | Name | Pos. | Ht. | Wt. | College |
|---|---|---|---|---|---|
| 1. | Dunbar, Vaughn | RB | 5-9 | 204 | Indiana |
| 3. | Legette, Tyrone | CB | 5-8 | 177 | Nebraska |
| 4. | McGuire, Gene | C | 6-2 | 284 | Notre Dame |
| 4. | Lumpkin, Sean | S | 6-0 | 206 | Minnesota |
| 5. | Small, Torrance | WR | 6-3 | 201 | Alcorn State |
| 6. | Vincent, Kary | CB | 5-9 | 175 | Texas A&M |
| 8. | Stewart, Robert | NT | 5-11 | 292 | Alabama |
| 9. | Jones, Donald | LB | 6-0 | 231 | Washington |
| 10. | Dowdell, Marcus | WR | 5-10 | 178 | Tennessee State |
| 11. | Gisler, Mike | G | 6-3 | 295 | Houston |
| 12. | Adell, Scott | T | 6-4 | 310 | North Carolina State |

## VETERAN ROSTER

| No. | Name | Pos. | Ht. | Wt. | NFL Year | College |
|---|---|---|---|---|---|---|
| 7 | Andersen, Morten | K | 6-2 | 221 | 11 | Michigan State |
| 28 | Atkins, Gene | S | 6-1 | 200 | 6 | Florida A&M |
| 6 | Barnhardt, Tommy | P | 6-2 | 207 | 6 | North Carolina |
| 85 | Brenner, Hoby | TE | 6-5 | 245 | 12 | Southern California |
| 67 | Brock, Stan | T | 6-6 | 278 | 13 | Colorado |
| 16 | Buck, Mike | QB | 6-3 | 227 | 3 | Maine |
| 26 | Buck, Vince | CB | 6-0 | 198 | 3 | Central State, Ohio |
| 80 | Carroll, Wesley | WR | 6-0 | 183 | 2 | Miami |
| 41 | Cook, Toi | CB | 5-11 | 188 | 6 | Stanford |
| 71 | Cooper, Richard | T | 6-5 | 290 | 3 | Tennessee |
| 72 | Dombrowski, Jim | G | 6-5 | 298 | 7 | Virginia |
| 89 | Early, Quinn | WR | 6-0 | 190 | 5 | Iowa |
| 22 | Fenerty, Gill | RB | 6-0 | 205 | 3 | Holy Cross |
| 91 | Goff, Robert | NT | 6-3 | 270 | 5 | Auburn |
| 74 | Haverdink, Kevin | T | 6-5 | 285 | 4 | Western Michigan |
| 3 | Hebert, Bobby | QB | 6-4 | 215 | 7 | Northwestern State, La. |
| 34 | Heyward, Craig | RB | 5-11 | 260 | 5 | Pittsburgh |
| 61 | Hilgenberg, Joel | C | 6-2 | 252 | 9 | Iowa |
| 21 | Hilliard, Dalton | RB | 5-8 | 204 | 7 | Louisiana State |
| 57 | Jackson, Rickey | LB | 6-2 | 243 | 12 | Pittsburgh |
| 68 | Jetton, Paul | G | 6-4 | 288 | 4 | Texas |
| 53 | Johnson, Vaughan | LB | 6-3 | 235 | 7 | North Carolina State |
| 27 | Jones, Reggie | CB | 6-1 | 202 | 2 | Memphis State |
| 23 | Jordan, Buford | RB | 6-0 | 223 | 7 | McNeese State |
| 78 | Keim, Mike | T | 6-7 | 285 | 1 | Brigham Young |
| 60 | Kennard, Derek | G | 6-3 | 300 | 7 | Nevada-Reno |
| 84 | Martin, Eric | WR | 6-1 | 207 | 8 | Louisiana State |
| 93 | Martin, Wayne | DE | 6-5 | 275 | 4 | Arkansas |
| 39 | Maxie, Brett | S | 6-2 | 194 | 8 | Texas Southern |
| 25 | McAfee, Fred | RB | 5-10 | 193 | 2 | Mississippi College |
| 69 | Miller, Les | NT | 6-7 | 285 | 6 | Fort Hays State |
| 51 | Mills, Sam | LB | 5-9 | 225 | 7 | Montclair State |
| 35 | Morse, Bobby | RB-PR | 5-10 | 213 | 5 | Michigan State |
| 86 | Newman, Pat | WR | 5-11 | 189 | 2 | Utah State |
| 38 | Nicholson, Calvin | CB | 5-9 | 183 | 2 | Oregon State |
| 45 | Petry, Stan | CB | 5-11 | 180 | 4 | Texas Christian |
| 20 | Pinkett, Allen | RB | 5-9 | 196 | 7 | Notre Dame |
| 70 | Port, Chris | G | 6-5 | 290 | 2 | Duke |
| 55 | Ross, Scott | LB | 6-1 | 235 | 2 | Southern California |
| 83 | Scales, Greg | TE | 6-4 | 253 | 4 | Wake Forest |
| 99 | Smeenge, Joel | LB | 6-5 | 255 | 3 | Western Michigan |
| 30 | Smith, Cedric | RB | 5-10 | 223 | 3 | Florida |
| 56 | Swilling, Pat | LB | 6-3 | 242 | 7 | Georgia Tech |
| 29 | Taylor, Keith | S | 5-11 | 206 | 5 | Illinois |
| 82 | Tice, John | TE | 6-5 | 249 | 10 | Maryland |
| 65 | Trapilo, Steve | G | 6-5 | 281 | 5 | Boston College |
| 97 | Turnbull, Renaldo | DE | 6-4 | 255 | 3 | West Virginia |
| 88 | Turner, Floyd | WR | 5-11 | 188 | 3 | Northwestern State, La. |
| 87 | Wainright, Frank | TE | 6-3 | 236 | 2 | Northern Colorado |
| 4 | Walsh, Steve | QB | 6-2 | 204 | 4 | Miami |
| 73 | Warren, Frank | DE | 6-4 | 290 | 11 | Auburn |
| 94 | Wilks, Jim | DE-NT | 6-5 | 275 | 12 | San Diego State |
| 90 | Williams, James | LB | 6-0 | 230 | 3 | Mississippi State |
| 92 | Winston, DeMond | LB | 6-2 | 239 | 2 | Vanderbilt |

### 1992 SCHEDULE OF GAMES

**September**

| | | |
|---|---|---|
| 6 | at Philadelphia | 1:00 |
| 13 | CHICAGO | 12:00 |
| 20 | at Atlanta | 1:00 |
| 27 | SAN FRANCISCO | 7:00 |

**October**

| | | |
|---|---|---|
| 4 | at Detroit | 1:00 |
| 11 | LOS ANGELES RAMS | 6:30 |
| 18 | at Phoenix | 1:00 |
| 25 | Open Date | |

**November**

| | | |
|---|---|---|
| 1 | TAMPA BAY | 12:00 |
| 8 | at New England | 1:00 |
| 15 | at San Francisco | 1:00 |
| 23 | WASHINGTON (Mon.) | 8:00 |
| 29 | MIAMI | 12:00 |

**December**

| | | |
|---|---|---|
| 3 | ATLANTA (Thurs.) | 7:00 |
| 13 | at Los Angeles Rams | 1:00 |
| 20 | BUFFALO | 12:00 |
| 26 | at New York Jets (Sat.) | 12:30 |

# SAN FRANCISCO 49ers

**Address** 4949 Centennial Boulevard, Santa Clara, California 95054.

**Stadium** Candlestick Park, San Francisco.
*Capacity* 66,455 *Playing Surface* Grass.

**Team Colours** Forty Niners Gold and Scarlet.

**Head Coach** George Seifert – 4th year.

**Championships** Division 1970,'71,'72,'81,'83,'84, '86,'87,'88,'89,'90; Conference 1981,'84,'88,'89; Super Bowl 1981,'84,'88,'89.

**History** AAFC 1946-49, NFL 1950-69, NFC 1970-

Even a six-game winning streak to close out the 1991 season could not overcome a disastrous 4-6 start and the 49ers failed by a whisker to reach the playoffs. Entering the 1992 campaign, they look almost as invincible as in their NFL Championship years.

Other than expressions of genuine sympathy for the great Joe Montana, the uncertainty surrounding his ability to return from a season-long absence through injury is of little concern. For in Steve Young, San Francisco has the 1991 NFL leading passer, while reserve Steve Bono has shown often enough that he can direct the offense with authority. Young has a rocket arm and, much in the manner of Denver's John Elway, is a fine runner to the extent that he came second in the club with 415 yards, despite playing in only 11 games. Bono is more a classic pocket passer. The latest information is that Montana will attempt to come back, leaving head coach George Seifert a difficult problem of personnel management.

Everyone would like his difficulties in sharing out the time among a set of wide receivers which start with Jerry Rice and end with fourth-stringer Odessa Turner, who was acquired as a Plan-B free agent from the Giants and could thrive on the West Coast. Rice needs only eight touchdown receptions to set the new all-time record currently held by the retired Steve Largent. He has taken seven years, compared with Largent's 14, and there are few sights quite like Rice, searing down the sideline or cutting across the middle.

His starting partner, John Taylor, may be even faster and, like Rice, caught his passes for over 1,000 yards, but included a 97-yard touchdown. Behind these two, Mike Sherrard comes in just often enough to keep him sharp.

One surprising aspect has been the club's inability to solve a problem which emerged when running back Roger Craig was lost to free agency. Dexter Carter is not the sort to play every down, despite his unquestioned elusiveness, and while Keith Henderson was the rushing leader at a good average of 4.1 yards per carry, he is not likely to emerge as a premier back. Another worry is that Carter had five fumbles and Henderson four, figures which are rather high for backs who averaged fewer than ten carries per game. This aspect might have been a deciding factor in persuading the club to draft Amp Lee, a back with good moves and who fumbled only once in his last 452 plays in college.

The offensive line is an enduring strength. In the 1991 preseason, right guard Roy Foster was scheduled to have a shoulder operation which would have meant missing the opening games. Tough veteran that he is, Foster decided to wait and ended up starting all 16 games, as did Steve Wallace, Guy McIntyre, Jesse Sapolu and Harris Barton.

For the defensive front, San Francisco was one of the first teams to use a whole variety of players, varying with circumstances, in the early 1980s. It means that while Pierce Holt and Larry Roberts are listed as the starting defensive ends, with Michael Carter at nose tackle, Tim Harris and Charles Haley also play the end position when used primarily as pass rushers. Haley also starts in the normal sense of outside linebacker, as part of a four-man unit with Keith DeLong, Mike Walter and Bill Romanowski. Harris's career has gone off line following his disgruntlement at Green Bay and

| 1992 SCHEDULE OF GAMES | September | |
|---|---|---|
| | 6 at New York Giants | 4:00 |
| | 13 BUFFALO | 1:00 |
| | 20 at New York Jets | 1:00 |
| | 27 at New Orleans | 7:00 |
| | October | |
| | 4 LOS ANGELES RAMS | 1:00 |
| | 11 at New England | 1:00 |
| | 18 ATLANTA | 1:00 |
| | 25 Open Date | |
| | November | |
| | 1 at Phoenix | 2:00 |
| | 9 at Atlanta (Mon.) | 9:00 |
| | 15 NEW ORLEANS | 1:00 |
| | 22 at Los Angeles Rams | 1:00 |
| | 29 PHILADELPHIA | 1:00 |
| | December | |
| | 6 MIAMI | 1:00 |
| | 13 at Minnesota | 12:00 |
| | 19 TAMPA BAY (Sat.) | 1:00 |
| | 28 DETROIT (Mon.) | 6:00 |

*John Taylor's talents are sometimes hidden by those of Jerry Rice.*

### 1992 Draft

| Round | Name | Pos. | Ht. | Wt. | College |
|---|---|---|---|---|---|
| 1. | Hall, Dana | CB-S | 6-2 | 206 | Washington |
| 2. | Lee, Amp | RB | 5-11 | 200 | Florida State |
| 3. | Bollinger, Brian | G | 6-5 | 285 | North Carolina |
| 4. | Thomas, Mark | DE | 6-5 | 264 | North Carolina State |
| 6. | Russell, Damien | S | 6-0 | 199 | Virginia Tech |
| 9. | Hagan, Darian | QB | 5-9 | 190 | Colorado |
| 10. | Mayfield, Corey | NT | 6-2 | 273 | Oklahoma |
| 11. | Covington, Tom | TE | 6-3 | 238 | Georgia Tech |
| 12. | LaBounty, Matt | DE | 6-3 | 261 | Oregon |

### VETERAN ROSTER

| No. | Name | Pos. | Ht. | Wt. | NFL Year | College |
|---|---|---|---|---|---|---|
| 79 | Barton, Harris | T | 6-4 | 280 | 6 | North Carolina |
| 65 | Boatswain, Harry | T | 6-4 | 295 | 1 | New Haven |
| 13 | Bono, Steve | QB | 6-4 | 215 | 8 | UCLA |
| 22 | Bowles, Todd | S | 6-2 | 205 | 7 | Temple |
| 96 | Brown, Dennis | DE | 6-4 | 290 | 3 | Washington |
| 64 | Burt, Jim | NT | 6-1 | 270 | 12 | Miami |
| 20 | Canley, Sheldon | RB | 5-9 | 195 | 1 | San Jose State |
| 35 | Carter, Dexter | RB-KR | 5-9 | 170 | 3 | Florida State |
| 95 | Carter, Michael | NT | 6-2 | 285 | 9 | Southern Methodist |
| 6 | Cofer, Mike | K | 6-1 | 160 | 5 | North Carolina State |
| | Crudup, Derrick | S | 6-2 | 215 | 3 | Oklahoma |
| 25 | Davis, Eric | CB | 5-11 | 178 | 2 | Jacksonville State |
| 59 | DeLong, Keith | LB | 6-2 | 235 | 4 | Tennessee |
| 54 | Donahue, Mitch | LB | 6-2 | 254 | 2 | Wyoming |
| 75 | Fagan, Kevin | DE | 6-3 | 260 | 6 | Miami |
| 67 | Foster, Roy | G | 6-4 | 290 | 11 | Southern California |
| | Gash, Thane | S | 6-0 | 195 | 4 | East Tennessee State |
| 98 | Goss, Antonio | LB | 6-4 | 228 | 4 | North Carolina |
| 29 | Griffin, Don | CB | 6-0 | 176 | 7 | Middle Tennessee State |
| 94 | Haley, Charles | LB-DE | 6-5 | 230 | 7 | James Madison |
| 36 | Hanks, Merton | CB | 6-2 | 185 | 2 | Iowa |
| 92 | Harris, Tim | LB | 6-6 | 258 | 7 | Memphis State |
| 30 | Henderson, Keith | RB | 6-1 | 220 | 4 | Georgia |
| | Hendrix, Manny | CB | 5-10 | 187 | 7 | Utah |
| 78 | Holt, Pierce | DE | 6-4 | 280 | 5 | Angelo State |
| 40 | Jackson, Johnnie | S | 6-1 | 204 | 4 | Houston |
| 55 | Johnson, John | LB | 6-3 | 230 | 2 | Clemson |
| 84 | Jones, Brent | TE | 6-4 | 230 | 6 | Santa Clara |
| 90 | Jordan, Darin | LB | 6-2 | 245 | 3 | Northeastern |
| 45 | Lewis, Kevin | CB | 5-11 | 173 | 3 | Northwestern State, La. |
| 83 | Lewis, Ronald | WR | 5-11 | 173 | 3 | Florida State |
| | Logan, Marc | RB | 5-11 | 222 | 6 | Kentucky |
| 62 | McIntyre, Guy | G | 6-3 | 265 | 9 | Georgia |
| 16 | Montana, Joe | QB | 6-2 | 195 | 13 | Notre Dame |
| 14 | Musgrave, Bill | QB | 6-2 | 196 | 2 | Oregon |
| 69 | Neville, Tom | G | 6-5 | 298 | 5 | Fresno State |
| 26 | Pollard, Darryl | CB | 5-11 | 187 | 5 | Weber State |
| 4 | Prokop, Joe | P | 6-2 | 225 | 7 | Cal-Poly Pomona |
| 44 | Rathman, Tom | RB | 6-1 | 232 | 7 | Nebraska |
| | Reichenbach, Mike | LB | 6-2 | 240 | 9 | East Stroudsburg State |
| 80 | Rice, Jerry | WR | 6-2 | 200 | 8 | Mississippi Valley State |
| 91 | Roberts, Larry | DE | 6-3 | 275 | 7 | Alabama |
| 53 | Romanowski, Bill | LB | 6-4 | 231 | 5 | Boston College |
| 61 | Sapolu, Jesse | C | 6-4 | 260 | 7 | Hawaii |
| 88 | Sherrard, Mike | WR | 6-2 | 187 | 5 | UCLA |
| 24 | Sydney, Harry | RB | 6-0 | 217 | 6 | Kansas |
| | Tamm, Ralph | G | 6-3 | 280 | 3 | West Chester State |
| 82 | Taylor, John | WR | 6-1 | 185 | 6 | Delaware State |
| 60 | Thomas, Chuck | C-G | 6-3 | 280 | 7 | Oklahoma |
| | Turner, Odessa | WR | 6-3 | 205 | 6 | Northwestern State, La. |
| 74 | Wallace, Steve | T | 6-5 | 276 | 7 | Auburn |
| 89 | Walls, Wesley | TE | 6-5 | 246 | 4 | Mississippi |
| 99 | Walter, Michael | LB | 6-3 | 238 | 10 | Oregon |
| 97 | Washington, Ted | NT-DE | 6-4 | 299 | 2 | Louisville |
| 32 | Watters, Ricky | RB | 6-1 | 212 | 1 | Notre Dame |
| 41 | Whitmore, David | S | 6-0 | 235 | 3 | Stephen F. Austin |
| 81 | Williams, Jamie | TE | 6-4 | 245 | 10 | Nebraska |
| 8 | Young, Steve | QB | 6-2 | 200 | 8 | Brigham Young |

subsequent move to San Francisco. But at top form he is a demon, quite capable of running a game.

Unaccountably, following on the heels of losing All-Pro safety Ronnie Lott to free agency in 1991, San Francisco has lost starting strong safety Dave Waymer in the same circumstances to the same club, the Raiders. Waymer was coming off a season in which he led the team with 86 tackles, four interceptions and 16 passes defensed, and earned the Ed Block award for unusual courage on the field. The 49ers are noted for giving youth its chance, meaning that draftee Dana Hall is probably penciled in to start in Waymer's spot. Todd Bowles is at free safety with the most likely partner for cornerback Don Griffin being Darryl Pollard. Several really fine backups include Johnnie Jackson, Kevin Lewis, Merton Hanks and Eric Davis.

Mike Cofer and Joe Prokop handle the placekicking and punting respectively. Taylor takes care of punt returns while Dexter Carter can focus on kickoff returns, now that he is no longer required to bear the brunt of the rushing offense. Last year he returned a kickoff 98 yards for a touchdown.

# HOW THE SEASON WORKS

The National Football League consists of 28 teams divided into two **Conferences**, the American Football Conference (AFC) and the National Football Conference (NFC). Each conference has 14 teams and is subdivided into two five-team **Divisions** and one four-team **Division**. These are essentially based on sensible geographical consider-ations but also take into account the traditional rivalries which were in existence when the expanded NFL was restructured in 1970. The teams are listed below in order of their final 1991 division standings since this is of importance in arriving at a team's schedule (fixture list) for 1992.

## THE SCHEDULE

When considering a team's schedule, it's best to set aside the four teams who each finished the 1991 season in fifth place in their divisions. Looking at the remaining 24, every team plays 12 games against others from its own con-ference. Again, excluding the four fifth-placed teams, every team will play four games against teams from the rival con-ference (known as interconference games), specifically to allow fans in the cities of one conference the opportunity of seeing the star players and teams of the other conference. The structure of a team's schedule depends on whether it plays in a four-team or a five-team division.

## AMERICAN FOOTBALL CONFERENCE

**Eastern Division**

|  |  | W | L | T |
|---|---|---|---|---|
| Buffalo | AE-1 | 13 | 3 | 0 |
| N.Y. Jets | AE-2 | 8 | 8 | 0 |
| Miami | AE-3 | 8 | 8 | 0 |
| New England | AE-4 | 6 | 10 | 0 |
| Indianapolis | AE-5 | 1 | 15 | 0 |

**Central Division**

|  |  | W | L | T |
|---|---|---|---|---|
| Houston | AC-1 | 11 | 5 | 0 |
| Pittsburgh | AC-2 | 7 | 9 | 0 |
| Cleveland | AC-3 | 6 | 10 | 0 |
| Cincinnati | AC-4 | 3 | 13 | 0 |

**Western Division**

|  |  | W | L | T |
|---|---|---|---|---|
| Denver | AW-1 | 12 | 4 | 0 |
| Kansas City | AW-2 | 10 | 6 | 0 |
| L.A. Raiders | AW-3 | 9 | 7 | 0 |
| Seattle | AW-4 | 7 | 9 | 0 |
| San Diego | AW-5 | 4 | 12 | 0 |

## NATIONAL FOOTBALL CONFERENCE

**Eastern Division**

|  |  | W | L | T |
|---|---|---|---|---|
| Washington | NE-1 | 14 | 2 | 0 |
| Dallas | NE-2 | 11 | 5 | 0 |
| Philadelphia | NE-3 | 10 | 6 | 0 |
| N.Y. Giants | NE-4 | 8 | 8 | 0 |
| Phoenix | NE-5 | 4 | 12 | 0 |

**Central Division**

|  |  | W | L | T |
|---|---|---|---|---|
| Detroit | NC-1 | 12 | 4 | 0 |
| Chicago | NC-2 | 11 | 5 | 0 |
| Minnesota | NC-3 | 8 | 8 | 0 |
| Green Bay | NC-4 | 4 | 12 | 0 |
| Tampa Bay | NC-5 | 3 | 13 | 0 |

**Western Division**

|  |  | W | L | T |
|---|---|---|---|---|
| New Orleans | NW-1 | 11 | 5 | 0 |
| Atlanta | NW-2 | 10 | 6 | 0 |
| San Francisco | NW-3 | 10 | 6 | 0 |
| L.A. Rams | NW-4 | 3 | 13 | 0 |

## Four-Team Division

A typical schedule, e.g., for the Houston Oilers, appears below. It is set out deliberately not in chronological order but to emphasize that the schedule has a quite definite structure.

### Houston Oilers (AFC Central)

| | | |
|---|---|---|
| Cincinnati Bengals | AFC Central | Home |
| Cincinnati Bengals | AFC Central | Away |
| Cleveland Browns | AFC Central | Home |
| Cleveland Browns | AFC Central | Away |
| Pittsburgh Steelers | AFC Central | Home |
| Pittsburgh Steelers | AFC Central | Away |
| Buffalo Bills | AFC East | Home |
| Indianapolis Colts | AFC East | Away |
| Miami Dolphins | AFC East | Away |
| Denver Broncos | AFC West | Away |
| Kansas City Chiefs | AFC West | Home |
| San Diego Chargers | AFC West | Home |
| Detroit Lions | NFC Central | Away |
| Chicago Bears | NFC Central | Home |
| Green Bay Packers | NFC Central | Home |
| Minnesota Vikings | NFC Central | Away |

The Oilers will always play their division rivals, the Cincinnati Bengals, Cleveland Browns and Pittsburgh Steelers, both home and away. The flavour of intra-conference competition is maintained by six games, every year, against teams from outside their division but within their conference. There will always be three games against the AFC East and three against the AFC West. Again, every year, there will be four games against teams from a particular division of the rival conference, based on a three-year cycle. In 1992 they play the NFC Central; in 1993 they will play teams from the NFC West and in 1994 the NFC East. For every NFL team, a complete list of opponents, other than those within a team's own division, is arrived at by applying the formula on page 157. The letters and numbers refer to Conference, Division and final standing in that division. Thus, the Dallas Cowboys, who are in the National Conference Eastern Division and finished second in that division, are identified as NE-2. Equally, the Pittsburgh Steelers, who are in the American Conference Central Division and finished second in that division, are labelled AC-2.

## Five-Team Division (Top Four Teams Only)

In the AFC West the schedules for the top four teams have identical structure and include home and away games against the other four teams in the division. Each of the top four teams plays two games against AFC Central teams and two against the AFC East. Also, they play the top four teams in the NFC East as part of their three-year cycle of interconference games. In 1993 they will play teams from the NFC Central, and in 1994 the NFC West. Below is the schedule structure for the Los Angeles Raiders.

### Los Angeles Raiders (AFC West)

| | | |
|---|---|---|
| Denver Broncos | AFC West | Home |
| Denver Broncos | AFC West | Away |
| Kansas City Chiefs | AFC West | Home |
| Kansas City Chiefs | AFC West | Away |
| San Diego Chargers | AFC West | Home |
| San Diego Chargers | AFC West | Away |
| Seattle Seahawks | AFC West | Home |
| Seattle Seahawks | AFC West | Away |
| Buffalo Bills | AFC East | Home |
| Miami Dolphins | AFC East | Away |
| Cincinnati Bengals | AFC Central | Away |
| Cleveland Browns | AFC Central | Home |
| Dallas Cowboys | NFC East | Home |
| New York Giants | NFC East | Home |
| Philadelphia Eagles | NFC East | Away |
| Washington Redskins | NFC East | Away |

## Fifth-Placed Teams

In the AFC, the two fifth-placed teams will each play eight games against teams from their own division and will always play single games against each of the four AFC Central division teams. In the NFC, the two fifth-placed teams each play eight games against teams within their own division and will always play single games against the four NFC West teams. Each of the four fifth-placed teams is guaranteed home and away games against the other fifth-placed team in its own conference, and single games against the two fifth-placed teams from the rival conference. The schedule structures for all four teams are set out as follows:

### Indianapolis Colts (AE-5)

| | | |
|---|---|---|
| AFC East | | 8 games |
| AFC Central | | 4 games |
| San Diego | (AW-5) | Home |
| San Diego | (AW-5) | Away |
| Tampa Bay | (NC-5) | Away |
| Phoenix | (NE-5) | Home |

### San Diego Chargers (AW-5)

| | | |
|---|---|---|
| AFC West | | 8 games |
| AFC Central | | 4 games |
| Indianapolis | (AE-5) | Home |
| Indianapolis | (AF-5) | Away |
| Tampa Bay | (NC-5) | Home |
| Phoenix | (NE-5) | Away |

### Tampa Bay (NC-5)

| | | |
|---|---|---|
| NFC Central | | 8 games |
| NFC West | | 4 games |
| Phoenix | (NE-5) | Home |
| Phoenix | (NE-5) | Away |
| Indianapolis | (AE-5) | Home |
| San Diego | (AW-5) | Away |

**Phoenix (NE-5)**

| | | |
|---|---|---|
| NFC East | | 8 games |
| NFC West | | 4 games |
| Tampa Bay | (NC-5) | Home |
| Tampa Bay | (NC-5) | Away |
| Indianapolis | (AE-5) | Away |
| San Diego | (AW-5) | Home |

# THE PLAYOFFS

On completion of the regular season, each conference holds an elimination competition known as the Playoffs. Under a playoff format introduced for the 1990 season, the teams involved will be the three division winners and three Wild Card teams, namely, those three, other than the division winners, who have the best won-lost-tied records. In 1992 the three Wild Cards, together with the division winner with the poorest record, will contest the first round of the playoffs, the victors joining the two division winners with the better records in the conference semi-finals. Operating on the best-versus-worst principle, the team with the best record will play the team which has the poorest record.

### Home-Field Advantage in the Playoffs

The game site is determined on the best-versus-worst principle, with the team which has the better won-lost-tied record always given home-field advantage. Taking the AFC as the example, in the 1991 playoffs the pecking order of teams was as follows:

| | W | L | T |
|---|---|---|---|
| Buffalo* | 13 | 3 | 0 |
| Denver* | 12 | 4 | 0 |
| Houston* | 11 | 5 | 0 |
| Kansas City** | 10 | 6 | 0 |
| Los Angeles Raiders** | 9 | 7 | 0 |
| New York Jets** | 8 | 8 | 0 |

\* Division Champions
\*\* Wild Card teams

# TIE-BREAKING PROCEDURES

Ties are broken by the following list of criteria:

### Teams in the same division

A: *Two teams*
1. Head-to-head (best record in games played between the two teams)
2. Best record in games played within the division
3. Best record in games played within the conference

4. Best record in common games
5. Best net points scored in division games (just like goal difference in soccer)
6. Best net points in all games

B: *Three or More Teams* (If two teams remain tied after all other teams are eliminated, the tie-breaking procedure reverts to A:1.)
1. Head-to-head (best record in games played between the teams)
2. Best record in games played within the division
3. Best record in games played within the conference
4. Best record in common games
5. Best net points in division games
6. Best net points in all games

### Tie-Breakers for the Wild Card places

(a) If the teams are from the same division, the division tie-breaker is applied.
(b) If the teams are from different divisions, the following procedure is adopted:

C: *Two Teams*
1. Head-to-head (if they have played each other)
2. Best record in games played within the conference
3. Best record in common games (minimum of four)
4. Best average net points in conference games
5. Best net points in all games

D: *Three or More Teams* (If two teams remain tied after all other teams are eliminated, the tie-breaking procedure reverts to A:1, or C:1, whichever is applicable.)
1. Head-to-head sweep (this applies only if one team has either beaten or lost to all the others)
2. Best record in games played within the conference
3. Best record in common games (minimum of four)
4. Best average net points in conference games
5. Best net points in all games

### 1991 Tie-Breakers

**New York Jets-Miami (third wild-card place):**
A:1; Order: New York (2-0), Miami (0-2).
**Atlanta-Philadelphia-San Francisco (third wild-card place):** D:2; Order: Atlanta (7-5) and San Francisco (7-5) (tied), Philadelphia (6-6).
A:1; Order: Atlanta (2-0), San Francisco (2-0).
**Chicago-Dallas (home-field advantage):**
C:2; Order: Chicago (9-3), Dallas (8-4).

## AFC EAST-AE

| AE-1 H | AE-1 A | AE-2 H | AE-2 A | AE-3 H | AE-3 A | AE-4 H | AE-4 A | AE-5 H | AE-5 A |
|---|---|---|---|---|---|---|---|---|---|
| AC-2 | AC-1 | AC-4 | AC-2 | AC-1 | AC-3 | AC-3 | AC-4 | AC-1 | AC-2 |
| AW-1 | AW-3 | AW-2 | AW-1 | AW-3 | AW-4 | AW-4 | AW-2 | AC-3 | AC-4 |
| NW-2 | NW-1 | NW-1 | NW-2 | NW-2 | NW-1 | NW-1 | NW-2 | AW-5 | AW-5 |
| NW-4 | NW-3 | NW-3 | NW-4 | NW-4 | NW-3 | NW-3 | NW-4 | NE-5 | NC-5 |

## AFC CENTRAL-AC

| AC-1 H | AC-1 A | AC-2 H | AC-2 A | AC-3 H | AC-3 A | AC-4 H | AC-4 A |
|---|---|---|---|---|---|---|---|
| AW-2 | AE-5 | AE-2 | AE-1 | AE-3 | AE-5 | AE-4 | AE-2 |
| AW-5 | AE-3 | AE-5 | AW-2 | AW-1 | AE-4 | AE-5 | AW-4 |
| AE-1 | AW-1 | AW-4 | AW-5 | AW-5 | AW-3 | AW-3 | AW-5 |
| NC-2 | NC-1 | NC-1 | NC-2 | NC-2 | NC-1 | NC-1 | NC-2 |
| NC-4 | NC-3 | NC-3 | NC-4 | NC-4 | NC-3 | NC-3 | NC-4 |

## AFC WEST-AW

| AW-1 H | AW-1 A | AW-2 H | AW-2 A | AW-3 H | AW-3 A | AW-4 H | AW-4 A | AW-5 H | AW-5 A |
|---|---|---|---|---|---|---|---|---|---|
| AC-1 | AC-3 | AC-2 | AC-1 | AC-3 | AC-4 | AE-3 | AC-2 | AC-2 | AC-1 |
| AE-2 | AE-1 | AE-4 | AE-2 | AE-1 | AE-3 | AC-4 | AE-4 | AC-4 | AC-3 |
| NE-2 | NE-1 | NE-1 | NE-2 | NE-2 | NE-1 | NE-1 | NE-2 | AE-5 | AE-5 |
| NE-4 | NE-3 | NE-3 | NE-4 | NE-4 | NE-3 | NE-3 | NE-4 | NC-5 | NE-5 |

## NFC EAST-NE

| NE-1 H | NE-1 A | NE-2 H | NE-2 A | NE-3 H | NE-3 A | NE-4 H | NE-4 A | NE-5 H | NE-5 A |
|---|---|---|---|---|---|---|---|---|---|
| NC-1 | NC-3 | NC-2 | NC-1 | NC-3 | NC-4 | NC-4 | NC-2 | NC-5 | NC-5 |
| NW-2 | NW-1 | NW-4 | NW-2 | NW-1 | NW-3 | NW-3 | NW-4 | NW-1 | NW-2 |
| AW-1 | AW-2 | AW-2 | AW-1 | AW-1 | AW-2 | AW-2 | AW-1 | NW-3 | NW-4 |
| AW-3 | AW-4 | AW-4 | AW-3 | AW-3 | AW-4 | AW-4 | AW-3 | AW-5 | AE-5 |

## NFC CENTRAL-NC

| NC-1 H | NC-1 A | NC-2 H | NC-2 A | NC-3 H | NC-3 A | NC-4 H | NC-4 A | NC-5 H | NC-5 A |
|---|---|---|---|---|---|---|---|---|---|
| NE-2 | NE-1 | NE-4 | NE-2 | NE-1 | NE-3 | NE-3 | NE-4 | NE-5 | NE-5 |
| NW-1 | NW-3 | NW-2 | NW-1 | NW-3 | NW-4 | NW-4 | NW-2 | NW-2 | NW-1 |
| AC-1 | AC-2 | AC-2 | AC-1 | AC-1 | AC-2 | AC-2 | AC-1 | NW-4 | NW-3 |
| AC-3 | AC-4 | AC-4 | AC-3 | AC-3 | AC-4 | AC-4 | AC-3 | AE-5 | AW-5 |

## NFC WEST-NW

| NW-1 H | NW-1 A | NW-2 H | NW-2 A | NW-3 H | NW-3 A | NW-4 H | NW-4 A |
|---|---|---|---|---|---|---|---|
| NC-2 | NC-1 | NC-4 | NC-2 | NC-1 | NC-3 | NC-3 | NE-2 |
| NC-5 | NE-3 | NE-2 | NC-5 | NC-5 | NE-4 | NE-4 | NC-4 |
| NE-1 | NE-5 | NE-5 | NE-1 | NE-3 | NE-5 | NE-5 | NC-5 |
| AE-1 | AE-2 | AE-2 | AE-1 | AE-1 | AE-2 | AE-2 | AE-1 |
| AE-3 | AE-4 | AE-4 | AE-3 | AE-3 | AE-4 | AE-4 | AE-3 |

# CHAPTER EIGHT

# 1992 NATIONAL FOOTBALL LEAGUE SCHEDULE

**(All times local)**

## FIRST WEEK

**Sunday, September 6**                   **Kickoff**

| | |
|---|---|
| Cincinnati at Seattle | 1:00 |
| Cleveland at Indianapolis | 12:00 |
| Detroit at Chicago | 12:00 |
| Kansas City at San Diego | 1:00 |
| Los Angeles Raiders at Denver | 6:00 |
| Los Angeles Rams at Buffalo | 1:00 |
| Minnesota at Green Bay | 12:00 |
| New England at Miami | 4:00 |
| New Orleans at Philadelphia | 1:00 |
| New York Jets at Atlanta | 1:00 |
| Phoenix at Tampa Bay | 4:00 |
| Pittsburgh at Houston | 12:00 |
| San Francisco at New York Giants | 4:00 |

**Monday, September 7**

| | |
|---|---|
| Washington at Dallas | 8:00 |

## SECOND WEEK

**Sunday, September 13**

| | |
|---|---|
| Atlanta at Washington | 1:00 |
| Buffalo at San Francisco | 1:00 |
| Chicago at New Orleans | 12:00 |
| Dallas at New York Giants | 1:00 |
| Green Bay at Tampa Bay | 1:00 |
| Houston at Indianapolis | 3:00 |
| Los Angeles Raiders at Cincinnati | 1:00 |
| Minnesota at Detroit | 1:00 |
| New England at Los Angeles Rams | 1:00 |
| New York Jets at Pittsburgh | 4:00 |
| Philadelphia at Phoenix | 5:00 |
| San Diego at Denver | 2:00 |
| Seattle at Kansas City | 12:00 |

**Monday, September 14**

| | |
|---|---|
| Miami at Cleveland | 9:00 |

## THIRD WEEK

**Sunday, September 20**

| | |
|---|---|
| Cincinnati at Green Bay | 12:00 |
| Cleveland at Los Angeles Raiders | 1:00 |
| Denver at Philadelphia | 1:00 |
| Detroit at Washington | 4:00 |
| Indianapolis at Buffalo | 8:00 |
| Kansas City at Houston | 12:00 |
| Los Angeles Rams at Miami | 4:00 |
| New Orleans at Atlanta | 1:00 |
| Phoenix at Dallas | 3:00 |
| Pittsburgh at San Diego | 1:00 |
| San Francisco at New York Jets | 1:00 |
| Seattle at New England | 1:00 |
| Tampa Bay at Minnesota | 12:00 |

**Monday, September 21**

| | |
|---|---|
| New York Giants at Chicago | 8:00 |

## FOURTH WEEK

Open Date: Five NFC East teams
and AFC East Fifth-Placed team

**Sunday, September 27**

| | |
|---|---|
| Atlanta at Chicago | 12:00 |
| Buffalo at New England | 1:00 |
| Denver at Cleveland | 1:00 |
| Miami at Seattle | 1:00 |
| Minnesota at Cincinnati | 1:00 |
| New York Jets at Los Angeles Rams | 1:00 |
| Pittsburgh at Green Bay | 3:00 |
| San Diego at Houston | 12:00 |
| San Francisco at New Orleans | 7:00 |
| Tampa Bay at Detroit | 1:00 |

**Monday, September 28**

| | |
|---|---|
| Los Angeles Raiders at Kansas City | 8:00 |

## FIFTH WEEK

Open Date: Four AFC Central teams

**Sunday, October 4**

| | |
|---|---|
| Chicago at Minnesota | 12:00 |
| Green Bay at Atlanta | 1:00 |
| Indianapolis at Tampa Bay | 1:00 |
| Kansas City at Denver | 2:00 |
| Los Angeles Rams at San Francisco | 1:00 |
| Miami at Buffalo | 1:00 |
| New England at New York Jets | 8:00 |
| New Orleans at Detroit | 1:00 |
| New York Giants at Los Angeles Raiders | 1:00 |
| Seattle at San Diego | 1:00 |
| Washington at Phoenix | 1:00 |

**Monday, October 5**

| | |
|---|---|
| Dallas at Philadelphia | 9:00 |

## SIXTH WEEK
Open Date: Five NFC Central teams
and AFC West Fifth-Placed team
**Sunday, October 11**
| | |
|---|---|
| Atlanta at Miami | 1:00 |
| Buffalo at Los Angeles Raiders | 1:00 |
| Houston at Cincinnati | 4:00 |
| Los Angeles Rams at New Orleans | 6:30 |
| New York Jets at Indianapolis | 3:00 |
| Philadelphia at Kansas City | 12:00 |
| Phoenix at New York Giants | 1:00 |
| Pittsburgh at Cleveland | 1:00 |
| San Francisco at New England | 1:00 |
| Seattle at Dallas | 12:00 |

**Monday, October 12**
| | |
|---|---|
| Denver at Washington | 9:00 |

## SEVENTH WEEK
Open Date: Four AFC East teams
**Thursday, October 15**
| | |
|---|---|
| Detroit at Minnesota | 6:30 |

**Sunday, October 18**
| | |
|---|---|
| Atlanta at San Francisco | 1:00 |
| Green Bay at Cleveland | 1:00 |
| Houston at Denver | 2:00 |
| Kansas City at Dallas | 12:00 |
| Los Angeles Raiders at Seattle | 1:00 |
| New Orleans at Phoenix | 1:00 |
| New York Giants at Los Angeles Rams | 1:00 |
| Philadelphia at Washington | 1:00 |
| San Diego at Indianapolis | 12:00 |
| Tampa Bay at Chicago | 12:00 |

**Monday, October 19**
| | |
|---|---|
| Cincinnati at Pittsburgh | 9:00 |

## EIGHTH WEEK
Open Date: Four NFC West teams
**Sunday, October 25**
| | |
|---|---|
| Chicago at Green Bay | 12:00 |
| Cincinnati at Houston | 12:00 |
| Cleveland at New England | 4:00 |
| Dallas at Los Angeles Raiders | 1:00 |
| Denver at San Diego | 1:00 |
| Detroit at Tampa Bay | 1:00 |
| Indianapolis at Miami | 4:00 |
| Phoenix at Philadelphia | 1:00 |
| Pittsburgh at Kansas City | 6:30 |
| Seattle at New York Giants | 1:00 |
| Washington at Minnesota | 12:00 |

**Monday, October 26**
| | |
|---|---|
| Buffalo at New York Jets | 9:00 |

## NINTH WEEK
Open Date: Four AFC West teams
**Sunday, November 1**
| | |
|---|---|
| Cleveland at Cincinnati | 4:00 |
| Green Bay at Detroit | 1:00 |
| Houston at Pittsburgh | 1:00 |
| Indianapolis at San Diego | 1:00 |
| Los Angeles Rams at Atlanta | 1:00 |
| Miami at New York Jets | 1:00 |
| New England at Buffalo | 1:00 |

| | |
|---|---|
| New York Giants at Washington | 8:00 |
| Philadelphia at Dallas | 3:00 |
| San Francisco at Phoenix | 2:00 |
| Tampa Bay at New Orleans | 12:00 |

**Monday, November 2**
| | |
|---|---|
| Minnesota at Chicago | 8:00 |

## TENTH WEEK
**Sunday, November 8**
| | |
|---|---|
| Cincinnati at Chicago | 7:00 |
| Cleveland at Houston | 12:00 |
| Dallas at Detroit | 1:00 |
| Green Bay at New York Giants | 1:00 |
| Los Angeles Raiders at Philadelphia | 1:00 |
| Miami at Indianapolis | 1:00 |
| Minnesota at Tampa Bay | 1:00 |
| New Orleans at New England | 1:00 |
| New York Jets at Denver | 2:00 |
| Phoenix at Los Angeles Rams | 1:00 |
| Pittsburgh at Buffalo | 4:00 |
| San Diego at Kansas City | 3:00 |
| Washington at Seattle | 1:00 |

**Monday, November 9**
| | |
|---|---|
| San Francisco at Atlanta | 9:00 |

## ELEVENTH WEEK
**Sunday, November 15**
| | |
|---|---|
| Chicago at Tampa Bay | 4:00 |
| Cincinnati at New York Jets | 1:00 |
| Detroit at Pittsburgh | 1:00 |
| Houston at Minnesota | 12:00 |
| Los Angeles Rams at Dallas | 12:00 |
| New England at Indianapolis | 1:00 |
| New Orleans at San Francisco | 1:00 |
| New York Giants at Denver | 6:00 |
| Philadelphia vs. Green Bay at Milwaukee | 12:00 |
| Phoenix at Atlanta | 1:00 |
| San Diego at Cleveland | 1:00 |
| Seattle at Los Angeles Raiders | 1:00 |
| Washington at Kansas City | 12:00 |

**Monday, November 16**
| | |
|---|---|
| Buffalo at Miami | 9:00 |

## TWELFTH WEEK
**Sunday, November 22**
| | |
|---|---|
| Atlanta at Buffalo | 1:00 |
| Cleveland at Minnesota | 12:00 |
| Dallas at Phoenix | 2:00 |
| Denver at Los Angeles Raiders | 1:00 |
| Detroit at Cincinnati | 1:00 |
| Green Bay at Chicago | 12:00 |
| Houston at Miami | 1:00 |
| Indianapolis at Pittsburgh | 1:00 |
| Kansas City at Seattle | 5:00 |
| New York Jets at New England | 4:00 |
| Philadelphia at New York Giants | 1:00 |
| San Francisco at Los Angeles Rams | 1:00 |
| Tampa Bay at San Diego | 1:00 |

**Monday, November 23**
| | |
|---|---|
| Washington at New Orleans | 8:00 |

**THIRTEENTH WEEK**
**Thursday, November 26**

| | |
|---|---|
| Houston at Detroit | 12:30 |
| New York Giants at Dallas | 3:00 |

**Sunday, November 29**

| | |
|---|---|
| Buffalo at Indianapolis | 4:00 |
| Chicago at Cleveland | 1:00 |
| Kansas City at New York Jets | 1:00 |
| Los Angeles Raiders at San Diego | 5:00 |
| Miami at New Orleans | 12:00 |
| Minnesota at Los Angeles Rams | 1:00 |
| New England at Atlanta | 1:00 |
| Philadelphia at San Francisco | 1:00 |
| Phoenix at Washington | 1:00 |
| Pittsburgh at Cincinnati | 1:00 |
| Tampa Bay vs. Green Bay at Milwaukee | 12:00 |

**Monday, November 30**

| | |
|---|---|
| Denver at Seattle | 6:00 |

**FOURTEENTH WEEK**
**Thursday, December 3**

| | |
|---|---|
| Atlanta at New Orleans | 7:00 |

**Sunday, December 6**

| | |
|---|---|
| Cincinnati at Cleveland | 1:00 |
| Dallas at Denver | 2:00 |
| Detroit vs. Green Bay at Milwaukee | 12:00 |
| Indianapolis at New England | 1:00 |
| Kansas City at Los Angeles Raiders | 1:00 |
| Los Angeles Rams at Tampa Bay | 8:00 |
| Miami at San Francisco | 1:00 |
| Minnesota at Philadelphia | 1:00 |
| New York Jets at Buffalo | 1:00 |
| San Diego at Phoenix | 2:00 |
| Seattle at Pittsburgh | 1:00 |
| Washington at New York Giants | 4:00 |

**Monday, December 7**

| | |
|---|---|
| Chicago at Houston | 8:00 |

**FIFTEENTH WEEK**
**Saturday, December 12**

| | |
|---|---|
| Denver at Buffalo | 12:30 |
| New York Giants at Phoenix | 2:00 |

**Sunday, December 13**

| | |
|---|---|
| Atlanta at Tampa Bay | 1:00 |
| Cincinnati at San Diego | 1:00 |
| Cleveland at Detroit | 1:00 |
| Dallas at Washington | 1:00 |
| Green Bay at Houston | 7:00 |
| Indianapolis at New York Jets | 1:00 |
| New England at Kansas City | 12:00 |
| New Orleans at Los Angeles Rams | 1:00 |
| Philadelphia at Seattle | 1:00 |

| | |
|---|---|
| Pittsburgh at Chicago | 12:00 |
| San Francisco at Minnesota | 12:00 |

**Monday, December 14**

| | |
|---|---|
| Los Angeles Raiders at Miami | 9:00 |

**SIXTEENTH WEEK**
**Saturday, December 19**

| | |
|---|---|
| Kansas City at New York Giants | 12:30 |
| Tampa Bay at San Francisco | 1:00 |

**Sunday, December 20**

| | |
|---|---|
| Buffalo at New Orleans | 12:00 |
| Chicago at Detroit | 4:00 |
| Houston at Cleveland | 1:00 |
| Los Angeles Rams at Green Bay | 12:00 |
| Minnesota at Pittsburgh | 1:00 |
| New England at Cincinnati | 1:00 |
| New York Jets at Miami | 8:00 |
| Phoenix at Indianapolis | 1:00 |
| San Diego at Los Angeles Raiders | 1:00 |
| Seattle at Denver | 2:00 |
| Washington at Philadelphia | 1:00 |

**Monday, December 21**

| | |
|---|---|
| Dallas at Atlanta | 9:00 |

**SEVENTEENTH WEEK**
**Saturday, December 26**

| | |
|---|---|
| Los Angeles Raiders at Washington | 4:00 |
| New Orleans at New York Jets | 12:30 |

**Sunday, December 27**

| | |
|---|---|
| Atlanta at Los Angeles Rams | 1:00 |
| Buffalo at Houston | 7:00 |
| Chicago at Dallas | 3:00 |
| Cleveland at Pittsburgh | 1:00 |
| Denver at Kansas City | 12:00 |
| Green Bay at Minnesota | 12:00 |
| Indianapolis at Cincinnati | 1:00 |
| Miami at New England | 1:00 |
| New York Giants at Philadelphia | 1:00 |
| San Diego at Seattle | 1:00 |
| Tampa Bay at Phoenix | 2:00 |

**Monday, December 28**

| | |
|---|---|
| Detroit at San Francisco | 6:00 |

**POSTSEASON**

| | |
|---|---|
| Saturday, Jan. 2 | AFC and NFC First-Round Playoffs |
| Sunday, Jan. 3 | AFC and NFC First-Round Playoffs |
| Saturday, Jan. 9 | AFC and NFC Divisional Playoffs |
| Sunday, Jan. 10 | AFC and NFC Divisional Playoffs |
| Sunday, Jan. 17 | AFC and NFC Championship Games |
| Sunday, Jan. 31 | Super Bowl XXVII at Rose Bowl, Pasadena, California |
| Sunday, Feb. 7 | AFC-NFC Pro Bowl at Honolulu, Hawaii |

# ALL-TIME SERIES RECORDS

| | Buffalo | Indianapolis | Miami | New England | N.Y. Jets | Cincinnati | Cleveland | Houston | Pittsburgh | Denver | Kansas City | L.A. Raiders | San Diego | Seattle |
|---|---|---|---|---|---|---|---|---|---|---|---|---|---|---|
| **Buffalo** | | 23-19-1 | 17-35-1 | 29-34-1 | 35-28-0 | 7-11-0 | 3-8-0 | 12-19-0 | 6-6-0 | 16-10-1 | 16-13-1 | 15-13-0 | 9-17-2 | 1-3-0 |
| **Indianapolis** | 19-23-1 | | 13-32-0 | 18-25-0 | 24-20-0 | 7-5-0 | 7-14-0 | 6-6-0 | 4-11-0 | 2-8-0 | 4-6-0 | 3-5-0 | 5-6-0 | 2-1-0 |
| **Miami** | 35-17-1 | 32-13-0 | | 31-21-0 | 27-25-1 | 10-3-0 | 6-4-0 | 10-12-0 | 9-5-0 | 5-2-1 | 8-10-0 | 4-16-1 | 6-10-0 | 4-2-0 |
| **New England** | 34-29-1 | 25-18-0 | 21-31-0 | | 28-35-1 | 7-6-0 | 2-8-0 | 17-14-1 | 3-8-0 | 12-17-0 | 7-12-3 | 13-13-1 | 13-12-2 | 6-4-0 |
| **N.Y. Jets** | 28-35-0 | 20-24-0 | 25-27-1 | 35-28-1 | | 8-6-0 | 6-9-0 | 12-17-1 | 1-11-0 | 11-10-1 | 13-14-1 | 11-13-2 | 9-16-1 | 3-8-0 |
| **Cincinnati** | 11-7-0 | 5-7-0 | 3-10-0 | 6-7-0 | 6-8-0 | | 23-20-0 | 25-21-1 | 21-22-0 | 6-10-0 | 9-10-0 | 5-16-0 | 9-11-0 | 6-5-0 |
| **Cleveland** | 8-3-0 | 14-7-0 | 4-6-0 | 8-2-0 | 9-6-0 | 20-23-0 | | 26-18-0 | 50-34-0 | 5-13-0 | 7-6-2 | 2-10-0 | 6-7-1 | 3-8-0 |
| **Houston** | 19-12-0 | 6-6-0 | 12-10-0 | 14-17-1 | 17-12-1 | 21-25-1 | 18-26-0 | | 16-30-0 | 20-12-1 | 15-22-0 | 13-22-0 | 15-17-1 | 4-4-0 |
| **Pittsburgh** | 6-6-0 | 11-4-0 | 5-9-0 | 8-3-0 | 11-1-0 | 22-21-0 | 34-50-0 | 30-16-0 | | 7-11-1 | 12-5-0 | 6-10-0 | 12-5-0 | 4-4-0 |
| **Denver** | 10-16-1 | 8-2-0 | 2-5-1 | 17-12-0 | 10-11-1 | 10-6-0 | 13-5-0 | 12-20-1 | 11-7-1 | | 27-36-0 | 19-43-2 | 33-30-1 | 17-13-0 |
| **Kansas City** | 13-16-1 | 6-4-0 | 10-8-0 | 12-7-3 | 14-13-1 | 10-9-0 | 6-7-2 | 22-15-0 | 5-12-0 | 36-27-0 | | 29-35-2 | 31-31-1 | 15-12-0 |
| **L.A. Raiders** | 13-15-0 | 5-3-0 | 16-4-1 | 13-13-1 | 13-11-2 | 16-5-0 | 10-2-0 | 22-13-0 | 10-6-0 | 43-19-2 | 35-29-2 | | 41-22-2 | 15-15-0 |
| **San Diego** | 17-9-2 | 6-5-0 | 10-6-0 | 12-13-2 | 16-9-1 | 11-9-0 | 7-6-1 | 17-15-1 | 5-12-0 | 30-33-1 | 31-31-1 | 22-41-2 | | 12-14-0 |
| **Seattle** | 3-1-0 | 1-2-0 | 2-4-0 | 4-6-0 | 8-3-0 | 5-6-0 | 8-3-0 | 4-4-0 | 4-4-0 | 13-17-0 | 12-15-0 | 15-15-0 | 14-12-0 | |
| **Dallas** | 3-1-0 | 6-3-0 | 2-5-0 | 6-0-0 | 4-1-0 | 3-2-0 | 10-16-0 | 4-3-0 | 12-13-0 | 3-2-0 | 2-2-0 | 1-3-0 | 4-1-0 | 3-1-0 |
| **N.Y. Giants** | 3-3-0 | 4-7-0 | 1-1-0 | 3-1-0 | 3-3-0 | 0-4-0 | 17-26-2 | 4-0-0 | 42-26-3 | 4-2-0 | 5-1-0 | 2-3-0 | 4-2-0 | 4-2-0 |
| **Philadelphia** | 4-2-0 | 5-6-0 | 2-5-0 | 5-2-0 | 4-0-0 | 1-5-0 | 12-30-1 | 5-0-0 | 44-25-3 | 4-2-0 | 1-0-0 | 3-3-0 | 2-3-0 | 3-1-0 |
| **Phoenix** | 3-3-0 | 6-4-0 | 0-6-0 | 6-1-0 | 2-1-0 | 1-3-0 | 10-31-3 | 3-2-0 | 21-29-3 | 0-3-1 | 1-3-1 | 1-2-0 | 1-4-0 | 3-0-0 |
| **Washington** | 5-2-0 | 6-16-0 | 3-5-0 | 4-1-0 | 4-0-0 | 4-2-0 | 9-32-1 | 3-3-0 | 42-27-3 | 3-3-0 | 1-2-0 | 2-5-0 | 5-0-0 | 4-1-0 |
| **Chicago** | 3-2-0 | 16-21-0 | 1-5-0 | 3-3-0 | 3-1-0 | 2-2-0 | 3-7-0 | 2-3-0 | 15-4-1 | 5-4-0 | 3-2-0 | 3-4-0 | 1-4-0 | 2-4-0 |
| **Detroit** | 2-1-1 | 17-17-2 | 2-2-0 | 2-2-0 | 3-3-0 | 2-3-0 | 13-4-0 | 2-3-0 | 13-10-1 | 3-4-0 | 3-4-0 | 2-5-0 | 3-2-0 | 1-4-0 |
| **Green Bay** | 1-4-0 | 19-18-1 | 0-7-0 | 2-2-0 | 1-5-0 | 2-4-0 | 8-5-0 | 2-3-0 | 16-11-0 | 1-4-1 | 2-3-1 | 2-5-0 | 3-1-0 | 3-3-0 |
| **Minnesota** | 4-2-0 | 6-12-1 | 1-5-0 | 2-3-0 | 1-3-0 | 3-3-0 | 7-3-0 | 3-2-0 | 6-5-0 | 4-3-0 | 2-3-0 | 2-6-0 | 3-3-0 | 2-3-0 |
| **Tampa Bay** | 4-2-0 | 2-4-0 | 1-4-0 | 0-3-0 | 1-5-0 | 1-3-0 | 0-4-0 | 1-3-0 | 0-4-0 | 0-2-0 | 2-4-0 | 0-2-0 | 0-4-0 | 0-2-0 |
| **Atlanta** | 3-2-0 | 0-10-0 | 1-4-0 | 3-3-0 | 2-3-0 | 2-5-0 | 1-8-0 | 5-2-0 | 1-8-0 | 3-4-0 | 0-3-0 | 3-4-0 | 3-1-0 | 1-4-0 |
| **L.A. Rams** | 3-2-0 | 16-20-2 | 1-4-0 | 2-3-0 | 4-2-0 | 2-4-0 | 8-9-0 | 4-2-0 | 13-5-2 | 3-3-0 | 3-1-0 | 2-5-0 | 3-2-0 | 4-1-0 |
| **New Orleans** | 2-2-0 | 2-3-0 | 1-4-0 | 1-5-0 | 2-4-0 | 4-3-0 | 3-8-0 | 3-3-1 | 5-5-0 | 1-4-0 | 3-2-0 | 2-3-1 | 1-4-0 | 3-2-0 |
| **San Francisco** | 2-2-0 | 16-21-0 | 2-4-0 | 5-1-0 | 5-1-0 | 7-1-0 | 6-8-0 | 5-2-0 | 7-7-0 | 3-4-0 | 4-1-0 | 2-5-0 | 3-3-0 | 4-1-0 |